COOKING FOR ALL SEASONS

MACMILLAN PUBLISHING COMPANY

◆

NEW YORK

◆

COLLIER MACMILLAN CANADA

◆

TORONTO

◆

MAXWELL MACMILLAN INTERNATIONAL

◆

NEW YORK · OXFORD · SINGAPORE · SYDNEY

COOKING

 FOR

ALL SEASONS

BY JIMMY SCHMIDT

ILLUSTRATIONS BY ROBERT SCHEFMAN

Macmillan Publishing Company
866 Third Avenue, New York, NY 10022

Collier Macmillan Canada, Inc.
1200 Eglinton Avenue East, Suite 200
Don Mills, Ontario M3C 3N1

Library of Congress Cataloging-in-Publication Data
Schmidt, Jimmy.
Cooking for all seasons / by Jimmy Schmidt;
Illustrations by Robert Schefman.
p.   cm.
Includes bibliographical references and index.
ISBN 0-02-607131-2
1. Cookery.   I. Title.
TX714.S355   1991
641.5—dc20   90-23867   CIP

Macmillan books are available at special discounts
for bulk purchases for sales promotions, premiums, fund-raising,
or educational use. For details, contact:

Special Sales Director
Macmillan Publishing Company
866 Third Avenue
New York, NY 10022

10 9 8 7 6 5 4 3 2 1

Designed by Liney Li

Printed in the United States of America

DEDICATION

◆

TO MY FAMILY,

DARLENE,

STEPHEN,

AND TAYLOR,

MADELEINE KAMMAN,

AND GOD FOR

THE INSPIRATION AND

LOVE OF LIFE.

Contents

Acknowledgments

IT IS MY PLEASURE to thank the wonderful people who helped make this book possible.

My parents enjoyed a great appreciation of the foods nature so generously presented during the course of the year. In my youth, many fond memories were born with my family picking corn, raspberries, strawberries, foraging for asparagus and walnuts, and many other activities revolving around wonderful food. My parents shared with me a special view of the bounty of nature that is close to my heart.

When I was eighteen years of age I met a very exceptional teacher who gave the gift of time, knowledge and, most importantly, a quest for quality that started my adventures in cuisine. Madeleine Kamman planted the seed for the love of food, nature, and life, so amazingly intertwined. Her patience and direction toward personal cuisine was the start of this book.

My wife, Darlene, provided inspiration and understanding as I researched for what seemed forever. She shared the secrets of life and friendship. My son Stephen's and daughter Taylor's laughter became the special spice of the seasons.

Christine Schefman coordinated my efforts into a form of simplicity. Her organization of the materials and production staff polished the book while keeping it simple and easy to use. Geri Morfino endured endless changes and brought the manuscript to fruition when all was thought to be caught in a permanent cycle of corrections.

Keith Josefiak and Michael Schram tested my ideas as well as being close friends through the process. They also kept the kitchens running in perfect shape with Greg Ervin, Jeff Drew, and John Iaconelli. David Neault, Sylvia Oestrike, Rozanne McGraw, Margarita Garcia, Kim Schwarz, and Susan Cosentino gave personal contributions to our patrons during my time with the book. All the staff at The Rattlesnake Club gave to the making of this book through the daily successes of the restaurant.

There are many more people too numerous to list here who influenced me with their knowledge and love of gastronomy. To all my close friends and associates a warm thanks.

SEASONAL BUYING CHARTS

E arly in my pursuit of eating I became entranced with capturing foods at their exact peak of taste and texture. By cataloging the seasonal attributes I was able to anticipate their peak arrival at the marketplace. With the largest supply in season these wonderful ingredients were also the best values the market had to offer.

These charts will guide you through the best buys of each season month by month. Their accuracy has been reinforced by state agricultural boards and farmers' guilds. Local fish and shellfish were tracked by landed poundage at the larger regional ports through the United States Government National Marine Fisheries Service. Foraged and more unusual foods were tracked through horticultural societies and guilds, seed catalogs, greenhouses for plant stock, and tree nurseries for root stock production, past and future. Early agricultural books offered past views of varieties of vegetables and fruits with noncommercial characteristics that were true gems. A little detective work uncovered their current sources.

These seasonal charts reflect more than just availability and value. Many commercially produced popular foods such as asparagus, tomatoes, and berries have had their production altered beyond their natural seasons to almost continuous availability. Although the accessibility has increased the casualty has been almost complete depletion of their natural flavors and characteristics. By selecting your foods in alignment with the natural seasons you offer your taste nature's true beauty while avoiding the manufactured pitfalls.

Once you are familiar with the natural cycles you will never again be satisfied with uncharacteristic food.

How to Use the Charts

The seasonal charts are organized by major food groups: Vegetables, Fruits, Exotic Fruits, Shellfish, Fish, Poultry, Meats, Edible Wild Plants, and Mushrooms. The top of each chart represents the seasons, month by month, as shown below. The individual food items are organized alphabetically within their major food group. A shaded bar indicates the food's seasonal peaks, with a darker bar denoting the very peak of the season. The state or region of cultivation or harvest is indicated where appropriate.

Mother Nature directs the seasons with changes in weather, so allow for some slight variations. Mankind has also been adding other negative variables to the seasons with the depletion of the ozone layer, stripping of the rain forests, and general high levels of pollution. I have attempted to be as thorough as possible by listing the food items that are most available throughout the mainland United States. Some items that are very limited in availability, less popular, or rather indistinct have been overlooked in order to keep the charts as easy to read as possible.

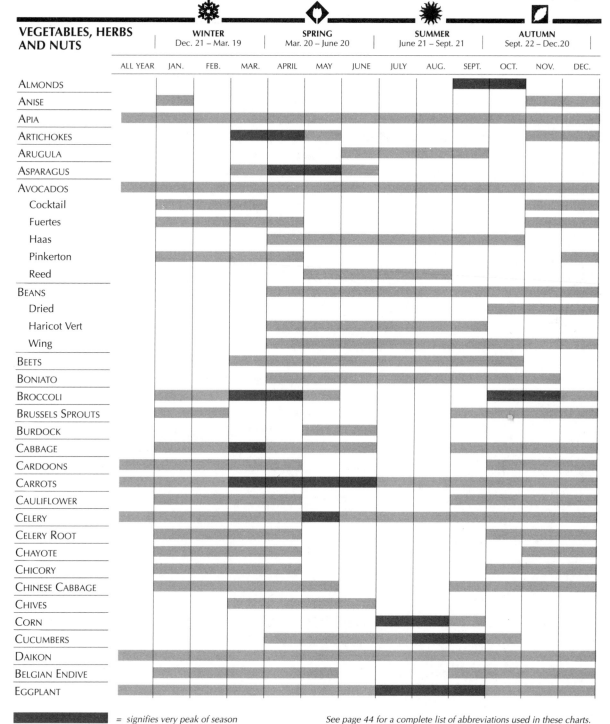

VEGETABLES, HERBS AND NUTS

		WINTER Dec. 21 – Mar. 19		SPRING Mar. 20 – June 20			SUMMER June 21 – Sept. 21			AUTUMN Sept. 22 – Dec.20		
	ALL YEAR	JAN.	FEB.	MAR.	APRIL	MAY	JUNE	JULY	AUG.	SEPT.	OCT.	NOV.	DEC.
ALMONDS													
ANISE													
APIA													
ARTICHOKES													
ARUGULA													
ASPARAGUS													
AVOCADOS													
Cocktail													
Fuertes													
Haas													
Pinkerton													
Reed													
BEANS													
Dried													
Haricot Vert													
Wing													
BEETS													
BONIATO													
BROCCOLI													
BRUSSELS SPROUTS													
BURDOCK													
CABBAGE													
CARDOONS													
CARROTS													
CAULIFLOWER													
CELERY													
CELERY ROOT													
CHAYOTE													
CHICORY													
CHINESE CABBAGE													
CHIVES													
CORN													
CUCUMBERS													
DAIKON													
BELGIAN ENDIVE													
EGGPLANT													

▬▬▬ = signifies very peak of season   *See page 44 for a complete list of abbreviations used in these charts.*

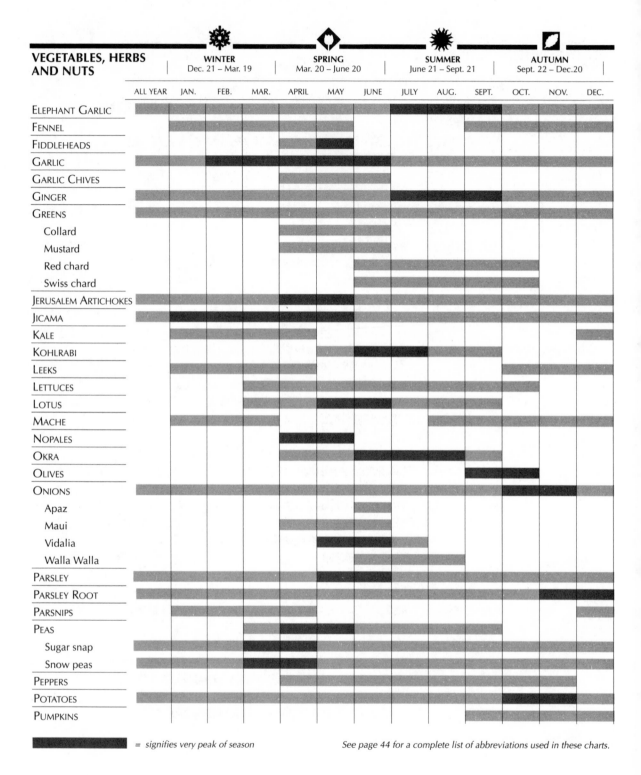

VEGETABLES, HERBS AND NUTS	WINTER Dec. 21 – Mar. 19			SPRING Mar. 20 – June 20			SUMMER June 21 – Sept. 21			AUTUMN Sept. 22 – Dec.20		
ALL YEAR	JAN.	FEB.	MAR.	APRIL	MAY	JUNE	JULY	AUG.	SEPT.	OCT.	NOV.	DEC.
ELEPHANT GARLIC												
FENNEL												
FIDDLEHEADS												
GARLIC												
GARLIC CHIVES												
GINGER												
GREENS												
Collard												
Mustard												
Red chard												
Swiss chard												
JERUSALEM ARTICHOKES												
JICAMA												
KALE												
KOHLRABI												
LEEKS												
LETTUCES												
LOTUS												
MACHE												
NOPALES												
OKRA												
OLIVES												
ONIONS												
Apaz												
Maui												
Vidalia												
Walla Walla												
PARSLEY												
PARSLEY ROOT												
PARSNIPS												
PEAS												
Sugar snap												
Snow peas												
PEPPERS												
POTATOES												
PUMPKINS												

■ = signifies very peak of season   See page 44 for a complete list of abbreviations used in these charts.

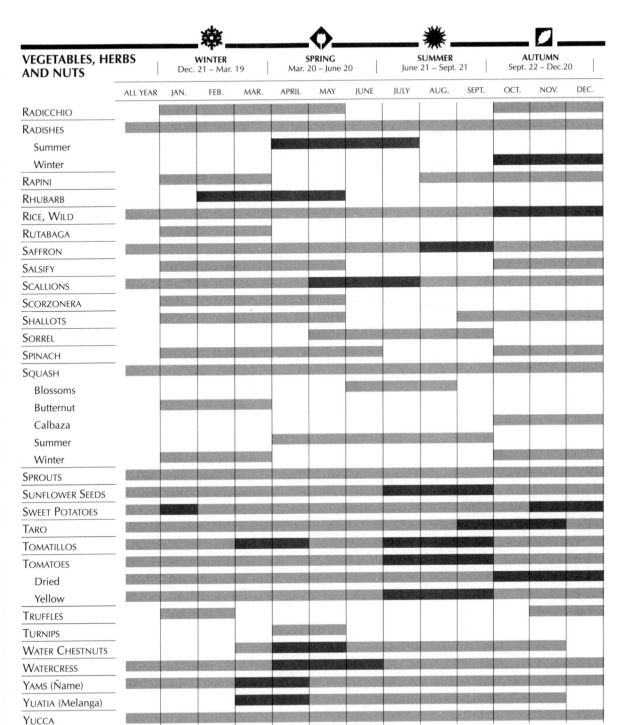

VEGETABLES, HERBS AND NUTS

	ALL YEAR	WINTER Dec. 21 – Mar. 19			SPRING Mar. 20 – June 20			SUMMER June 21 – Sept. 21			AUTUMN Sept. 22 – Dec.20		
		JAN.	FEB.	MAR.	APRIL	MAY	JUNE	JULY	AUG.	SEPT.	OCT.	NOV.	DEC.
RADICCHIO		▓	▓	▓	▓	▓					▓	▓	▓
RADISHES	▓												
Summer					█	█	█	█			▓		
Winter											█	█	█
RAPINI		▓	▓	▓	▓	▓					▓	▓	▓
RHUBARB			█	█	█	█					▓	▓	▓
RICE, WILD	▓										▓	▓	▓
RUTABAGA		▓	▓	▓									
SAFFRON	▓								█	█	▓		
SALSIFY		▓	▓	▓	▓						▓	▓	▓
SCALLIONS	▓												
SCORZONERA		▓	▓	▓	▓	▓	▓						
SHALLOTS		▓	▓	▓	▓	▓	▓						
SORREL					▓	▓	▓	▓	▓	▓	▓		
SPINACH	▓												
SQUASH	▓												
Blossoms							▓	▓	▓				
Butternut		▓											
Calbaza											▓	▓	▓
Summer					▓	▓	▓						
Winter		▓											
SPROUTS	▓												
SUNFLOWER SEEDS	▓								█	█			
SWEET POTATOES	▓	█										█	█
TARO	▓								█	█			
TOMATILLOS	▓		█	█				█	█				
TOMATOES	▓										▓	▓	█
Dried	▓										▓	▓	█
Yellow	▓							█	█		▓		
TRUFFLES		▓	▓									▓	▓
TURNIPS					▓	▓							
WATER CHESTNUTS					█	█	▓						
WATERCRESS	▓				█	█	▓						
YAMS (Ñame)				█	█	▓	▓						
YUATIA (Melanga)				█	█	▓	▓					▓	
YUCCA	▓												

█ = *signifies very peak of season*

See page 44 for a complete list of abbreviations used in these charts.

EXOTICS

| | WINTER Dec. 21 – Mar. 19 | | SPRING Mar. 20 – June 20 | | SUMMER June 21 – Sept. 21 | | AUTUMN Sept. 22 – Dec.20 | |

	ALL YEAR	JAN.	FEB.	MAR.	APRIL	MAY	JUNE	JULY	AUG.	SEPT.	OCT.	NOV.	DEC.
ACEROLA													
ASIAN PEARS													
CA													
WA													
ATEMOYA													
BABACO													
BANANAS													
BREADFRUIT													
CANISTEL													
CALAMONDIN													
CARAMBOLA													
CERIMAN													
CHERIMOYA													
COCONUTS													
DATES, CHINESE													
DURIAN													
FEIJOA													
CA													
NZ													
GUAVAS													
CA													
HA													
NZ													
GUAVA, STRAWBERRY													
JUJUBE													
KIWI													
CA													
NZ													
KUMQUATS													
CA													
FL													
LONGONS													
LOQUATS													
CA													
FL													
HA													

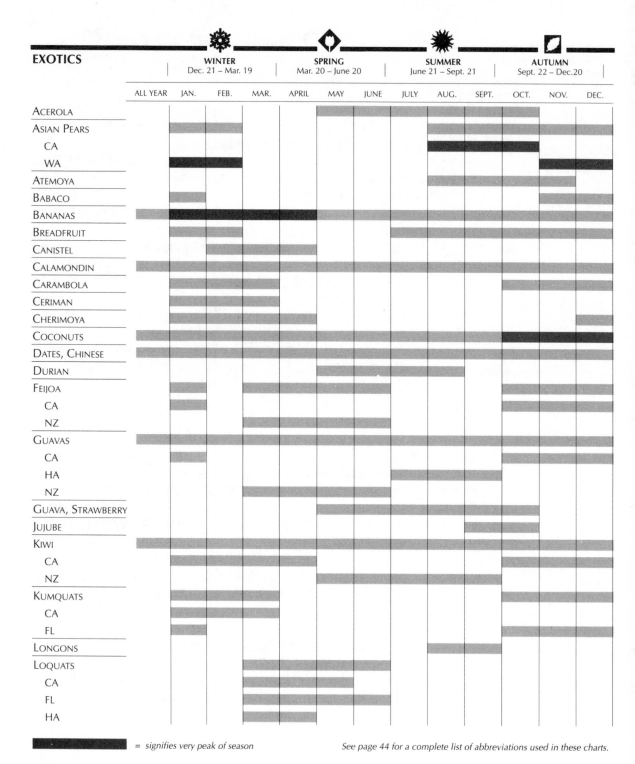

= signifies very peak of season   See page 44 for a complete list of abbreviations used in these charts.

EXOTICS

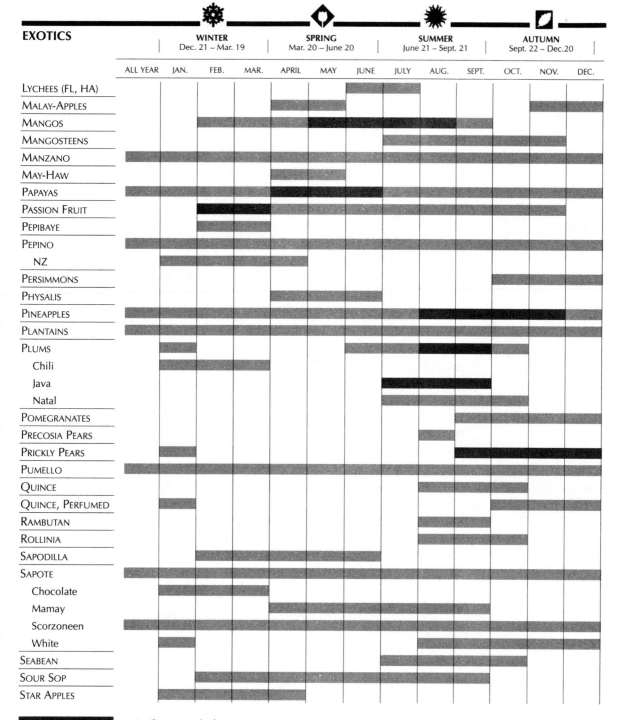

	WINTER Dec. 21 – Mar. 19			SPRING Mar. 20 – June 20			SUMMER June 21 – Sept. 21			AUTUMN Sept. 22 – Dec.20		
ALL YEAR	JAN.	FEB.	MAR.	APRIL	MAY	JUNE	JULY	AUG.	SEPT.	OCT.	NOV.	DEC.

- LYCHEES (FL, HA)
- MALAY-APPLES
- MANGOS
- MANGOSTEENS
- MANZANO
- MAY-HAW
- PAPAYAS
- PASSION FRUIT
- PEPIBAYE
- PEPINO
-   NZ
- PERSIMMONS
- PHYSALIS
- PINEAPPLES
- PLANTAINS
- PLUMS
-   Chili
-   Java
-   Natal
- POMEGRANATES
- PRECOSIA PEARS
- PRICKLY PEARS
- PUMELLO
- QUINCE
- QUINCE, PERFUMED
- RAMBUTAN
- ROLLINIA
- SAPODILLA
- SAPOTE
-   Chocolate
-   Mamay
-   Scorzoneen
-   White
- SEABEAN
- SOUR SOP
- STAR APPLES

▬▬▬ = signifies very peak of season

See page 44 for a complete list of abbreviations used in these charts.

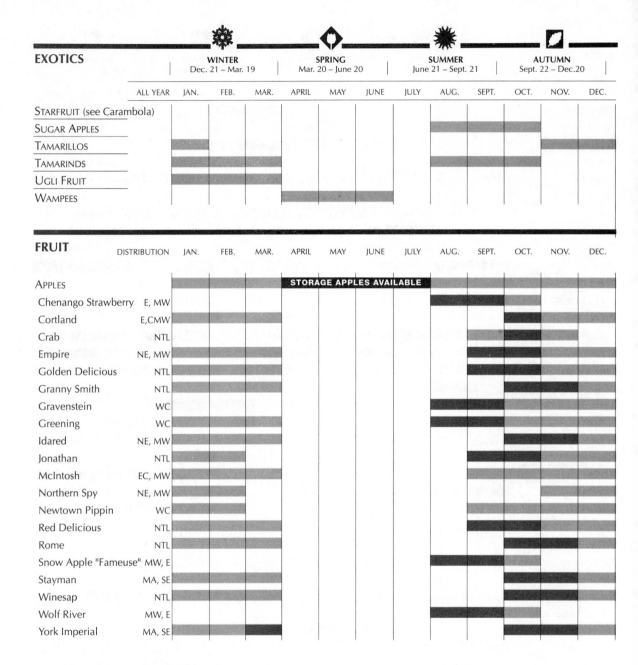

| EXOTICS | WINTER Dec. 21 – Mar. 19 | | | SPRING Mar. 20 – June 20 | | | SUMMER June 21 – Sept. 21 | | | AUTUMN Sept. 22 – Dec.20 | | |

	ALL YEAR	JAN.	FEB.	MAR.	APRIL	MAY	JUNE	JULY	AUG.	SEPT.	OCT.	NOV.	DEC.
STARFRUIT (see Carambola)													
SUGAR APPLES									■	■	■		
TAMARILLOS		■							■	■	■	■	■
TAMARINDS		■	■	■					■	■	■		
UGLI FRUIT		■	■	■									
WAMPEES					■	■	■						

FRUIT	DISTRIBUTION	JAN.	FEB.	MAR.	APRIL	MAY	JUNE	JULY	AUG.	SEPT.	OCT.	NOV.	DEC.
APPLES				STORAGE APPLES AVAILABLE									
Chenango Strawberry	E, MW								■	■			
Cortland	E,CMW									■	■	■	■
Crab	NTL									■	■		
Empire	NE, MW									■	■	■	■
Golden Delicious	NTL									■	■	■	■
Granny Smith	NTL										■	■	■
Gravenstein	WC								■	■			
Greening	WC								■	■	■		
Idared	NE, MW										■	■	■
Jonathan	NTL									■	■	■	
McIntosh	EC, MW									■	■	■	■
Northern Spy	NE, MW									■	■	■	■
Newtown Pippin	WC									■	■		
Red Delicious	NTL									■	■	■	■
Rome	NTL										■	■	■
Snow Apple "Fameuse"	MW, E								■	■	■		
Stayman	MA, SE										■	■	■
Winesap	NTL										■	■	■
Wolf River	MW, E								■	■	■		
York Imperial	MA, SE										■	■	■

■ = signifies very peak of season

See page 44 for a complete list of abbreviations used in these charts.

FRUIT

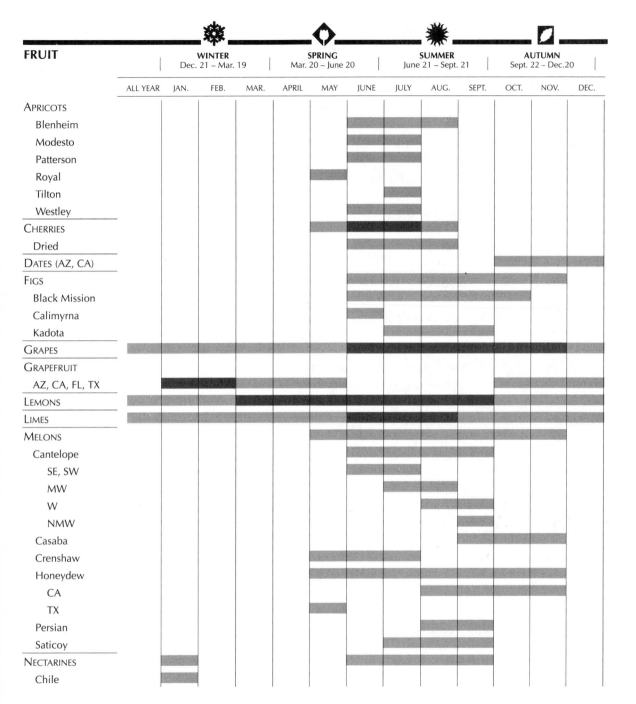

	WINTER Dec. 21 – Mar. 19			SPRING Mar. 20 – June 20			SUMMER June 21 – Sept. 21			AUTUMN Sept. 22 – Dec.20		
ALL YEAR	JAN.	FEB.	MAR.	APRIL	MAY	JUNE	JULY	AUG.	SEPT.	OCT.	NOV.	DEC.

APRICOTS
  Blenheim
  Modesto
  Patterson
  Royal
  Tilton
  Westley
CHERRIES
  Dried
DATES (AZ, CA)
FIGS
  Black Mission
  Calimyrna
  Kadota
GRAPES
GRAPEFRUIT
  AZ, CA, FL, TX
LEMONS
LIMES
MELONS
  Cantelope
    SE, SW
    MW
    W
    NMW
  Casaba
  Crenshaw
  Honeydew
    CA
    TX
  Persian
  Saticoy
NECTARINES
  Chile

■■■■■ = signifies very peak of season   See page 44 for a complete list of abbreviations used in these charts.

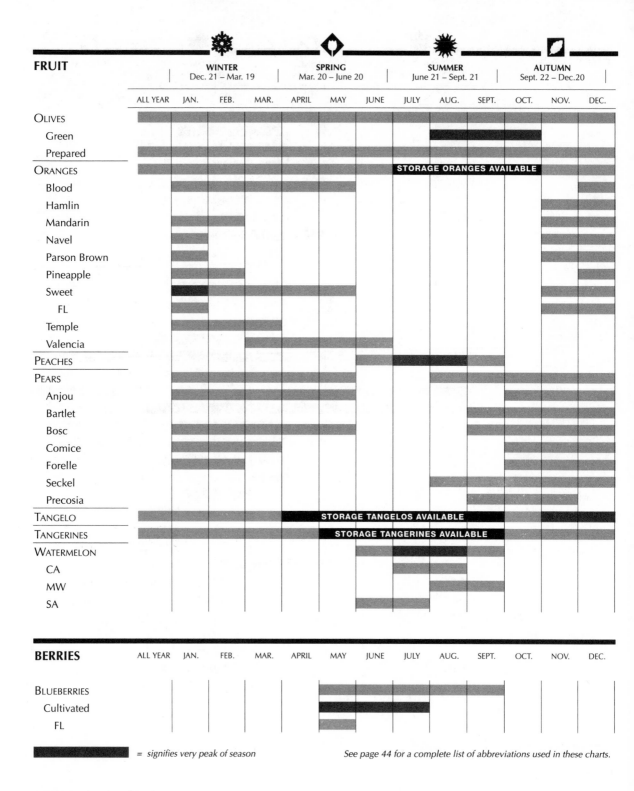

FRUIT

	WINTER Dec. 21 – Mar. 19	SPRING Mar. 20 – June 20	SUMMER June 21 – Sept. 21	AUTUMN Sept. 22 – Dec.20

	ALL YEAR	JAN.	FEB.	MAR.	APRIL	MAY	JUNE	JULY	AUG.	SEPT.	OCT.	NOV.	DEC.
OLIVES													
Green													
Prepared													
ORANGES								STORAGE ORANGES AVAILABLE					
Blood													
Hamlin													
Mandarin													
Navel													
Parson Brown													
Pineapple													
Sweet													
FL													
Temple													
Valencia													
PEACHES													
PEARS													
Anjou													
Bartlet													
Bosc													
Comice													
Forelle													
Seckel													
Precosia													
TANGELO						STORAGE TANGELOS AVAILABLE							
TANGERINES						STORAGE TANGERINES AVAILABLE							
WATERMELON													
CA													
MW													
SA													

BERRIES

	ALL YEAR	JAN.	FEB.	MAR.	APRIL	MAY	JUNE	JULY	AUG.	SEPT.	OCT.	NOV.	DEC.
BLUEBERRIES													
Cultivated													
FL													

= signifies very peak of season   See page 44 for a complete list of abbreviations used in these charts.

BERRIES

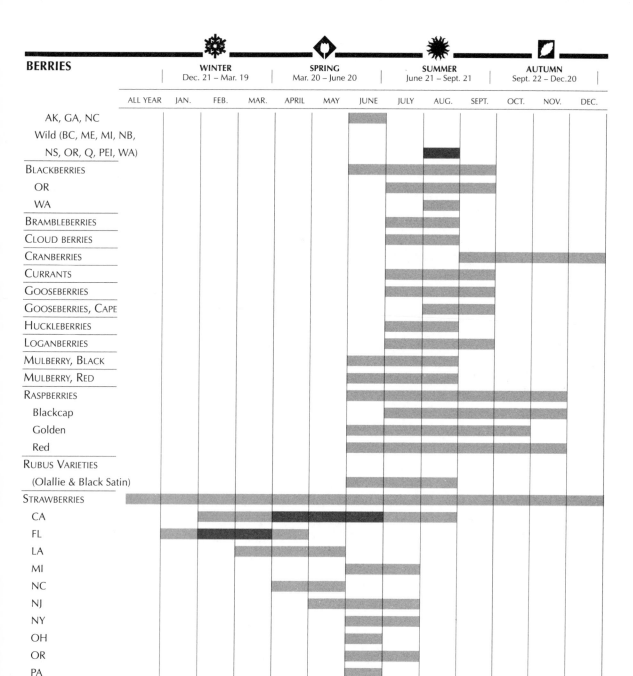

	WINTER Dec. 21 – Mar. 19			SPRING Mar. 20 – June 20			SUMMER June 21 – Sept. 21			AUTUMN Sept. 22 – Dec.20		
	ALL YEAR	JAN.	FEB.	MAR.	APRIL	MAY	JUNE	JULY	AUG.	SEPT.	OCT.	NOV.	DEC.
AK, GA, NC													
Wild (BC, ME, MI, NB, NS, OR, Q, PEI, WA)													
BLACKBERRIES													
OR													
WA													
BRAMBLEBERRIES													
CLOUD BERRIES													
CRANBERRIES													
CURRANTS													
GOOSEBERRIES													
GOOSEBERRIES, CAPE													
HUCKLEBERRIES													
LOGANBERRIES													
MULBERRY, BLACK													
MULBERRY, RED													
RASPBERRIES													
Blackcap													
Golden													
Red													
RUBUS VARIETIES (Olallie & Black Satin)													
STRAWBERRIES													
CA													
FL													
LA													
MI													
NC													
NJ													
NY													
OH													
OR													
PA													
White													

■ = signifies very peak of season   *See page 44 for a complete list of abbreviations used in these charts.*

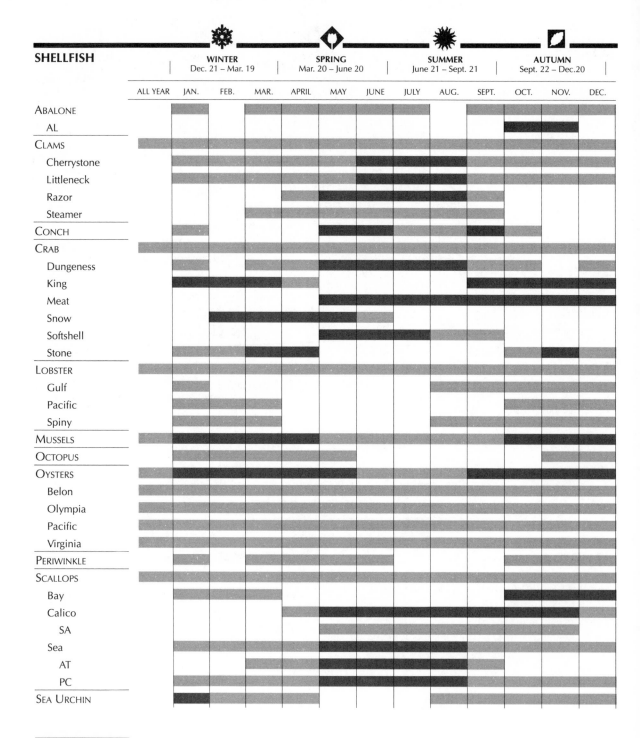

SHELLFISH

	WINTER Dec. 21 – Mar. 19			SPRING Mar. 20 – June 20			SUMMER June 21 – Sept. 21			AUTUMN Sept. 22 – Dec.20		
	ALL YEAR	JAN.	FEB.	MAR.	APRIL	MAY	JUNE	JULY	AUG.	SEPT.	OCT.	NOV.	DEC.
ABALONE													
AL													
CLAMS													
Cherrystone													
Littleneck													
Razor													
Steamer													
CONCH													
CRAB													
Dungeness													
King													
Meat													
Snow													
Softshell													
Stone													
LOBSTER													
Gulf													
Pacific													
Spiny													
MUSSELS													
OCTOPUS													
OYSTERS													
Belon													
Olympia													
Pacific													
Virginia													
PERIWINKLE													
SCALLOPS													
Bay													
Calico													
SA													
Sea													
AT													
PC													
SEA URCHIN													

= signifies very peak of season   *See page 44 for a complete list of abbreviations used in these charts.*

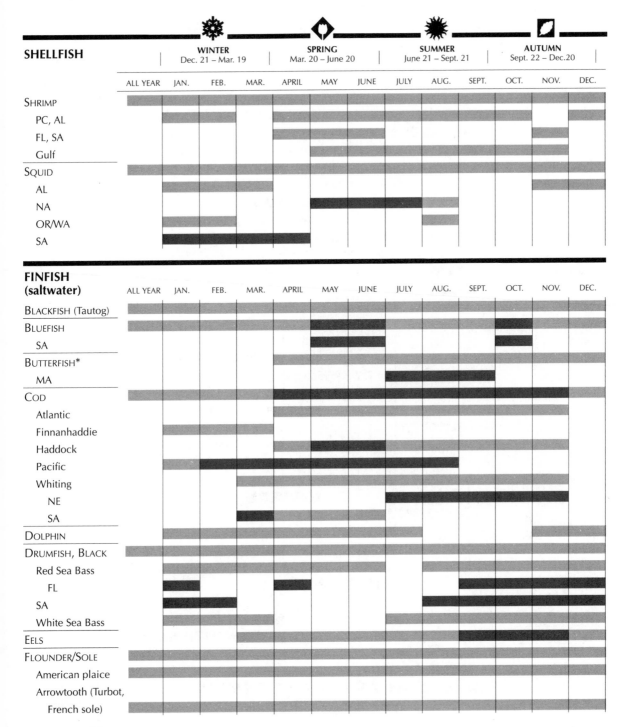

SHELLFISH

		WINTER Dec. 21 – Mar. 19			SPRING Mar. 20 – June 20			SUMMER June 21 – Sept. 21			AUTUMN Sept. 22 – Dec.20	
	ALL YEAR	JAN.	FEB.	MAR.	APRIL	MAY	JUNE	JULY	AUG.	SEPT.	OCT.	NOV.	DEC.
SHRIMP													
PC, AL													
FL, SA													
Gulf													
SQUID													
AL													
NA													
OR/WA													
SA													

FINFISH (saltwater)

	ALL YEAR	JAN.	FEB.	MAR.	APRIL	MAY	JUNE	JULY	AUG.	SEPT.	OCT.	NOV.	DEC.
BLACKFISH (Tautog)													
BLUEFISH													
SA													
BUTTERFISH*													
MA													
COD													
Atlantic													
Finnanhaddie													
Haddock													
Pacific													
Whiting													
NE													
SA													
DOLPHIN													
DRUMFISH, BLACK													
Red Sea Bass													
FL													
SA													
White Sea Bass													
EELS													
FLOUNDER/SOLE													
American plaice													
Arrowtooth (Turbot, French sole)													

= signifies very peak of season   See page 44 for a complete list of abbreviations used in these charts.

* The butterfish referred to in this chart is the Atlantic pomfret variety.

	WINTER Dec. 21 – Mar. 19		SPRING Mar. 20 – June 20		SUMMER June 21 – Sept. 21		AUTUMN Sept. 22 – Dec.20	

	ALL YEAR	JAN.	FEB.	MAR.	APRIL	MAY	JUNE	JULY	AUG.	SEPT.	OCT.	NOV.	DEC.
Butter sole													
Curlfin sole													
Dover sole													
English sole													
Gray sole													
Lemon sole													
NE													
Rex sole													
Sand dabs													
Summer flounder													
Winter flounder													
SA													
Yellowfin sole													
HALIBUT													
Atlantic													
Pacific													
GOATFISH													
GROUPER													
SA													
HERRING													
MACKEREL													
Atlantic													
MA													
NE													
SA													
Pacific													
HA													
Spanish													
Gulf													
PC													
Wahoo													
MARLIN													
MONKFISH (Lotte)													
AT													
MULLET													
AT, PC													

= signifies very peak of season   See page 44 for a complete list of abbreviations used in these charts.

FINFISH (saltwater)

	ALL YEAR	JAN.	FEB.	MAR.	APRIL	MAY	JUNE	JULY	AUG.	SEPT.	OCT.	NOV.	DEC.

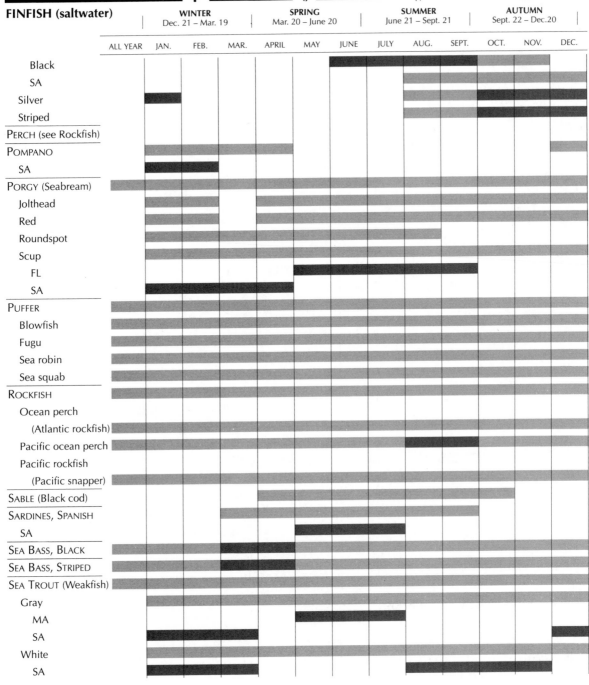

Black
SA
Silver
Striped
PERCH (see Rockfish)
POMPANO
SA
PORGY (Seabream)
Jolthead
Red
Roundspot
Scup
FL
SA
PUFFER
Blowfish
Fugu
Sea robin
Sea squab
ROCKFISH
Ocean perch
(Atlantic rockfish)
Pacific ocean perch
Pacific rockfish
(Pacific snapper)
SABLE (Black cod)
SARDINES, SPANISH
SA
SEA BASS, BLACK
SEA BASS, STRIPED
SEA TROUT (Weakfish)
Gray
MA
SA
White
SA

■ = signifies very peak of season   *See page 44 for a complete list of abbreviations used in these charts.*

FINFISH (saltwater)

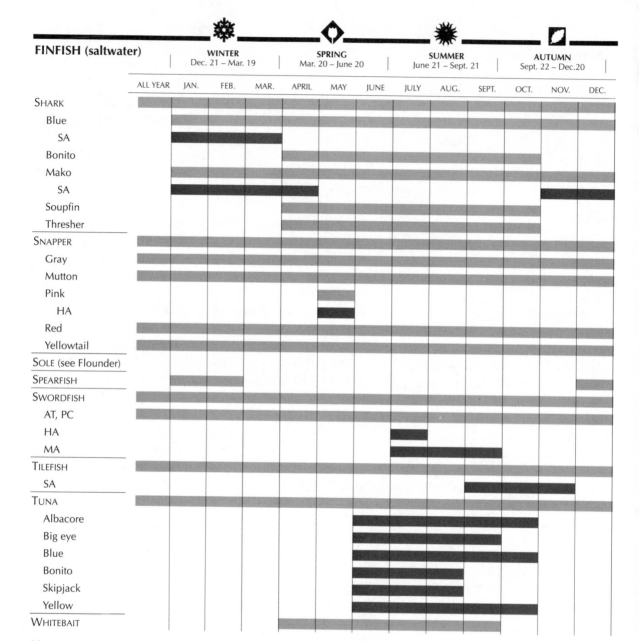

	ALL YEAR	JAN.	FEB.	MAR.	APRIL	MAY	JUNE	JULY	AUG.	SEPT.	OCT.	NOV.	DEC.
WINTER Dec. 21 – Mar. 19													
SPRING Mar. 20 – June 20													
SUMMER June 21 – Sept. 21													
AUTUMN Sept. 22 – Dec.20													

SHARK
  Blue
    SA
  Bonito
  Mako
    SA
  Soupfin
  Thresher

SNAPPER
  Gray
  Mutton
  Pink
    HA
  Red
  Yellowtail

SOLE (see Flounder)

SPEARFISH

SWORDFISH
  AT, PC
  HA
  MA

TILEFISH
  SA

TUNA
  Albacore
  Big eye
  Blue
  Bonito
  Skipjack
  Yellow

WHITEBAIT

HAWAIIAN NAMES FOR SALTWATER FINFISH

BLUE MARLIN – *KAJIKI*
MACKEREL (similar to the king mackerel) – *WAHOO*
POMPANO – *PAPIO*

GRAY SNAPPER – *UKU*
PINK SNAPPER – *LEHI OR OPAKAPAKA*
RED SNAPPER – *ONAGA*
YELLOW SNAPPER – *GENDAI*

ALBACORE – *TOMBO*
BIG EYE TUNA – *AHI*
BLUE TUNA (Pacific variety) – *AHI*
BONITO TUNA – *KAWAKAWA*

(Hawaii)
SKIPJACK TUNA – *AKU (Hawaii)*
YELLOW TUNA (Atlantic and Pacific varieties) – *AHI*

■ = *signifies very peak of season*

See page 44 for a complete list of abbreviations used in these charts.

FINFISH (freshwater)

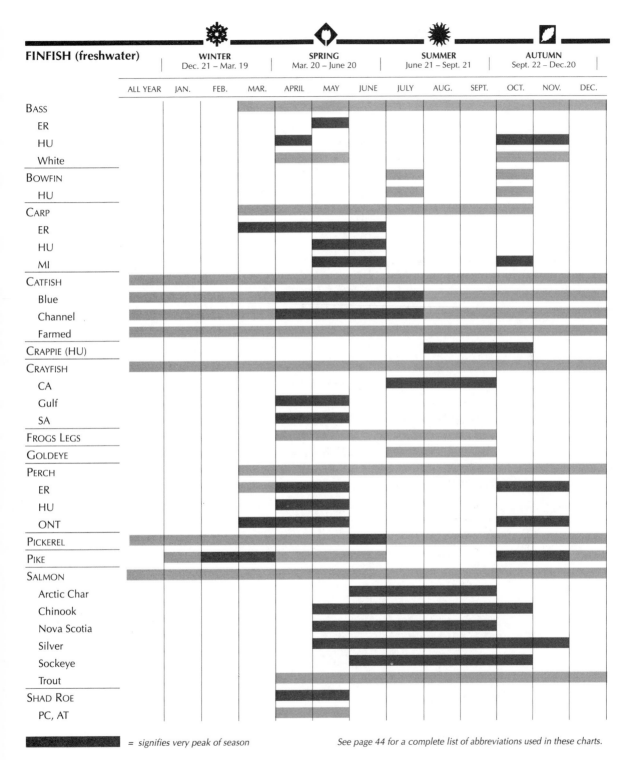

	WINTER Dec. 21 – Mar. 19			SPRING Mar. 20 – June 20			SUMMER June 21 – Sept. 21			AUTUMN Sept. 22 – Dec.20		
	ALL YEAR	JAN.	FEB.	MAR.	APRIL	MAY	JUNE	JULY	AUG.	SEPT.	OCT.	NOV.	DEC.

Fish species chart:

- BASS
  - ER
  - HU
  - White
- BOWFIN
  - HU
- CARP
  - ER
  - HU
  - MI
- CATFISH
  - Blue
  - Channel
  - Farmed
- CRAPPIE (HU)
- CRAYFISH
  - CA
  - Gulf
  - SA
- FROGS LEGS
- GOLDEYE
- PERCH
  - ER
  - HU
  - ONT
- PICKEREL
- PIKE
- SALMON
  - Arctic Char
  - Chinook
  - Nova Scotia
  - Silver
  - Sockeye
  - Trout
- SHAD ROE
  - PC, AT

■ = signifies very peak of season

See page 44 for a complete list of abbreviations used in these charts.

FINFISH (freshwater)

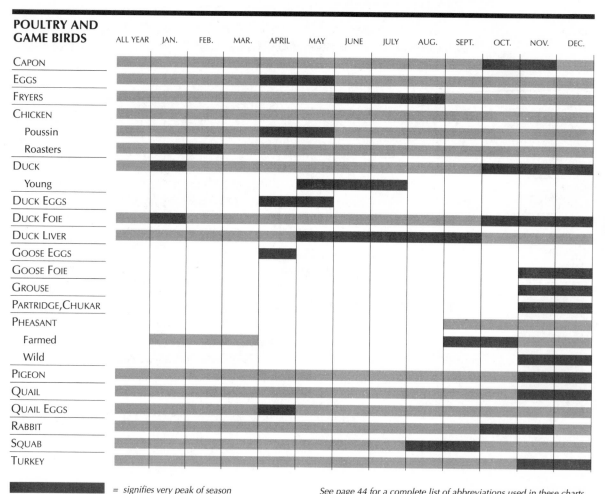

	ALL YEAR	JAN.	FEB.	MAR.	APRIL	MAY	JUNE	JULY	AUG.	SEPT.	OCT.	NOV.	DEC.
SMELT													
STURGEON													
TROUT													
Brook													
Gasque, Rainbow													
Lake													
WALLEYE													
WHITEFISH													

POULTRY AND GAME BIRDS

	ALL YEAR	JAN.	FEB.	MAR.	APRIL	MAY	JUNE	JULY	AUG.	SEPT.	OCT.	NOV.	DEC.
CAPON													
EGGS													
FRYERS													
CHICKEN													
Poussin													
Roasters													
DUCK													
Young													
DUCK EGGS													
DUCK FOIE													
DUCK LIVER													
GOOSE EGGS													
GOOSE FOIE													
GROUSE													
PARTRIDGE, CHUKAR													
PHEASANT													
Farmed													
Wild													
PIGEON													
QUAIL													
QUAIL EGGS													
RABBIT													
SQUAB													
TURKEY													

▬ = *signifies very peak of season*

See page 44 for a complete list of abbreviations used in these charts.

	WINTER Dec. 21 – Mar. 19	SPRING Mar. 20 – June 20	SUMMER June 21 – Sept. 21	AUTUMN Sept. 22 – Dec.20

BEEF PRICES

• Briskets up • Liver stable • Loin stable/low • Oxtails decline • Rounds low • Shanks low • Shortribs low • Strips decline • Tenderloin stable/low	• Briskets decline • Liver up • Loin rises to peak • Oxtails decline • Rounds rise to peak • Shanks rise • Shortribs rise • Strips rise • Tenderloin rise	• Briskets low • Liver declines • Loin declines • Oxtails start to rise • Rounds decline • Shanks decline • Shortribs decline • Strips highest • Tenderloin high	• Briskets rise • Liver up • Loin stable • Oxtails up • Rounds decline • Shanks stable • Shortribs stable • Strips stable or some decline • Tenderloin stable

VEAL PRICES

Through May: • Briskets, chuck/hinds, shanks are best buys • Premium cuts higher	May through August: • Spring veal available • Premium cuts begin to decline	May through August: • Spring veal available • Premium cuts begin to decline	Starting in August: • Prices usually rise on premium loin cuts • Other cuts more stable or lower

LAMB PRICES

• Chucks, legs, shanks, mutton/yearlings are best buys	• Spring lamb available; born February/March, all cuts small and tender. • Lamb prices peak across the board	• Late spring lamb available; born April/May, all cuts small and tender. • Early spring lamb chops available • Lamb prices decline	• Premium loin cuts increase. Racks, loin chops, loins/tenderloins. • Other cuts lower

PORK PRICES

• Bacon/pancetta, hams/legs, full loin roasts, sausages are best buys	• Suckling pigs available. • Pork prices generally lowest overall of the year • Spareribs increasing	• Young pork available. • Smaller loins and chops, whole roasts are best buys. • Spareribs at their highest prices	• Pork prices usually rise • Spareribs declining

BUFFALO/GOAT/ DEER/VENISON AVAILABILITY

	ALL YEAR	JAN.	FEB.	MAR.	APRIL	MAY	JUNE	JULY	AUG.	SEPT.	OCT.	NOV.	DEC.
BUFFALO		▓									▓	█	█
KIDS (20–35 lbs.)					█	█	█						
GOATS (35–55 lbs.)								█	█	█			
DEER											▓	█	█
VENISON											▓	█	█

█ = signifies very peak of season

See page 44 for a complete list of abbreviations used in these charts.

These charts are organized similarly to the regular charts. Since these are wild crops the regional peaks of season with weather fluctuations may exhibit some slight variation.

The Edible Wild Plant Application Guide

Wild foods have properties similar to standard foods. This chart is organized alphabetically to reference the preparation instructions. Suggestions are offered for substituting wild foods for common ingredients, creating new dishes with unusual personalities and flavors.

The charts list the wild plants generally considered to be safe to eat and many are found at your local specialty store. This chart does not represent that these plants are not toxic, only the plants' approximate season. The user must be responsible for interpreting the information within and for any identifications made therefrom. Neither the author nor the publisher accept responsibility for the identifications made by the user of this book or for the consequences of eating any of these species.

PLANT	APPLICATION
Acorns	Boil to leach bitterness
	Roast, grind, then mix with cornmeal for cakes, polentas, flapjacks
Arrowhead (Duck Potatoes)	Roast, bake, or boil like potatoes
Barberry	Use in preserves and tart sauces
Bayberry (Sweet Gale)	Use as a spice
Beechnuts	Use nuts, raw or cooked
Birch	Use seeds toasted
Bitterroot (Purslane)	Roast or boil the roots
Black walnuts	Use like walnuts
Buffalo berry (Oleaster)	Use in jams/preserves
Bunchberry (Dogwood)	Use in jams/preserves

PLANT	APPLICATION
Burdock	Peel stem, simmer 20 minutes with ¼ teaspoon baking soda, slice, then use like potatoes
Butternuts (White Walnuts)	Use like walnuts
Cattail	Peel well and use like leeks, raw or lightly cooked
Chia	Grind seeds as spice or use as drink
Chickweed	Use as salad greens
Chicory	Use root as a coffee stretcher
	Use leaves as greens
Chokecherry	Use as fresh fruit or in jams and preserves
	Pits are poisonous (cyanogenetic)
Christmas berries	Roast or use as berries
Chufa (Sedge)	Use as a vegetable, raw or cooked
	Use as a drink—Spanish
Clover (Pea)	Use blossoms, raw or dried, in breads
	Steam greens
	Dry or roast roots
Cranberries (Wild)	Use like commercial cranberries, even though these have more flavor and color
Dandelion	Use as salad greens or roast fresh for coffee
Dock	Cook or use greens in salads
Elderberries	Use in jellies and jams
Evening Primrose	Pick roots before blossoms emerge
	Boil with lots of salted water
Fireweed (Evening Primrose)	Boil very young stems as you would asparagus
Glasswort	Use for pickles
Grapes (Wild)	Use in juice, jams, preserves, and tarts
Ground-cherry (Tomatillos)	Use raw in preserves and tarts
Groundnuts (Pea)	Use like potatoes
Hawthorns	Use in jellies and jams

Hickories (Wild)	Use like walnuts	Rum cherries	Use in juice, jams, or spirits
Highbush cranberries	Use just like regular cranberries	Saxifrage	Use as salad greens
Iceplants	Use the leaves and twigs in salads	Scurvy grass (Mustard)	Use as greens
Juniper	Use as spice	Serviceberry (Rose)	Use in jams, jellies, or baked goods such as pies
Knotweed (Buckwheat)	Boil roots Boil young sprouts in salted water	Shepherd's purse (Mustard)	Use as salad greens Grind seeds, mix with grains
Lambs quarters	Use as salad greens	Silverweed (Rose)	Use roots like potatoes
Madrone	Boil tender shoots in spring Use berries raw in jams	Sow thistle	Use young greens in salads like dandelions
Maples	Use sap for syrup and jams		
Mayapple (Barberry)	Use juice raw Use in preserves	Spicebush (Laurel)	Use as spice
Manzanita	Use raw berries in jam	Spring beauty (Purslane)	Use root like potatoes
Milkweed	Boil sprouts well, treat like asparagus	Strawberry spinach (Loosefoot)	Use greens in salad
Miners lettuce	Use as salad greens		
Mountain sorrel (Buckwheat)	Use as salad greens	Sumac (Cashew)	Use berries to make tea
Mulberry	Use raw or in jams and preserves	Sunflower	Use seeds as nuts or grind into meal
Mustard	Before flowering use as salad greens After flowering, cook greens; use flowers in salads Use seeds for pickles or garnishes	Sweet flag (Arum)	Candy the root, as for ginger
		Toothwort (Mustard)	Chop raw root for salads
Nettles	Boil young sprouts	Wild watercress	Boil or steam
Orpine	Slice tubers raw into salads	Wild apple (Rose)	Bake like an apple or make into applesauce
Papaws (Custard apple)	Use raw or cooked in desserts	Wild celery	Use greens in salads
Partridgeberry	Use in jams and preserves	Wild ginger (Birthwort)	Use like ginger
Pin cherry	Use in jams and preserves		
Pine nuts	Toast and use like other nuts	Wild lettuce	Steam or use as salad greens
Pokeweed	Boil young shoots	Wild onions (Lily)	Blanch in salted water or use mild ones raw
Prairie turnips (Pulse)	Use raw or cook like turnips	Wild rice (Grass)	Use like rice
Purslane	Use greens, raw or cooked Mix seeds with grains for breads	Wintercress (Mustard)	Use greens raw
Ramps	Blanch, use like leeks		
Rose	Use rose hips (haws) in teas or sorbets; jams or jellies		

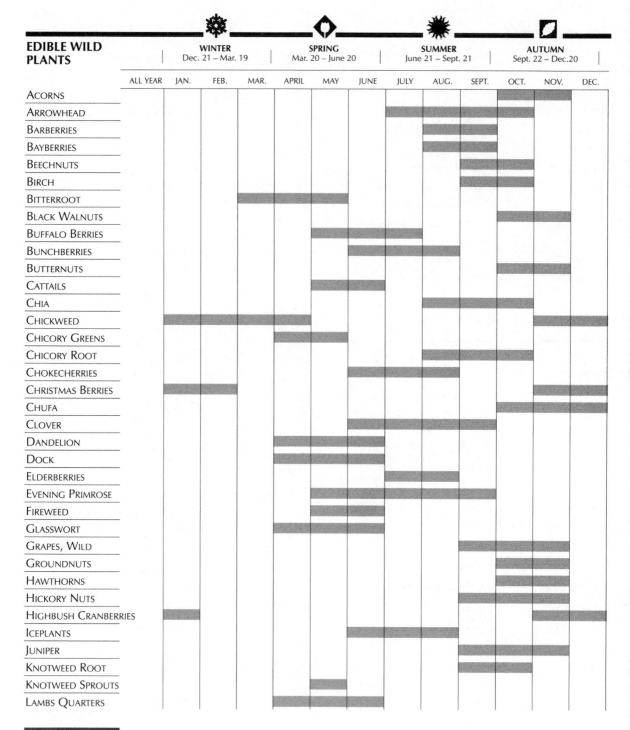

EDIBLE WILD PLANTS

		WINTER Dec. 21 – Mar. 19			SPRING Mar. 20 – June 20			SUMMER June 21 – Sept. 21			AUTUMN Sept. 22 – Dec.20		
	ALL YEAR	JAN.	FEB.	MAR.	APRIL	MAY	JUNE	JULY	AUG.	SEPT.	OCT.	NOV.	DEC.
Acorns											■	■	
Arrowhead								■	■	■	■		
Barberries									■	■			
Bayberries									■	■			
Beechnuts										■	■		
Birch										■	■		
Bitterroot				■	■	■							
Black Walnuts											■	■	
Buffalo Berries						■	■	■					
Bunchberries							■	■	■				
Butternuts											■	■	
Cattails						■	■						
Chia									■	■	■		
Chickweed		■	■	■	■							■	■
Chicory Greens					■	■							
Chicory Root									■	■	■		
Chokecherries							■	■	■				
Christmas Berries		■	■									■	■
Chufa											■	■	■
Clover							■	■	■	■			
Dandelion					■	■	■						
Dock					■	■	■						
Elderberries								■	■				
Evening Primrose						■	■	■	■	■			
Fireweed						■	■						
Glasswort					■	■	■						
Grapes, Wild										■	■	■	
Groundnuts											■	■	
Hawthorns											■	■	
Hickory Nuts										■	■	■	
Highbush Cranberries		■										■	■
Iceplants							■	■	■				
Juniper										■	■	■	
Knotweed Root										■	■		
Knotweed Sprouts						■							
Lambs Quarters					■	■	■						

■ = *signifies very peak of season*

See page 44 for a complete list of abbreviations used in these charts.

EDIBLE WILD PLANTS

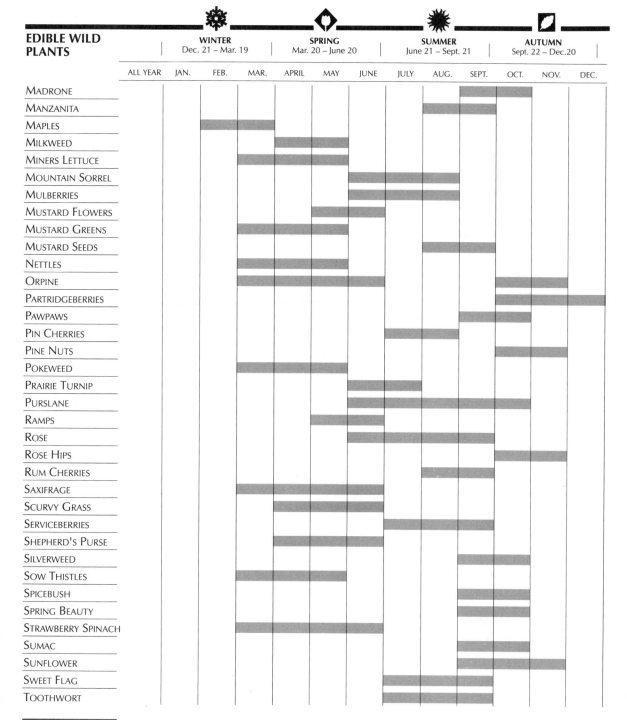

	ALL YEAR	JAN.	FEB.	MAR.	APRIL	MAY	JUNE	JULY	AUG.	SEPT.	OCT.	NOV.	DEC.
WINTER Dec. 21 – Mar. 19													
SPRING Mar. 20 – June 20													
SUMMER June 21 – Sept. 21													
AUTUMN Sept. 22 – Dec.20													
MADRONE										▓	▓		
MANZANITA									▓	▓			
MAPLES			▓	▓									
MILKWEED					▓	▓							
MINERS LETTUCE				▓	▓								
MOUNTAIN SORREL							▓	▓	▓				
MULBERRIES							▓						
MUSTARD FLOWERS					▓								
MUSTARD GREENS				▓	▓	▓							
MUSTARD SEEDS									▓	▓			
NETTLES				▓	▓	▓							
ORPINE				▓	▓	▓					▓	▓	
PARTRIDGEBERRIES											▓	▓	▓
PAWPAWS										▓	▓		
PIN CHERRIES								▓	▓				
PINE NUTS											▓	▓	
POKEWEED				▓	▓	▓	▓						
PRAIRIE TURNIP							▓	▓					
PURSLANE								▓	▓	▓			
RAMPS					▓	▓							
ROSE							▓	▓	▓				
ROSE HIPS											▓	▓	
RUM CHERRIES									▓				
SAXIFRAGE				▓	▓	▓							
SCURVY GRASS					▓	▓							
SERVICEBERRIES								▓	▓				
SHEPHERD'S PURSE					▓	▓							
SILVERWEED										▓	▓		
SOW THISTLES				▓	▓	▓							
SPICEBUSH										▓	▓		
SPRING BEAUTY										▓	▓		
STRAWBERRY SPINACH				▓	▓	▓							
SUMAC										▓			
SUNFLOWER										▓	▓	▓	
SWEET FLAG							▓	▓	▓				
TOOTHWORT								▓	▓	▓			

▓ = signifies very peak of season

See page 44 for a complete list of abbreviations used in these charts.

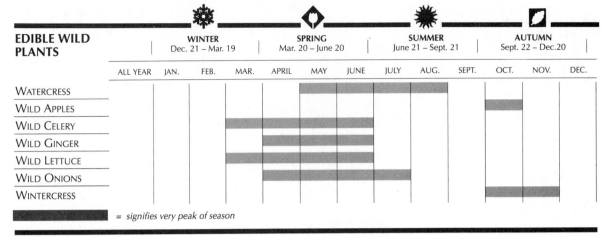

EDIBLE WILD PLANTS

		WINTER Dec. 21 – Mar. 19			SPRING Mar. 20 – June 20			SUMMER June 21 – Sept. 21			AUTUMN Sept. 22 – Dec.20	
	ALL YEAR	JAN.	FEB.	MAR.	APRIL	MAY	JUNE	JULY	AUG.	SEPT.	OCT.	NOV.	DEC.
WATERCRESS						■	■	■	■				
WILD APPLES											■		
WILD CELERY				■	■	■	■						
WILD GINGER					■	■	■						
WILD LETTUCE				■	■	■	■						
WILD ONIONS					■	■	■	■					
WINTERCRESS											■	■	

■ = *signifies very peak of season*

LIST OF ABBREVIATIONS

AK – Arkansas
AZ – Arizona
BC – British Columbia
CA – California
EC – East Coast
ER – Erie
FL – Florida
GA – Georgia
HA – Hawaii
HU – Huron
LA – Louisiana
MA – Massachusetts
ME – Maine
MI – Michigan
MW – Midwest
NB – New Brunswick
NC – North Carolina
NE – Northeast
NJ – New Jersey
NMW – North Midwest
NS – Nova Scotia
NTL – Nationally
NY – New York
NZ – New Zealand
OH – Ohio
ONT – Ontario
OR – Oregon
PA – Pennsylvania
PEI – Prince Edward Island
Q – Quebec
SA – South Atlantic
SE – Southeast
TX – Texas
WA – Washington
WC – West Coast
WI – Wisconsin

WILD MUSHROOMS

These charts are organized by the seasons beginning with spring. Each chart lists alphabetically, by the Latin name, most of the edible mushrooms in that season. With each mushroom is given the common name where applicable, the flavor and texture rating, whether each is edible raw, where they are commonly found, and coloration. To discover the edible mushrooms at their peak simply proceed to the current season and follow the charts. Those edible mushrooms are then available through specialty food stores and even some supermarkets.

Wild edible mushrooms offer flavors and textures that are absolutely wonderful. Morels, chanterelles, cepes, and truffles announce the seasons in grand style. These treasures of nature elevate food to new highs.

The mushrooms listed in these charts are a small portion of the ten thousand species that grow in the United States. Most of the wild mushrooms listed are difficult to properly identify except by experts. Because of the potential for serious or fatal poisoning care must be taken in collecting, identifying, and preparing the mushrooms as well as moderation in eating certain species. It is important to recognize the source of the mushrooms for if they have come in contact with and absorb manmade toxic substances such as pesticides even edible mushrooms can be very dangerous. Many wild mushrooms are available from specialty stores although we recommend verifying their source to avoid potential problems. It is safer to eat single varieties of wild mushrooms rather than mixing, so if a problem develops, the cause may be quickly identified.

Care should also be taken in eating any wild mushroom raw. Most edible mushrooms are toxic in the raw stage and should be cooked thoroughly. The wild mushrooms which are considered safe to eat raw may be toxic to certain people.

The charts list the wild mushrooms generally considered safe to eat. Those with asterisks next to their Latin name are widely distributed commercially and should be relatively easy to find. This chart does not represent that these mushrooms are not toxic, only the mushroom's approximate season. The user must be responsible for interpreting the information within and for any identifications made therefrom. Neither the author nor the publisher accept responsibility for the identifications made by the user of this book or for the consequences of eating any of these species.

SPRING WILD MUSHROOMS

RATING KEY	BEST	LEAST
FOR TASTE	1	4
TEXTURE	FIRM++++	SOFT+

LATIN NAME	COMMON NAME	RATING	EAT RAW?	HABITAT	COLOR/COMMENTS
*Cantharellus cibarius**	Chanterelle	1/+++	X	Woods, moss	Golden yellow
*Cantharellus friesii**	Chanterelle, girolles	1/+++	X	Woods, moss	Orange
*Cantharellus subal bidus**	Chanterelle	2/++		Woods, moss	Yellow
*Cantharellus tubae formis**	Chanterelle	1/+++		Latifoliate woods	Brown, turning yellow
*Cantharellus tubae formis**	Chanterelle	2/++		Wood fragments	Yellow
Coprinus comatus	Shaggy mane	1/++		Sandy soils	White/brownish gray (eat when young)
Coprinus ovatus	Shaggy mane	1/++		Sandy soils	White/brownish (more delicate tasting)
Hygrophorus (Camarophyllus) marzuolos		3/+++		Mountains	Blackish, spotted
Hygrophorus (Linacium) poetarum		2/++		Latifoliate woods/mtns.	Rosy cream
Hygrophorus pratensis		1/+++		Mountains	Pale tan
Lactarius camphorates	Candy cap	2/++		Conifers	Deep red-brown
*Lepiota procera**	Parasol mushroom	1/++		Meadows	Tan/brown
Lyophyllum (Tricholoma) georgii		1/+++		Under bushes	Pale cream/gray
Lyophyllum var. albellum		1/+++		Under bushes	White
Lyophyllum var. gambosum		1/+++		Under bushes	With reddish gills
Lyophyllum var. graveolens		1/+++		Under bushes	Grayish

LATIN NAME	COMMON NAME	RATING	EAT RAW?	HABITAT	COLOR/COMMENTS
Lyophyllum var. pallumbinim		1/+++		Under bushes	Amethyst-colored center
Lyophyllum decastes	Fried chicken mushroom	2/++		Under bushes	White
Lyophyllum goniospermum		1/+++		Mtns. and woods	Amethyst-colored gills
Marasmius oreades*	Fairy ring, Scotch bonnets	1/+++		Sandy/grassy	Tan
Morchella conica*	Morel	1/+++		Woods	Reddish brown
Morchella costata*	Morel	1/+++		Woods	Light brown, black
Morchella deliciosa*	Morel	1/+++		Woods	Gray
Morchella deliciosa*	Morel	1/+++		Woods	White
Morchella elata*	Morel	1/+++		Woods	Olive-brown
Morchella rotunda*	Morel	1/+++		Woods	Reddish
Morchella umbrina*	Morel	1/+++		Woods	Dark brown
Morchella vulgaris*	Morel	1/+++		Woods	Light gray/white
Pleurotus cornucopiae	Oyster mushroom	1/+++		On trees	Whitish red tinge, larvae-like
Pleurotus eryngii*	Oyster mushroom	1/+++		Sandy soils	Whitish
Pleurotus var. ferular	Oyster mushroom	1/+++		Sandy soils	Brownish gray
Pleurotus nebrodensis	Oyster mushroom	1/+++		Mtns./Alps	Whitish
Pleurotus ostreatus*	Oyster mushroom	1/+++		On trees	Black/brown/gray
Pleurotus porrigens*	Angels' wings	1/+++		On trees	White
Polyporus (Polypilus) frondosus	Hen of the woods	3/+		On trees	Gray/brown
Polyporus (Polypilus)* sulphureus	Chicken mushroom	3/++		On trees	Yellow (edible unripe)
Psalliota campestris*	Meadow mushroom	2/+++	X	Meadows	Silky white
Russula cyanoxantha		1/+++		Woods	Slate gray

LATIN NAME	COMMON NAME	RATING	EAT RAW?	HABITAT	COLOR/COMMENTS
Russula cyanoxantha grisea		1/+++		Woods	Violet-gray
Russula cyanoxantha grisea ionochlora		1/+++		Woods	Violet-gray
Russula lutea		1/+++		Latifoliate woods	Red/orange-red, golden/lemon-yellow
Russula vesca		1/++		Woods/plains	Amaranth brown
Russula virescens		1/+++		Woods	Green/yellow-gray/gray
Russula xerampelina	Shrimp mushroom	2/++		Coniferous woods	Purple/crimson
Stropharia coronilla		4/+		All kinds	Light yellow/violet spores
Stropharia ferrii		2/++		All kinds	Yellow/brick red
Tricholomopsis edodes*	Shiitake	1/+++		Cultivated	Tan-brown

SUMMER WILD MUSHROOMS

LATIN NAME	COMMON NAME	RATING	EAT RAW?	HABITAT	COLOR/COMMENTS
Boletus aereus*	Cepes, Tête de Negre	1/+++		Mixed woods	Bronze-brown
Boletus appendiculatus*	Butter cepes	1/+++		Latifoliate woods	Reddish brown/flesh-yellow
Boletus castaneus*	Cepes	1/+++		Latifoliate woods	Chestnut
Boletus cyanescens*	Cepes	1/+++		Woods	Olive
Boletus edulis*	Porcini	1/+++		Latifoliate woods	Tawny brown (best commercial boletus)
Boletus mirabilis*	Admirable cepes	1/+++		On wood, woods	Garnet-brown with reddish stem

LATIN NAME	COMMON NAME	RATING	EAT RAW?	HABITAT	COLOR/COMMENTS
Boletus pinicola*	Cepes	1/+++		Mtns.	Garnet-brown
Boletus reticulatus*	Cepes	1/+++		Latifoliate woods	Hazel-gray, brown top
Boletus rubiginosus*	Cepes	1/+++		Latifoliate woods	Reddish brown
Cantharellus amethysteus*	White chanterelle	2/++		Humid woods	White
Cantharellus carbonarius*	Black chanterelle, gray chanterelle	1/++		Humid woods	Grayish with white stems
Cantharellus cibarius*	Chanterelle	1/+++	X	Woods and moss	Gold
Cantharellus cinereus*	Black chanterelle, gray chanterelle	1/++		Humid woods	Grayish
Cantharellus cinnabarinus*	Cinnabar chanterelle	1/+++		Woods and moss	Vermillion
Cantharellus (Craterellus) cornucopioides*	Trump de la Mort (Trumpet of death)	1/++		Woods/wood pieces	Black/gray-brown
Cantharellus friesii*	Chanterelle	1/+++	X	Woods and moss	Orange
Cantharellus tubarformis*	Chanterelle	1/+++		Latifoliate woods	Brown/yellow
Cantharellus tubarformis* var. lutescens	Chanterelle	1/+++		Wood pieces	Yellow
Clitopilus prunulus	Sweetbread mushroom	1/+++		Near Boletus edulis	White
Coprinus comatus*	Shaggy mane	1/+++		Sandy soils	White/brown-green
Coprinus ovatus*	Shaggy mane	1/+++		Sandy soils	White (more delicate tasting)
Gyrocephalus rufus		2/++	X	Mtns., coniferous forests	Rosy red
Hydnum repandum	Hedgehog	2/++		Woods	Red
Hydnum umbilicatun	Hedgehog			Woods	White/yellow
Lactarius deliciosus*	Saffron milk cap	2/++		Coniferous woods	Orange/green when ripe
Lactarius deliciosus		2/++		Coniferous woods	Indigo
Lactarius deliciosus		2/++		Coniferous woods	Orange

LATIN NAME	COMMON NAME	RATING	EAT RAW?	HABITAT	COLOR/COMMENTS
Lactarius sanguifluus		2/++		Coniferous woods	Orange-vermillion
Lepiota americana*		1/++		Latifoliate woods	Pallid red-brown
Lepiota excoriata	Gray parasol	1/+++		Fields	Cuticle gray
Lepiota procera*	Parasol mushroom	1/+++		Fields	Tan-brown
Lepiota umbonata		1/++		Latifoliate woods	Ocher/tan
Lycoperdon maximum	Puff ball	2/+++		Pastures/woods	Cream
Lyophyllum goniospermum		1/+		Mtn. woods	Amethystine/ cream
Marasmius oreades*	Fairy ring, Scotch bonnets	1/+++		Sandy/grassy	Tan
Peziza aurantia	Orange peel	2/++	X	Sandy/grassy	Rosy/orange
Pleurotus erungii*	Oyster mushroom	1/+++		Sandy soil	White
Pleurotus eryngii verferulae*	Oyster mushroom	1/+++		Sandy soil	Brown-gray
Pleurotus nebrodensis*	Oyster mushroom	1/+++		Mtns./Alps	White
Pleurotus cornucopiae*	Oyster mushroom	3/+		On trees	White/red
Polyporus (Grifola) frondosus*	Hen of the woods	3/+		On trees	Gray/brown
Polyporus ovinus*	Sheep mushroom	2/++		Coniferous woods	Olive
Polyporus pes caprae*	Sheep mushroom	2/++		Coniferous woods	Brown
Polyporus (Laetiporus) sulphureus*	Chicken mushroom	3/++		On trees	Yellow
Polyporus (Grifola) umbellatus*	Sheep mushroom	2/++		Latifoliate woods	Hazel/gray (spoils quickly)
Psalliota (Agaricus) arvensis*	Horse mushroom	2/++	X	Grassy and sunny ground	White with hazel center
Psalliota bispora*	Regular domesticated mushroom	2/++	X	Cultivated	White/brown
Psalliota campestris	Meadow mushroom	2/++	X	Coniferous woods	Silky white
Psalliota silvicola	Woodland mushroom	2/++	X	Coniferous woods	White
Psalliota agusta*	Prince mushroom	1/++	X	Coniferous woods	White/yellow
Russula cyanoxantha		1/+++		Woods	Slate gray

LATIN NAME	COMMON NAME	RATING	EAT RAW?	HABITAT	COLOR/COMMENTS
Russula cyanoxantha grisea		1/+++		Woods	Violet-gray
Russula cyanoxantha grisea ionochlora		1/+++		Woods	Violet-gray
Russula lutea		1/+++		Latifoliate woods	Red/orange red, yellow golden
Russula vesca		2/++		Woods/plains	Amaranth brown
Russula virescens		1/+++		Woods	Green/yellow, green/gray
Suillus brevipes		2/++		Pine woods	Yellow/brown
Suillus cavipes*		1/+++		Pine woods	Rusty brown/yellow
Suillus granulatus		2/++		Pine woods	White/orange
Suillus lakei*		1/+++		Pine woods	Red/gray
Suillus luteus*	Brown ring boletus	1/+++		Pine woods	Yellow/brown
Suillus pictus	Slippery jacks	2/++		Pine woods	Deep red
Tricholoma caligatum		1/++		Woods	Gray/red-brown
Tricholoma columbetta		2/++		Woods	White with spots
Tricholoma flavovirens	Man on horseback	2/++		Pine trees	Yellow/brown
Tricholoma matsutake		2/++		Pine trees	Yellow/brown
Tricholomopsis edodes*	Shiitake	1/+++		Cultivated	Tan-brown
Volvariella bombycina	Silky volvaria	1/+++		On wood knotholes	White/yellow

AUTUMN WILD MUSHROOMS

LATIN NAME	COMMON NAME	RATING	EAT RAW?	HABITAT	COLOR/COMMENTS
Armillaria caesarea	Caesars mushroom	1/+++		Coniferous woods	Orange-red
Armillaria mellea	Honey mushroom, Tête de Meduce	2/++		Coniferous woods	Yellow
Armillaria ponderosa	Pine mushroom, American matsutake	1/+++		Pines	White
*Boletus aereus**	Cepes, Tête de Negre	1/+++		Mixed woods	Bronze-brown
Boletus	Butter cepes	1/+++		Latifoliate woods	Reddish
*Boletus castaneus**	Cepes	1/+++		Latifoliate woods	Chestnut
*Boletus cyanescens**	Cepes	1/+++		Woods	Olive
*Boletus edulis**	Porcini	1/+++		Latifoliate woods	Tawny brown (best commercial boletus)
*Boletus mirabilis**	Admirable cepes	1/+++		On wood/USA, woods	Garnet-brown with reddish stem
*Boletus reticulatus**	Cepes	1/+++		Latifoliate woods	Hazel/gray-brown on top
*Boletus rubiginosus**	Cepes	1/+++		Latifoliate woods	Reddish brown
*Boletus zelleri**	Cepes	1/+++		Pine woods	Olive-brown
*Cantharellus amethysteus**	White chanterelle	2/++		Humid woods	White
*Cantharellus carbonarius**	Black chanterelle, gray chanterelle	1/++		Humid woods	Grayish with white stems
*Cantharellus cibarius**	Chanterelle	1/+++	X	Woods and moss	Gold
*Cantharellus cinereus**	Black chanterelle, gray chanterelle	1/++		Humid woods	Grayish

LATIN NAME	COMMON NAME	RATING	EAT RAW?	HABITAT	COLOR/COMMENTS
Cantharellus (Craterellus) Cornuco-pioides*	Trump de la Mort (Trumpettes of death)	1/++		Woods/wood pieces	Black/green-brown
Cantharellus friesii*	Chanterelle	1/+++	X	Woods and moss	Orange
Cantharellus olidus	Rosy chantarelle	2/+++		Spruces	Rosy
Cantharellus tubarformis*	Chanterelle	1/+++		Latifoliate woods	Brown/yellow
Cantharellus tubarformis var. lutescens*	Chanterelle	1/+++		Wood pieces	Yellow
Clitopilus prunulus	Sweetbread mushroom	1/+++		Near boletus	White
Coprinus comatus*	Shaggy mane	1/+++		Sandy soils	White/brown-green
Coprinus ovatus*	Shaggy mane	1/+++		Sandy soils	White (more delicate tasting)
Hydnum albidus*	Hedgehog	2/++		Woods	White
Hydnum repandum*	Hedgehog	2/++		Woods	Red
Hydnum rufescens*	Hedgehog	2/++		Woods	Orange with white stem
Hydnum umbilicatum*	Hedgehog	2/++		Woods	White/yellow
Hygrocybe bresadolae		2/++		Meadows	Yellow with orange center
Hygrophorus marzuolos		1/+++		Mtns.	Black spotted
Lactarius deliciosus*	Saffron milk cap	2/++		Coniferous woods	Orange/green when ripe
Lactarius deliciosus		2/++		Coniferous woods	Indigo
Lactarius deliciosus		2/++		Coniferous woods	Orange
Lactarius sanguifluus		2/++		Coniferous woods	Orange-vermillion
Lepiota americana*		1/++		Latifoliate woods	Pallid red-brown
Lepiota excoriata	Gray parasol	1/+++		Fields	Cuticle gray
Lepiota procera*	Parasol mushroom	1/+++		Fields	Tan-brown

LATIN NAME	COMMON NAME	RATING	EAT RAW?	HABITAT	COLOR/COMMENTS
Lyophyllum goniospermum		1/+		Mtn. woods	Amethystine/ cream
*Marasmius oreades**	Fairy ring, Scotch bonnets	1/+++		Sandy/grassy areas	Tan
Peziza Aurantia	Orange peel	2/++		Sandy/grassy	Rosy/orange
*Pleurotus cornucopiae**	Oyster mushroom	3/+		On trees	White/red
*Pleurotus erungii**	Oyster mushroom	1/+++		Sandy soil	White
*Pleurotus eryngii verferulae**	Oyster mushroom	1/+++		Sandy soil	Brown-gray
*Pleurotus nebrodensis**	Oyster mushroom	1/+++		Mtns./Alps	White
*Pleurotus ostreatusae**	Oyster mushroom	1/+++		Trunks, stumps	Yellow/brown
*Polyporus (Grifola) frondosus**	Hen of the woods	3/+		On trees	Gray/brown
*Polyporus ovinus**	Sheep mushroom	2/++		Coniferous woods	Olive
*Polyporus pes caprae**	Sheep mushroom	2/++		Coniferous woods	Brown
*Polyporus (Grifola) umbellatus**	Sheep mushroom	2/++		Latifoliate woods	Hazel/gray (spoils quickly)
*Polyporus (Laetiporus) sulphureus**	Chicken mushroom	3/++		On trees	Yellow
*Psalliota bispora**	regular domesticated mushroom	2/++	X	Cultivated	White/brown
*Psalliota agusta**	Prince mushroom	1/++	X	Coniferous woods	White/yellow
*Rozites caperata**	Gypsy mushroom, Pigeon mushroom, Chicken of the woods	2/++		Woods, near mosses and huckleberries	Yellow/tan
Russula cyanoxantha		1/+++		Woods	Slate gray
Russula cyanoxantha grisea		1/+++		Woods	Violet-gray

LATIN NAME	COMMON NAME	RATING	EAT RAW?	HABITAT	COLOR/COMMENTS
Russula cyanoxantha grisea ionochlora		1/+++		Woods	Violet-gray
Russula virescens		1/+++		Woods	Green/yellow or green/gray
Russula vesca		2/++		Woods/plains	Amaranth brown
Sparassis crispa		2/++		Old pines	White/brown
Suillus brevipes		2/++		Pine woods	Yellow/brown
*Suillus cavipes**		1/+++		Pine woods	Rusty brown/yellow
Suillus granulatus		2/++		Pine woods	White/orange
*Suillus luteus**	Brown ring boletus, Slippery jacks	1/+++		Pine woods	Yellow/brown
*Suillus lakei**		1/+++		Pine woods	Red/gray
Suillus pictus		2/++		Pine woods	Deep red
Tricholoma columbetta		2/++		Woods	White with spots
Tricholoma caligatum		1/++		Woods	Gray/red-brown
Tricholoma equestre		2/++		Pine trees	Sulfur-yellow
Tricholoma flavovirens	Man on horseback	2/++		Pine trees	Yellow/brown
Tricholoma matsutake		2/++		Pine trees	Yellow/brown
Tricholoma portentosum		2/++		Latifoliate woods	Violet to black
Tricholoma terreum		2/++		Coniferous woods	Gray/brown
*Tricholomopsis edodes**	Shiitake	1/+++		Cultivated	Tan-brown
*Tuber magnatum**	White truffle	1/++++	X	Oaks, latifoliate woods	Rosy white
Volvariella bombycina	Silky volvaria	1/+++		On wood	White/yellow

WINTER WILD MUSHROOMS

LATIN NAME	COMMON NAME	RATING	EAT RAW ?	HABITAT	COLOR
Armillaria mellea	Honey mushroom, Tête de Meduce	2/++	.	Coniferous woods	Yellow
Armillaria ponderosa	Pine mushroom, American matsutake	1/+++		Pines	White
*Boletus zelleri**	Cepes	1/+++		Pine woods	Olive-brown
Collybia velutipes		2++		Latifoliate woods	Honey/orange
Hydnum rufescens	Hedgehog	2++		Woods	Orange with white stems
*Pleurotus ostreatusae**	Oyster mushroom	1/+++		Trunks, stumps	Yellow/brown
*Tricholoma edodes**	Shiitake	2/++		Cultivated	Tan-brown
Tricholoma terreum		2/++		Coniferous woods	Gray/brown
*Tuber brumale**	Winter truffle	1/++++	X	Oaks	Black/brown
*Tuber magnatum**	White truffle	1/++++	X	Oaks, latifoliate woods	Rosy white
*Tuber melano-sporum**	Black truffle	1/++++	X	Oaks	Black/brown

THE BASICS

VEGETABLE BLANCHING GUIDE

When cooking all of these vegetables, a few simple guidelines will produce wonderful results. Blanch or cook the vegetables uncovered in large quantities of lightly salted boiling water, until just tender, usually a few minutes. The large amount of water dilutes the natural acids released by the vegetables, helping to maintain their bright green color. Covering the pot condenses these same natural acids, causing discoloration of the vegetables. Avoid overcooking, for the flavors, composed of volatile compounds and vitamins, are driven off, resulting in bland vegetables with little nutritional value.

How to Use the Chart

1. Look up the vegetable of your choice.

2. Locate the size of the vegetable to determine the proper timing.

3. *Peel* or *Unpeeled*—the X designates how the vegetables are best served. Peeling should be done before blanching, removing only the exterior membrane.

4. Cooking textures (all figures indicate minutes)
   Crudité—Used primarily raw or quite crisp and firm. Usually served chilled or at room temperature. *1/RAW* indicates blanch for 1 minute for crudité. *2/RAW* indicates you can blanch for 2 minutes if you wish, depending on use. The color will be very intense and natural.
   Al dente—Means firm to the bite but without raw texture. Most vegetables are best served at this texture for optimum flavor and nutrition. The color will still be bright.
   Tender—Resilient to the bite but without resistance. Vegetables are technically overcooked at this point, although some people prefer their vegetables this way. Color begins to fade.
   Puree—No texture to bite. Mostly used for puree. Color paler.

5. *Acid*—This indicates that acids (like lemon or lime juice) should be added to the cooking liquids to prevent discoloration.

VEGETABLE	SIZE	PEEL	UNPEELED	CRUDITÉ	AL DENTE	TENDER	PUREE	ACID
ASPARAGUS	SML	X	X	RAW	2	4	7	NO
ASPARAGUS	MED	X	X	1 ½	3	5	8	NO
ASPARAGUS	LRG	x		2	4	6	9–10	NO
ARTICHOKES	SML		x	10	12	15	18	YES
ARTICHOKES	MED		X	12	15	18	20	YES
ARTICHOKES	LRG		X	15	17	20	25	YES
ANISE BULB	MED		X	5	8	12	15	NO
BROCCOLI	PC	X	X	1/RAW	3	5	10	NO
BRUSSELS SPROUTS	MED	X		2	3	5	10	NO
CARROTS, SLICED	MED	X		RAW	7	10	15	NO

VEGETABLE	SIZE	PEEL	UNPEELED	CRUDITÉ	AL DENTE	TENDER	PUREE	ACID
CAULIFLOWER	PC		X	1/RAW	3	5	10	NO
CELERY ROOT	MED	X	X	10	13	18	25	NO
CELERY STALK	PC	X	X	RAW	2	5	8	NO
CHAYOTE	LRG	X	X	10	15	19	25	NO
CORN ON COB	MED		HUSKED		3	5	8	NO
CORN KERNELS	PC		X	RAW	2	4	6	NO
ENGLISH PEAS	MED	X (SHELL)		RAW	2	3	6	NO
FENNEL BULB	MED		X	RAW	15	20	25	NO
HARICOT VERT	SML			RAW	1 1/2	4	9	NO
JICAMA, SLICED	MED	X		RAW	3	6	10	YES
KOHLRABI	MED	X		RAW	8	12	20	NO
LEEKS	MED	X			4	6	12	NO
PARSLEY ROOT	MED	X		3	4	6	10	NO
PARSNIP, SLICED	MED	X		2/RAW	3	5	10	NO
POTATOES, DICED	MED	X			10	20	20	NO
POTATOES, NEW	SML	X	X		15	25	30	NO
RADISHES	MED		X	RAW	3	5	10	NO
RADISHES, DIAKON, SLICED	MED	X		RAW	2	5	10	NO
RAPINI	PC	X		RAW	2	4	8	NO
SNOW PEAS	MED	STRING		RAW	1/2	1 1/2	3	NO
SPINACH	SML	STEM		RAW	1/2	2	3	NO
SQUASH, ACORN, DICED	MED	X		3	5	9	15	NO
SQUASH, BUTTERNUT, DICED	MED	X		3	5	9	15	NO
SQUASH, HUBBARD, DICED	MED	X		3	5	9	15	NO

NUT BLANCHING AND TOASTING GUIDE

To develop the full flavor of nuts, proper toasting is necessary to bring out their taste and crunchy texture.

How to Use the Chart

1. Select the nut of your choice.

2. *Skins* designates if the flavor of the nut is improved by removing the skin.

3. *Blanch* is the time in minutes in boiling water necessary to remove the skins easily.

4. *Toast* refers to the time in minutes it takes to toast the nut to its best flavor and crunchy texture. To toast the nuts, place on an ungreased cookie sheet and in a preheated 300°F oven on the lower rack. Stir frequently until nuts are light tan in color. If nuts are to be infused into a sauce, they should be toasted till deeper in color to develop the nut's full flavor. Cool on a rack to room temperature. Do not refrigerate.

5. *Infuse* means the time in minutes the nut should be toasted for the best flavor release when the nut is to be used for infusion into creams for desserts and ice creams.

6. *Cups/lb* provides cup-to-pound equivalents (how many cups of a particular nut in a pound) for easy home conversion.

NUT	SKINS	BLANCH	TOAST	INFUSE	CUPS/LB
ALMOND, SLICED	NO	N/A	30	40	4¼
ALMOND, WHOLE	YES	5	35	45	3¼
CHESTNUT	YES	25	N/A	N/A	
HAZELNUT	YES	5	25	45	4
MACADAMIA	NO	N/A	30	40	3¼
PEANUT	YES	3	35	35	3¼
PEANUT, DRY ROASTED	NO	N/A	N/A	5	3¼
PECAN	NO	N/A	35	45	4½
PINE NUT	NO	N/A	25	30	3¼
PISTACHIO	YES	3	40	50	3¼
WALNUT	NO	N/A	50	50	4½
WHITE WALNUT, BUTTERNUT	NO	N/A	50	50	4½

SEED AND SPICE TOASTING CHART

To develop the true, rich flavors of spices and seeds, it is best to toast them to drive off flavor-inhibiting moisture. Avoid overheating as volatile oils will escape. It is best to use fresh—meaning this season's—spices.

How to Use the Chart

1. Select the seed or spice of your choice.

2. *Toast* refers to the time it takes to toast whole seeds and spices with normal moisture content. To toast, place on an ungreased cookie sheet and in a pre-heated 325°F oven on the lower rack. Stir frequently until seeds or spices are light in tan color. Cool on a rack to room temperature. Do not refrigerate.

3. *Cups/lb* provides cup-to-pound equivalents (how many cups of a particular seed or spice in a pound) for easy home conversion.

SEEDS OR SPICES	TOAST	CUPS/LB
CARAWAY	12	4
CELERY	5	4
CORIANDER	13	6
CUMIN	13	4½
DILL	5	5
FENNEL	10	4½
MUSTARD	12	2½
PAPAYA	7	N/A
POPPY	10	3
PUMPKIN	15	4
SESAME	10	3
SUNFLOWER	12	3½
SZECHUAN PEPPERCORN	10	8

PREPARING AN ARTICHOKE

To prepare an artichoke, you should

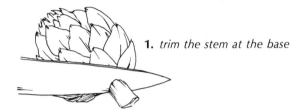

1. trim the stem at the base

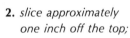

2. slice approximately one inch off the top;

3. cut the spiky tops off the outer leaves

4. rub the trimmed artichoke with lemon or lime juice to retard the enzymatic browning

Roasting Peppers

Roasting peppers develops their natural flavors and allows you to peel them easily. If you want your peppers crisp and not roasted, you can peel them by hand.

Choose the type of pepper you need for the recipe you are making.

Place the whole pepper on an open gas flame or outdoor grill or under a broiler and cook until the pepper's skin is black. Rotate the pepper until all the skin is black. Place the pepper in a bowl and cover the bowl with plastic wrap. Allow the pepper to cool for 15 minutes, then remove it to a counter top. Using your hands (except with hot chiles which should only be handled with rubber gloves), remove the skin. Prepare the pepper as your recipe requires.

Roasting Garlic, Shallots, Leeks, and Onions

Roasting develops the natural flavors and sugars of vegetables. Once you try them roasted, you will want to incorporate them into your favorite recipes. Choose the vegetable you need for the recipe you are making.

1 **whole head of garlic**
1 **onion, with skin on**
1 **shallot, with skin on**
2 **cups pearl onions, with skin on**
1 **leek, trimmed**
  Virgin olive or corn oil

Preheat the oven to 400° F.

In a large ovenproof skillet, combine the vegetable with enough oil to coat. Place on the lower rack of the oven and cook until the skin is brown and the vegetable tender, about 30 to 60 minutes, depending on the size.

(The shallots, garlic, and pearl onions take the least time, while the onion and leek take about twice as long.) Let cool. With a little pressure from your hand, the vegetable will easily come away from its skin. The vegetable will hold its natural shape but will mash under the pressure of a utensil like a fork. You may refrigerate the roasted vegetables with or without their skins for up to 3 days.

Grilled Eggplant

Eggplant is a native of India and was so named because of the resemblance the smaller white variety has to its namesake. It is made up of a large portion of intercellular air pockets capable of absorbing large volumes of olive oil. The old lore in parts of the Mediterranean culture was that people showed wealth by the amount of olive oil on the eggplant they served to their guests; the more olive oil, the richer they were.

1 **large eggplant**
¼ **cup kosher salt**
1 **cup virgin olive oil**

Peel and slice the eggplant ½ inch thick. Sprinkle all the surfaces of the eggplant with the salt. Place the eggplant in a colander and allow the salt to draw out the moisture for 1 hour. Rinse the eggplant off under cold running water, pat dry with paper toweling, and rub with ½ cup of the olive oil.

Preheat the grill.

Place the eggplant slices on the grill and sear well, about 4 minutes. Turn over and cook until tender, about 4 minutes. Remove to a dish and add the remaining olive oil. Refrigerate until ready to use.

Poultry Stock

1 **gallon (or more) water**
4 **pounds chicken bones**
2 **large onions, diced**
2 **large carrots, diced**
2 **bunches fresh parsley stems**
2 **bay leaves**
2 **teaspoons black peppercorns**

Combine the water with the bones in an 8-quart or larger stockpot. Bring to a simmer over medium heat, skimming the surface. Add the remaining ingredients and simmer for 5 hours, adding more water if necessary to keep the ingredients covered. Strain through a fine sieve. Refrigerate and spoon off the fatty stock that rises to the top. (This can be prepared ahead and refrigerated for up to 3 days or frozen for up to 1 month.)

MAKES ABOUT 10 CUPS ■

Duck Stock

4 **pounds duck bones**
1 **gallon (or more) water**
2 **large onions, diced**
2 **large carrots, diced**
2 **bunches fresh parsley stems**
2 **bay leaves**
2 **teaspoons black peppercorns**

Preheat the oven to 400° F.

In a large ovenproof skillet, add the duck bones. Place on the lower rack of the oven and cook until browned, about 30 minutes.

Combine the water with the bones in an 8-quart or larger stockpot. Bring to a simmer over medium heat,

skimming the surface. Add the remaining ingredients and simmer for 4 hours, adding more water if necessary to keep the ingredients covered. Strain through a fine sieve. Refrigerate and spoon off the fatty stock that rises to the top. (This can be prepared ahead and refrigerated for up to 3 days or frozen for up to 1 month.)

MAKES ABOUT 10 CUPS ■

Beef Stock

2 **pounds beef breast or meaty beef bones**
2 **pounds veal breast or meaty veal bones**
1 **gallon (or more) water**
2 **large onions, diced**
2 **large carrots, diced**
2 **bunches fresh parsley stems**
2 **bay leaves**
2 **teaspoons black peppercorns**

Preheat the oven to 400°F.

In a large ovenproof skillet, add the beef and veal breasts or bones. Place on the lower rack of the oven and cook until browned, about 45 minutes.

Combine the water with the bones in an 8-quart or larger stockpot. Bring to a simmer over medium heat, skimming the surface. Add the remaining ingredients and simmer for 12 hours, adding more water if necessary to keep the ingredients covered. Strain through a fine sieve. Refrigerate and spoon off the fatty stock that rises to the top. (This can be prepared ahead and refrigerated for up to 3 days or frozen for up to 1 month.)

VARIATION: To make lamb stock, substitute 2 pounds lamb breast or meaty bones for the beef breast and brown with the veal breast for only 30 minutes. Proceed as for the beef stock.

MAKES ABOUT 10 CUPS ■

Veal Stock

1 gallon (or more) water
4 pounds veal breast or meaty veal bones
2 large onions, diced
2 large carrots, diced
2 bunches fresh parsley stems
2 bay leaves
2 teaspoons black peppercorns

Combine the water with the veal breast or bones in an 8-quart or larger stockpot. Bring to a simmer over medium heat, skimming the surface. Add the remaining ingredients and simmer for 24 hours, adding more water if necessary to keep the ingredients covered. Strain through a fine sieve. Refrigerate and spoon off the fatty stock that rises to the top. (This can be prepared ahead and refrigerated for up to 3 days or frozen for up to 1 month.) For a more intense color and flavor, roast the bones at 400°F for about 45 minutes prior to making the stock.

MAKES ABOUT 10 CUPS ■

Speedy Vegetable Stock

 1 large onion, diced
1½ cups roasted (see page 62) shallots, finely diced
 ½ bunch parsley stems
 3 bay leaves
 ¼ cup black peppercorns
 ½ cup tomato paste
 4 cups (or more) water
One 750-ml bottle dry white wine, preferably Chardonnay

Combine all the ingredients in a 12-cup or larger stock pot. Bring to a simmer over medium-high heat, stirring occasionally. Cook for 1 hour, then strain through a fine sieve. Allow to cool, then refrigerate for up to 5 days or freeze for up to 1 month.

To prepare for sauce concentration and easier storage: In a 12-cup stock pot bring the stock to a boil over high heat. Cook until reduced to 1 to 1½ cups. Remove from the heat and allow to cool. Refrigerate for up to 10 days or freeze for up to 1 month.

COOKING NOTES: By reducing the stock it will shorten the cooking or reduction time of your sauce recipes, as well as take up less space in your refrigerator or freezer. ■ Since tomato paste is an ingredient in this recipe, the final dish will have the taste of tomato. If, by your taste, the recipe is not enhanced by the tomato flavor, it may be replaced with an additional ½ cup roasted shallots.

MAKES ABOUT 8 CUPS ■

Vegetable Stock

2 large leeks, cleaned of sand and diced
2 large onions, diced
1 cup chopped shallots
1 large carrot, diced
1 celery root, peeled and diced
3 quarts (or more) water
3 cups dry white wine
1 bunch fresh parsley stems
2 bay leaves
2 tablespoons black peppercorns

Combine the vegetables with the water and wine in an 8-quart or larger stock pot. Bring to a simmer over medium heat, skimming the surface. Add the parsley stems, bay leaves, and peppercorns. Return to a simmer and cook for 4 hours, adding more water if necessary to keep the ingredients covered. Strain through a fine sieve. Refrigerate. (This can be prepared ahead and refrigerated for up to 3 days or frozen for up to 1 month.)

MAKES ABOUT 10 CUPS ■

Fish Stock (Fumet)

Select sole or salmon for the best fish fumet. Avoid oily, smelly fish or the stock will taste the same way.

5   pounds fresh lean fish heads and frames
3   quarts (or more) water
3   cups dry white wine
1   large leek, cleaned of sand and diced
2   large onions, diced
1   cup chopped shallots
1   large carrot, diced
1   bunch fresh parsley stems
2   bay leaves
2   tablespoons black peppercorns

Wash the fish bones under cold running water until the water is clear. Combine the fish bones with the water and wine in an 8-quart or larger stock pot. Bring to a simmer, skimming the surface. Add the leek, onions, shallots, carrot, parsley stems, bay leaves, and peppercorns. Return to a simmer and cook for 45 minutes. Strain through a fine sieve. Refrigerate. (Can be prepared ahead. Refrigerate for up to 3 days or freeze for up to 1 month.)

MAKES ABOUT 10 CUPS ■

Crème Fraîche

1   cup heavy cream
1   cup sour cream

Scald the heavy cream, then whisk in the sour cream. Maintain at a temperature of 110°F for 12 hours in a water bath in an oven turned to the lowest setting of warm. Refrigerate to cool overnight. (Can be prepared 3 days ahead.)

MAKES 2 CUPS ■

Tomato Concasse

The word *concasse* is from the French *concasser,* meaning to chop.

6   large ripe tomatoes (smell and feel them!)
    Salt to taste
    Freshly ground black pepper to taste

Add the tomatoes to a large pot of boiling salted water and cook for 30 seconds to loosen the skins. Remove and drain. With a paring knife, score the tomato skins and remove.

Cut the tomatoes in half horizontally. Squeeze out the seeds, then dice into 1/4-inch pieces and place in a colander to drain while you're dicing the remaining tomatoes.

Add salt and pepper. Refrigerate until ready to serve, or up to 24 hours.

VARIATIONS: Make with equal parts yellow and red tomatoes or blend with diced dried tomatoes to your taste.

Substitute red and yellow pepper concasse as a brighter and crisper alternative to the tomato concasse. Make it from 1 red and 1 yellow diced pepper in place of the tomatoes.

MAKES 2 CUPS ■

Cranberry Puree

Great blended with crème anglaise for a topping for desserts, with vinaigrettes for salads, and salsas for grilled meats.

- **2 cups fresh cranberries**
- **½ cup sugar**
- **2 cups water**

In a small saucepan, combine all the ingredients. Bring to a simmer over high heat, then cook until the cranberries are soft, about 30 minutes. Transfer to a food processor and puree until smooth. Strain through a fine sieve. Reserve in the refrigerator for up to 2 weeks.

MAKES 1 CUP ∎

Ginger Puree

- **1½ cups peeled and diced fresh ginger**
- **½ cup fresh lemon juice**
- **2 tablespoons sugar**

In a small saucepan, combine all the ingredients. Bring to a simmer over high heat and cook until tender, about 30 minutes. Transfer to a food processor and puree until smooth. Strain. Reserve in the refrigerator for up to 1 month.

MAKES 1 CUP ∎

Quatre Épices

Select fresh ground spices for they lose their essential oils quickly while in storage. If the spices smell strong, they will taste great. Trust your nose. This is the traditional pâté spice so commonly associated with France. It is a great seasoning for game and poultry.

- **2 teaspoons ground cinnamon**
- **4 teaspoons ground allspice**
- **2 teaspoons freshly grated nutmeg**
- **4 teaspoons ground coriander**
- **4 teaspoons ground tarragon**
- **1 teaspoon ground cloves**
- **1 teaspoon ground marjoram**

Combine all the ingredients. Store in a sealed jar in a cool location or under refrigeration for up to a month.

MAKES 6 TABLESPOONS ∎

Rattlesnake Chili Powder

Select fresh ground spices for they lose their essential oils quickly while in storage. If the spices smell strong, they will taste great. Trust your nose.

- **¼ cup ground coriander**
- **½ cup ground cumin**
- **¼ cup hot Hungarian paprika**
- **1 tablespoon ground ginger**
- **2 tablespoons ground telecherry black pepper (see note below)**
- **1 tablespoon ground jalapeño powder**
- **1 tablespoon ground cayenne pepper**

Sift the spices together. Store in an airtight jar under refrigeration for up to 2 months.

COOKING NOTES: Telecherry is an especially fragrant type of peppercorn and my favorite. The name refers to where it's produced, Telecherry, India.
- Jalapeño powder can be bought in specialty spice stores.

MAKES 1¼ CUPS ■

Rattlesnake Curry Powder

Select fresh ground spices for they lose their essential oils quickly while in storage. If the spices smell strong, they will taste great. Trust your nose.

- ¼ cup ground coriander
- 3 tablespoons ground cumin
- 1 tablespoon ground turmeric
- 1 tablespoon ground ginger
- 1 tablespoon ground telecherry black pepper (see note below)
- 1 tablespoon ground jalapeño powder
- 1 tablespoon ground mustard seed
- 1 tablespoon ground cardamom seed
- 1 tablespoon ground fenugreek
- 1 tablespoon ground cayenne pepper
- 1½ teaspoons ground cloves
- 1½ teaspoons ground cassia (see note below)

Sift the spices together. Store in an airtight jar under refrigeration for up to 2 months.

COOKING NOTES: Telecherry is an especially fragrant type of peppercorn and my favorite. The name refers to where it's produced, Telecherry, India.
- Cassia is the dried flower bud of the cassia tree whose bark is sold commercially as cinnamon. It has a pronounced flavor, much like that of "red hots" candy. You can purchase it in spice or specialty food stores, as you can jalapeño powder.

MAKES 1 CUP ■

Blue Corn Tortillas

- ¾ cup blue corn masa
- 1 tablespoon corn oil
  Pinch of salt
  Up to 2 tablespoons hot water

In a small bowl, combine the masa, oil, and salt until just blended. Add enough of the water to just form a ball. Roll into 8 small balls. If you don't have a tortilla press, roll out to a thickness of ¹⁄₁₆ of an inch between layers of wax paper. Place between wax paper and flatten each one in a tortilla press. (If the masa crumbles or cracks around edges, add more water and reform.)

Heat a skillet or a griddle until very hot and glaze with corn oil to prevent sticking. Peel off one layer of the wax paper, press the tortilla onto the skillet, and cook for 2 minutes. Remove the remaining wax paper. Turn over and cook until slightly tanned and firm, about 2 minutes.

Keep warm, wrapped in a towel, in a 175°F oven.

VARIATION: Make yellow corn tortillas by substituting an equal amount of yellow cornmeal for the blue corn masa.

MAKES 8 TORTILLAS ■

Blue Corn Tortilla Chips

- 6 blue corn tortillas, quartered (best if undercooked)
  Corn oil for frying

Fill a large deep skillet with 3 inches of corn oil and heat to 325°F over medium-high. Add half of the tortilla quarters and cook until crisp while stirring, about 3 minutes. Remove to paper towels to drain. Repeat with the remaining tortillas.

VARIATION: Use the same technique to make yellow corn chips, using yellow corn tortillas.

MAKES 24 CHIPS ■

Egg Pasta Dough

1½ **cups all-purpose flour**
2 **large eggs, beaten**

On a large flat surface, sift the flour into a mound and make a well in the center. Pour the eggs into the well. Start mixing the flour into the eggs with a fork until the eggs and flour are combined. Begin working with your hands to combine the remaining flour into a ball. Knead the ball with your palms, pushing it away from your body. Fold and turn the pasta after each away motion until the texture is smooth and supple, about 8 minutes. Form into a smooth ball, cover with plastic wrap, and refrigerate until ready to use. Can be made up to 3 days ahead.

MAKES ½ POUND ■

Spinach Pasta Dough

½ **cup blanched (see pages 57–59) spinach**
1 **large egg, beaten**
1¾ **cups high-gluten flour**

In a food processor, combine the spinach and the egg. Puree on high speed until smooth, about 5 minutes.

On a large flat surface, sift the flour into a mound and make a well in the center. Pour the spinach mixture into the well. Start mixing the flour into the spinach with a fork until well blended. Begin working with your hands to

combine the remaining flour into a ball. Knead the ball with your palms, pushing it away from your body. Fold and turn the pasta after each away motion until the texture is smooth and supple, about 8 minutes. Form into a smooth ball, cover with plastic wrap, and refrigerate until ready to use. Can be made up to 3 days ahead.

VARIATIONS: For a light green pasta, substitute 2 to 2¼ cups all-purpose flour for the high-gluten flour. The high-gluten flour absorbs more moisture than the all-purpose flour, thus making a greener colored pasta.

Substitute ½ cup Italian tomato paste for the spinach to make tomato pasta.

MAKES ½ POUND ■

Beet Pasta Dough

1 **medium-size beet**
1 **large egg, beaten**
1½ **cups high-gluten flour**

Preheat the oven to 400°F.

Place the beet in a small baking pan, set in the lower third of the oven, and cook until a skewer inserted in the beet meets no resistance, about 30 minutes. Remove and allow to cool to room temperature. Peel off the toughened outer skin.

In a food processor, combine the beet and the egg and puree until smooth, about 3 minutes.

On a large flat surface, sift the flour into a mound and make a well in the center. Pour the beet mixture into the well. Start mixing the flour into the beet mixture with a fork until well blended. Begin working with your hands to combine the remaining flour into a ball. Knead the ball with your palms, pushing it away from your body. Fold and turn the pasta after each away motion until the texture is smooth and supple, about 8 minutes. Form into a smooth ball, cover with plastic wrap, and refrigerate until ready to use. Can be made up to 3 days ahead.

VARIATIONS: For a light pink pasta, substitute 2 to 2¼ cups all-purpose flour for the high-gluten flour. The high-gluten flour absorbs more moisture than the all-purpose flour, thus making a redder colored pasta.

Substitute ½ cup pumpkin puree for the beet in the processor to make pumpkin pasta. Add 1 teaspoon ground nutmeg or 1 tablespoon Ginger Puree (see page 66) to the beet or pumpkin pasta for a spicier variation.

MAKES ½ POUND ∎

the dough in plastic and refrigerate again for 20 minutes.

Repeat the rolling and the folding technique for two final turns, wrap in plastic, and refrigerate the dough for at least 20 minutes before rolling out for baking. Refrigerate up to 3 days. If you freeze the dough, thaw it overnight in the refrigerator.

Flour and roll the dough out to ¼- to ⅛-inch thickness, depending on your application. Bake on a greased cookie sheet in a preheated 400°F oven until golden, about 12 minutes.

MAKES 1½ POUNDS ∎

Puff Pastry

3 cups all-purpose flour, sifted
½ teaspoon salt
¾ pound (3 sticks) unsalted butter,
  cut into 1½-teaspoon pieces
10 tablespoons ice water

Combine the flour and salt on a table. Mix in the butter until coated with the flour. Make a trough or long well in the flour. Add 2 tablespoons of the ice water to the trough. With your fingertips extended and palms upward, distribute the water through the flour by putting your fingertips together while gently tossing the flour. Continue the technique until the dough just holds together without being sticky. Flatten the dough into a rectangle with the palm of your hand in a downward motion. Refrigerate the dough for 20 minutes.

On a floured surface, roll the pastry into a rectangle three times longer than it is wide, ⅜ to ½ inch thick. Dust to remove any excess flour. Fold the top third of the rolled dough over the center third. Then fold the bottom third of the rolled dough over the center third to complete a "turn." Rotate the pastry clockwise 90° and repeat the rolling and the folding technique for a second turn. Wrap the dough in plastic and refrigerate for 20 minutes. Repeat the rolling and folding technique for two additional turns. Wrap

Black Walnut Bread

Great for croutons in winter salads.

1 package dry yeast
¼ cup pure maple syrup
1 cup lukewarm water (about 110°F)
2 cups all-purpose flour, sifted
1 cup whole wheat flour, sifted
¾ teaspoon salt
½ tablespoon coarsely ground black pepper
3 cups black walnut pieces
2 tablespoons virgin olive oil

In a small bowl, combine the yeast, syrup, and warm water. Allow the yeast to activate and foam.

In a food processor, combine the flours, salt, and pepper. Add 2 cups of the walnuts, chopping until very fine. Add the yeast mixture and process until a ball forms; work just until the dough pulls away from the side of the bowl. Add the remaining walnuts and the olive oil.

Remove immediately to an oiled bowl, cover with a clean cloth, and allow to rise in a warm, draft-free place till doubled, about 30 minutes. Punch down.

Place a baking stone on the lower rack of the oven and preheat the oven to 400°F.

Form the dough into a long, thin ficelle. In a warm, draft-free place, covered with a clean cloth, allow to rise 1½ times in volume, about 10 minutes. Place on the stone on the lower rack of the oven. Bake for 10 minutes, reduce the heat to 350°F, and continue to bake until golden, about 10 minutes. Remove to a rack to cool.

COOKING NOTE: *Ficelle* is a French term for a loaf of bread that is approximately half the diameter of a baguette of French bread.

MAKES 1 FICELLE LOAF (ABOUT 1½ INCHES IN DIAMETER BY 16 INCHES LONG) ■

Lemon Bread

1 package dry yeast
2 tablespoons sugar
¾ cup lukewarm water (about 110°F)
½ cup grated lemon rind
3 cups all-purpose flour, sifted
½ teaspoon salt
¼ cup fresh lemon juice
1½ tablespoons coarsely ground black pepper
2 tablespoons virgin olive oil

In small bowl, combine the yeast, sugar, and warm water. Allow the yeast to activate and foam.

In a food processor, combine the flour, pepper, and salt. Add the lemon rind and chop until very fine. Add the yeast mixture and lemon juice, and process until a ball forms; work just until the dough pulls away from the side of the bowl. Add the olive oil. Remove immediately to an oiled bowl, cover with a clean cloth, and allow to rise in a warm, draft-free place until doubled, about 10 minutes. Punch down.

Place a baking stone on the lower rack of the oven and preheat to 400°F. Form the dough into a long, thin ficelle. Allow to rise to 1½ times in volume, about 10 minutes. Place on the stone on the lower rack of the oven. Bake for 10 minutes, reduce the heat to 350°F, and

continue to bake until golden, about 10 minutes. Remove to a rack to cool.

MAKES 1 FICELLE LOAF (ABOUT 1½ INCHES IN DIAMETER BY 16 INCHES LONG) ■

Toasted Croutons

1 loaf French bread, sliced ¼ inch thick
¼ cup virgin olive oil

Rub the surfaces of the sliced bread with the olive oil. Place in a preheated 350°F oven and cook until golden, about 2 minutes. Reserve.

VARIATIONS:
Lemon Croutons: Substitute one loaf of Lemon Bread (see left) and either toast as described above or on a grill.
Walnut Bread Croutons: Substitute one loaf Black Walnut Bread (see page 69).
Grilled Garlic Croutons: Substitute one loaf French bread, rub the surfaces of the cut bread with 2 roasted cloves garlic (see page 62), and then brush with the olive oil. Place on a grill and toast until golden, about 2 minutes.

Clarified Butter

½ pound (2 sticks) unsalted butter

In a small pan, melt the butter. Remove from the heat and pour into a clear measuring cup. Skim off the white froth, which is whey, and discard. Skim off the butter fat and reserve. Cover and refrigerate for up to 2 weeks.

MAKES ½ CUP ■

Acetification is caused by the bacteria acetobacter aceti (mycoderma aceti) as well as a few related vinegar bacteria. They attack the alcohol in wine or other liquids and convert it into acetic acid and/or the ester ethyl acetate. The original bacteria usually gain access to the wine through fruit flies who act as host, unsterilized equipment, or by airborne bacteria cells or spores (though this is rare). The bacteria colony grows on the surface of the wine until quite thick, then sinks into the wine or vinegar. This colony is called the vinegar mother and is available from specialty stores. The colony will reform until all the alcohol is converted to vinegar. The colony then will become dormant until new wine is added.

Other bacteria and yeasts can also attack the wine prior to acetification, causing the wine to be unpalatable. This can be prevented by the introduction of the vinegar mother, which establishes the preferred bacteria colony in the wine that is to be converted to vinegar.

Vinegars are great to grow at home using leftover wines or favorite wines or ciders. Combine the vinegar mother and the wine or cider in a large glass jar and cover with cheesecloth. Allow it to develop for about 2 months in a warm, ventilated area. Draw off not more than half the vinegar, bottle it, and store at room temperature. Replace the drawn-off vinegar with additional wine. Blends of different wines can be used, the flavor of the vinegar reflecting the varietal of the wine itself.

Seasoned Vinegars

Vinegars can be seasoned with herbs, spices, vegetables, and fruits. Introduce the seasonings into a neutral vinegar, allow them to macerate for some length of time, then strain off the seasoned vinegar. Use this seasoned vinegar to make special dressings that enhance the flavor of the greens or vegetables they will accompany. This technique is especially tasty with salsas. For more unusual tastes, seasoned vinegars can be paired with seasoned oils, such as ginger vinegar with Szechuan corn oil.

Some suggestions for complementary flavorings for seasoned vinegars are as follows:

Apple or pear vinegar	Spices such as cinnamon, allspice, nutmeg, mace, ginger, Szechuan peppercorns, and vanilla
Sauvignon blanc vinegar	Dill, chervil, caraway, parsley, and sorrel
Chardonnay vinegar	Basil, ginger, dried red peppers, achiote, coriander, fennel, marjoram, oregano, and tarragon
Riesling or gewürztraminer vinegar	Juniper, hot peppers, paprikas, onions, and chives
Pinot noir vinegar	Rosemary, shallots, garlic, marjoram, angelica, and tarragon
Cabernet sauvignon or full-bodied red wine vinegar	Citrus rinds, peppercorns, chives, scallion greens, garlic, hot peppers, thyme, juniper, star anise, bay, ginger, currants, and berries

Rattlesnake Vinegar

2 cups red wine vinegar
1 cup white wine vinegar
1 cup cider vinegar
1 cup chopped garlic
1 cup chopped shallots
½ cup crushed red peppers

Combine all the ingredients in a gallon glass jar. Cover the jar with cheesecloth tightly. Store in a cool location for 2 months until the flavors develop. Ladle the vinegar from the jar and strain through a coffee filter into a glass container to remove the sediments. The vinegar is now ready to use with your favorite recipes. Store at room temperature, well covered to prevent evaporation. It will store for approximately a year.

Chardonnay and Fennel Vinegar

2 **quarts chardonnay vinegar (or substitute white wine vinegar)**
One **750-ml bottle chardonnay**
1 **medium-size fennel bulb, trimmed and coarsely chopped**
½ **cup fennel seeds, toasted (see page 61)**

Combine the ingredients in a large saucepan. Bring to a boil over high heat. Allow to cool to room temperature. Pour into a gallon glass jar. Cover the top with cheesecloth tightly. Store in a cool location for 2 months until the flavor develops. Ladle the vinegar from the jar and strain through a coffee filter into a glass container to remove the sediments. The vinegar is now ready to use in your favorite recipes. Store at room temperature, well covered to prevent evaporation. It will store for approximately a year.

VARIATIONS:
Cabernet Sauvignon and Orange Vinegar: Substitute equal amounts of cabernet vinegar or red wine vinegar and cabernet wine, the peel of 4 oranges without the pith, ¼ cup whole black peppercorns, and ¼ cup crushed juniper berries and proceed as described above.
Chardonnay, Ginger, and Coriander Vinegar: Substitute equal amounts of chardonnay or white wine vinegar and chardonnay wine, 1 cup sliced fresh ginger, and ½ cup toasted (see page 61) coriander seeds and proceed as described above.

MAKES 2 QUARTS ■

Apple and Szechuan Vinegar

2 **quarts apple cider vinegar**
1 **quart fresh apple cider**
2 **cups Szechuan peppercorns**

Combine the ingredients in a gallon glass jar. Cover the top with cheesecloth tightly. Store in a cool location for two months until the flavor develops. Ladle the vinegar from the jar and strain through a coffee filter into a glass container to remove the sediments. The vinegar is now ready to use in your favorite recipes. Store at room temperature, well covered to prevent evaporation. It will store for approximately a year.

VARIATIONS: For substitutions of specialty white wine vinegars, use half champagne or white wine vinegar and half wine, allowing the combination to age for 3 months to further develop the flavors. For specialty red wine vinegars, substitute half red wine vinegar and half varietal red wine and also allow to age for 3 months.
Gewürztraminer and Juniper Vinegar: Substitute equal amounts of gewürztraminer vinegar, gewürztraminer wine, and crushed juniper berries and proceed as described above.
Pinot Noir and Rosemary Vinegar: Substitute equal amounts of pinot noir vinegar, pinot noir, and crushed fresh rosemary and proceed as described above. For extra spunk, add a couple of crushed heads of garlic and 2 or 3 serrano peppers.

MAKES 2 QUARTS ■

Select a firm salmon or fish fillet free of tears in the flesh. Chill in the refrigerator before handling. Place the fillet on a cleanable cutting surface. Trim bones and fat from the belly section of the fillet. Run your finger or the back of a paring knife lightly across the surface of the fillet from head to tail to lift and expose the remaining bones. Remove the bones with needlenose pliers, tweezers, or hemostats.

Cut the escalope by positioning the knife perpendicular to the fish fillet on approximately a 30° angle and making a slice ½ inch thick, cutting down through the flesh to the skin. Without cutting through the skin, turn the knife flat away from the fillet, cutting to release the escalope. Place escalopes on a parchment- or wax paper–covered cookie sheet, cover with plastic wrap, and refrigerate until ready to use.

I prefer to smoke the fillets of lake trout or salmon trout. These fish smoke very well because of their higher oil content, which protects the flesh from drying out during the brining and smoking process.

The average weight per fillet should be 24 to 32 ounces. This allows the brining to season the fish properly. These medium thickness fillets have shorter smoking times with better smoke-to-flesh flavor balance. Smaller fillets often dry out or become too smoky. Larger fillets, because of the longer cooking time required, will have a greater concentration of smoke in the surface of their flesh, resulting in a bitter flavor.

To prepare the fillets, trim the inner surface of the fillet to expose the flesh to the brine. Remove the scales but leave the skin on. Cure the fish in the brine (see page 74) for an average of 1 hour per pound of fillets for lean fish, 2 hours per pound for fatter fish, like trout. The brine is used to firm up the flesh, season the fish, and preserve it against spoilage. The first two goals are of primary importance to us. Keep the brine and fish under refrigeration while curing.

After curing, remove the fillets from the brine. Rinse with cold water to remove the excess brine. Transfer the fillets to the racks of the smoker, skin-side down. Place the rack near the fan in the refrigerator for approximately 4 hours to develop the dull pellicle, a thin skin or film, on the surface of the fillet. This pellicle, caused by the reaction of the brine with the air flow, helps retain the moisture of the fish.

Smoke in a low or cold temperature smoker for approximately 4 hours. Technically, a cold smoker is one between 32° and 85°F and does not cook the fish. This allows the fish to be infused by the smoky flavor without the fish cooking and drying out. I prefer to smoke between 32° and 40°F.

The smoke generated by wood chips flavors the fish and different wood chips result in different flavors. I prefer hickory and apple or pear wood chips. There are many other types, so experiment to find your own blend of wood.

Refrigerate the fish after smoking until ready to cook.

To cook, preheat the oven to 325°F. Lay the fillets on a cookie sheet and place on the lower rack of the oven. Cook until done, when the flesh is approximately 130° to 140°F, about 15 minutes. Remove from the oven and refrigerate.

After chilling, flip the fillets over and peel off the skin, starting at the tail. With a pairing knife, scrape the fatty (dark colored) tissue from the fillet. Turn the fillet back over and trim the belly of fatty tissue. Slice the fillet into portions for serving of about 5 ounces each. Refrigerate until serving.

Remember to handle the fish at all times as a fresh product, which means keep it cold. This will preserve the flavor as well as the texture.

Brine for Smoking Fish

You can vary the brine to your tastes and to match the fish to certain sauces. For more unusual flavors, add spices such as fresh ginger, hot peppers, peppercorns, and strong herbs to the basic brine recipe. Select these spices to coordinate with the spices in the sauce or dressing to be served with the smoked fish. The flavor match will be terrific.

You can also vary the flavors by using different proportions of salt to sugar. Different types of sugar, such as maple, will introduce other flavors.

> 1 **gallon ice water**
> ½ **cup fresh lemon juice**
> 1 **cup packed dark brown sugar**
> 1½ **cups kosher salt**
> 2 **heads garlic, cut in half (optional)**

In a large bowl or pan, combine the ingredients until the sugar and salt are dissolved. Add the fish. Refrigerate. Cure for designated time based on size, density, and usage of the smoked fish.

MAKES 1½ GALLONS, ENOUGH FOR ABOUT 5 POUNDS OF FISH FILLETS ■

SPRING

The golden rays of the sun, a warming breeze, and green sprouts pushing away a blanket of snow announce the arrival of spring. This thaw releases the next generation of life, anxious to grow and discover the world. New young flavors and colors are bright additions to our menus and landscapes. The crisp textures and earthy flavors are robust enough to ward off the lingering chill of spring nights.

In my younger years, I would walk the railroad tracks in search of wild asparagus, the woods for morel mushrooms, and the fields for tender baby mustard greens. Each day a new edible would appear from the woods and edges of the fields. I would eat like a king, celebrating the rebirth of the earth.

The farmers' markets also come alive in the spring with all the fresh offerings of spring's renewed promise, such as wonderful asparagus and morel mushrooms perfect for a gratin or salad. Baby artichokes yield tender leaves for a soup vibrant with the flavor of cumin and in a salad of ginger and smoked salmon. Tender emerging greens such as mizuni, watercress, mâche, sorrel, and scallions become wonderful bright flavors for salads and sauces.

Spring announces the return of the birds and fish from their winter migrations. This wakeup call arouses the hibernating species. It is time for all species to find mates and give birth to the next generation.

The soft-shell crabs explode from their old shell for the next series of growth, giving luscious tender meat perfect for a protection of tempura batter. Young smelt are never sweeter than the first few days of their mating run. Perch and salmon are firm from winter's cold water but shed their fat layers for the warmer weather. Salmon flavors are brilliant with the sweet flavor of Vidalia onions or port and peppercorns.

Young chicken is moist and full flavored enhanced with a mustard and spice rub. Tender veal, its mother's milk produced from grass not hay, is lush in its marriage to the wild earthy mushrooms. In spring lamb chops framed with baby artichokes and celery root are a highlight of the season.

Desserts of the spring offer bright rich indulgences before it is time for the summer swimsuit. The last of the exotics add a crisp bite to unusual combinations such as Ginger and Passion Fruit Crème Brûlée, Passion Ice Cream with White Chocolate Sauce, or Kiwi Ice Cream. Twists on more traditional desserts include a Pressed Chocolate Cake, where the air is forced out for a denser chocolate taste, Sour Cherry Tart made with pepper vodka, and Gratin of Strawberries and Rhubarb.

Spring is the time to celebrate the renewal of nature. These delicate flavors occur only once each year—catch them before they mature and vanish into the flowers and greenery of the summer.

Steamer Clams with Watercress and Shallots

Steamer clams are also known as soft-shell clams. You can apply the same technique to littlenecks and cherrystone clams, as well as any shellfish, especially mussels. Try mixing and matching oysters, clams, mussels, and shucked scallops. Start with steaming the heaviest shelled fish, such as oysters, first, then add the remaining lighter shelled fish so all the shellfish open about the same time. Remove and shuck shellfish as they open to prevent overcooking.

Remember to choose the freshest shellfish since this dish reveals the natural flavors rather than masks them. Do not eat shellfish that hasn't opened during steaming, as it may be spoiled.

48 **steamer clams**
 1 **cup clam juice, canned or bottled**
 1 **cup Fish Stock (see page 65)**
 1 **cup dry white wine**
    Pinch of saffron threads to color or taste
½ **cup coarsely chopped watercress**
½ **cup chopped shallots, rinsed under cold running water and squeezed dry (see note below)**
 1 **teaspoon coarsely ground white pepper**
¼ **cup Clarified Butter (see page 70)**

In a medium-size saucepan, combine the clams, clam juice, stock, wine, and saffron. Bring to a simmer over high heat. Cover and allow the clams to steam until opened, about 5 minutes. Remove from the heat. Divide the clams with their attached shells into four serving bowls. Spoon the steaming broth over the clams and divide the watercress, shallots, pepper, and butter between them. Serve immediately.

COOKING NOTE: Rinsing the shallots removes their strong flavor.

MAKES 4 SERVINGS ■

Crab, Grapefruit, and Jicama Salad

Bright clean flavors really show off crab. This is especially flavorful with the stone crab claws available through mid-May.

20 **asparagus spears, lower two-thirds peeled and blanched (see pages 57–58)**
20 **large grapefruit segments**
½ **cup Grapefruit Mayonnaise (recipe follows)**
 1 **cup peeled and julienned jicama (see note below)**
¾ **pound jumbo lump crabmeat, carefully picked over for shells**
¼ **cup roasted, peeled (see page 62), seeded, and diced red bell pepper**
 1 **tablespoon chopped fresh mint**

Arrange the asparagus, spears pointing outward, on four salad plates. Position the grapefruit segments in the center to form a well. Spoon the mayonnaise into each well and distribute the jicama, crab, and peppers around the grapefruit. Sprinkle the mint over the salad. Serve.

COOKING NOTE: Keep the jicama covered with moistened toweling to prevent it from drying out, if cut ahead of time.

MAKES 4 SERVINGS ∎

Grapefruit Mayonnaise

Grapefruit Mayonnaise complements grilled fish or chilled shellfish, and makes a wonderful light salad dressing.

¾ **cup fresh grapefruit juice**
2 **large egg yolks**
2 **tablespoons Dijon mustard**
  Pinch of salt
1 **cup corn oil**
2 **dashes Angostura bitters**
2 **dashes Peychauds bitters**
  Tabasco sauce to taste
  Freshly ground black pepper and salt to taste

In a small saucepan over medium-high heat, simmer the grapefruit juice until reduced to 2 tablespoons, about 7 minutes.

In a food processor (using a food processor will keep the texture much lighter and thinner than traditional mayonnaise), combine the reduced grapefruit juice, egg yolks, mustard, and salt by pulsing for 15 seconds. Slowly add the oil in a steady stream, then add the bitters and Tabasco. Adjust the salt and pepper to taste.

COOKING NOTES: The bitters are quite fragrant. As you develop a taste for the flavors, you may want to add more. You can use both types or just one of the bitters for this recipe (or bitters of your own choice).
∎ The mayonnaise will hold under refrigeration for approximately 5 days. The thinner texture allows spooning over the salad unlike traditional thick mayonnaises.

MAKES 1¼ CUPS ∎

Smoked Salmon and Artichoke Salad with Ginger Dressing

This is an interesting combination of the smoked salmon and earthy artichoke. I like to keep the artichoke firm for the contrast to the silky texture of the fish.

½ **pound smoked salmon, sliced thin and julienned (see note below)**
4 **medium-size artichokes, blanched (see pages 57–58), prepared (see page 61), and cut into eighths**
¼ **cup julienned red onion**
1 **large red bell pepper, roasted, peeled (see page 62), seeded, and julienned**
½ **cup peeled and julienned jicama (see note below)**
½ **cup Ginger Dressing (recipe follows)**
2 **heads red oakleaf lettuce**
2 **tablespoons snipped fresh chives**

In a medium-size bowl, combine the salmon, artichokes, onion, pepper, and jicama. Toss with the Ginger Dressing. Arrange the lettuce leaves on four salad plates. Mound the salmon and artichoke salad atop the greens and sprinkle with the chives. Serve.

COOKING NOTES: Remember to trim the fatty darker flesh from the salmon. This area carries most of the oily "fishy" flavor.
∎ Keep the jicama covered with moistened toweling to prevent it from drying out, if cut ahead of time.

MAKES 4 SERVINGS ∎

Ginger Dressing

Poaching the ginger in vinegar provides a spicy base to this spunky mayonnaise. Used sparingly, it enhances the smoky flavor of salmon and roast peppers, as well as any smoked or spicy fish served hot or cold. Keep the acid high in the dressing with lemon juice when pairing it with artichoke to balance its characteristic sweetness.

> 2 **tablespoons peeled and diced fresh ginger**
> 2 **tablespoons balsamic vinegar**
> 1/4 **cup fresh lemon juice**
> 2 **large egg yolks**
> 1 **tablespoon extra-strong Dijon mustard**
> 1 **cup virgin olive oil**
> 1 **tablespoon waterpacked green peppercorns, drained, crushed, and minced**
> **Salt to taste**
> **Tabasco sauce to taste**
> 2 **tablespoons chopped fresh dill**

In a small saucepan combine the ginger and vinegar. Bring to a simmer over medium heat, cooking until tender, about 10 minutes. (Add water to replace evaporation as necessary.) Transfer to a blender, add the lemon juice, and puree until smooth. Strain.

In a medium-size bowl, combine the puree, egg yolks, and mustard. Whisk in the oil in a slow steady stream. When thickened, add the peppercorns. Add the salt and Tabasco, then add the dill and refrigerate.

COOKING NOTE: The mayonnaise will hold under refrigeration for approximately 5 days. Using the traditional technique of whisking the oil in results in a thicker texture which clings to the smoked salmon and artichokes, as well as reinforcing the mounding of the salad on the plate.

MAKES 1 1/2 CUPS ■

Smoked Trout with Horseradish Sauce

The smoked trout is a great contrast to the crunchy raw artichoke and fennel. I prefer lake trout or salmon trout because of its moist flesh.

> 1 **large artichoke**
> 1/2 **cup fresh lemon juice**
> 1 **small fennel bulb, trimmed (reserve 2 tablespoons chopped fennel greens)**
> 3/4 **cup virgin olive oil**
> **Salt to taste**
> **Freshly ground black pepper to taste**
> 1 **bunch watercress**
> 4 **fillets smoked trout (see pages 73–74), deboned, skinned, and trimmed of fat**
> 1/2 **cup Horseradish Sauce (recipe follows)**

Peel the artichoke until only the heart remains. Quarter the heart and remove and discard the choke. Slice the artichoke quarters paper thin. In a medium-size bowl, immediately toss the sliced artichoke in the lemon juice to prevent discoloring. Prepare the fennel bulb, slicing paper thin and discarding the core and coarse outer leaves, then combine with the artichoke. Add the olive oil, fennel greens, salt, and pepper. Refrigerate until ready to serve.

Divide the watercress onto four serving plates. Place a trout fillet on each plate and garnish with the artichoke and fennel salad. Spoon the Horseradish Sauce in a band over each trout. Serve.

MAKES 4 SERVINGS ■

Horseradish Sauce

This creamy horseradish sauce is a big favorite over smoked and grilled fish and shellfish, as well as beef and grilled fresh vegetables.

2 large egg yolks
1 tablespoon Dijon mustard
1 tablespoon fresh lemon juice
½ cup virgin olive oil
Salt to taste
Freshly ground white pepper to taste
½ cup prepared white horseradish, drained
2 tablespoons snipped fresh chives

In a mixer, combine the egg yolks, mustard, and lemon juice. On high speed, gradually add the olive oil in a steady stream. Add salt and pepper, then mix in the horseradish and chives. Refrigerate until ready to serve, or up to 5 days.

COOKING NOTE: If you prefer to use fresh horseradish, select firm roots that are not sprouting. When grated, the horseradish has an intense flavor that will soon dissipate into the air, therefore it must be used immediately. Prepared horseradish is grated then preserved in vinegar to prevent this loss of mustard oils to oxidation. The strong flavors are also heightened by the vinegar. The addition of the horseradish results in a thinner texture more like a thick sauce than a traditional thick mayonnaise, which allows the coating of the fish.

MAKES 1 CUP ■

Ragout of Snails and Artichokes

The vermouth, which is actually wine seasoned with herbs, pulls the flavors of the snails, artichokes, and peppers together. A simple but elegant dish.

12 baby artichokes, less than 2 inches in diameter (see note below)
¼ pound (1 stick) unsalted butter
4 large cloves garlic, roasted (see page 62) and smashed

28 canned helix snails, drained
1 cup dry vermouth
2 tablespoons fresh lemon juice
½ cup roasted, peeled (see page 62), seeded and finely julienned red bell pepper
1 tablespoon fresh thyme leaves
1 tablespoon chopped fresh parsley
Salt to taste
Freshly ground black pepper to taste
1½ teaspoons grated lemon rind
Sprigs fresh thyme for garnish
8 Toasted Croutons (see page 70)

Cook the artichokes in a medium-size nonaluminum pot of boiling salted water until tender, about 10 minutes. Check for doneness by inserting a skewer into the heart. Drain well. Remove the outer tougher leaves. Quarter the artichoke, trim the spiny tops of the leaves, and remove the choke, if any.

In a medium-size skillet over high heat, combine the artichokes, 2 tablespoons of the butter, the garlic, and snails. Cook for 2 minutes, then add the vermouth and lemon juice, cooking until reduced by half, about 3 minutes. Whisk in the remaining butter, cooking until thickened enough to lightly coat the back of a spoon. Add the peppers, thyme, parsley, salt, and pepper. Remove from the heat and add the lemon rind. Spoon onto serving plates and garnish with sprigs of thyme and the croutons.

COOKING NOTES: If baby artichokes are unavailable, substitute 4 large artichokes. Also, avoid using aluminum pots with artichokes or you will end up with aluminum-flavored artichokes.
■ The snails can be marinated in the vermouth and thyme for up to 3 days under refrigeration for extra flavor.
■ If the sauce separates, remove the snails, artichokes, and peppers to a side plate, add a little more vermouth or lemon juice, and simmer, until thickened, with an additional tablespoon of butter at the end. Return snails and vegetables and serve.

MAKES 4 SERVINGS ■

Gratin of Asparagus, Morels, and Celery Root

It's the true awaking of spring when the morels arrive.

- **1 medium-size celery root**
- **24 large asparagus spears, blanched (see pages 57–58) and cut in half lengthwise (see note below)**
- **4 tablespoons (½ stick) unsalted butter**
- **¾ pound morel mushrooms, stems trimmed**
- **½ cup Fino sherry**
- **3 tablespoons heavy cream**
- **¾ cup Crème Fraîche (see page 65)**
- **Salt to taste**
- **Freshly ground white pepper to taste**
- **¼ cup snipped fresh chives**

Cook the celery root in a medium-size pot of boiling salted water until tender, about 15 minutes. Test for doneness with a skewer. Drain well. Peel and trim into a rounded shape. With a knife or mandolin, make twelve ⅛-inch slices or, for a more abstract presentation, cut the celery root into shapes such as triangles or diamonds. Pat dry and keep warm in a low oven at 150°F.

In a small nonaluminum pan, reheat the asparagus in simmering water. Turn off and let sit in water until draining on paper towels right before assembly.

In a large skillet over high heat, cook the butter until it just begins to brown. Add the morels, cooking until browned, about 5 minutes. Add the sherry and cream, cooking until reduced by half, about 4 minutes. Add the Crème Fraîche, cooking just until thickened enough to coat the back of a spoon, about 1 minute. Add salt and pepper.

Place one slice of the celery root in the center of each serving plate. Distribute half of the asparagus, with tips outward, on the celery root. Spoon half of the morels with their sauce over the asparagus, then top with another slice of celery root and the remaining asparagus and morels, leaving some sauce for topping the gratin. Top once again with a slice of celery root, then spoon the remaining sauce over the gratin. Sprinkle with chives and serve.

VARIATION: Fiddlehead ferns are terrific in place of or in addition to the asparagus. Make sure your fiddleheads are from the ostrich fern; bracken ferns are known to cause animal poisoning when raw and are thought to be potentially carcinogenic.

COOKING NOTE: Aluminum will intensify the natural sulfur flavor of asparagus, so it is best to avoid cooking in it.

MAKES 4 SERVINGS ∎

Asparagus with Citrus Vinaigrette

A simple salad to celebrate asparagus.

- **24 asparagus spears, lower two-thirds peeled, blanched (see pages 57–58), and brought to room temperature**
- **1½ cups Citrus Vinaigrette (recipe follows)**
- **2 tablespoons snipped fresh chives**
- **½ cup shaved Parmesan cheese**

Arrange the asparagus on serving plates, spoon over the vinaigrette, top with the chives and Parmesan, and serve.

MAKES 4 SERVINGS ∎

Citrus Vinaigrette

Great on salads, smoked salmon, and poached shellfish.

2 tablespoons roasted (see page 62) and minced shallots
2 tablespoons raspberry vinegar
1 cup orange juice, reduced to 1/4 cup over medium heat
1/2 teaspoon salt
1 cup virgin olive oil
Freshly ground black pepper to taste

In a blender, combine the shallots, vinegar, reduced orange juice, and salt, and puree until smooth. With the blender running, gradually add the olive oil in a steady stream until thickened. Add salt and pepper. Will keep in the refrigerator up to 2 weeks.

MAKES 1 1/2 CUPS ■

Frog Legs with Twice Fried Garlic

The fried garlic cloves are as popular as the frog legs.

1/4 pound (1 stick) unsalted butter, at room temperature
2 tablespoons smashed roasted (see page 62) garlic
3 tablespoons chopped scallion greens
1/4 cup fresh lime juice
1 teaspoon kimchee base (see note below)
1 teaspoon Tabasco sauce
Corn oil for frying
2 cups all-purpose flour
2 tablespoons paprika
1 teaspoon salt
3/4 teaspoon freshly ground white pepper
2 large eggs, lightly beaten
1 cup milk
12 to 16 medium-size frog legs
12 cloves roasted garlic, peeled
1 bunch fresh parsley, coarsely chopped
1 head red oakleaf lettuce

With a mixer, combine the butter, smashed roasted garlic, scallions, lime juice, kimchee base, and Tabasco. Set aside.

Fill a large, heavy, deep skillet with corn oil to a depth of 3 inches. Heat over medium-high heat to 350°F.

In a medium-size bowl, sift together the flour, paprika, salt, and pepper. In another medium-size bowl, combine the eggs and milk. Drench the frog legs and whole garlic cloves in the egg and milk mixture, shake off the excess, then dredge in the seasoned flour, coating evenly. Shake to remove any excess. Slip the frog legs and garlic into the corn oil, stirring occasionally, and cooking until evenly golden, about 4 minutes. Transfer to a bowl and toss with the parsley. Arrange the lettuce on four serving plates, and top with the frog legs and garlic cloves. Distribute the butter mixture over the frog legs, allowing it to melt slightly. Serve immediately.

COOKING NOTES: I prefer medium-size frog legs that average 16 to 20 per pound. The larger legs are a little tough and smaller legs have less meat to the bones.
■ The compound butter is very bright with lime juice and blends well with the lettuce and fried legs and garlic. I choose to increase the acid in the accompaniments to the fried foods for this purpose.
■ If you can't find kimchee base (available in oriental food stores), use this homemade substitute: combine 1 tablespoon garlic powder, 1 teaspoon Ginger Puree (see page 66), 1 tablespoon Tabasco sauce, and 1/2 cup Hunt's chili sauce in a small bowl. Use sparingly. Tightly cover and refrigerate for up to a month. Kimchee base can be used to spice up mayonnaise, vinaigrettes, salsas, and sauces. Be adventurous.

MAKES 4 SERVINGS ■

Rainbow Ravioli with Saffron Sauce

This technique makes "striped" pasta of different colors. You can cut the different colors in odd shapes and roll them on the top of the egg pasta to produce abstract results. Remember to keep your patterns small so they translate onto the individual ravioli.

<table>
<tbody>
<tr><td>¼</td><td>pound (1 stick) unsalted butter</td></tr>
<tr><td>¼</td><td>cup trimmed and diced fennel bulb</td></tr>
<tr><td>1</td><td>large red bell pepper, roasted, peeled (see page 62), seeded, and diced</td></tr>
<tr><td>½</td><td>pound scallops, foot removed (see note below) and diced</td></tr>
<tr><td>¾</td><td>pound lobster meat, chunked</td></tr>
<tr><td>¼</td><td>cup snipped fresh chives</td></tr>
<tr><td>1½</td><td>teaspoons tomato paste</td></tr>
<tr><td>¼</td><td>teaspoon ground fennel seed</td></tr>
<tr><td>2</td><td>tablespoons plain dry bread crumbs</td></tr>
<tr><td>½</td><td>teaspoon salt</td></tr>
<tr><td>½</td><td>teaspoon coarsely ground black pepper</td></tr>
<tr><td>3</td><td>large egg yolks</td></tr>
<tr><td>¼</td><td>pound Egg Pasta (see page 68)</td></tr>
<tr><td>¼</td><td>pound Spinach Pasta (see page 68)</td></tr>
<tr><td>¼</td><td>pound Beet (or Tomato) Pasta (see page 68)</td></tr>
<tr><td>1</td><td>tablespoon heavy cream</td></tr>
</tbody>
</table>

FOR THE SAUCE

<table>
<tbody>
<tr><td>½</td><td>cup dry white wine</td></tr>
<tr><td>½</td><td>cup fresh lemon juice</td></tr>
<tr><td>1</td><td>cup heavy cream</td></tr>
<tr><td></td><td>Pinch of saffron or to taste</td></tr>
<tr><td>1</td><td>tablespoon grated lemon rind</td></tr>
<tr><td></td><td>Salt to taste</td></tr>
<tr><td></td><td>Freshly ground black pepper to taste</td></tr>
</tbody>
</table>

To make the filling, cook the butter over high heat in a medium-size skillet until very brown, almost burnt and smoking. Add the fennel and red pepper, cooking for 30 seconds. Add the scallops, cooking until opaque, about 2 minutes. Keep the filling cooked medium-rare so that the inside will be "just cooked" when the pasta is done.

Transfer to a medium-size bowl and combine with the lobster meat, 2 tablespoons of the chives, the tomato paste, fennel seed, bread crumbs, salt, and ¼ teaspoon of the black pepper. Mix in 2 of the egg yolks, then set aside.

Using a pasta machine, roll each color pasta once to flatten, then cut lengthwise into ½ inch wide by 12 inch long (see note below) strips. Align strips of alternating colors, allowing them to slightly overlap; roll once with a rolling pin to set the colors together. Roll the multicolor sheets through the pasta machine until very thin and approximately 2½ inches wide by 24 inches long. Repeat the process to yield four sheets.

Place 1 tablespoon of the filling mixture every 2½ inches down the center of a sheet of pasta. In a small bowl, mix the remaining egg yolk with the heavy cream and brush the egg wash on the pasta around the filling. Cover with another sheet of pasta, pressing together to seal in the filling. With a crinkle ravioli cutter, cut the filled pasta into ravioli. Repeat with the other sheets of pasta till all the dough and filling are gone. Refrigerate to firm for at least 1 hour.

To start the sauce, bring the wine and lemon juice to a boil over high heat in a medium-size saucepan until reduced to ¼ cup. Add the cream, cooking until reduced enough to coat the back of a spoon, then add the saffron and lemon rind. Adjust the salt and pepper to taste. Remove from the heat and keep warm till needed.

Cook the ravioli in a large skillet in 3 inches of boiling salted water until al dente, about 4 minutes. With a slotted spoon, remove to paper towels to drain. Position the ravioli in the center of warm serving plates, spoon the saffron sauce around the ravioli, sprinkle with the remaining chives, and serve.

COOKING NOTES: The "foot" is the tough muscle on the side of the scallop.
- If you use 2 colors of pasta, roll the initial piece out to ¾ inch by 12 inches.

MAKES 4 SERVINGS ∎

Fried Smelts with Lemon and Brown Butter

Smelts must be freshly caught and smell very "sweet." My old fishmonger always swore that the best smelled just like watermelon. The most well known smelt for good eating is the rainbow, found primarily in the Midwest, Northeast, and Canada. The eulachon, or hooligan, from Alaska is also highly esteemed.

½ pound (2 sticks) unsalted butter
¼ cup fresh lemon juice
¼ cup nonpareil capers, drained
   Corn oil for frying
2 cups all-purpose flour
2 tablespoons paprika
1 teaspoon salt
¾ teaspoon freshly ground white pepper
2 large eggs, lightly beaten
1 cup milk
1 pound smelts, cleaned
2 lemons, sliced very thin
½ cup snipped fresh chives

In a medium-size skillet over high heat, cook the butter until just browned, about 6 minutes. Remove from the heat, then carefully add the lemon juice. When the foam recedes, add the capers. Keep warm. Fill a large, heavy, deep skillet with corn oil to a depth of 3 inches and heat over medium-high to 350°F.

In a medium-size bowl, sift together the flour, paprika, salt, and pepper.

In another medium-size bowl, combine the eggs and milk. Drench smelts and lemon slices in the egg and milk mixture; shake off the excess. Dredge in the seasoned flour, coat evenly, then shake to remove the excess.

Slip the smelts and the lemon slices into the oil, stirring occasionally, and fry until evenly golden, about 3 minutes. Transfer to a large bowl and toss with chives.

Mound on a serving plate and spoon over the browned butter.

Serve immediately.

VARIATIONS: You can fry in any citrus juice for a brighter approach to fried dishes. Try different spices in the flour, such as dry mustard, ground ginger, caraway seeds, or ground cumin.

MAKES 4 SERVINGS ■

Chicken Linguine with Peas and Tarragon

This is a great, simple recipe for spring pasta. Remember to keep the meat tender, pasta al dente, and vegetables crisp for the best contrast. Your palate will distinguish the ingredients by texture. If all the textures are the same, on the palate they will be indistinguishable from one another.

One 2½- to 3-pound whole chicken
2 tablespoons unsalted butter
2 tablespoons chopped shallots
1 cup chanterelles, quartered, stems trimmed
½ cup dry white wine
1¼ cups heavy cream
   Salt to taste
   Coarsely ground black pepper to taste
1½ cups fresh peas, blanched to tender, about 3 minutes (see pages 57–59)
1 tablespoon fresh tarragon leaves
1 pound linguine noodles, flavor of your choice (see page 68)
¼ cup grated Pecorino Romano cheese
¼ cup grated Parmesan cheese

Preheat oven to 400°F. Roast the chicken on a rack in a roasting pan set on the lower rack of the oven. Cook until golden brown, about 1¼ hours. Remove, let cool, and pull off all the meat. Dice into ½-inch pieces.

In a large skillet over high heat, combine the butter, shallots, and mushrooms and cook until browned, about

5 minutes. Add the wine and cook until reduced by half, about 3 minutes. Add the cream, cooking until thickened enough to coat the back of a spoon, about 10 minutes. Stir in the chicken and heat thoroughly. Adjust salt and pepper to taste, add the peas and tarragon, and heat through. Remove from the heat.

In a large amount of boiling water, cook the pasta until al dente. Transfer to a strainer, rinse with warm water, and drain well. Add the pasta to the skillet with the cheeses and toss until evenly coated. Serve immediately.

MAKES 4 SERVINGS ■

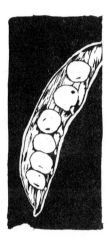

Artichoke Soup with Hazelnut Butter

This soup is pure artichokes with a frame of cumin.

   2 **pounds baby artichokes, each no more than 2**
     inches in diameter
  12 **cups Poultry Stock (see page 63)**
   2 **lemons, juiced**
 ¼ **cup heavy cream**
 ¾ **cup sour cream**
 ¾ **teaspoon ground cumin**
     Salt to taste
     Freshly ground white pepper to taste
 ¾ **cup Hazelnut Butter (recipe follows)**

Discard the tough outer leaves and stems from the artichokes. Place the artichokes in a large acid-resistant pot with the stock and lemon juice (avoid using an aluminum pot, as the artichokes will pick up an aluminum flavor). Bring to a simmer over medium-high heat and cook until the artichokes are tender, about 15 minutes. Test for doneness by inserting a skewer.

Puree the artichokes with the stock in a blender in batches. Strain through a medium sieve into a saucepan, pressing to extract as much pulp as possible. Whisk in the cream, sour cream, and cumin, then adjust the salt and pepper. Ladle into warm bowls, garnish with Hazelnut Butter, and serve.

COOKING NOTE: You can substitute larger artichokes; just quarter them and remove the choke after cooking them in the stock.

MAKES 8 SERVINGS ■

Hazelnut Butter

Toast the nuts until golden to develop the richest flavor. You can use blanched hazelnuts to save time. They are usually worth the difference in price for the effort saved in rubbing off the skins one by one.

 ¼ **pound (1 stick) unsalted butter, at room**
     temperature
 ¼ **cup chopped toasted (see page 61) hazelnuts**
   2 **tablespoons chopped fresh parsley**

Using a mixer, combine the butter, hazelnuts, and parsley. Refrigerate until ready to serve or up to 1 week.

COOKING NOTE: Hazelnut butter is a great topping for other dishes such as soups and croutons for salads. Add up to ¼ cup lemon juice and the butter complements grilled fish and poultry.

MAKES ABOUT ¾ CUP ■

Sorrel and Celery Root Soup

Celery root is the thickener providing the starch and body in this soup. Its earthy flavor goes so well with sorrel.

2 **large celery roots, peeled and cut into 1-inch cubes**
8 **cups Poultry Stock (see page 63)**
1 **pound sorrel, stemmed**
1 **cup sour cream**
1 **cup heavy cream**
2 **lemons, juiced**
  Salt to taste
  Freshly ground white pepper to taste

In a large pot, combine the celery root and stock and bring to a simmer over medium-high heat. Cook until tender, testing for doneness by inserting a skewer, about 30 minutes.

Combine the celery root, stock, and sorrel in a blender in batches, pureeing until smooth, then return to the pot. Whisk in the sour cream and heavy cream. Season with the lemon juice, and adjust the salt and pepper. Ladle the soup into warm bowls and serve.

COOKING NOTE: Add the sorrel at the end of cooking your dish so that the bright lemon flavor is not cooked out. If you plan to serve the soup at a later time, allow the soup to cool to room temperature before adding the sorrel and pureeing.

MAKES 8 SERVINGS ■

Fennel and Shallot Soup

After your first spoonful this will be one of your favorites.

 2 **tablespoons unsalted butter**
 2 **cups shallots, chopped**
18 **cups Poultry Stock (see page 63)**
 4 **large fennel bulbs (about 4½ pounds), trimmed and sliced (reserve ¼ cup minced fennel greens)**
¼ **cup fennel seeds**
 1 **cup heavy cream**
½ **cup sour cream**
  Salt to taste
  Freshly ground white pepper to taste
¼ **cup freshly grated Parmesan cheese**

Melt the butter in a large pot over low heat. Add the shallots and sauté until they begin to soften, about 10 minutes. Add the stock, fennel bulbs, and fennel seeds. Simmer until tender, about 2½ hours.

Puree the soup in a blender in batches and strain through a fine sieve. Whisk in the heavy cream and sour cream, and adjust the salt and pepper. Stir in the fennel greens. Ladle the soup into warm bowls, garnish with the grated cheese, and serve.

VARIATION: For the strong of heart, or on a full moon, substitute roasted garlic for the shallots. Add red wine vinegar to taste to balance the sweetness of the garlic and fennel combination.

COOKING NOTE: Trim away only the coarse brown outer bulb of the fennel. After the fennel has been cooked, the blender will make soup of all the parts while the strainer will remove the ribs.

MAKES 8 SERVINGS ■

Asparagus Soup with Pistachio Butter

This soup is a great utilizer of asparagus trimmings. Serve the top 2 inches of the asparagus as a luxurious side dish and reserve the remainder for this wonderful soup.

 10 **tablespoons (1¼ sticks) unsalted butter**
  2 **cups chopped shallots**
  8 **cups Poultry Stock (see page 63)**
  4 **pounds asparagus, bottoms trimmed, tips reserved for garnish**
  2 **tablespoons chopped fresh chives**
  ¼ **cup chopped toasted (see page 60) pistachios**
  1 **cup heavy cream**
     Salt to taste
     Freshly ground white pepper to taste

Melt 2 tablespoons of the butter in a large acid-resistant pot (see note below) over low heat. Add the shallots and sauté until they begin to soften, about 10 minutes. Then add the stock and asparagus and simmer until just tender, about 30 minutes.

Meanwhile, in a blender, combine the remaining butter, the chives, and pistachios and puree until smooth. Refrigerate until ready to use.

To preserve the bright green color, immediately puree the stock and asparagus in batches in a blender and strain through a fine sieve. Return to the pot, whisk in the heavy cream, and adjust the salt and pepper. Add the asparagus tips to warm bowls and ladle the soup over. Garnish with the pistachio butter and serve.

COOKING NOTE: Aluminum will intensify the natural sulfur flavor of asparagus if it is overcooked, so it is best to use an acid-resistant pot such as stainless steel or enameled.

MAKES 8 SERVINGS ■

Spinach and Sweetbread Salad

Sweetbreads, the thymus glands of young animals, are usually thought of as rich and heavy. When teamed up with this spinach salad they take on a new, silky, light personality. Veal sweetbreads have the best taste.

  1 **large sweetbread, about ¾ to 1 pound**
  1 **large onion, diced**
  3 **cups hot Veal or Poultry Stock (see page 63)**
     Salt to taste
     Coarsely ground black pepper to taste
  6 **tablespoons (¾ stick) unsalted butter**
  1 **large egg, lightly beaten**
  ½ **cup milk**
  1 **cup plain dry bread crumbs**
  ¼ **pound pancetta, diced (or substitute slab or regular bacon)**
  ¼ **cup red wine vinegar**
  2 **tablespoons honey**
  2 **tablespoons coarse-grained prepared mustard**
  ½ **cup diced, roasted (see page 62) shallots**
  ½ **bunch fresh parsley, stemmed and chopped**
  ½ **cup virgin olive oil**
  4 **cups spinach, stemmed and torn into bite-size pieces**
  2 **tablespoons mustard seeds, toasted (see page 61)**

In a medium-size saucepan, cover the sweetbread with cold water. Bring to a simmer over high heat and cook for 5 minutes. Remove from the heat and cool under cold running water. Drain. Place the sweetbread between two plates and weight it down with 1½ pounds of canned goods. Refrigerate like this overnight to press the sweetbreads to an equal thickness so they will cook evenly. Preheat oven to 375°F.

In a medium-size ovenproof saucepan, combine the sweetbread, onions, and hot stock. Adjust the salt and pepper. Cover the surface of the stock with aluminum foil. Cover the pot with a lid, then place on the lower rack of the oven and cook until tender, about 45 minutes, testing for doneness by inserting a skewer. Remove from the oven and allow to cool to room temperature in the stock. With your hands, clean the sweetbread of all its membranes while dividing into walnut-size pieces.

In a medium-size skillet heat 4 tablespoons of the butter over medium-high heat.

In a small bowl, combine the egg and milk, whisking until homogeneous. Dip the sweetbreads in the egg mixture and transfer to the bread crumbs to coat evenly. Carefully drop the sweetbreads, one at a time, into the butter. Sauté until brown on all sides, about 3 minutes. Remove to paper toweling to drain. Season with salt and pepper and keep warm in the oven on low.

In another medium-size skillet, combine the remaining butter and the pancetta. Cook until golden, about 5 minutes. Remove from the heat, drain the pancetta on paper towels, and pour off the fat. Return the pancetta to the pan and add the vinegar, honey, mustard, shallots, parsley, and olive oil. Adjust the salt and pepper to taste and add pancetta drippings to your own taste.

In a metal bowl, toss the spinach with the warm pancetta dressing, reserving some. Distribute the wilted spinach salad on serving plates, and apportion the sweetbreads across the salads. Drizzle the sweetbreads with the remaining dressing and sprinkle with the mustard seeds. Serve.

COOKING NOTE: Covering the stock with the aluminum foil prevents the stock from boiling which produces silkier, moister sweetbreads.

MAKES 4 SERVINGS ◼

Radicchio, Watercress, and Walnut Salad

The spicy watercress is a colorful contrast to the ruby radicchio, for both the eye and palate. Salads do not get much better than this.

- ¼ **cup balsamic vinegar**
- 2 **tablespoons red wine vinegar**
- ¾ **cup walnut oil**
  Salt to taste
  Coarsely ground black pepper to taste
- 1 **head radicchio (see note below), trimmed**
- 3 **bunches watercress, stemmed**
- ½ **cup black walnuts, toasted (see page 60)**
- ½ **cup shaved Parmesan cheese**

In a small bowl, whisk together the vinegars and walnut oil. Add salt and pepper.

Carefully peel off the leaves from the head of radicchio. Select four of the best large leaves and place in the center of the serving plates, and cut the remaining leaves into ¼-inch-wide julienne.

In a medium-size bowl, combine the julienned radicchio with the watercress leaves. Add the dressing and toss, then arrange on the large radicchio leaves. Sprinkle the walnuts over the salads, top with the shaved Parmesan cheese, and serve.

VARIATION: Try different nut oils and shaved hard cheese combinations, such as hazelnut oil and Romano cheese.

COOKING NOTE: Avoid soaking radicchio in water. It turns more bitter and loses flavor.

MAKES 4 SERVINGS ◼

Endive, Mizuni, and Beet Salad

- 4 **medium-size beets**
- 4 **Belgian endives**
- 2 **bunches mizuni (baby mustard greens)**
- ¼ **cup red wine vinegar**
- 2 **tablespoons coarse-grained prepared mustard**
- ¾ **cup virgin olive oil**
  Salt to taste
  Coarsely ground black pepper to taste

Preheat the oven to 375°F. Place the beets in a small roasting pan on the lower rack in oven. Roast until tender, about 30 minutes, testing for doneness by inserting a skewer. Cool, peel, and cut into ¼-inch sticks.

Arrange the Belgian endive leaves on serving plates, and distribute the mizuni across it. Sprinkle the beets on top.

In a small bowl, whisk together the vinegar, mustard, and olive oil. Add salt and pepper to taste, then drizzle over the salad, and serve.

COOKING NOTES: The roasting of the beets develops their rich flavors rather than diluting them through the process of boiling. After roasting, they are very easy to peel.

■ Avoid soaking Belgian endive in water or exposing it to sunlight, as both will result in a bitter taste. The dark blue wrapping in the case of endive is to shield it from the light.

MAKES 4 SERVINGS ■

Fennel, Hearts of Palm, and Onion Salad

Roasted fennel is great in any salad but with hearts of palm and onions you can't go wrong. Try adding chopped radicchio for more color; its bitterness is a striking contrast to the sweet fennel. You can also try substituting picaija blossoms for the hearts of palm. The picaija is the blossom of the palm which has firmer, tentacle-shaped leaves that taste similar to the heart.

> 2 **large fennel bulbs, trimmed (reserve ¼ cup chopped tender fennel greens and sprigs for garnish) and quartered**
> 1 **cup water**
> ¼ **cup balsamic vinegar**
> ¾ **cup virgin olive oil**
> **Salt to taste**
> **Coarsely ground black pepper to taste**

One 28-ounce can hearts of palm, drained and cut on an angle
½ **cup finely julienned red onions**
¼ **cup grated Asiago or Parmesan cheese**

Preheat the oven to 375°F. Place the fennel bulbs in a small roasting pan with the water and place on the lower rack of the oven. Cook until tender, about 30 minutes. Cool, peel, and cut into ¼-inch sticks.

In a small bowl, combine the vinegar, olive oil, salt and pepper for the dressing.

In a medium-size bowl, combine the fennel, hearts of palm, red onion, and the fennel greens. Add the dressing and toss. Position in the center of the serving plates, and top with the grated cheese. Garnish with sprigs of fennel greens and serve.

MAKES 4 SERVINGS ■

Lake Perch with Herbed Tartar Sauce

Few dishes satisfy as simply and consistently as this one.

> 2 **cups all-purpose flour**
> 2 **tablespoons paprika**
> 1 **teaspoon salt**
> ¾ **teaspoon freshly ground white pepper**
> 2 **large eggs, lightly beaten**
> 1 **cup milk**
> 1½ **pounds lake perch fillets, skinned**
> 16 **thin slices lemon**
> ½ **cup Clarified Butter (see page 70)**
> **Sprigs fresh parsley for garnish**
> 1 **cup Herbed Tartar Sauce (recipe follows)**

In a medium-size bowl, sift together the flour, paprika, salt, and pepper.

In another medium-size bowl, combine the eggs and milk. Drench the perch and lemon slices in the egg-and-milk mixture, then shake off any excess and dredge them in the seasoned flour. Coat evenly, then shake to remove excess flour.

In a large skillet over high heat, warm the butter until just about smoking. Lay in the perch fillets, one by one, cooking until golden, about 2 minutes. Turn the fillets over, cooking until done, about 1 minute. Remove to a rack or paper toweling to drain. Repeat with the remaining perch and lemon slices. Mound the perch fillets on serving plates, garnish with the lemons and parsley, and serve with the tartar sauce.

MAKES 4 SERVINGS ■

Herbed Tartar Sauce

The average commercial version pales against this tartar sauce. Choose your ingredients wisely, such as plump, bright anchovy fillets and great pickles. You can vary the spices to create your own proprietary tartar sauce.

- 2 **large egg yolks**
- 1 **tablespoon Dijon mustard**
- ¼ **cup fresh lemon juice**
- 1 **cup corn oil**
- 1 **hard-boiled egg, chopped**
- 2 **tablespoons diced green bell pepper**
- 2 **tablespoons diced red onion**
- 2 **tablespoons sweet relish, drained**
- 2 **tablespoons diced dill pickle**
- 2 **tablespoons capers, drained and minced**

- 2 **anchovy fillets, minced**
- 1 **tablespoon minced scallion greens**
- 1 **tablespoon minced fresh parsley**
- ½ **teaspoon ground anise**
- ½ **teaspoon chopped fresh thyme**
- ½ **teaspoon salt**
- 1 **teaspoon freshly ground black pepper**

In the bowl of a mixer, combine the yolks, mustard, and lemon juice. On high speed, gradually add the corn oil in a steady stream. On slow speed, mix in the remaining ingredients. Adjust the salt and pepper to taste. Refrigerate until ready to use. Can be made up to 5 days ahead.

MAKES 2 CUPS ■

Escalope of Sea Bass with Fennel and Peppers

The fennel, peppers, and capers bring out the rich spicy flavors of the bass.

- 1 **cup Fish Stock (see page 65)**
- 1 **cup dry white wine**
- 2 **lemons, juiced**
- 1½ **cups heavy cream**
- ½ **cup trimmed and diced fennel bulb**
- ½ **cup roasted, peeled (see page 62), seeded, and diced yellow bell pepper**
- ½ **cup roasted, peeled, seeded, and diced red bell pepper**
- ¼ **cup nonpareil capers, drained**
  Salt to taste
  Coarsely ground black pepper to taste
- ¼ **cup packed fresh basil leaves, coarsely chopped**
- 8 **escalopes sea bass, about 3 ounces each**
- 1 **tablespoon virgin olive oil**
- 4 **sprigs fresh basil for garnish**

Preheat the grill or broiler.

In a medium-size saucepan, combine the stock, wine, and lemon juice, bring to a simmer over high heat, and cook until reduced to ½ cup, about 6 minutes. Add the cream and cook until thick enough to coat the back of a spoon, about 8 minutes. Add the fennel, peppers, and capers, and adjust the salt and pepper. Stir in the chopped basil, then reduce the heat to low.

Rub the surfaces of the sea bass with the olive oil, then place on the grill, cooking until well seared, about 2 minutes. Turn over and cook until done, about 3 minutes.

Spoon the sauce across warm plates, position the sea bass atop the sauce, and garnish with basil sprigs. Serve.

MAKES 4 SERVINGS ■

Swordfish with Ginger and Grapefruit

The bright grapefruit brings the rich swordfish alive.

 1   **cup Fish Stock (see page 65)**
 ¾   **cup dry white wine**
 1   **cup fresh grapefruit juice**
 ¼   **cup chopped shallots**
 2   **tablespoons Ginger Puree (see page 66)**
 ¼   **cup peeled and finely julienned fresh ginger**
 ½   **cup sugar**
 1   **cup water**
 12 **tablespoons (1½ sticks) unsalted butter, at
     room temperature**
 1   **tablespoon Angostura bitters**
     Salt to taste
     Freshly ground white pepper to taste

 2   **tablespoons grated grapefruit rind**
 12 **large grapefruit sections**
 4   **swordfish steaks, about 7 ounces each,
     trimmed of skin and fat**
 2   **tablespoons virgin olive oil**
 2   **tablespoons chopped scallion greens, cut on
     an angle**

Preheat the grill or broiler.

In a medium-size saucepan over high heat, combine the stock, wine, grapefruit juice, and shallots, and cook until reduced to 1 cup, about 9 minutes. Mix in the Ginger Puree. Strain through a fine sieve.

In a small saucepan, combine the ginger, sugar, and water. Bring to a simmer over medium heat, cooking until the ginger is tender, about 15 minutes. Drain.

In a large saucepan over high heat, bring the grapefruit reduction to a boil. Whisk in the butter, 1 tablespoon at a time, cooking until the sauce is thickened enough to coat the back of a spoon, about 4 minutes. Add the bitters and adjust the salt and pepper. Add the grapefruit rind, cooked ginger, and the grapefruit sections. Remove from the heat.

Rub the surfaces of the swordfish with the olive oil. Place on the grill and cook until seared, about 3 minutes. Turn over to finish, about 2 minutes, depending on the thickness of the swordfish.

Position the swordfish on warm serving plates. Rewarm the sauce for 1 minute and spoon the sauce over the fish, placing three grapefruit sections on each piece. Sprinkle with the scallions and serve.

VARIATION: Substitute ugli fruit, thought to be a cross between a bitter orange, mandarin orange, and grapefruit or pummelo, for the grapefruit.

COOKING NOTES: The bitters are quite fragrant, so adjust the amount to your taste. You can also substitute aperitifs such as Campari, Punt e Mes, or Pimm's Cup for the bitters.

■ Choose swordfish that has been cut into thick steaks so that more moisture is maintained during cooking. If you prefer more well done fish, select wider, thinner steaks that will cook through faster.

■ If the sauce separates, remove the grapefruit with a

slotted spoon, add more juice, and reduce over high heat until thickened. Add more butter and bitters to balance. Return the segments and serve.

MAKES 4 SERVINGS ■

Swordfish with Cracked Peppercorns and Scallions

A brilliant contrast of colors and flavors.

  1 **cup Fish Stock (see page 65)**
  1 **cup dry white wine**
1½ **cups heavy cream**
  1 **bunch scallion greens, chopped**
  1 **tablespoon black peppercorns, cracked**
  1 **tablespoon white peppercorns, cracked**
 ¼ **cup Szechuan peppercorns, cracked**
  4 **swordfish steaks, about 6 to 8 ounces each, trimmed of skin and fat**
    Salt to taste
 ¼ **cup snipped fresh chives**
  4 **red radishes, thinly sliced**

Preheat the broiler. In a medium-size saucepan, combine the stock and wine. Bring to a simmer over high heat and cook until reduced to ½ cup, about 8 minutes. Add the cream and cook until reduced to 1 cup, about 10 minutes. Pour into a blender, add the scallion greens, and let steep for 5 minutes. (The sauce will break down some of the acids from the scallions so that when pureed they won't break the cream.) Puree until smooth and strain through a fine sieve into another saucepan.

In a small bowl, combine the peppercorns, then distribute over the tops of the swordfish steaks, pressing them firmly into the surface of the fish. Place the fish on a broiler pan, pepper-side up. Adjust the salt.

Broil the swordfish until desired doneness is reached,

about 4 to 6 minutes, depending on the thickness of the steaks.

Meanwhile, return the sauce to a simmer over medium-high heat. Allow to reduce until thickened enough to coat the back of a spoon, about 2 minutes.

Spoon the sauce onto warm serving plates. Sprinkle the chives and radishes over the sauce and position the swordfish on top. Serve immediately.

COOKING NOTES: Choose swordfish that has been cut into thick steaks so that more moisture is maintained during cooking. If you prefer more well done fish, select wider, thinner steaks that will cook through faster.
■ The peppercorns, when heated, will lose their "hot" characteristics because the broiler heat drives the volatile oils out. What remains is their rich peppercorn flavor.
■ If you reheat the sauce, avoid long boiling to prevent the loss of its bright green color.

MAKES 4 SERVINGS ■

Bluefish with Red Wine, Shallots, and Juniper Berries

Bluefish, although a "fatty" fish, is wonderful for broiling. Be sure to remove all the dark tissue under the skin prior to cooking. This will reduce the oily "fishy" flavor. It's wonderful with red wine and juniper flavors.

½ cup Fish Stock (see page 65)
¾ cup dry red wine, preferably pinot noir
¼ cup coarsely chopped shallots
¼ cup coarsely chopped onions
1 bunch fresh parsley stems
2 tablespoons juniper berries
12 tablespoons (1½ sticks) unsalted butter, at
   room temperature
   Salt to taste
   Coarsely ground white pepper to taste
¼ cup finely diced shallots, rinsed under cold
   running water and squeezed dry
2 tablespoons snipped fresh chives
4 bluefish fillets, about 7 ounces each, trimmed
   of skin and fat
2 tablespoons virgin olive oil

Preheat the broiler.

In a medium-size saucepan, combine the stock, wine, chopped shallots, onions, parsley stems, and juniper berries, and cook over high heat until reduced to ¼ cup, about 10 minutes. Strain through a sieve into a large saucepan.

In a large saucepan over high heat, bring the wine reduction to a boil. Whisk in the butter, 1 tablespoon at a time, cooking until the sauce is thick enough to coat the back of a spoon, about 4 minutes. Adjust the salt and pepper, and reduce the heat to low. Stir in the diced shallots and chives.

Rub the surface of the bluefish with the olive oil. Place on a broiler pan and cook until done, about 7 minutes, depending on the thickness of the fish, testing with a skewer for firmness and internal temperature.

Place the bluefish on warm serving plates, spoon the sauce over the fish, and serve.

COOKING NOTE: Rinsing the shallots removes the strong flavor.

MAKES 4 SERVINGS ■

Mahi Mahi with Lime and Papaya Salsa

Also known as dolphin (though mahi mahi is a fish, not the mammal) or dorado, mahi mahi (the Hawaiian name) has a firm, white flesh with a delicate flavor. In the salsa, the heat is dictated by the poblanos and the Tabasco, while cooling contrast is provided by the papayas. The flavors just keep going and going.

2 ripe papayas, peeled, seeded, and diced
2 medium-size poblano peppers, roasted, peeled
   (see page 62), seeded, and diced
1 large red bell pepper, roasted, peeled, seeded,
   and diced
¼ cup chopped fresh cilantro
¼ cup fresh lime juice
1 clove garlic, minced
¾ cup virgin olive oil
   Salt to taste
   Tabasco sauce to taste
8 escalopes mahi mahi, about 3 ounces each
   Sprigs fresh cilantro for garnish

Preheat the grill or broiler.

To make the salsa, combine the papayas, peppers, cilantro, lime juice, garlic, and olive oil in a medium-size bowl. Season with salt and Tabasco. Refrigerate until ready to use or up to 2 days.

Rub the surfaces of the mahi mahi with the olive oil. Place on the grill and allow to sear, about 3 minutes. Turn the escalopes over and cook until done, about 3 minutes, depending on thickness, testing for firmness and warmth by inserting a skewer.

Spoon the salsa onto the serving plates, reserving ¼ cup for the garnish. Place 2 escalopes over the salsa on each plate, spoon the remaining salsa over the fish, garnish with sprigs of cilantro, and serve.

MAKES 4 SERVINGS ■

Salmon Cakes with Vidalias and Dill

The spring season welcomes the wonderful Nova Scotia Atlantic salmon, as well as the Western chinook, or king salmon, both valued for their superior quality. Look for them.

- **1 cup diced Vidalia or other sweet onion**
- **½ pound (2 sticks) plus 1 tablespoon unsalted butter**
- **¾ pound firm skinless salmon (see note below)**
- **¼ pound sea scallops, foot removed (see note below)**
- **1 large egg**
- **¾ teaspoon salt**
- **¼ teaspoon freshly ground white pepper**
- **2 cups heavy cream**
- **¼ cup coarsely chopped fresh dill**
  All-purpose flour for dusting
- **1 cup dry white wine**
- **1 cup Fish Stock (see page 65)**
- **¼ cup coarse-grained prepared mustard**
- **4 sprigs fresh dill for garnish**

In a small skillet over medium-high heat, sauté the onions in 1 tablespoon of the butter until softened. Cool and set aside.

In a food processor, puree ¼ pound of the salmon, cut into 1-inch pieces, with the scallops. Add the egg and continue to puree until smooth. Refrigerate.

With a mixer on high speed, cream 1 stick of the butter, together with the salt and pepper. Gradually add the fish puree, mixing until homogeneous. With the mixer on slow speed, gradually add 1 cup of the cream until just incorporated. (Do not overwork the mousse or it will become grainy.) Julienne the remaining ½ pound of the salmon and fold it into the cream mixture with the onions and dill. Form into 8 cakes and coat with flour. Place on a cookie sheet lined with parchment paper and refrigerate for at least 2 hours.

In a medium-size saucepan, combine the wine and stock. Over high heat, reduce to ¼ cup, about 3 minutes. Add the remaining 1 cup cream, cooking until thick-

ened enough to coat the back of a spoon, about 5 minutes. Reduce heat to low, stir in the mustard, and adjust the salt and pepper.

In a heavy skillet, heat the remaining 1 stick of butter over medium-high heat. Add the salmon cakes (flouring again if it's been absorbed into the cakes), cooking until golden, about 3 minutes. Turn over, cover the skillet, and cook until done, about 5 minutes. Remove and drain on paper towels.

Spoon the sauce onto warm serving plates, place the salmon cakes in the center, garnish with the sprigs of dill, and serve.

VARIATION: For smoked salmon cakes, increase the scallops to ½ pound (omitting the salmon) and use ½ pound smoked salmon, julienned, for the garnish.

COOKING NOTES: Remember to trim the fatty darker flesh from the salmon. This carries the oily "fishy" flavor.
- The "foot" is the tough muscle on the side of the scallop.
- The crucial step in making the mousse for the cakes is to slowly add the fish puree into the creamed butter, making sure it is *completely* combined. Scrape the bowl and whisk well. You cannot overwork it at this point. Then add the cream on slow speed in as short a time as possible, finishing by hand. This step is easy to overwork, so be gentle.

MAKES 4 SERVINGS ■

Salmon with Port, Lime, and Green Peppercorns

½ cup Fish Stock (see page 65)
½ cup fresh lime juice
½ cup tawny port
½ cup heavy cream
 2 tablespoons waterpacked green peppercorns, drained
   Salt to taste
 2 tablespoons chopped fresh tarragon
 2 tablespoons minced lime rind
 8 escalopes salmon, about 3 ounces each (see note below)
 2 tablespoons virgin olive oil
   Sprigs fresh tarragon for garnish

Preheat the grill or broiler.

In a medium-size saucepan, combine the stock, lime juice, and port, and cook over high heat until reduced to ½ cup, about 8 minutes. Add the heavy cream and cook until thickened enough to coat the back of a spoon, about 5 minutes. Add the peppercorns, adjust the salt, then stir in the tarragon and rind. Reduce heat to low.

Rub the surfaces of the salmon with the olive oil. Place on the grill, allowing to sear, about 3 minutes. Turn the escalopes over and cook until done, approximately 3 minutes, depending on thickness, testing for firmness and warmth by inserting a skewer.

Spoon the sauce onto warm serving plates, reserving ¼ cup for garnish. Place 2 escalopes over the sauce on each plate, spoon the remaining sauce over the fish, garnish with sprigs of tarragon, and serve.

VARIATION: Try substituting Madeira for the port, along with blood orange juice and zest for the lime.

COOKING NOTE: Remember to trim the fatty darker flesh from the salmon. This carries the oily "fishy" flavor.

MAKES 4 SERVINGS ■

Soft-Shell Crabs with Ginger Tempura

The secret here is to keep the batter thin, coating the crabs just enough that they fry up crisp.

   Corn oil for frying
 2 cups tempura mix (see note below)
 2 tablespoons Ginger Puree (see page 66) or to taste
½ cup diced scallion greens
   Salt to taste
   Tabasco sauce to taste
12 soft-shell crabs, cleaned (see note below)
 1 cup packed fresh cilantro leaves
 1 cup Citrus Aioli Sauce (recipe follows)

Fill a large, heavy, deep skillet with corn oil to a depth of 3 inches. Heat over medium-high to 350°F.

In a medium-size bowl, prepare the tempura mix according to directions. Add the Ginger Puree, scallions, salt, and Tabasco. Dip the crabs in the batter, then remove them to a rack set over a cookie sheet, allowing the excess batter to drip off. Lower the crabs into the hot corn oil and cook until golden, about 4 minutes. Drain on paper toweling, then transfer the crabs to a large bowl and toss with the cilantro.

Divide onto serving plates. Drizzle with the aioli sauce and serve.

COOKING NOTES: Tempura mix is available at oriental markets or you can make your own. Combine 1 large egg yolk with 2 cups ice cold water and ¼ teaspoon baking soda. Whisk in slowly 1⅔ cups sifted all-purpose flour. The batter should be just thick enough to coat the crabs. Add water to thin or a little flour to thicken as necessary.
■ Clean the crabs by pulling the key (lower belly flap) and opening the body shell. Remove the lungs and guts, then replace the body shell. Snip off the face, if you choose. Keep well refrigerated until ready to cook.

MAKES 4 SERVINGS ■

Citrus Aioli Sauce

Keep this sauce high in acid for balancing off the sweetness of fried foods. It's also great for steamed or fried vegetables.

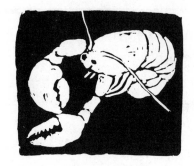

½ cup fresh lime juice
½ cup fresh lemon juice
2 large egg yolks
2 cloves garlic, roasted (see page 62) and minced
1 tablespoon Dijon mustard
1 cup virgin olive oil
½ cup prepared salsa (your choice on the heat!)
Salt to taste
Tabasco sauce to taste

In a small pan, combine the lime and lemon juices. Bring to a simmer over high heat, cooking until reduced to ¼ cup, about 5 minutes. Cool.

In the bowl of a mixer, combine the yolks, garlic, mustard, and reduced juice. On high speed gradually add the olive oil in a steady stream, then stir in the salsa. Season with salt and Tabasco. Refrigerate until ready to use. Can be made 2 days ahead.

MAKES 2 CUPS ■

Grilled Lobster with Herb Vinaigrette

With clean light flavors and a vinaigrette rather than the traditional butter, this is very long on flavor. During spring, lobsters are full in the shell, preparing for the molting that will take place during the summer. So enjoy lobsters before Memorial Day. Select hard-shelled lobsters with firm flesh rather than the soft-shell ones that are stringier fleshed from molting. When broiling lobster, cook quickly and at a very hot temperature to capture all the flavor.

6 tablespoons raspberry vinegar
1 tablespoon fresh lemon juice
½ teaspoon salt
1 cup plus 2 tablespoons extra virgin olive oil
3 tablespoons snipped fresh chives
3 tablespoons minced fresh basil
½ to ¾ teaspoon crushed red pepper
Four 1¼- to 1½-pound lobsters, halved lengthwise with sand sac removed
¼ cup plain dry bread crumbs
4 decoratively cut lemon halves
Sprigs fresh basil for garnish

To make the vinaigrette, combine the vinegar, lemon juice, and salt in a small bowl. Slowly whisk in the oil in a thin stream. Add the chives, basil, and crushed red peppers, and set aside. (The vinaigrette can be prepared 1 day ahead. Cover tightly and refrigerate until ready to use.)

Position a rack 4 inches from the broiler and preheat. Arrange the lobsters cut-side up on the broiler pan. Stir the vinaigrette and spoon 2 tablespoons over each half, then sprinkle with the bread crumbs. Broil until the lobster meat is opaque and the topping golden brown, about 10 minutes. Transfer the lobster to the serving plates and garnish with lemon and basil sprigs. Serve immediately, and pass the remaining vinaigrette separately.

VARIATIONS: Mix ground almond or hazelnut dust into the bread crumbs. For a tastier vinaigrette, substitute lemon balm for the basil and malt vinegar for the raspberry vinegar.

MAKES 4 SERVINGS ■

Chicken with Mustard and Spice Rub

¼ cup ground cumin
3 tablespoons achiote paste (see note below)
1½ cups coarse-grained prepared mustard
2 tablespoons Coleman's dry mustard
¼ pound (1 stick) unsalted butter, at room temperature
1 cup chopped fresh parsley
Salt to taste
2 chicken halves, boned, except for the wings and drumsticks (your butcher can do this)
2 tablespoons virgin olive oil
2 red bell peppers, roasted, peeled (see page 62), seeded, and cut into ½-inch strips
2 tablespoons fresh lime juice

Preheat the broiler to 450°F. Preheat the oven to 400°F (if separate).

With an electric mixer, combine the cumin, achiote, and mustards, then the butter, mixing until a smooth paste is formed. Mix in the parsley, and season with salt. Divide the butter into two containers. Using your fingers, lift the skin of the chicken breast and leg away from the meat and distribute one half of the butter mixture under the skin. Rub the chicken surfaces very lightly with the olive oil, then place on a roasting pan with the skin-side up. Broil until seared and golden, about 7 minutes. Lower the temperature to 375°F and cook until done, about 5 minutes, testing by inserting a skewer and observing clear juices. (Turn over if the skin gets too brown.) Place the roasted peppers in the oven for several minutes to warm.

Arrange the chicken on warm serving plates, brush with the lime juice, and spread with the remaining butter mixture. Garnish with the warmed grilled peppers and serve.

VARIATION: For a lower fat version, replace all the butter with 2 tablespoons of Dijon mustard. Roast, then remove the chicken skin.

COOKING NOTE: Achiote paste is a Central American condiment made from ground annatto seeds (the achiote), garlic, vinegar, salt, and sometimes chiles. It can be found in Spanish and Mexican markets. If you can't locate it, for 2 tablespoons achiote paste, substitute a mixture of 1 tablespoon mild Hungarian paprika, 1 tablespoon red bell pepper puree, 1 teaspoon minced garlic, and 1 teaspoon red wine vinegar. *Do not* use the annatto seed itself as a direct substitution—its flavor is much too strong.

MAKES 4 SERVINGS ■

Chicken Hash with Artichokes and Mushrooms

This style is chunkier compared to the traditional ground-pancake style. It's a great way to use leftover cooked chicken or turkey. A hash after the holidays is wonderful. Simply add the cooked meat to the sauce at the end to warm.

1 pound baby artichokes, maximum 2 inches in diameter
3 quarts Poultry Stock (see page 63)
3¼ pounds boneless chicken breasts
½ cup corn oil
2 cups ½-inch-cubed peeled baking potatoes
4 tablespoons (½ stick) unsalted butter
2 cups diced onion
2 cups ¾-inch pieces stemmed morel or button mushrooms
1½ cups Crème Fraîche (see page 65), plus a little extra for garnish
6 tablespoons cream sherry
¾ teaspoon salt
¼ teaspoon freshly ground black pepper
½ cup minced fresh parsley
8 sprigs fresh parsley for garnish

Cook the artichokes in a large nonaluminum pot of boiling water until tender, testing for doneness by inserting a skewer, about 10 minutes. Drain, rinse under cold water, and drain well. Discard the tough outer leaves, trim off any dark green skin, and quarter each artichoke. Remove any choke, using a teaspoon.

In a large saucepan, bring the stock to a simmer, then add the chicken. Adjust the heat so the liquid barely simmers. Cook until the chicken is opaque on the outside and just pink inside, 4 to 10 minutes, depending on size. Using a slotted spoon, transfer the chicken to a plate, and let cool completely. Simmer the stock until reduced to 1 cup, about 40 minutes. Discard the chicken skin and cut the meat into ¾-inch pieces.

In a large, heavy skillet, heat the oil over medium-high. Add the potatoes and cook until light brown, stirring frequently, about 5 minutes. Using a slotted spoon, transfer the potatoes to paper toweling to drain. Reserve the oil in the skillet.

Melt the butter in another large, heavy skillet over high heat, then add the onion and mushrooms. Cook until light brown, stirring frequently, about 8 minutes. Transfer the onion and mushrooms to a bowl. Add the artichokes and reduced stock to the skillet. Simmer until the liquid coats artichokes, about 5 minutes.

Add the Crème Fraîche, sherry, salt, and pepper, and simmer for 5 minutes. Add the mushrooms and onions and simmer until the sauce thickens slightly, stirring occasionally, about 8 minutes. Add the chicken and stir until heated.

Meanwhile, reheat the oil in the skillet over medium-high heat. Add the potatoes and stir until crisp and tender, about 4 minutes. Drain on paper toweling. Add the potatoes and minced parsley to the chicken mixture, simmering until the sauce coats the hash, 1 to 2 minutes. Spoon onto serving plates and garnish with sprigs of parsley and a dollop of Crème Fraîche.

COOKING NOTE: Avoid using aluminum pots with artichokes or you will end up with aluminum-flavored artichokes.

MAKES 8 SERVINGS ■

Roast Duck with Blood Oranges

Two 5- to 6-pound ducks
7 large blood oranges, peeled
2 cups Duck or Veal Stock (see page 63 or 64)
2 lemons, peeled and quartered
½ cup dry red wine, preferably pinot noir
4 tablespoons (½ stick) unsalted butter
1 tablespoon snipped fresh chives
Salt to taste
Coarsely ground black pepper to taste
1 recipe Vidalia Onion Rings (recipe follows)

Preheat the oven to 425°F.

Place the ducks on a rack in a deep roasting pan, on the lower shelf of the oven, and cook for 20 minutes. Turn the heat down to 350°F, and cook until the breast is medium-rare, about 15 minutes. Remove the ducks from the oven. Allow the ducks to cool slightly and carefully pour off the fat. Cut the breasts from the duck, and return the legs and carcass to the oven, cooking until medium degree of doneness, about 45 minutes. Remove from the oven, carve the legs from the carcass, and trim the fat from the breast and legs.

Cut 4 of the oranges into quarters, and break the remaining oranges into segments.

In a medium-size saucepan over medium-high heat, bring the stock to a simmer. Cook until reduced to ½ cup, about 8 minutes, then add the quartered oranges, the lemons, and wine. Cook until thickened enough to coat the back of a spoon, about 10 minutes, and strain through a fine sieve into another saucepan. Return to a simmer over high heat, then whisk the butter into the sauce, cooking until thickened, about 4 minutes. Adjust the salt and pepper, reduce the heat to low, and add the orange segments and chives.

Crisp the legs and breast in a 450°F oven for 8 to 10 minutes. Thinly slice the breast.

Spoon the sauce onto warm plates, distribute the onion rings across the sauce, then position the leg and breast meat over the onion rings. Spoon the remaining sauce with the orange segments over the duck. Serve.

VARIATION: For a fruitier version, substitute orange juice for the wine.

COOKING NOTE: This technique for cooking ducks keeps the breast medium-rare and the legs well done. For a well-done duck, continue cooking the whole duck for 1 hour after turning down the temperature to 350°F.

MAKES 4 SERVINGS ■

Vidalia Onion Rings

If you can't get Vidalias, substitute a mild flavored onion, such as Walla Walla, Maui, or Ossa.

    Corn oil for frying
1 cup all-purpose flour
1 tablespoon paprika
1/2 teaspoon salt
1/4 teaspoon freshly ground white pepper

1 large egg, lightly beaten
1/2 cup milk
1 large Vidalia or other sweet onion, sliced into thin rings

Fill a small heavy skillet with corn oil to a depth of 2 inches. Heat over medium-high to 350°F.

In a medium-size bowl, sift together the flour, paprika, salt, and pepper, and set aside. In another medium-size bowl, combine the egg and milk. Dredge the onion rings in the flour and dip into the egg batter. Then, using a slotted spoon, lift them out, allowing the excess liquid to drain back into the bowl. Transfer the onion rings to the flour mixture. Coat well and shake off the excess. Slip into the oil and fry until golden brown, about 2 minutes. Drain on paper toweling and store in a warm oven until ready to use.

Lamb Chops with Artichokes and Celery Root

4 tablespoons (1/2 stick) unsalted butter
1 cup coarsely chopped red onion
2 cups dry red wine, preferably cabernet sauvignon
4 cups Veal Stock (see page 64)
    Salt to taste
    Freshly ground black pepper to taste
1 3/4 cups baby artichoke hearts, blanched (see pages 57–58), prepared (see page 61), and quartered
1 cup water
1 tablespoon cumin seeds
1 medium-size celery root, peeled, cut into 1/4-by-1-inch sticks, and blanched
2 tablespoons finely chopped fresh parsley
1 tablespoon finely chopped fresh rosemary
8 lamb loin chops, about 4 ounces each

Preheat the grill or broiler.

In a medium-size saucepan, heat 2 tablespoons of the butter over high heat. Add the onions and cook until translucent, about 5 minutes. Add the wine and bring to a simmer over medium heat. Cook until reduced by half, about 10 minutes. Add 3 cups of the stock and cook until thickened enough to coat the back of a spoon, about 15 minutes. Adjust salt and pepper. Transfer to a blender and puree until smooth. Strain through a fine sieve into another skillet and keep warm.

Meanwhile, in a nonaluminum (see note below) medium-size saucepan, combine 1 cup of artichokes, the remaining stock, the water, and cumin. Bring to a simmer over high heat, cooking until the artichokes are tender, about 20 minutes. Transfer the artichokes and cooking juices to a blender, and puree until smooth, adding additional water if too thick to process. Strain through a fine sieve. Adjust salt and pepper. Keep warm over low heat.

In another medium-size skillet, melt the remaining butter over high heat. Add the remaining baby artichokes and the celery root, and sauté until heated through, about 3 minutes. Season with salt and pepper, then stir in the parsley and rosemary. Keep warm over low heat.

Place the chops on the grill or under the broiler and cook until well seared, about 5 minutes. Turn over and cook to desired doneness, about 4 minutes for medium-rare, 9 minutes for medium-well. Spoon the sauce in the center of the plate, then top with the artichoke puree. Distribute the artichoke and celery root garnish over the sauces. Lay two chops over sauce per plate. Serve.

COOKING NOTES: Select lamb loin chops that resemble a beef porterhouse steak, with the sirloin and tenderloin. The tenderloin will cook faster than the sirloin so check the tenderloin for doneness first; the sirloin will always be rarer.

▪ Avoid using aluminum pans with artichokes as you will end up with aluminum-flavored artichokes.

MAKES 4 SERVINGS ▪

Grilled Beef Tenderloin with Red Wine and Pistachios

The crunchy topping is a wonderful texture contrast to the tender meat.

  2 **cups Beef or Veal Stock (see page 63 or 64)**
  2 **cups dry red wine, preferably pinot noir**
  ½ **cup garlic cloves, roasted (see page 62)**
  ½ **cup chopped shallots**
  ½ **cup chopped fresh parsley**
     Salt to taste
     Freshly ground black pepper to taste
  ¼ **cup pistachios, toasted (see page 60) and chopped**
  ¼ **cup sunflower seeds, toasted (see page 61) and chopped**
  8 **tenderloin steaks, about 8 ounces each**
  2 **tablespoons virgin olive or corn oil**
     Sprigs fresh parsley for garnish

Preheat the grill or broiler.

In a large saucepan, combine the stock, wine, 3 tablespoons of the roasted garlic, the shallots, and ¼ cup of the chopped parsley. Bring to a simmer over medium heat and cook until reduced enough to coat the back of a spoon, about 20 minutes. Transfer to a blender and puree until smooth. Strain through a fine sieve into another saucepan, then adjust the salt and pepper. Stir in the remaining parsley, then reduce the heat to low.

In a small bowl, combine the remaining garlic, the pistachios, sunflower seeds, and 2 tablespoons of the red wine sauce. Mix well.

Rub the surface of the steaks with the oil. Grill until well seared on the surface, about 5 minutes. Turn over and cook until you reach desired doneness, about 4 minutes for medium-rare, depending on the thickness.

Brush the tops of the steaks with a small amount of sauce, then press the steaks, top-side down, into the pistachio mixture, coating the surface well. Position the steaks on serving plates, spoon the remaining sauce around them, garnish with parsley sprigs, and serve.

COOKING NOTES: The nut garnish/topping can be added to the sauce, just before adjusting the salt and pepper.
• Avoid very dark colored beef for the cow may have been excited prior to its termination. This raised activity depletes the muscles of their glycogen supply, resulting in less lactic acid, yielding gummy textured meat that spoils quickly.

MAKES 4 SERVINGS ■

Rack of Veal with Wild Mushrooms

This recipe contains all the rich flavors of the morels and the veal, and the lightness of the greens.

2   **pounds bone-in loin of veal**
2   **cups Veal Stock (see page 64)**
2   **large red bell peppers, roasted, peeled (see page 62), and seeded**
1   **cup heavy cream**
3   **tablespoons balsamic vinegar**
    Salt to taste
    Freshly ground black pepper to taste
6   **ounces wild mushrooms, preferably morels, trimmed**
2   **tablespoons unsalted butter**
1   **head mizuni (baby mustard greens)**
1   **yellow bell pepper, roasted, peeled, seeded, and julienned**
1   **tablespoon chopped fresh tarragon**
1   **tablespoon snipped fresh chives**
1   **tablespoon waterpacked green peppercorns, drained**
4   **sprigs fresh flatleaf parsley or tarragon**

Preheat the oven to 400°F. Place the veal in a roasting pan and cook until medium-rare, an internal temperature of 120°F, about 50 minutes.

While the veal is cooking, in a 12-inch skillet bring the stock to a simmer over medium-high heat and cook until reduced to 1/2 cup, about 15 minutes.

Puree 1 of the red peppers in a blender and set aside. Julienne the other one and set aside.

In a medium-size saucepan, bring the heavy cream to a simmer over medium-high heat and cook until thickened enough to coat the back of a spoon, about 15 minutes. Add the red pepper puree and the reduced stock, and cook again until thickened enough to coat the back of a spoon, about 5 minutes. Strain through a medium sieve, then add the vinegar, and adjust the salt and pepper.

In a large skillet over high heat, sauté the mushrooms in the butter until browned, about 8 minutes. Season with salt and pepper, and drain.

Arrange the greens on serving plates and distribute the julienned red pepper, yellow pepper, mushrooms, tarragon, chives, and peppercorns over them. Slice the veal off the bone into sixteen slices. Lay the slices over the greens, spoon the sauce over them, garnish with parsley sprigs, and serve.

VARIATIONS: The sauce adapts well to variations using other types of peppers and richer vegetables, such as fennel and sorrel. Match corresponding herbs to your sauce-vegetable combination.

COOKING NOTE: Roasting the veal at 400°F keeps it moist and pink. For a more well done roast, turn the oven down to 350°F after 15 minutes. You will need to cook the veal a little longer but the meat will be moist because of the initial searing.

MAKES 4 SERVINGS ■

Basic Polenta

This recipe provides the basic proportions for any polenta, no matter the type of cornmeal, liquid, or extra seasonings added.

Leftover soups make a great liquid base for polentas. For example, artichoke soup can be converted into artichoke polenta with Romano or Parmesan cheese.

3½ cups liquid
2 teaspoons salt
1 teaspoon freshly ground black pepper
2 cups yellow cornmeal
½ cup grated cheese of your choice (optional)
2 tablespoons unsalted butter, plus more for sautéing

In a large saucepan, combine the liquid and seasonings. Bring to a simmer over medium-high heat. Gradually whisk in the cornmeal. Stir with a spatula or wooden spoon until the polenta is thick enough to allow the spoon to stand up in it, about 15 minutes. Add the cheese and butter. Adjust the salt and pepper.

Pour the polenta mixture into a parchment-lined 16- by 12- by 1-inch sheet pan. Smooth and level the surface, cover with plastic wrap, and refrigerate until firm, about 4 hours.

Remove the plastic wrap and, with a knife or cookie cutter, cut the polenta into desired shapes (triangles, rectangles, diamonds, moons, etc.). Invert the pan to unmold. Refrigerate until ready to cook, covering with plastic wrap if more than 1 hour.

In a nonstick skillet, heat butter (as much as is necessary to cover the bottom of the pan) over high heat. Carefully add the polenta and cook until seared, about 2 minutes. Turn over to lightly brown the other side, about 2 minutes. Pat with paper towels, then serve immediately.

MAKES TWENTY-FOUR 2-INCH PIECES ■

Fennel Polenta

3 large fennel bulbs, trimmed (reserve and chop the greens)
1 cup water
2½ cups milk
3 cups Poultry Stock (see page 63)
1 tablespoon salt
1 teaspoon freshly ground black pepper
1 teaspoon freshly grated nutmeg
3½ cups yellow cornmeal
¼ pound (1 stick) unsalted butter, plus more for sautéing

Preheat the oven to 400°F.

Place fennel bulbs and water in a roasting pan on the lower rack of the oven. Bake until very well done and tender, about 1 hour, testing for doneness by inserting a skewer. Remove and allow to cool slightly. Transfer to a food processor, add ¼ cup of the milk, and puree until smooth. Reserve in a warm area.

In a large saucepan, combine the remaining milk, the stock, salt, pepper, and nutmeg. Bring to a simmer over medium-high heat, then gradually whisk in the cornmeal. Stir with a spatula or wooden spoon until the polenta is thick enough to allow the spoon to stand up in it, about 15 minutes. Add the fennel puree, chopped fennel greens, and butter. Adjust the seasonings.

Pour the polenta mixture into a parchment-lined 16- by 12- by 1-inch sheet pan. Smooth and level the surface, cover with plastic wrap, and refrigerate until firm, about 4 hours.

Remove the plastic wrap and, with a knife or cookie cutter, cut the polenta into desired shapes (triangles, rectangles, diamonds, moons, etc.). Invert the pan to unmold and refrigerate until ready to cook, covering with plastic wrap if more than 1 hour. In a nonstick skillet, heat butter (as much as is necessary to cover the bottom of the pan) over high heat. Carefully add the polenta and cook until seared, about 2 minutes. Turn over to lightly brown the other side, about 2 minutes. Pat with paper towels, then serve immediately.

VARIATIONS: Fennel polenta can also include Parmesan cheese, basil, roasted garlic, roasted tomatoes, and other complementary ingredients. Choose rich, strong flavors for the best results.

COOKING NOTE: Fennel can also be cooked by boiling. Cut the fennel into quarters and simmer in the Poultry Stock until tender, about 12 minutes. Add water or white wine to replenish evaporated Poultry Stock.

MAKES TWENTY-FOUR 2-INCH PIECES ■

Sweet Potato Polenta

4 large sweet potatoes (Louisiana Orange yam
    variety), about 3 pounds
2½ cups milk
3 cups Poultry Stock (see page 63)
1 tablespoon salt
1 teaspoon freshly ground black pepper
1 teaspoon freshly grated nutmeg
3½ cups yellow cornmeal
¼ pound (1 stick) unsalted butter, plus enough
    for sautéing

Preheat the oven to 400°F.

Place the sweet potatoes in a roasting pan on the lower rack of the oven. Bake until very well done and tender, about 1 hour. Remove and allow to cool slightly. Scoop the meat of the potatoes into a food processor, add ¼ cup of the milk, and puree until smooth. Reserve in a warm area.

In a large saucepan, combine the remaining milk, the stock, salt, pepper, and nutmeg, and bring to a simmer over medium-high heat. Gradually whisk in the cornmeal. Stir with a spatula or wooden spoon until the polenta is thick enough to allow the spoon to stand up in it, about 15 minutes. Add the sweet potato puree and the butter. Adjust the salt and pepper.

Pour the polenta mixture into a parchment-lined 16- by 12- by 1-inch sheet pan. Smooth and level the surface, cover with plastic wrap, and refrigerate until firm, about 4 hours.

Remove the plastic wrap and, with a knife or cookie cutter, cut the polenta into desired shapes (triangles, rectangles, diamonds, moons, etc.). Invert the pan to unmold, and refrigerate until ready to cook, covering with plastic wrap if more than 1 hour.

In a nonstick skillet, heat butter (as much as is necessary to cover the bottom of the pan) over high heat. Carefully add the polenta and cook until seared, about 2 minutes. Turn over to lightly brown the other side, about 2 minutes. Pat with paper towels, then serve immediately.

COOKING NOTES: Add more liquid if the mixture gets dry, as there are natural variations in the amount of starch in sweet potatoes.

■ You can stir a little cranberry puree in at the end with the butter to produce a marbling effect. Be careful not to totally combine or you'll just end up with a light pink cast.

MAKES TWENTY-FOUR 2-INCH PIECES ■

Blue Corn Polenta

Blue corn produces a beautiful purple-blue colored polenta. I prefer a medium grind for a little coarser texture. You can blend different color polentas for unusual taste combinations.

3 cups Poultry Stock (see page 63)
2 teaspoons salt
1 teaspoon freshly ground black pepper
1½ cups blue cornmeal
½ cup masa-harina
1 clove garlic, roasted (see page 62) and
    minced
2 tablespoons unsalted butter, plus enough for
    sautéing

In a large saucepan combine the stock and seasonings. Bring to a simmer over medium-high heat, then gradually whisk in the cornmeal and masa-harina. Stir with a spatula or wooden spoon until the polenta is thick enough to allow the spoon to stand up in it, about 15 minutes. Add the garlic and butter, and adjust the salt and pepper.

Pour the polenta mixture into a parchment-lined 16- by 12- by 1-inch sheet pan. Smooth and level the surface, cover with plastic wrap, and refrigerate until firm, about 4 hours.

Remove the plastic wrap and, with a knife or cookie cutter, cut the polenta into desired shapes (triangles, rectangles, diamonds, moons, etc.). Invert the pan to unmold and refrigerate until ready to cook, covering with plastic wrap if more than 1 hour.

In a nonstick skillet, heat the butter (as much as is necessary to cover the bottom of the pan) over high heat. Carefully add the polenta and cook until seared, about 2 minutes. Turn over to lightly brown the other side, about 2 minutes. Pat with paper towels, then serve immediately.

MAKES TWENTY-FOUR 2-INCH PIECES ∎

cutter, cut the polenta into desired shapes (triangles, rectangles, diamonds, moons, etc.). Invert the pan to unmold and refrigerate until ready to cook, covering with plastic wrap if more than 1 hour.

In a nonstick skillet, heat butter (as much as is necessary to cover the bottom of the pan) over high heat. Carefully add the polenta and cook until seared, about 2 minutes. Turn over to lightly brown the other side, about 2 minutes. Pat with paper towels, then serve immediately.

MAKES TWENTY-FOUR 2-INCH PIECES ∎

Yellow Corn Polenta

This is a great base recipe for adding ingredients to, such as sautéed chanterelles, or other wild mushrooms, and asparagus or artichoke pieces. Cook the vegetable garnish until tender so that when the polenta is chilled the textures are similar, which will allow the polenta to be cut evenly and smoothly.

   2 cups Poultry Stock (see page 63)
1½ cups milk
   2 teaspoons salt
   1 teaspoon freshly ground black pepper
   2 cups yellow cornmeal
½ cup finely grated Parmesan cheese
   2 tablespoons unsalted butter, plus enough for sautéing

In a large saucepan, combine the stock, milk, and seasonings. Bring to a simmer over medium-high heat, then gradually whisk in the cornmeal. Stir with a spatula or wooden spoon until the polenta is thick enough to allow the spoon to stand up in it, about 15 minutes. Add the Parmesan and butter. Adjust the salt and pepper.

Pour the polenta mixture into a parchment-lined 16- by 12- by 1-inch sheet pan. Smooth and level the surface, cover with plastic wrap, and refrigerate until firm, about 4 hours.

Remove the plastic wrap and, with a knife or cookie

Passion Fruit Ice Cream with White Chocolate Sauce

The ice cream captures all the passion fruit perfume while the chocolate sauce enriches the flavors of the ice cream.

   1 cup half-and-half, scalded
   1 tablespoon cassia buds (see note below), coarsely crushed
   3 large egg yolks
   2 tablespoons sugar
   1 teaspoon vanilla extract
     Pinch of salt
   5 ounces white chocolate, broken into ½-ounce pieces
½ cup heavy cream
¼ cup raspberry puree (see note on page 108)
     Passion Fruit Ice Cream (recipe follows)
     Sprigs fresh mint for garnish

To make the white chocolate sauce, combine the scalded half-and-half with the cassia. Allow to infuse until cool. Reheat to scald again.

In a medium-size saucepan, combine the egg yolks, sugar, vanilla, and salt, then stir in the scalded half-and-half mixture. Cook over medium-low heat until thickened enough to coat the back of a spoon, about 4 minutes. Do not boil. Remove from the heat and add the chocolate, stirring until melted. Stir in the heavy cream, then strain, cover, and refrigerate.

To serve, spoon the sauce onto the serving plates. Decorate the sauce with the raspberry puree, then position a scoop of Passion Fruit Ice Cream on top of the sauce. Garnish with mint sprigs and serve immediately.

COOKING NOTE: Cassia is the dried flower bud of the cassia tree whose bark is sold commercially as cinnamon. Cassia buds have a pronounced flavor, often compared with that of "red hots" candy. It's available in spice or specialty food stores.

MAKES 4 SERVINGS ■

Passion Fruit Ice Cream

   ½ **cup sugar**
  12 **large egg yolks**
      Pinch of salt
   1 **teaspoon vanilla extract**
  2½ **cups frozen passion fruit puree (see note below)**
   2 **cups heavy cream**

In a medium-size saucepan, combine the sugar, egg yolks, salt, vanilla, and passion fruit puree. Cook over medium-low heat until thickened enough to coat the back of a spoon, about 6 minutes; do not boil. Remove from the heat, add the cream, and strain through a fine sieve. Refrigerate to chill.

Transfer the custard to an ice-cream maker and process according to the manufacturer's instructions. Freeze in a covered container overnight to a firm texture.

COOKING NOTE: Frozen passion fruit puree is available at specialty food stores at a relatively modest price; fresh passion fruit yields about 2 to 3 tablespoons puree per average-size fruit and will result in greater expense.

MAKES 1 QUART ■

Kiwi Ice Cream

Although the kiwi is most kindly referred to as the ex-star of nouvelle cuisine, it works well in this ice cream. Grown on vines, most kiwis come from California or New Zealand, though they originated in China. Select supple, unbruised fruit with a soft fragrance.

   8 **large egg yolks**
  1¼ **cups sugar**
      Pinch of salt
   1 **teaspoon vanilla extract**
   2 **cups half-and-half, scalded**
   6 **large ripe kiwis, peeled and cut into pieces**
   1 **cup heavy cream**

In a medium-size saucepan, combine the egg yolks, sugar, salt, and vanilla. Whisk in the scalded half-and-half. Stir over medium-low heat until thickened enough to coat the back of a spoon, about 10 minutes; do not boil. Remove from the heat and strain into a blender. Add the kiwis and cream, and puree until smooth. Cover and refrigerate until well chilled.

Transfer the custard to an ice-cream maker and process according to the manufacturer's instructions until thickened. Freeze in a covered container overnight. If frozen solid, allow to soften slightly before serving.

MAKES 1½ QUARTS ■

Pressed Chocolate Cake with Hazelnut Ice Cream and Hot Fudge Sauce

The "pressing" technique used here produces a denser chocolate cake by pushing the air out from the cake.

  7 ounces extra bittersweet chocolate (do not use baking chocolate)
 14 tablespoons (1³/₄ sticks) unsalted butter
  5 large eggs, separated
  1 tablespoon vanilla extract
³/₄ cup sugar
    Pinch of salt
  2 tablespoons unsweetened dark cocoa powder
  8 scoops Hazelnut Ice Cream (recipe follows)
  2 cups Rattlesnake Hot Fudge Sauce (see page 107)

Preheat the oven to 350°F. Grease a 10-inch springform pan.

In the top of a double boiler over simmering water, combine the chocolate and butter. Heat until melted and smooth. Transfer to a medium-size bowl and whisk in the egg yolks and vanilla. Sift in the sugar, salt, and cocoa while continuing to whisk.

With a mixer, whip the egg whites to soft peaks. Fold one third of them into the chocolate mixture. Repeat with the remaining whites, then pour the mixture into the prepared pan. Place on the lower rack of the oven and bake for 25 minutes.

Remove to a cake rack and immediately loosen the springform collar (sides). Slip a plate inside the collar on top of the cake and push down slightly to push the air from the cake. Remove the plate and springform collar, and allow the cake to cool before serving.

To serve, cut the cake into eight pieces and place on serving plates. Position a scoop of ice cream on each piece of cake and spoon hot fudge sauce over the top. Serve immediately.

COOKING NOTE: Please observe the folding technique to capture the maximum amount of air which will create a superior texture during baking.

MAKES 8 SERVINGS ■

Hazelnut Ice Cream

2¹/₂ cups half-and-half, scalded
 ¹/₂ cup hazelnuts, blanched (see page 60), toasted, and chopped
   8 large egg yolks
³/₄ cup sugar
     Pinch of salt
   1 tablespoon vanilla extract
   2 cups heavy cream

Combine the scalded half-and-half and hazelnuts in a blender and puree for 2 minutes. Allow to steep together until cool.

In medium-size saucepan, combine the egg yolks, sugar, salt, and vanilla. Whisk in the half-and-half mixture. Stir over medium-low heat until the custard thickens enough to coat the back of a spoon, about 10 minutes; do not boil. Remove from the heat and whisk in the heavy cream. Strain through a fine sieve into a medium-size bowl, cover, and refrigerate until well chilled.

Transfer the custard to an ice-cream maker and process according to the manufacturer's instructions. Freeze in a covered container overnight. If frozen solid, allow to soften slightly before serving.

COOKING NOTE: You reheat the hazelnut-infused cream to scalding for the best flavor and yield. If you strain it while the cream and nuts are cool, you will lose 10 to 25 percent of the volume and the ice cream's texture will be dense and chalky.

MAKES 1¹/₂ QUARTS ■

Rattlesnake Hot Fudge Sauce

You can vary this using different types of chocolates and coffees. My preference is for the bittersweet flavor. If you choose a sweeter chocolate, reduce the sugar by half in the recipe. This can be prepared up to 1 week ahead.

  1 **cup sugar**
  1 **cup water**
16 **ounces extra bittersweet chocolate (do not use baking chocolate)**
¼ **pound (1 stick) unsalted butter**
  1 **cup condensed or evaporated milk**
  1 **tablespoon vanilla extract**
     Strong coffee to taste

Cook the sugar and water in a medium-size saucepan over low heat, stirring until the sugar dissolves. Increase the heat and bring to a boil. Cool the syrup slightly.

In the top of a double boiler over simmering water, combine the chocolate and butter. Heat until melted and smooth, then transfer to a medium-size bowl. Whisk in the sugar syrup, condensed milk, and vanilla. Thin with coffee to desired consistency. Cover and refrigerate until ready to use.

Reheat gently in the top of a double boiler before serving.

MAKES APPROXIMATELY 3 CUPS ■

Ginger and Passion Fruit Crème Brûlée

This recipe is perfect with exotic spring flavors, especially the bright, rich fruits, such as the mango. Simply substitute the exotic fruit purees for the passion fruit.

  2 **cups heavy cream**
½ **cup half-and-half**
10 **large egg yolks**
½ **cup superfine sugar**
  1 **tablespoon vanilla extract**
½ **cup frozen passion fruit puree (see note below)**
  1 **tablespoon Ginger Puree (see page 66)**
¼ **cup packed light brown sugar**

Preheat the oven to 300°F.

In a medium-size saucepan, scald the cream and half-and-half over medium heat. Remove from the heat.

In a large bowl, combine the egg yolks, sugar, and vanilla, and beat rapidly with a wire whisk until light. Slowly add the hot cream and passion fruit and ginger purees while continuing to whisk, until smooth. Strain through a fine sieve. Fill 4 custard dishes to ¼ inch below the top edge.

Place the custards in a water bath, in the lower third of the oven. Cook until lightly tanned on top and a skewer inserted into the center is hot to the touch, about 15 to 20 minutes. Remove to a cake rack and allow to cool. Cover with plastic wrap and chill for at least 8 hours before serving.

To serve, preheat the broiler. Evenly spread the brown sugar across the tops of the custards. Place the custards under the broiler, allowing the tops to caramelize but not burn. (A brûlée iron also works well. To use a brûlée iron, heat over an open flame on high until white hot, about ½ hour. Spread the brown sugar over the custard, then lightly press the brûlée iron to the sugar, just to carmelize it to a dark brown color.) Allow to cool for several minutes before serving.

COOKING NOTES: Frozen passion fruit puree is available in specialty food stores at a relatively modest price; fresh passion fruit yields only about 2 to 3 tablespoons of puree per average-size fruit and will be more expensive.

■ Whipping the eggs to a foamy state and then adding the hot cream creates a light, smooth brûlée texture. Avoid overwhipping the eggs to a "ribbon" or the brûlée will drop a large volume in the molds after cooking.

MAKES 4 SERVINGS ■

Cassis Bavarois with Berries

This is packed with pure berry flavor. Currants are often overlooked but deserve to be paired with blueberries and raspberries.

    Almond oil for mold (see note below)
¾ **cup double crème de cassis liqueur**
1 **tablespoon gelatin**
1½ **cups black currant or raspberry puree (see note below)**
5 **large egg yolks**
2 **tablespoons sugar or to taste**
1 **cup half-and-half, scalded**
1¼ **cups heavy cream**
1 **pint blueberries**
1 **pint strawberries, cut in half if large**
1 **pint raspberries**
    Splash of brandy or cognac
    Sprigs fresh mint for garnish

Wipe 8 custard cups or molds with the almond oil. Turn upside down on paper toweling until ready to fill.

In a small bowl, combine ½ cup of the crème de cassis with the gelatin. Heat the mixture in a water bath until the gelatin is dissolved.

In a large bowl, combine the remaining crème de cassis and the berry puree. Warm over medium heat, then remove from the heat and stir in the gelatin mixture. In a small saucepan, combine the egg yolks and sugar,

then add the scalded half-and-half. Heat over medium until thickened enough to coat the back of a spoon, about 5 minutes; do not boil. Strain through a fine sieve into a bowl.

In a large bowl, whip the cream until thickened but still fluid. Fold into the berry mixture. Place the bowl over an ice bath and, using a rubber spatula, stir constantly until heavily thickened. Immediately pour into the molds, cover, and refrigerate overnight.

Run a knife around the edges of the molds to loosen the bavarois and position them in the center of the serving plates. Toss the fresh berries with the brandy and distribute over the bavarois. Garnish with mint sprigs and serve.

COOKING NOTES: To make the berry puree, thaw frozen berries in a strainer over a saucepan, allowing the juices to collect in the pan. Reserve the berries. Reduce the juices over medium heat until thickened enough to coat the back of a spoon, about 10 minutes, depending on the original volume. Using a blender, puree the berries with the juice until smooth. Strain.

■ For the best results, the whipped cream and berry mixture should have the *same* texture when combined.

■ Almond oil is available from specialty food stores and baking suppliers.

MAKES 8 SERVINGS ■

Sour Cherry Tart

This recipe combines pepper vodka with sour cherries in a bright tart. Sour cherries are also known as "pie cherries," with two thirds of the production coming from Michigan. They taste best when cooked and are extremely fragile when fresh, so use immediately.

One 11-inch Hazelnut Tart Shell (recipe follows)
- 1/2 **cup sugar**
- 2 **large eggs, lightly beaten**
- 2 **large egg yolks**
- 1 **teaspoon vanilla extract**
- **Pinch of salt**
- 1 **cup half-and-half, scalded**
- 1/2 **cup pepper vodka**
- 4 **tablespoons (1/2 stick) unsalted butter**
- 3 **cups sour cherries, pitted**
- **Confectioners' sugar for dusting**

Preheat the oven to 375°F.

Line the tart shell with foil, shiny-side down. Fill with pie weights or dried beans, then bake until set, about 20 minutes. Remove the beans and foil and continue baking until browned, about 15 minutes.

In a medium-size bowl, combine the sugar, eggs, egg yolks, vanilla, and salt. Add the hot half-and-half, then the vodka. Strain through a fine sieve.

In a large skillet over high heat, melt the butter, then add the cherries. Cook until the cherries are warm and the juices have thickened enough to coat the fruit, about 5 minutes.

Spoon the cherries into the tart shell, then pour in the custard. Bake until the custard sets, about 10 minutes.

Cool on a rack. Dust the tart with confectioners' sugar, then serve.

COOKING NOTE: This fruit sautéing technique works well on almost all firm or sour fruit. Fruits that contain less moisture will require less cooking time. Those fruits with a lot of moisture will need a longer cooking time over high continuous heat to concentrate their juices.

MAKES ONE 11-INCH TART ∎

Hazelnut Tart Shell

This recipe works with most nuts. Avoid oily nuts or, if you do use them, reduce the volume of butter in the recipe to maintain a pastry texture. Also, adjust the amount of sugar to balance any bitter qualities.

- 1/2 **cup hazelnuts, toasted and skinned (see page 60)**
- 1/2 **cup confectioners' sugar**
- 3/4 **pound (3 sticks) unsalted butter**
- 1 **large egg**
- 2 **tablespoons grated orange rind**
- 1/4 **teaspoon salt**
- 2 **cups pastry flour**

In a food processor, grind the nuts and sugar together until fine. Add the butter and whip until light. Add the egg, orange rind, and salt. Add the flour, mixing until just combined. Transfer the dough to a piece of parchment or wax paper and flatten into a disc. Cover with another piece of parchment, and refrigerate until firm, at least 8 hours.

Dust the dough with flour, then roll the dough out between sheets of parchment to a thickness of 1/4 inch. Fit into an 11-inch tart pan, trim, and finish edges. Refrigerate at least 30 minutes before baking.

COOKING NOTE: Keep the pastry cool for easy handling.

MAKES ONE 11-INCH TART SHELL ∎

Gratin of Strawberries and Rhubarb

½ cup superfine sugar
10 large egg yolks
2 teaspoons vanilla extract
2 cups heavy cream, scalded
½ cup cognac
2 tablespoons unsalted butter
2 cups 1-inch rhubarb pieces
2 pints strawberries, sliced

Preheat the broiler.

In a large bowl, combine ¼ cup of the sugar, the egg yolks, and vanilla. Stir in the hot cream, then add the cognac. Strain through a fine sieve. Keep warm.

In a large skillet over high heat, melt the butter. Add the rhubarb and the remaining sugar. Cook until warm and all the juices are reduced over the fruit, about 5 minutes.

Spoon the rhubarb into 4 hot ovenproof soup plates and distribute the strawberries over it. Pour the custard over to fill, then bake until the custard sets and the tops are golden, about 8 minutes. Serve. (Watch out, the plates are very hot.)

VARIATIONS: If you substitute liquors, keep the sugar content in mind and adjust the sugar in the custard to taste. One of my favorite versions is tiny wild blueberries with old bourbon substituted for the strawberries, rhubarb, and cognac. Another variation is tiny wild strawberries and grappa.

COOKING NOTES: The gratin works best when the soup plates are hot, the fruit is warm or at room temperature, and the custard is warm. When that is the case, the top of the gratin will brown quickly and the custard thickens almost immediately when placed under the broiler. Cold ingredients in cold soup plates will take forever to heat up and then cook with poor results. Keep it hot!

▪ When using fresh berries and tender fruit, do not cook before covering with the custard. Use the rhubarb sauté technique for firm and sour fruit only.

▪ Select ovenproof soup plates or shallow ovenproof ramekins to withstand the heat of the broiler. Dishes by Corning or Pillevuit work well.

MAKES 4 SERVINGS ▪

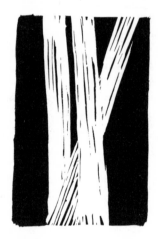

SPRING MENUS

Smoked Salmon and Artichoke Salad with Ginger Dressing
Robert Mondavi Reserve Sauvignon Blanc

◆

Grilled Beef Tenderloin with Red Wine and Pistachios
Asparagus
Heitz Cellars Bella Oaks Cabernet Sauvignon

◆

Gratin of Strawberries and Rhubarb

Crab, Grapefruit, and Jicama Salad
Cakebread Cellars Sauvignon Blanc

◆

Sorrel and Celery Root Soup

◆

Salmon Cakes with Vidalias and Dill
Asparagus
Fennel Polenta
Jordan Vineyard Chardonnay

◆

Sour Cherry Tart

Gratin of Asparagus, Morels, and Celery Root
Neyers Chardonnay

◆

Radicchio, Watercress, and Walnut Salad

◆

Roast Duck with Blood Oranges
Yellow Corn and Sweet Potato Polentas
Pine Ridge Merlot

◆

Pressed Chocolate Cake with Hazelnut
Ice Cream and Hot Fudge Sauce

Steamer Clams with Watercress and Shallots
Frog's Leap Sauvignon Blanc

◆

Lake Perch with Herbed Tartar Sauce
Leaf Spinach
New Potatoes
Rombauer Chardonnay

◆

Ginger and Passion Fruit Crème Brûlée

S U M M E R

Nature's most loving personality is summer. The warm air and beautiful flowers cast a spell to lure you outside to the calming comfort of paradise. Food grows everywhere. The special delights of delicate berries and fruits reflect all the beauty of nature. A ripe peach eaten out of hand becomes a sublime experience. Savoring a fresh fig can be the source of a tranquil moment in a busy day.

Summer is the most bountiful season of the year. Fresh vegetables and fruits from the garden are difficult to surpass. The flavors of naturally ripened produce are pure and forward, easy to season, and simple to serve, complements to a spontaneous lifestyle.

So many wonderful techniques are applicable to summer foods. It is a great time for simple preparations and capturing summer flavors with seasoned vinegars and dressings. The dishes require short preparation times, with an emphasis on grilling techniques to take full advantage of the great outdoors.

Welcome your guests with simple but elegant appetizers of chilled shellfish salads, squash blossoms with eggplant and peppers, and salmon carpaccio with tiny, crunchy papaya seed garnishes. Cook garden pizzas in an oven or grill them.

Chilled summer soups capture the new clean flavors of the produce. Grilling and barbecuing are raised to an art form. The sublime burger is elevated to new heights. Special seasonings and techniques are used to capture all the flavors of steaks on the grill. Even the traditionally inspired pickles and cold salads are elegant in their summer spendor.

This is the time for light meat and poultry dishes with simple marinades, grilled or poached. Fun preparations of tamales and tortillas match the heat. Main course salads with salmon or crab cakes with tomatillos reflect this light attitude.

There is something so wonderful about walking the fields and gardens, filled with foods so great that you can just pick and eat them. Capture these just picked flavors in wonderful sorbet preparations. Easy to make with wonderful fruit and tea flavors, they are the most refreshing way to end a meal. Ice creams abound with the tree- and bush-ripened fruits encased in creamy silk. Does ice cream taste any better than in the summer?

Summer is the season to be with nature in the great outdoors, the time to celebrate that the true meaning of life has been captured in a tomato or an ear of corn.

Chilled Roast Veal with Capers and Basil

This salad is a terrific appetizer or main course. It is perfect for the picnic basket for a luxurious retreat to the fields.

1½ pounds loin of veal
  1 bunch arugula, trimmed and pulled apart
 ½ cup Tomato Concasse (see page 65)
 ½ cup nonpareil capers, drained
 ¾ cup Basil Vinaigrette (recipe follows)
 ¼ cup pine nuts, toasted (see page 60)
 ¼ cup grated Pecorino Romano cheese

Preheat the oven to 450°F or the grill.

Place the veal in a roasting pan and cook until medium-rare, an internal temperature of 120°F, about 25 minutes (or grill to desired level of doneness). Set aside.

Lay the arugula across the serving plates. Slice the veal very thin and flatten with a meat bat or the side of a knife until paper thin. Lay the slices across the arugula, then distribute the tomatoes and capers across them and drizzle with the vinaigrette. Top with the pine nuts and Romano cheese. Serve.

COOKING NOTE: Cook the veal to a temperature slightly lower than that you would prefer to keep the veal moist and tender when served chilled.

MAKES 4 SERVINGS ■

Basil Vinaigrette

Great used as a dressing over sliced tomatoes, vegetables, or grilled poultry. The blender technique captures the fresh flavor of the basil within the oil and vinegar. It is a good way to make use of extra herbs from your garden and carry their flavors into fall. Refrigerate the dressing in an airtight jar; it will keep for weeks.

¼ cup balsamic vinegar
 2 cloves garlic, roasted (see page 62)
¼ teaspoon salt
¼ teaspoon freshly ground black pepper
¾ cup virgin olive oil
½ cup packed fresh basil leaves
 1 tablespoon grated lemon rind

In a blender, combine the vinegar, garlic, salt, pepper, and olive oil. Add the basil and lemon rind, and puree until smooth. Strain through a medium sieve into a small bowl.

MAKES 1½ CUPS ■

Salmon Carpaccio

The combination of smoked and fresh salmon is wonderful with playful garnishes of jicama and papaya seeds.

¼ cup balsamic vinegar
¼ teaspoon salt
 1 tablespoon coarse-grained prepared mustard
 1 tablespoon waterpacked green peppercorns, drained, crushed, and minced
½ cup nonpareil capers, drained
¼ cup snipped fresh chives
½ cup virgin olive oil
½ cup papaya seeds
½ pound salmon fillet, cleaned of all skin and fatty tissue
½ pound smoked salmon, thinly sliced
 1 cup peeled and diced jicama (see note below)
16 Toasted Croutons (see page 70)

In a medium-size bowl, whisk together the vinegar and salt. Add the mustard, peppercorns, capers, chives, and olive oil. Adjust the seasonings to taste.

Pinch the papaya seeds to break the membranes and remove (see note below). Place the seeds in a strainer and rinse under cold running water. Drain on paper toweling. Place the seeds on a cookie sheet and toast in a preheated 400°F oven until crunchy, about 7 minutes. Allow to cool.

Slice the salmon fillet very thinly (see below) on an angle to resemble smoked salmon. Lay the slices on opposite sides of the serving plates. Place the smoked salmon slices between the fresh salmon slices. Sprinkle the jicama over the salmon and drizzle on the sauce. Top with the papaya seeds, garnish with the croutons, and serve.

VARIATIONS: In the summer, I prefer only raw salmon. During the winter months, my preference is to flash cook the raw salmon under a preheated broiler *only* until the color has changed. You can also mix and match the raw and smoked salmon as you wish.

COOKING NOTES: Use the freshest and firmest salmon taken from the coldest water for best results. Remember to trim the fatty darker flesh from the salmon as this carries the oily "fishy" flavor.

■ The papaya seeds, when mature, add a taste similar to the spice flavors in watercress. My preference is the

seeds that are black-gray when mature. They are white or light gray when immature; these should be discarded. The membrane can be easily removed by rubbing a wooden spoon over the seeds in a strainer. Rinse well under water to separate. After toasting they are crunchy and provide a great color contrast.

■ Keep the jicama covered with moist toweling to prevent it from drying out if diced ahead of time.

MAKES 4 SERVINGS ■

Mussel, Scallop, and Corn Salsa Salad

This salad can include any shellfish, such as lobster, shrimp, and crab meat, with equal success.

4	**ears sweet corn**
½	**cup water**
½	**cup dry white wine**
4	**sprigs fresh thyme or 1 teaspoon dried, crumbled**
1	**small dried red chile**
½	**bunch fresh parsley stems**
24	**mussels, scrubbed and debearded**
¾	**pound scallops, foot removed (see note below)**
1	**cup virgin olive oil**
¼	**cup fresh lime juice**
½	**medium-size red bell pepper, roasted, peeled (see page 62), seeded, and cut into ¼-inch dice**
½	**jalapeño chile, roasted, peeled, seeded, and minced (or substitute serrano chiles)**
¼	**cup diced scallion greens**
¼	**cup snipped fresh chives**
2	**tablespoons minced fresh mint**
	Tabasco sauce to taste
	Salt to taste
1½	**heads red oakleaf lettuce, curly endive, or Boston lettuce**

Slice the corn kernels from the cob and blanch them in boiling water until just tender, about 3 minutes. Drain thoroughly. Bring the water, wine, thyme, dried chile, and parsley to a boil in a large saucepan over high heat. Add the mussels, cover, and cook 4 minutes. Remove the opened mussels, cover, and cook any remaining closed mussels 5 minutes longer. Remove the mussels, discarding any that do not open. Add the scallops to the pan and simmer over medium heat until just opaque, about 2 minutes. Drain.

Remove the mussels from their shells and place in a large bowl. Add the scallops, then mix in the oil and lime juice, then the bell pepper, jalapeño chile, corn, scallions, chives, and mint. Season with Tabasco and salt. Refrigerate at least 2 hours, stirring occasionally. (Can be prepared 6 hours ahead.)

Let the salad stand at room temperature 30 minutes. Line a serving platter with the lettuce leaves. Stir the salad and spoon it onto the serving platter. Serve.

COOKING NOTES: The "foot" is the tough muscle on the side of the scallop.

- The best sweet corn is picked in the evening when the sugar levels are the highest. Also, night's cooler weather helps to slow the biochemical changes after the corn has been picked.

- If the mussels have spawned, which occurs in early summer as water temperatures rise, substitute other shellfish until the mussel meat is plumped back up, usually by late summer. The spawning depletes much of their weight and they taste very metallic.

MAKES 8 SERVINGS ∎

Shrimp and Scallop Salad with Champagne Mayonnaise

A refreshing summer salad of light delicate flavors.

12	**large shrimp, poached (see note below), peeled, deveined, and chilled**
12	**large scallops, foot removed (see note below), poached and chilled**
1/2	**cup diced, roasted, peeled (see page 62), and seeded red bell pepper**
1/2	**cup diced red onion**
1/4	**cup chopped fresh dill**
1	**cup Champagne Mayonnaise (recipe follows)**
2	**medium-size ripe avocados**
4	**radicchio leaves (see note below), trimmed**
2	**bunches watercress**
1/2	**cup Tomato Concasse (see page 65)**
4	**sprigs fresh dill for garnish**

In a medium-size bowl, combine the shrimp, scallops, peppers, onions, and chopped dill, and toss with 3/4 cup of the mayonnaise to coat. Quarter and peel the avocados, then thinly slice each quarter and fan out slightly. Position the avocado fans on each side of the serving plate and place a leaf of radicchio in the center. Spoon the shrimp and scallop salad onto the radicchio. Position 1/2 bunch of the watercress opposite each radicchio leaf. Drizzle the remaining mayonnaise over the salads. Top with the Tomato Concasse and a dill sprig.

COOKING NOTES: Poach the shrimp in court bouillon as described in the recipe for Chilled Poached Salmon Medallions on page 132. Poach with the shells on and clean after poaching, for the best flavor and texture. Avoid soaking the shrimp in the water to prevent soggy flesh. For better flavor, scallops can be poached in the same bouillon.

- The "foot" is the tough muscle on the side of the scallop.

- Avoid soaking radicchio in water; it will turn more bitter and lose flavor.

MAKES 4 SERVINGS ∎

Champagne Mayonnaise

This is a light, flavorful mayonnaise with the consistency of a sauce, not a heavy sandwich spread. It is great on all poached or steamed fish and shellfish.

2 tablespoons fresh lemon juice
2 tablespoons champagne vinegar
2 large egg yolks
2 tablespoons Dijon mustard
¼ teaspoon salt
¼ teaspoon freshly ground white pepper
½ cup corn oil
½ cup virgin olive oil
½ cup brut champagne or sparkling wine

With a mixer on high speed, combine the lemon juice, vinegar, egg yolks, mustard, salt, and pepper. Slowly add the oils in a steady stream. Add the champagne to lighten the mayonnaise to sauce consistency. Adjust salt to taste. Refrigerate until ready to serve, or up to 1 week.

VARIATION: You can delete the egg yolks by replacing them with 2 tablespoons prepared mustard. The flavor will be stronger, so adjust the other ingredients accordingly to your taste.

MAKES 1½ CUPS ■

Grilled Squid and Vegetable Salad

¼ cup fresh lime juice
4 cloves garlic, roasted (see page 62) and chopped
¼ cup fresh thyme leaves
½ cup virgin olive oil
4 medium-size squid, cleaned (see note below)
1 medium-size zucchini, center core discarded (see art bottom left)
1 medium-size summer squash, quartered lengthwise
½ cup quartered artichoke hearts, blanched (see pages 57–58)
¼ cup chanterelles, stemmed
1 bunch greens, such as mizuni (baby mustard greens), mâche, or red oakleaf, trimmed
Salt to taste
Freshly ground black pepper to taste
½ cup Mushroom-Shallot Vinaigrette (recipe follows)

In a medium-size bowl, combine the lime juice, garlic, 3 tablespoons of the thyme, and the olive oil. Add the squid and allow to marinate for at least 2 hours.

Preheat the grill or broiler. Rub the surfaces of the squashes with the olive oil. Place on the grill and allow to sear, about 3 minutes. Remove and cut into ¼-inch julienne.

Slice the body of the squid once lengthwise, allowing it to lay flat. Place it on the grill (the inside toward the heat) with the tentacles. Cook until seared, about 3 minutes. (If the squid begins to curl, weight it down with a small sauté pan to keep flat.) Turn over and cook until done, about 3 minutes. The tentacles will usually cook faster than the body. Remove to a cutting board. Slice the body into ½-inch julienne and tentacles into quarters.

In a medium-size bowl, combine the squid, squashes, artichoke hearts, chanterelles, the remaining thyme, and the trimmed greens. Add the vinaigrette and toss. Adjust the salt and pepper. Divide among serving plates and serve.

COOKING NOTES: To clean squid, separate the head and tentacles from the body. Cut the tentacles from the head and discard the head. Remove the beak—also known as the pen or sword—which is the hard rudimentary shell. Remove the purplish skin with your hands. The body and tentacles are now ready to cook. Refrigerate until ready to use. Marinating squids adds lots of flavor. The small amount of acid (the lime juice) does less to tenderize it than to flavor it. Grill fast and hot until just cooked to keep the squid moist and tender. Grilling also adds a smoky flavor that blends well with the grilled vegetables.

MAKES 4 SERVINGS ■

Mushroom-Shallot Vinaigrette

The shallots and mushrooms (leftover stems work great) add flavor and depth beyond the traditional vinaigrette. It complements any salad, especially those with grilled ingredients.

¼ **cup chanterelles**
1 **cup plus 2 tablespoons virgin olive oil**
1 **tablespoon prepared mustard**
¼ **cup balsamic vinegar**
⅛ **teaspoon salt**
⅛ **teaspoon freshly ground black pepper**
2 **tablespoons chopped roasted (see page 62) shallots**

In a small skillet over high heat, sauté the mushrooms in 2 tablespoons of the oil. Stir occasionally until golden, about 5 minutes. Remove from the heat. In a blender combine the mustard, vinegar, salt, pepper, and olive oil. Add the mushrooms and shallots, pureeing until smooth. Adjust the salt and pepper to taste. Refrigerate until serving or up to 2 weeks.

VARIATION: You can vary the flavors by substituting full flavored vegetables such as fennel and peppers. Be sure to sauté or blanch vegetables before pureeing to concentrate their flavors.

MAKES 1½ CUPS ■

Squash Blossoms with Pepper Tapenade

The blossoms accompanied by the tapenade flavors are reflective of summer's bounty.

1 **small red bell pepper, roasted, peeled (see page 62), and seeded**
½ **small eggplant, sliced, salted, drained, and grilled (see page 62)**
½ **cup black olives, pitted**
4 **cloves garlic, roasted (see page 62) and minced**
1 **tablespoon anchovy paste**
½ **teaspoon freshly ground black pepper**
½ **cup virgin olive oil**
16 **to 20 squash blossoms, about 3 inches long (see note below)**
  Corn or virgin olive oil for frying
2 **cups all-purpose flour**
2 **tablespoons paprika**
1 **teaspoon salt**
¾ **teaspoon freshly ground white pepper**
2 **large eggs, beaten**
1 **cup milk**
1 **cup Roast Pepper Vinaigrette (recipe follows)**
  Sprigs fresh herbs for garnish

In a food processor, finely chop the pepper, eggplant, olives, garlic, anchovy paste, and black pepper. Slowly add the olive oil, then adjust the salt as necessary (it will depend on the saltiness of the olives).

Working with one squash blossom at a time, carefully peel back one petal for filling. Stuff approximately 1 tablespoon of the pepper mixture into the blossom, then fold the petals back over the stuffing. Refrigerate until ready to cook.

Fill a large, heavy, deep skillet with oil to a depth of 3 inches. Heat over medium-high heat to 350°F.

In a medium-size bowl, sift together the flour, paprika, salt, and pepper. In another medium-size bowl, combine the eggs and milk. Carefully drench the blossoms, one at a time, in the egg mixture. Shake the excess from the blossoms and transfer to the seasoned flour. Coat evenly, then shake to remove the excess flour. Place the blossoms in the oil and cook until golden, about 4 minutes. Transfer to paper toweling to drain.

Arrange the blossoms in the center of the serving plates, spoon the Roast Pepper Vinaigrette over the top, garnish with herbs, and serve.

COOKING NOTE: Select squash blossoms that are closed and bright in color. They deteriorate quickly after being cut from the plant, so use immediately. The blossoms can also be sautéed instead of fried.

MAKES 4 SERVINGS ∎

Roast Pepper Vinaigrette

1   **red bell pepper, deeply roasted, peeled (see page 62), and seeded**
¼   **cup balsamic vinegar**
¼   **teaspoon salt**
1   **cup virgin olive oil**
    Freshly ground black pepper to taste

In a blender, combine the bell pepper, vinegar, and salt, and puree until smooth. Still processing, gradually add the olive oil. Adjust the salt and pepper.

VARIATIONS: You can substitute any rich roasted vegetable for the pepper. Bright-colored vegetables are the best visually, as the colors reflect the summer garden. Try 1 cup roasted or grilled pumpkin.

MAKES 1½ CUPS ∎

Terrine of Corn, Squash, and Peppers with Roasted and Sundried Tomato Salsa

This nontraditional light summer terrine is fast to make and bake.

8   **cups Poultry or Vegetable Stock (see page 63 or 64)**
10⅔ **tablespoons (1⅓ sticks) unsalted butter**
1   **teaspoon freshly ground white pepper**
1   **teaspoon ground cumin**
1   **teaspoon ground coriander**
½   **teaspoon ground jalapeño or cayenne pepper**
2½ **teaspoons salt**
2¼ **cups yellow cornmeal**

¾ **pound skinless chicken breasts**
1 **large egg**
½ **cup heavy cream**
2 **medium-size chayote squash,**
   blanched al dente (see pages 57–58)
   and diced
1 **medium-size butternut squash, blanched**
   al dente and diced
1 **medium-size red bell pepper,**
   roasted, peeled (see page 62), seeded,
   and diced
1 **medium-size poblano pepper,**
   roasted, peeled, seeded, and diced
   (or substitute Anaheim chiles)
1 **cup sweet white corn kernels,**
   cut from the cob
2 **cups Roasted and Sundried Tomato Salsa**
   (recipe follows)
   Sprigs fresh herbs for garnish

In a medium-size saucepan over high heat, bring the stock to a simmer, then add the butter and spices. Whisk in the cornmeal in a steady stream, cooking until thickened, about 5 minutes. Remove from the heat. Cover with plastic wrap and refrigerate until chilled, about 1 hour.

Preheat the oven to 350°F. Line a 3- by 5- by 9-inch terrine mold with parchment.

In a food processor, puree the chicken with the egg until smooth, about 2 minutes.

Using a mixer, on high speed, blend together the cornmeal mixture. Slowly add the chicken puree, making sure it is well combined. On low speed, add the cream until just combined. Transfer to a large bowl and add the chayote and butternut squashes, peppers and the corn. Adjust the salt and pepper. Transfer to the prepared terrine mold. Smooth the top and cover with buttered parchment. Bake in a water bath until a thermometer inserted into the center reads 160° to 170°F, about 1½ hours. Remove to a cake rack. Cool for 30 minutes.

Unmold the terrine onto a cookie sheet. Using a sharp knife cut into ½-inch slices. Spoon the salsa onto serving plates. Position the terrine on top of the salsa, garnish with fresh herbs, and serve.

VARIATIONS: You can make a meatless version by simply substituting 2 whole eggs for the chicken in the recipe. The texture will be lighter, more like firm polenta.

The recipe is very adaptive to other meats, such as duck, squab, or even veal in place of the chicken. Your imagination is the only limit to vegetable garnishes that can be incorporated. Select the vegetables for crisp textures and avoid mushy ones. Blanch or sauté them to the correct texture and to concentrate flavors.

COOKING NOTE: Ground jalapeño is available at specialty spice stores.

MAKES 16 SERVINGS ■

Roasted and Sundried Tomato Salsa

The blend of the two tomato textures and flavors gives this salsa a new identity. Select sundried tomatoes in olive oil that are tender and supple rather than dry and hard. The best are rich in deep tomato flavors, a true delicacy.

6 **large, ripe tomatoes**
½ **cup virgin olive oil**
¼ **cup ⅛-inch diced, oil-packed sundried**
   tomatoes
3 **tablespoons fresh lime juice**
1 **clove garlic, minced**
¼ **cup chopped fresh marjoram or oregano**
   Salt to taste
   Freshly ground black pepper to taste

Preheat the oven to 550°F or fire up the grill.

Cut the tomatoes in half horizontally, squeeze out the seeds, and rub with olive oil. Place in an ovenproof skillet and cook until shrunken, about 15 minutes.

Dice the tomatoes into ¼-inch pieces. In a small bowl, combine the roasted and sundried tomatoes, the lime juice, garlic, olive oil, and marjoram. Add salt and pepper. Refrigerate until ready to serve or up to 3 days.

COOKING NOTE: Rubbing the tomato in olive oil before roasting helps transfer the oven's heat to the tomato, speeding up the roasting process.

MAKES 2 CUPS ▪

Chilled Shellfish and Angel Hair Pasta

Using different flavors of pasta and herbs provides an infinite range of combinations. Add the shellfish of your choice, preferably tender varieties to contrast with the crisp vegetables and al dente pasta.

1 **pound angel hair pasta, mixed flavors (see index)**
½ **cup virgin olive oil**
2 **tablespoons minced roasted (see page 62) garlic**
1 **pound shelled crawfish tails (or substitute shrimp)**
1 **tablespoon anchovy paste (optional)**
 Salt to taste
 Freshly ground black pepper to taste
2 **tablespoons chiffonaded fresh lemon basil (or substitute sweet basil)**
2 **tablespoons chiffonaded fresh dark opal basil (or substitute sweet basil)**
1 **large red bell pepper, roasted, peeled (see page 62), seeded, and julienned**
1 **large yellow bell pepper, roasted, peeled, seeded, and julienned**

1 **cup Roasted Tomato Vinaigrette (recipe follows)**
¾ **cup grated Parmesan cheese**

In a large amount of boiling water, cook the pasta until al dente. Transfer to a strainer, rinse with warm water and then cold to chill. Drain well, then toss with ¼ cup of the olive oil. Refrigerate.

In a medium-size saucepan over medium-high, heat the remaining olive oil with the garlic, cooking until tender, about 2 minutes. Add the crawfish and cook until hot, about 3 minutes. Remove from the heat and season with salt and pepper. Transfer to a large bowl and stir in the basils and peppers. Refrigerate.

To serve, combine the crawfish mixture with the pasta and tomato vinaigrette and toss with half of the Parmesan. Adjust the salt and pepper. Distribute onto serving plates, top with the remaining Parmesan, and serve.

MAKES 4 SERVINGS ▪

Roasted Tomato Vinaigrette

Roasting or grilling tomatoes concentrates their flavor.

2 **large ripe tomatoes**
1 **clove garlic, roasted (see page 62) and minced**
1 **tablespoon tomato paste**
3 **tablespoons red wine vinegar**
¾ **cup virgin olive oil**
 Salt to taste
 Freshly ground black pepper to taste

Preheat the oven to 500°F or fire up the grill.

Cut the tomatoes in half horizontally, squeeze out the seeds, and rub with olive oil. Place in an ovenproof skillet and cook in the oven or on the grill until shrunken, about 15 minutes.

In a food processor, finely chop the garlic. Add the tomatoes, tomato paste, and vinegar, pulsing until chopped. Slowly add the olive oil, salt, and pepper.

Refrigerate until ready to serve or up to 1 week.

MAKES 2 CUPS ■

Pizza Dough

1 package dry yeast
2 tablespoons sugar
1 cup lukewarm water (about 110°F)
4 cups all-purpose flour
Pinch of salt
2 large eggs, beaten
2 tablespoons virgin olive oil

In a small bowl, combine the yeast, sugar, and warm water. Set aside until it foams.

In a food processor with a plastic dough blade or regular blade, combine the flour and salt. Mix in the eggs, then the yeast, until a ball forms. Work just until the dough pulls away from the side of the bowl, then add the olive oil while running just to combine. Remove the dough immediately to an oiled bowl, cover with a clean cloth, and allow to rise in a dry, warm place until doubled in size, about 45 minutes. Punch down, then allow to double again, about 20 minutes. Form into five balls.

Lightly flour the dough and counter. Roll into very thin 9-inch circles.

Proceed with toppings and bake or grill according to individual recipes or hold between wax paper in the refrigerator till needed, up to 3 days.

VARIATION: Black olive dough can be made by adding 1 cup pitted olives to the flour and salt. Puree until finely chopped, then proceed with the dough as directed.

COOKING NOTES: The pizza dough is quite fluffy when baked the same day. The following day, the dough pro-duces a flatter, more crackerlike crust. It can also be frozen in rolled out form, between parchment, wrapped in plastic wrap. Thaw in the refrigerator overnight.

MAKES FIVE 9-INCH PIZZAS ■

Grilled Pizza Technique

Roll the pizza dough out on parchment to the desired size. Turn the dough-side down onto an oiled grill. The dough will generate enough steam to separate it from the parchment within the first 2 minutes. Remove the parchment, then turn the pizza over and cook until firmed, about 2 minutes. Add the desired toppings. If you are using cheese, cover the top with a pan until the cheese is melted. Watch the bottom of the crust to keep it from burning. You may need to raise the grill grate or lower the temperature, if you're grilling with gas.

This is great for outside cooking during the summer. The crust is very crisp and has a smoky grilled flavor. The dough is also great for hors d'oeuvres since the crust is easy to handle.

Grilled Pizza Crust/Oven Finish

Remove the grilled pizza crust to a plate before adding the toppings (it can be held for a few hours under a damp towel). Add the toppings just before serving and finish in the oven at 400°F, cooking until the cheese bubbles, about 5 minutes. Remove from the oven, cut into wedges, top with herbs, if appropriate, and serve. This is a more effective method of heating toppings than grilling. It's also a great method for transporting your pizza to cook somewhere else (like a friend's house). Just pop it in the oven to melt and warm the toppings and you're set.

Bresaola, Tomato, and Olive Pizza

- 1 ball Pizza Dough, rolled out (see page 123)
  Cornmeal for dusting bottom of pizza
- 2 tablespoons virgin olive oil
- ¼ cup grated fontinella cheese
- ¼ cup grated mozzarella cheese
- ½ cup very thinly julienned bresaola (or substitute prosciutto, bunderflaise, or Smithfield ham)
- ¼ cup niçoise black olives, pitted
- ¼ cup Tomato Concasse (see page 65)
- ¼ cup grated Asiago cheese
- 2 tablespoons chopped fresh basil

Place a pizza stone in the lower third of the oven and preheat to 550°F. When the stone is hot, carefully pull it out of the oven.

Dust the bottom of the crust with cornmeal, then lay it on the stone. Spread the olive oil across the dough and cover with the fontinella and mozzarella cheeses. Distribute the bresaola, olives, and tomatoes over the cheese. Top with the Asiago.

Place the stone back in the oven and bake 8 to 12 minutes, until the crust is golden. Remove from the oven, sprinkle with the basil, and serve.

MAKES ONE 9-INCH PIZZA ■

Tomato, Caper, and Basil Pizza

- 1 ball Pizza Dough, rolled out (see page 123)
  Cornmeal for dusting the pizza
- 2 tablespoons virgin olive oil
- ¼ cup grated fontinella cheese
- ¼ cup grated mozzarella cheese
- ¼ cup nonpareil capers, drained
- ¼ cup Tomato Concasse (see page 65)
- ¼ cup grated Asiago cheese
- 2 tablespoons chopped fresh basil

Place a pizza stone in the lower third of the oven and preheat to 550°F. When the stone is hot, carefully pull it out of the oven.

Dust the bottom of the crust with cornmeal, then lay it on the stone. Spread the olive oil across the dough, then cover with the fontinella and mozzarella cheeses. Distribute the capers and Tomato Concasse over the cheeses. Top with the Asiago.

Place the stone back in the oven and bake 8 to 12 minutes, until the crust is golden. Remove from the oven, sprinkle with the basil, and serve.

MAKES ONE 9-INCH PIZZA ■

Eggplant, Pepper, and Goat Cheese Pizza

- 1 ball Pizza Dough, rolled out (see page 65)
  Cornmeal for dusting bottom of pizza
- 2 tablespoons Pepper Sauce (recipe follows)
- ¼ cup grilled (see page 62) and diced eggplant
- ¼ cup grated fontinella cheese
- ¼ cup grated mozzarella cheese
- ¼ cup crumbled goat cheese

¼ cup roasted, peeled (see page 62), seeded, and diced red bell peppers
1 tablespoon chopped fresh basil
1 tablespoon chopped fresh thyme
2 tablespoons virgin olive oil

Place a pizza stone in the lower third of the oven and preheat to 550°F. When the stone is hot, carefully pull it out of the oven.

Dust the bottom of the crust with cornmeal, then lay it onto the stone. Spread the pepper sauce across the dough, cover with the eggplant, and top with the cheeses and peppers.

Place the stone back in the oven and bake 8 to 12 minutes, until the crust is golden. Remove from the oven, top with the basil and thyme, and drizzle on the olive oil. Cut and serve.

COOKING NOTE: The drizzle of olive oil balances the dry characteristics of the goat cheese.

MAKES ONE 9-INCH PIZZA ■

Pepper Sauce

A terrific alternative to the standard tomato-based pizza sauce.

1 large red bell pepper, deeply roasted, peeled (see page 62), and seeded
1 cup dry white wine
¼ teaspoon salt
Freshly ground black pepper to taste
Crushed red pepper (hot!) to taste

In a small saucepan combine the bell pepper and wine. Bring to a simmer over medium heat and cook until the pepper is tender and the wine is reduced to ¼ cup,

about 15 minutes. Transfer to a food processor and puree until smooth. Season with salt, black pepper, and red pepper.

VARIATION: You can substitute any variety of peppers for the bell pepper. Why don't you experiment with the full range of the chile family? My favorites are the poblanos and the serranos, although their heat is for the strong of heart.

MAKES 1¼ CUPS ■

Artichoke, Olive, and Fontinella Cheese Pizza

1 ball Pizza Dough, rolled out (see page 123)
  Cornmeal for dusting bottom of pizza
½ cup Pizza Sauce (recipe follows)
1 cup blanched (see pages 57–58) and quartered artichokes
¼ cup niçoise black olives, pitted
¾ cup grated fontinella cheese
½ cup grated mozzarella cheese
2 tablespoons grated Pecorino Romano cheese

Place a pizza stone in the lower third of the oven and preheat to 550°F. When the stone is hot, carefully pull it out of the oven.

Dust the bottom of the crust with cornmeal, then lay it onto the stone. Spread the pizza sauce across the dough, then distribute the artichokes and olives over the sauce. Top with the cheeses.

Place the stone back in the oven and bake 8 to 12 minutes, until the crust is golden. Cut and serve.

MAKES ONE 9-INCH PIZZA ■

Pizza Sauce

This is a more traditional pizza sauce. It is very simple when made in a food processor.

- 1 **clove garlic**
- 1 **cup canned, seeded, and drained Italian plum tomatoes**
- 1 **tablespoon tomato paste**
- 2 **tablespoons chopped fresh basil**
- 2 **tablespoons chopped fresh oregano**
- 1 **teaspoon crushed red pepper (hot!)**
- 1 **teaspoon sugar**
- 1/2 **teaspoon salt**

In a food processor, puree the garlic until smooth. Add the tomatoes and tomato paste and process until chopped. Slowly add the remaining ingredients until blended. Refrigerate until ready to use or up to 5 days.

VARIATION: Try substituting roasted or sundried tomatoes for different flavor intensities.

MAKES 1 1/2 CUPS ■

Potato and Leek Soup

This white and green presentation is tasty and visually dynamic.

- 4 **tablespoons (1/2 stick) unsalted butter**
- 1 **small onion, diced**
- 2 **leeks, white part only, diced**
- 1 **large potato, peeled and diced**
- 2 1/2 **cups Poultry or Vegetable Stock (see page 63 or 64)**
- 1/4 **cup buttermilk**
- 1 **teaspoon salt**
- 1/2 **teaspoon freshly ground white pepper**
- 1 **bunch scallion greens, coarsely chopped**
  Vegetable oil for frying
- 1/2 **cup all-purpose flour**
- 1 **tablespoon paprika**
- 1 **small Vidalia, Walla Walla, or other sweet onion, sliced into rings**
- 1/8 **cup snipped fresh chives, cut 2 inches long**

Melt 3 tablespoons of the butter in a medium-size saucepan, over medium-high heat. Lightly sauté the diced onions and leeks until tender, about 5 minutes. Add the potatoes and stock, and simmer over medium heat until the potatoes and leeks are very tender, about 20 to 25 minutes. Season with the salt and pepper.

Pour the potato-and-leek mixture into a blender and puree on high speed until smooth. Strain two thirds of the soup through a fine sieve into a container set in an ice bath to chill. Stir in the buttermilk, then refrigerate until ready to serve.

In a small skillet over medium heat, sauté the scallions in the remaining butter until tender, then add to the remaining soup in the blender. Puree until smooth. Strain through a fine sieve into a bowl and refrigerate.

In a medium-size skillet, heat oil, at a depth of 2 inches, to 350°F over medium-high heat. In a small bowl, combine the flour and paprika. Lightly dust the onion rings in the seasoned flour mixture, then fry in the hot oil until golden brown and crisp. Drain on paper towels.

Place the chives in a small strainer that will fit into the skillet. Dip the chives into the hot oil and fry until crisp, about 1 minute. Drain on paper toweling.

Ladle the white soup into bowls, then swirl in the scallion-scented soup. Top with the fried onions and chive garnish. Serve.

COOKING NOTES: If the soup thickens too much in the refrigerator, add more buttermilk or stock to lighten.
• The Vidalia, Walla Walla, and Maui onions have a sweet flavor ideal for the onion rings in this delicate leek-flavored soup. They also serve as a crunchy contrast to the silky soup texture. If you really love onions, puree a Vidalia or other sweet onion in a food processor, strain the juice, and add it to your taste into the soup for a fresh onion taste.

MAKES 4 SERVINGS ■

Chilled Cucumber and Dill Soup

This is an unusual combination of flavors but extremely refreshing for a hot summer day. The cucumbers add a fresh garden flavor while the pickles add a mature flavor dimension. Choose your favorite sour pickles as they will provide the backbone of the soup. Check the pickle juice to be sure it is not too salty. If it is, add more vinegar to balance it.

4	**tablespoons (½ stick) unsalted butter**
1	**small onion, diced**
1	**large cucumber, peeled, seeded, and coarsely chopped**
2	**large dill pickles, peeled, seeded, and coarsely chopped**
¼	**cup all-purpose flour**
2½	**cups Poultry or Vegetable Stock (see page 63 or 64), scalded**
¼	**cup champagne vinegar**
¼	**cup dill pickle juice**
1	**teaspoon salt**
½	**teaspoon freshly ground black pepper**
¼	**cup sour cream**
½	**cup chopped fresh dill**
4	**sprigs fresh dill for garnish**

Melt the butter in a large saucepan over medium-high heat and lightly sauté the diced onions, cucumbers, and pickles, about 2 minutes. Add the flour and sauté another 5 minutes. Remove from the heat and whisk in the stock. Return to a simmer and cook until the soup is thickened and the vegetables are tender, about 20 to 25 minutes. Pour the soup mixture into a blender and puree on high speed until smooth.

Strain the soup through a fine sieve into a bowl set in an ice bath to chill. Stir in vinegar and pickle juice; season with the salt and pepper. Stir in the sour cream and chopped dill and refrigerate until ready to serve.

Ladle the soup into bowls, garnish with a sprig of dill, and serve.

MAKES 4 SERVINGS ■

Summer Gazpacho

    1 large red bell pepper, seeded and diced
    1 medium-size green bell pepper, seeded and diced
    1 large cucumber, peeled, seeded, and diced
    1 small zucchini, diced
    1 medium-size red onion, diced
    2 cloves garlic, minced
  ½ cup fresh lime juice
Two 46-ounce cans tomato juice
  ¼ cup Worcestershire sauce
  ¼ cup cider vinegar
  ½ cup dry sherry
    Salt to taste
    1 tablespoon Tabasco sauce
  ½ cup chopped scallions, white part only
  ½ cup diced papaya
  ½ cup diced blanched (see pages 57–59) haricots vert
  ½ cup diced blanched white corn
  ½ cup virgin olive oil
    Chopped fresh herbs for garnish
    Sliced limes for garnish

In a blender, combine half of the red and green peppers, cucumber, and zucchini. Add all of the red onion, garlic, lime juice, and tomato juice. Puree until smooth. Transfer to a large bowl or pot and add the Worcestershire, vinegar, and sherry. Adjust the salt. Add the Tabasco, the remaining vegetables, papaya, and the olive oil. Refrigerate overnight.

The next day, season again with salt and Tabasco. Add more lime juice and sherry as necessary, as the vegetables absorb the flavors overnight.

Serve with chopped fresh herbs and a slice of lime.

VARIATIONS: Substitute all sorts of summer vegetables; just avoid the wet or mushy textured ones. Fun garnishes include garlic croutons or ice cubes of the pureed gazpacho blended with pepper vodka.

MAKES 16 SERVINGS ■

Tomato and Arugula with Grilled Onions

Sometimes the simplest dishes are the warmest to our hearts.

  2 tablespoons fresh lemon juice
  2 tablespoons balsamic vinegar
  1 cup virgin olive oil
    Salt to taste
    Coarsely ground black pepper to taste
  1 large Vidalia, Walla Walla, or other sweet onion, cut into 8 thick slices
  1 bunch arugula, trimmed and separated into leaves
  2 large, ripe tomatoes, cut into 12 slices
  4 large sprigs fresh basil

In a small bowl, whisk together the lemon juice, vinegar, and ¾ cup of the olive oil. Season with salt and pepper.

Preheat the grill. Rub the onion slices with the remaining olive oil, place on the grill, and let sear, about 3 minutes. Turn over and cook until crisp, about 3 minutes. Drain on paper towels.

Position the arugula at the top of the serving plates. Alternate 3 tomato slices with 2 onion slices to create a fan shape below the arugula on each serving plate. Spoon the vinaigrette over the salads, top with sprigs of basil, and serve.

MAKES 4 SERVINGS ■

Willy's Salad

This salad was named after the best garlic peeler ever. He made this dressing possible with the volume of garlic needed.

1 **head romaine lettuce, trimmed and cut into 2-inch pieces**
1 **cup grated Parmesan cheese**
1 **cup Toasted Croutons (see page 70)**
1 **cup Willy's Dressing (recipe follows)**

In a large bowl, combine the lettuce, croutons, and dressing. Toss, then add the Parmesan, tossing just to combine. Distribute on plates. Serve.

MAKES 4 SERVINGS ■

Willy's Dressing

2 **tablespoons minced garlic**
2 **tablespoons anchovy fillets (see note below), minced into paste**
2 **tablespoons red wine vinegar**
¼ **cup fresh lemon juice**
2 **large egg yolks**
2 **tablespoons Dijon mustard**
¾ **cup corn oil**
¾ **cup virgin olive oil**
2 **tablespoons Worcestershire sauce**
  Pinch of salt
1 **teaspoon coarsely ground black pepper**
  Tabasco sauce to taste

In a medium-size mixing bowl, combine the garlic, anchovies, vinegar, lemon juice, egg yolks, and mustard with a mixer set on medium speed. On high speed, add the oils, one at a time, in a steady stream until thickened.

Add the Worcestershire and season with the salt, black pepper, and Tabasco. Refrigerate overnight to develop flavor or hold up to 5 days.

VARIATION: You can substitute an equal amount of roasted shallots for the garlic and experiment with various vinegars. Select a gold or very green olive oil, depending on the strength of the condiments added to the dressing. Also try adding ½ cup minced sundried tomatoes for fun.

COOKING NOTE: Choose tender anchovies rather than the firm, canned fishy ones from dusty shelves. It makes a big difference.

MAKES 2 CUPS ■

Bean, Artichoke, and Asparagus Salad

The best crudités come right from the garden. Blanch as necessary (see the chart on pages 57–59) to balance the textures and flavors. You can also add greens to the salad but not to exceed 25 percent by volume of the salad. Arugula, watercress, and mustard greens or firm lettuces lend themselves best to this salad.

2 **tablespoons virgin olive oil**
1 **cup chanterelles, stemmed and sliced**
1 **cup haricot vert beans, blanched and halved**
1 **cup artichoke hearts, blanched**
½ **cup julienned Vidalia, Walla Walla, or other sweet onion**
12 **asparagus spears, blanched and cut in half lengthwise**
½ **cup radishes, sliced very thin**
¾ **cup Chive Vinaigrette (recipe follows)**
¼ **cup chopped fresh chervil (or substitute fresh parsley)**
½ **cup shaved Parmesan cheese**

To a small skillet over high heat, add the olive oil and the chanterelles and cook until golden, about 4 minutes. Remove to a strainer to drain.

In a medium-size bowl, combine the chanterelles, haricots vert, artichokes, onion, asparagus, and radishes. Add the vinaigrette and toss. Distribute among serving plates, top with chervil and Parmesan, and serve.

MAKES 4 SERVINGS ■

Chive Vinaigrette

This is wonderful on fresh vegetables. The blender technique used here captures the fresh herb flavors within the oil and vinegar. This is a great method to use with extra herbs from your garden. Refrigerate the dressings in airtight jars and they'll last up to 2 weeks.

1 **cup snipped fresh chives**
2 **tablespoons balsamic vinegar**
½ **teaspoon salt**
1 **cup virgin olive oil**
Freshly ground black pepper to taste

In a blender, combine the chives, vinegar, and salt, and puree until smooth. Gradually add the olive oil in a steady stream until thickened. Adjust the salt and add pepper to taste.

VARIATION: Substitute ¾ cup chopped fresh tarragon for the chives to make a tarragon vinaigrette.

MAKES 1½ CUPS ■

Grilled Tuna with Tomatoes and Saffron

½ **cup fresh lime juice**
½ **cup fresh lemon juice**
1 **cup heavy cream**
¼ **teaspoon saffron threads**
Salt to taste
Freshly ground black pepper to taste
4 **tuna steaks, about 6 ounces each**
2 **tablespoons virgin olive oil**
1 **cup Tomato Concasse (see page 65)**
¼ **cup Calamata olives, pitted and julienned**
¼ **cup chopped fresh basil**
Sprigs fresh basil for garnish

Preheat the grill or broiler.

In a medium-size saucepan, combine the juices and bring to a simmer over high heat. Cook until reduced to ¼ cup, about 3 minutes. Add the cream and cook until thickened enough to coat the back of a spoon, about 10 minutes. Add the saffron, remove from the heat, and season with salt and pepper.

Rub the surfaces of the tuna steaks with the olive oil. Place on the grill, allowing to sear, about 3 minutes. Turn the tuna over and cook until done, approximately 3 minutes, depending on the thickness of the steaks and the desired level of doneness.

Return the sauce to a simmer. Stir in the tomatoes, olives, and chopped basil, and warm through, then spoon onto serving plates, reserving ¼ cup of the sauce. Place the tuna steaks on top of the sauce, then spoon the remaining sauce over the tuna. Garnish with basil and serve.

COOKING NOTES: Cook tuna less than for most fish for it becomes quite dry when fully cooked. Tuna lends itself to medium-rare doneness because of its fine texture.

▪ Keep the acidic qualities of the sauce quite high, with emphasis on flavor strength, not on quantity.

MAKES 4 SERVINGS ▪

Escalope of Salmon with Ginger and Peppers

3 **tablespoons achiote paste (see note below)**
2 **tablespoons Ginger Puree (see page 66)**
1 **tablespoon virgin olive oil**
8 **escalopes salmon, about 3 ounces each (see note below)**
1 **cup Fish Stock (see page 65)**
1 **cup dry white wine, preferably chardonnay**
1 **cup heavy cream**
1 **dried pasilla pepper (or substitute anchos chiles)**
1 **lime, juiced**
   Salt to taste
   Freshly ground black pepper to taste
1 **head baby frisée or young curly endive, trimmed**
1 **head red oakleaf lettuce**
1 **large red bell pepper, roasted, peeled (see page 62), seeded, and diced**
1 **medium-size poblano pepper, roasted, peeled, seeded, and diced**
½ **cup chopped fresh cilantro**
½ **cup chopped fresh parsley**

In a small bowl, combine the achiote, 1 tablespoon of the Ginger Puree, and the olive oil, and rub across the surfaces of the salmon escalopes. Refrigerate until ready to cook.

Preheat the grill or broiler.

In a medium-size saucepan, combine the stock and wine. Bring to simmer over high heat and cook until reduced to ¼ cup, about 6 minutes. Add the cream and remaining ginger and cook until thickened enough to coat the back of a spoon, about 8 minutes. Transfer to a blender, add the dried pepper, and allow to steep for 5 minutes. Puree until smooth. Strain through a fine sieve into another saucepan and return to a simmer. Add the lime juice, adjust the salt and pepper, and reduce the heat to low.

Place the salmon on the grill and cook until well seared, about 2 minutes. Turn over and cook to medium-rare, about 4 minutes, or to your desired doneness.

Arrange the lettuces across the serving plates, distribute the red and poblano pepper over them, then sprinkle with the cilantro and parsley. Position the escalopes of salmon over the greens, then spoon the sauce over the salmon, and serve.

VARIATION: Substitute dried tomatoes and other dried tart fruits for the Ginger Puree. Blend wine or vinegars to match the main dried flavors.

COOKING NOTES: Choose the firmest and freshest salmon fillets possible, especially during the summer. Remember to trim the fatty darker flesh from the salmon, as it carries the oily "fishy" flavor. The sauce complements both the salmon and the greens.

▪ Achiote paste is a Central American condiment made from ground annatto seed (the achiote), garlic, vinegar, salt, and sometimes chiles. The flavor is similar to rich, mild paprika. It is available in Mexican and Spanish markets. If you can't locate it, substitute 1 tablespoon of mild Hungarian paprika mixed with 1 tablespoon red bell pepper puree and 1 teaspoon red wine vinegar, for 2 tablespoons of achiote. *Do not* substitute the annatto seed itself as it has a very strong flavor.

MAKES 4 SERVINGS ▪

Chilled Poached Salmon Medallions

Chilled poached fish is a summer refresher both in taste and texture. This is great with Cucumber and Dill Salad (see page 149).

3   **cups red wine (or substitute cider vinegar)**
3   **cups dry white wine**
1   **large onion, cut into 1-inch pieces**
2   **bay leaves**
1   **tablespoon fresh or dried thyme**
¼   **cup white peppercorns**
2   **tablespoons salt**
One   **¾-pound salmon fillet, boned and skinned (see note below)**
12   **long toothpicks**
1   **head red oakleaf lettuce, trimmed and separated into leaves**
4   **sprigs fresh dill for garnish**
  Lime-Ginger Mayonnaise (recipe follows)

In a fish poacher or an acid-resistant pot, combine the wines, onion, bay leaves, thyme, peppercorns, and salt. Bring to a simmer over medium heat and cook for 1 hour.

Cut the salmon fillet across the grain (#1) into eight equal portions. On a flat surface, position two of the portions, spine surfaces touching (#2). Wrap the belly sections around the corresponding portion to form a medallion. Secure the two portions in a medallion shape with three toothpicks placed horizontally through the fish (#3). Repeat for the remaining portions.

Place the medallions in the simmering liquid and cook until firm, about 8 minutes. Remove to a plate and twist the toothpicks to remove. Using a soft brush, dip into the poaching liquid and brush any herbs from the surface of medallions. Cover and refrigerate.

Arrange the lettuce leaves and dill sprigs on the serving plates. Position the medallions over the greens. Serve the mayonnaise over the fish or on the side.

COOKING NOTES: Remember to trim the fatty darker flesh from the salmon, as it carries the oily "fishy" flavor.
- Court bouillons (the poaching liquid) always are high in acid from the wine and vinegar, they contain salt, and are not made with fish bones, in contrast to a fish stock (fumet) which is low in acid, has no salt, wine, or vinegar added, and is made from lots of fish bones. Make sure to taste the court bouillon for salt so that the fish won't be depleted of its natural salt content if the court bouillon is lacking in it.
- Crimping, a technique similar to poaching, produces a more delicate texture in the fish. Add the fish to the simmering court bouillon, return to a simmer, then turn off the heat and allow it to cook on the stored heat, which will take an additional 2 or 3 minutes over poaching. The pressure that a liquid below a boil exerts is significantly lower than at a boil, resulting in a more tender fish. For consistent results, whether poaching or crimping, please make sure that the volume of the court bouillon is a minimum of eight times the volume of the fish to be cooked.
- This medallion technique can be applied to just about all fish fillets.

MAKES 4 SERVINGS ■

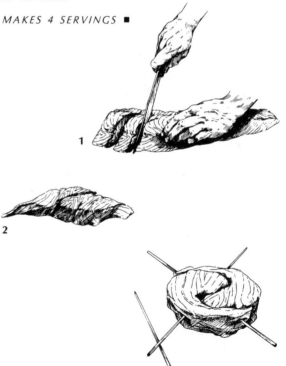

Lime-Ginger Mayonnaise

This complements smoked fish, such as salmon, as well as grilled shrimp or lobster.

2 **large egg yolks**
1 **tablespoon Dijon mustard**
¼ **cup fresh lime juice**
½ **cup corn oil**
  Salt to taste
  Freshly ground white pepper to taste
2 **tablespoons grated lime rind**
½ **cup Ginger Puree (see page 66)**
¼ **cup chopped fresh dill**

With a mixer on medium speed, combine the egg yolks, mustard, and lime juice in a medium-size bowl. On high speed, gradually add the oil in a steady stream. Add salt and pepper, then mix in the lime rind, ginger, and dill. Adjust the texture to sauce consistency as necessary with water or more lime juice. Refrigerate until ready to serve or up to 5 days.

MAKES 1¼ CUPS ■

Swordfish with Olive-Tomato Salsa

4 **swordfish steaks, about 7 ounces each, trimmed of skin and fat**
2 **tablespoons virgin olive oil**
1 **cup Olive-Tomato Salsa (recipe follows)**
4 **sprigs fresh thyme for garnish**

Preheat the grill or broiler.

Rub the surfaces of the swordfish steaks with the olive oil. Place on the grill and cook until seared, about 3 minutes. Turn over and cook until done, testing by firmness and slight beading of moisture on the surface, about 4 minutes for medium, depending on its thickness and the desired level of doneness. Position the swordfish on warm serving plates, then spoon the salsa over it. Garnish with the thyme and serve.

COOKING NOTE: Choose swordfish that has been cut into thick steaks so that during cooking more moisture is maintained. If you prefer more well done fish, select wider, thinner steaks that will cook through faster.

MAKES 4 SERVINGS ■

Olive-Tomato Salsa

Choose your favorite olives to customize the salsa to your taste.

¼ **cup diced green olives**
¼ **cup diced oil-cured black olives**
½ **cup Tomato Concasse (see page 65)**
2 **tablespoons chopped fresh thyme**
2 **tablespoons chopped fresh basil**
1 **teaspoon salt**
½ **teaspoon freshly ground black pepper**
2 **tablespoons red wine vinegar**
¼ **cup virgin olive oil**
  Tabasco sauce to taste

In a small bowl, combine the olives, Tomato Concasse, herbs, salt, pepper, vinegar, and olive oil. Add the Tabasco. Refrigerate until ready to serve or hold up to 2 days.

MAKES 1 CUP ■

Mahi Mahi with Spiced Couscous

A great make-ahead dish with a fun presentation.

> 3 tablespoons hot Hungarian paprika
> 1 tablespoon ground cumin
> 3 tablespoons corn oil
> 8 escalopes mahi mahi, about 3 ounces each
> 6 cups Spiced Couscous (recipe follows)
> 4 small brown or white paper bags (not lacquered, waxed, or made from recycled paper)
> 2 limes, juiced
> 1/2 cup fresh cilantro leaves

Preheat the grill or the broiler to 475°F. Preheat the oven to 400°F.

In a small bowl, combine the paprika, cumin, and corn oil to form a smooth paste. Rub over the surfaces of the fish.

Grill the mahi mahi, searing well, about 1 minute. Turn over and sear well, about 1 minute, keeping it rare to medium-rare.

Place 1 1/2 cups of the couscous into each paper bag. Place two mahi mahi escalopes over each portion of couscous. Collapse the upper portion of the bag flat, fold it over, and staple tightly to secure. Place the bags on a cookie sheet on the lower rack of the oven. Cook until the bag expands slightly, about 12 minutes. Remove from the oven and cut off stapled edge.

To serve, open the paper bag to expose the mahi mahi. Spoon the lime juice across the mahi mahi and couscous, garnish with the cilantro, and serve.

COOKING NOTES: If the fish is grilled and the couscous is made ahead and held in the refrigerator till needed, add a couple more minutes to the cooking time.

▪ The paper bags trap the steam from the ingredients, blending their flavors. This technique works well with all light-textured fish, especially salmon. You can also submerge the bag in a fryer for the same effect, cooking until the bag expands from the steam, about 8 minutes.

MAKES 4 SERVINGS ▪

Spiced Couscous

> 1/4 cup virgin olive oil
> 1/4 cup diced shallots
> One 15- to 17-ounce box couscous
> 3 cups boiling Fish Stock (see page 65)
> 2 tablespoons ground turmeric
> 1 tablespoon ground cumin
> 3 tablespoons hot Hungarian paprika
> 1 cup roasted, peeled (see page 62), seeded, and diced green bell pepper
> 1 cup trimmed and diced fennel bulb
> 1 cup coarsely chopped fresh cilantro
> 1 cup coarsely chopped scallion greens
> Salt to taste
> Freshly ground black pepper to taste

In a large skillet, heat the olive oil over medium heat. Add the shallots and sauté until translucent, about 5 minutes. Turn the heat to high and add the couscous. Stir until coated with olive oil and very hot, about 3 minutes.

Remove the skillet from the heat, add the stock, turmeric, cumin, and paprika, stirring to mix. Return to the heat, cooking until most of the liquid is absorbed, about 2 minutes. Remove from the heat and cover with a tight-fitting lid. Allow to stand for 5 minutes, then remove the lid. Using a whisk, stir to break up the larger clumps of couscous. Allow to cool. Add the pepper, fennel, cilantro, and scallions, then adjust salt and pepper. Refrigerate until ready to use.

COOKING NOTES: Prepared cooked couscous can be reheated and served as a starch by simply sautéing it in butter or olive oil. To avoid forming lumps, make sure your butter or olive oil is very hot before slowly adding the couscous. A nonstick pan makes this technique easier.

▪ Cooked couscous can be blended with just about any vegetable. Remember, though, to keep the vegetables small in size so the couscous will be hot at the same time the vegetables are cooked. If you use firmer vegetables you will need to blanch them before mixing them in.

MAKES 6 CUPS ▪

Lake Trout with Mole Verde

This recipe works with all fish by selecting greens to complement the fish.

  5 tomatillos, husked and quartered
  1 clove garlic, minced
  1 small onion, quartered
  1 cup stemmed and chopped spinach
  1 small head romaine lettuce, trimmed and chopped
  1 poblano pepper, roasted, peeled (see page 62), seeded, and diced
  1 tablespoon chopped fresh mint
  1 cup trimmed and chopped sorrel
  1 cup trimmed and chopped arugula
  2 tablespoons walnut oil
  3 tablespoons pine nuts, toasted (see page 60)
     Salt to taste
     Freshly ground black pepper to taste
 1/4 cup achiote paste (see note below)
 1/4 cup virgin olive oil
  8 escalopes lake trout, about 3 ounces each
  4 sprigs fresh mint for garnish

In a food processor, combine the tomatillos, garlic, and onion by pulsing until finely chopped. With the processor running, add the spinach, romaine, poblano pepper, mint, sorrel, and arugula, and process until just coarsely chopped. Mix in the walnut oil and pine nuts. Adjust salt and pepper. Transfer to a small saucepan and warm over medium heat. Remove from heat.

Preheat the grill or broiler.

In a small bowl, combine the achiote and olive oil. Dip the lake trout in the mixture, place on the grill, and cook until seared, about 2 minutes. Turn over and cook until done, about 4 minutes, testing for firmness and warmth by inserting a skewer.

Spoon the sauce onto warm serving plates. Position two escalopes on top of the sauce, allowing to slightly overlap. Garnish with mint and serve.

VARIATION: The substitutions of mizuni or mustard greens, mâché, and other varieties for the lettuce quantities above will produce interesting flavor combinations.

COOKING NOTES: Achiote paste is a Central American condiment made from ground annatto seed (the achiote), garlic, vinegar, salt, and sometimes chiles. The flavor is similar to rich, mild papika. It is available in Mexican and Spanish markets. If you can't locate it, substitute 1 tablespoon of mild paprika mixed with 1 tablespoon red bell pepper puree and 1 teaspoon red wine vinegar for 2 tablespoons of achiote. *Do not* substitute the annatto seed itself as it has a very strong flavor.

■ For the best sauce texture always place the coarsest greens in the food processor first. Add the tender greens last and do not overwork.

MAKES 4 SERVINGS ■

Soft-Shell Crabs with Capers and Lemon

The simplest and the best.

 1/2 pound (2 sticks) unsalted butter, at room temperature
 1/2 cup fresh lemon juice
     Salt to taste
     Tabasco sauce to taste
 3/4 cup nonpareil capers, drained
  2 cups all-purpose flour
  1 tablespoon freshly ground white pepper
 12 medium-size soft-shell crabs, cleaned (see note below)
 1/4 cup chopped fresh parsley

With a mixer, whip 1 stick of the butter until light. Slowly add the lemon juice, then season with salt and Tabasco. Add the capers and set aside.

In a medium-size bowl, combine the flour and pepper. Dredge the crabs in the flour, coating evenly, then shake off the excess.

In a large skillet, heat the remaining butter over medium-high heat until brown. Carefully add the crabs and cook until golden, about 3 minutes. Turn over and cook until the other side is golden, about 2 minutes. Remove to paper toweling to drain.

Arrange the soft-shells on warm serving plates. Spoon on the caper butter, allowing to melt over the crabs. Sprinkle with the parsley and serve.

COOKING NOTES: Clean the crabs by pulling the key (lower belly flap) and opening the body shell. Remove the lungs and guts, then replace the body shell (see art below). Snip off the face, if you choose. Keep well refrigerated until ready to use.

▪ Soft-shells also can be grilled or cooked on coals. To cook on coals, form a pouch of aluminum foil and place in it one or two crabs and some of the compound caper butter. Fold the edges over to seal well. Place right on the coals and cook until done, about 10 minutes, depending on the crab's size and the temperature of the coals. Easy for picnics and appetizers.

MAKES 4 SERVINGS ▪

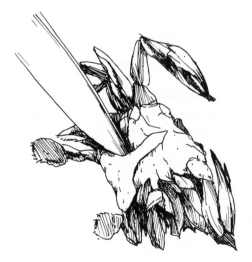

Crab Cakes with Tomatillos and Mint

This blends the more traditional style of crab cakes with some unusual flavors.

  4 **tablespoons (½ stick) unsalted butter**
  2 **tablespoons roasted, peeled (see page 62), seeded, and diced green bell peppers**
  2 **tablespoons roasted, peeled, seeded, and diced yellow bell peppers**
  2 **tablespoons roasted, peeled, seeded, and diced red bell peppers**
  2 **tablespoons diced celery**
  1 **clove garlic, minced**
  2 **large eggs, beaten**
4½ **teaspoons heavy cream**
  1 **tablespoon dry mustard**
 ½ **teaspoon Worcestershire sauce**
  1 **teaspoon ground cumin**
  1 **teaspoon fresh thyme leaves**
 ⅛ **teaspoon ground cayenne pepper**
  2 **tablespoons minced scallion greens**
  1 **tablespoon chopped fresh parsley**
 ¼ **cup mayonnaise**
  1 **pound lump crab meat, carefully picked over for shells**
  2 **cups ground oyster crackers**

FOR THE SAUCE

 ½ **cup husked and diced tomatillos**
  2 **cups heavy cream**
 ¼ **cup chopped fresh mint**
  2 **tablespoons champagne vinegar**
  6 **tablespoons roasted, peeled, seeded, and diced yellow bell peppers**
  6 **tablespoons roasted, peeled, seeded, and diced red bell peppers**
    Salt to taste
    Freshly ground black pepper to taste

In a medium-size heavy skillet, heat 1 tablespoon of the butter over high heat. Add the green, yellow, and red peppers, and the celery and garlic, and sauté until tender, about 2 minutes. Drain.

In a medium-size bowl, combine the sautéed vegetables, the eggs, cream, mustard, Worcestershire, cumin, thyme, and cayenne. Stir in the scallions, parsley, and mayonnaise, then fold in the crab meat and 2 tablespoons of the oyster cracker crumbs. Form into eight cakes and coat evenly with the remaining crumbs. Place on parchment and chill for 2 hours.

Meanwhile, in a medium-size saucepan, combine 1/4 cup of the tomatillos, the cream, and mint. Bring to a simmer over medium heat and cook until reduced enough to coat the back of a spoon, about 10 minutes. Strain through a fine sieve into another saucepan. Return the sauce to a simmer over high heat. Stir in the vinegar, the yellow and red peppers, and the remaining tomatillos, and cook until reduced enough to coat the back of a spoon, about 4 minutes. Season with salt and pepper. Remove from the heat.

In a heavy skillet, heat the remaining butter over medium-high. Add the crab cakes and cook until golden and hot, about 5 minutes. Remove to paper towels to drain.

Spoon the sauce onto warm serving plates. Position the crab cakes in the center, sprinkle with the mint, and serve.

VARIATIONS: Crab cakes also can be made like the salmon cakes on page 94 with a scallop mousse rather than the mayonnaise and bread crumbs. Use 1/2 pound scallops to 1/2 pound cleaned crab meat for the garnish. For another summer flavor, substitute equal amounts of diced tomatoes and citrus juice for the tomatillos and vinegar.

MAKES 4 SERVINGS ■

Tamale of Shrimp and Corn

Great to make ahead, with the fish and starch cooked together.

> 2 **cups shrimp shells (or substitute lobster shells)**
> 4 **cups Fish Stock (see page 65)**
> 1 **teaspoon salt**
> 1/2 **teaspoon freshly ground black pepper**
> 4 **tablespoons (1/2 stick) unsalted butter**
> 1 3/4 **cups yellow cornmeal**
> 1 **pound shrimp, shelled, deveined, and cut into 1/2-inch pieces**
> 3/4 **cup roasted, peeled (see page 62), seeded and diced poblano peppers**
> 3/4 **cup fresh corn, blanched (see pages 57–58)**
> 2 **teaspoons ground coriander**
> **Salt to taste**
> **Freshly ground black pepper to taste**
> 8 **large corn husks, soaked in warm water until supple, if dried**
> 1 **cup Tomato and Papaya Salsa (recipe follows)**

In a medium-size saucepan, combine the shrimp shells and stock. Bring to a simmer over medium heat and cook for 20 minutes. Strain into another saucepan and add the salt, pepper, and 3 tablespoons of the butter. Return to a simmer over medium-high heat. Slowly whisk in the cornmeal while constantly stirring. Cook until thick, about 5 minutes. Transfer to a bowl to cool.

In a medium-size bowl, combine the shrimp, peppers, corn, and coriander. Adjust salt and pepper to taste.

Lay the corn husks flat. Spread half of the cornmeal mixture over the center of the husks. Spread the shrimp mixture over the cornmeal and cover with the remaining cornmeal, to completely enclose. Wrap the husks with string.

Place the tamales seam-side down in a steamer over high heat and cook until hot, about 8 minutes.

Position a tamale in the center of a warm plate. Fold back the corn husks to reveal the filling. Serve the salsa over it.

To heat on a grill, wrap the tamale in an aluminum pouch with a little wine and cook directly on top of the coals for about 10 to 15 minutes. Be careful not to burn.

MAKES 8 TAMALES ▪

Tomato and Papaya Salsa

The cinnamon basil adds a great fragrant taste.

- ½ **cup seeded and diced tomatoes**
- ½ **cup peeled, seeded, and diced papaya**
- 2 **tablespoons chopped fresh cinnamon basil (or substitute sweet basil)**
- 2 **tablespoons snipped fresh chives**
- 2 **tablespoons fresh lime juice**
- 2 **tablespoons virgin olive oil**

In a small bowl, combine all the ingredients. Allow the flavors to blend for at least 30 minutes. Serve at room temperature. If not using immediately, refrigerate for up to 3 days.

MAKES 1 CUP ▪

Grilled Chicken with Misantle Butter

The nutty flavors of pumpkin and sesame seeds add richness to this summer-grilled chicken, while placing the butter under the skin gets the flavors into the meat rather than seasoning just the skin. The name *misantle* comes from a small village in the state of Veracruz, where a misantle spread is a local specialty. Remember to adjust the heat or the rack on the grill for high heat to sear and lower heat to penetrate if the chicken gets too dark or is large.

- ½ **cup pumpkin seeds, toasted (see page 61)**
- ¼ **cup sesame seeds, toasted**
- ½ **chipotle pepper, dried and rehydrated or canned (or substitute Tabasco or Pick-a-Pepper sauce to taste)**
- ½ **poblano pepper, roasted, peeled (see page 62), and seeded**
- 4 **tablespoons (½ stick) unsalted butter**
- 1 **tablespoon red wine vinegar**
- 2 **tablespoons fresh lime juice**
  Salt to taste
- 4 **chicken halves, boned, except for the wings and drumsticks (your butcher can do this)**
- 2 **tablespoons virgin olive oil**
- 4 **Red and Poblano Pepper Tamales (recipe follows)**
- 4 **sprigs fresh herbs for garnish**

To make the misantle butter, combine ¼ cup of the pumpkin seeds, 2 tablespoons of the sesame seeds, and the chipotle pepper in a food processor, and process until it is a smooth paste. Add the poblano pepper and butter, and puree until combined. Add the vinegar, lime juice, and salt. Transfer to a small bowl and fold in the remaining pumpkin and sesame seeds. Reserve under refrigeration until needed, up to 1 week.

Preheat the grill or broiler.

Lift up the chicken skin and rub 1 tablespoon of the misantle compound butter underneath. Rub the chicken all over very lightly with olive oil. Place skin-side to the heat until seared and golden, about 7 minutes. Turn over and cook until the desired doneness is reached, about 13 minutes. Remove to a plate, and spread the remaining misantle butter across the skin, allowing it to melt.

Meanwhile, remove the tamales from the steamer and position on the upper half of warm serving plates. Arrange the chicken on the lower half of the plate. Garnish with herbs and serve.

MAKES 4 SERVINGS ▪

Red and Poblano Pepper Tamales

You can use any vegetable to substitute for the tomatillos in the center of this colorful tamale. Just small-dice it so it's easy to cover with the masa-harina mix. Blanch firmer vegetables before using.

- 1 **cup milk**
- 2 **tablespoons unsalted butter**
- 1½ **teaspoons salt**
- ½ **cup rice flour**
- ¼ **cup masa-harina**
- ¼ **cup yellow cornmeal**
- ½ **cup roasted, peeled (see page 62), seeded, and pureed poblano peppers (1 large pepper should be enough—you can substitute Anaheim chiles)**
- ½ **cup roasted, peeled, seeded, and pureed red bell peppers (1 large pepper should be enough)**
- 8 **large corn husks, soaked in warm water until supple, if dried**
- ½ **cup husked and diced tomatillos**

In a medium-size saucepan, combine the milk, butter, and salt, and bring to a simmer over medium-high heat. Stir in the rice flour, masa-harina, and cornmeal. While constantly stirring, cook until very thick, about 4 minutes. Divide the masa mixture into two bowls. Mix the poblano puree into one bowl and the red pepper puree into the other.

Place 2 corn husks on a flat surface, allowing them to overlap. Spoon 2 tablespoons of each pepper masa over the center of the husks. Spoon 2 tablespoons of tomatillos over the masa. Cover the tomatillos with additional masa as necessary. Fold the husks around the masa to form a tamale.

Place the tamales seam-side down in a steamer over high heat and cook until hot, about 5 minutes. Serve by opening the husks to reveal the filling.

MAKES 4 TAMALES ∎

Lamb Loin Chops with Mint Pesto

Which came first, the mint or the lamb? This pesto variation made with mint and parsley beats any summer heat.

Spring lamb is born in February and March and arrives at market starting in May and continuing through the summer. This wonderful young lamb is delicately flavored because it has been fed on milk and grass rather than hay. Select two small chops per person to equal about 8 ounces per serving.

- 6 **cloves garlic, roasted (see page 62) and minced**
- ¾ **cup virgin olive oil**
- 8 **lamb loin chops, about 4 ounces each**
- 1 **cup chopped fresh mint**
- ½ **cup chopped fresh parsley**
- ¼ **teaspoon freshly ground black pepper**
- 2 **tablespoons chopped hazelnuts**
- 1 **tablespoon balsamic vinegar**
  Salt to taste
- 4 **sprigs fresh mint for garnish**

In a small bowl, combine 2 cloves of the minced garlic and 2 tablespoons of the olive oil. Rub the mixture on the surfaces of the lamb chops.

Preheat the grill or broiler.

In a blender, combine the remaining garlic and olive oil, the mint, parsley, pepper, and hazelnuts, and puree until finely chopped. Add the vinegar and salt. Reserve at room temperature.

Place the chops on the grill and cook until well seared, about 5 minutes. Turn over and cook until the desired level of doneness, about 4 minutes for medium-rare, depending on their thickness and the heat of the fire. Position the chops on warm serving plates and spoon the pesto over them. Garnish with mint sprigs and serve.

VARIATION: You can substitute your favorite herbs for the mint and parsley to make other "pestos."

MAKES 4 SERVINGS ∎

Lamb and Papaya Tortilla

1½ pounds lean lamb, from the leg, cut into
strips (see note below)
1 cup pomegranate juice (or substitute
unsweetened cranberry juice)
3 tablespoons crumbled bucheron or goat
cheese
3 tablespoons sour cream
8 Blue Corn Tortillas (see page 67; or substitute
yellow corn tortillas)
2 cups trimmed and shredded mixed romaine
and red oakleaf lettuces
2 cups Papaya-Pepper Salsa (recipe follows)
2 tablespoons chopped fresh cilantro or parsley

Place the lamb in a flat pan, add the pomegranate juice,
and refrigerate overnight.

Preheat the grill.

Remove the lamb from the marinade, pat dry with
paper towels, and grill until seared, about 2 minutes. Turn
over and cook to desired doneness, about 1 minute. Remove to a cutting board and julienne.

Meanwhile, combine the cheese and sour cream and
spread on 4 of the tortillas. Place the tortillas on a cookie
sheet and warm in a preheated 300°F oven for about 4
minutes, then place on serving plates. Cover with the
lettuce and half of the salsa. Distribute the lamb over the
salsa and cover with the remaining tortillas. Top with the
remaining salsa and cilantro and serve.

COOKING NOTES: Select meat from small young spring
lambs, 2 to 5 months old. Trim all the muscles out, clean
all the membranes, and cut against the grain into strips
(small scaloppine).

▪ The pomegranate marinade is used primarily for seasoning, although some denaturing (breaking down) of surface proteins by acids takes place to tenderize meat.
Remember to cook over very high heat to sear in the
remaining juices. The lamb strips will cook very quickly,
so check doneness frequently.

MAKES 4 SERVINGS ▪

Papaya-Pepper Salsa

1 medium-size ripe papaya, peeled, seeded, and
diced
2 medium-size poblano peppers, roasted, peeled
(see page 62), seeded, and diced
1 red bell pepper, roasted, peeled, seeded, and
diced
2 tablespoons snipped fresh chives
¼ cup fresh lime juice
1 clove garlic, minced
½ cup virgin olive oil
Salt to taste
Tabasco sauce to taste

Combine all the ingredients in a bowl. Adjust the salt and
Tabasco. Refrigerate for 1 hour or more before serving or
for up to 2 days.

VARIATIONS: Add diced avocado for a richer salsa.
Avocados contain up to 20 percent fat, so you may want
more lime juice to balance the flavors. Clean and toast
the papaya seeds (see page 61) and sprinkle over the salsa
when served for a great crunch.

MAKES 2 CUPS ▪

Lamb and Black Bean Tortilla

A heartier summer dish with the earthy black beans.

1½ pounds lean lamb, from the leg, cut into
strips
Virgin olive oil
3 tablespoons sour cream
8 Blue Corn Tortillas (see page 67; or substitute
Yellow Corn Tortillas)

2 cups stemmed and shredded spinach
2 cups Black Bean Salsa (recipe follows)
2 tablespoons chopped scallion greens

Preheat the grill.

Rub the lamb with olive oil, then place on the grill and cook until seared, about 2 minutes. Turn over and cook to desired doneness, about 1 minute. Remove to a cutting board and julienne.

Meanwhile, spread the sour cream on 4 of the tortillas. Place the tortillas on a cookie sheet and warm in a preheated 300°F oven for about 4 minutes, then place on serving plates. Cover with the spinach and half of the salsa. Distribute the lamb over the salsa and cover with the remaining tortillas. Top with the remaining salsa and the scallions, and serve.

VARIATION: Try different greens, such as arugula or mizuni, for spicier tones. Avoid soft leaf lettuces as their texture becomes unidentifiable on the palate with the beans and lamb.

COOKING NOTE: Select meat from small, young spring lambs, 2 to 5 months old. Trim all the muscles out, clean all the membranes, and cut into strips (small scaloppine) against the grain.

MAKES 4 SERVINGS ∎

Black Bean Salsa

Select black turtle beans for consistent size and cooking times.

1 cup dried black beans, soaked in cold water overnight
1 medium-size poblano pepper, roasted, peeled (see page 62), seeded, and diced
1 large red bell pepper, roasted, peeled, seeded, and diced

½ cup husked, roasted (see note below), and diced tomatillos
2 cloves garlic, roasted (see page 62) and minced
¼ cup snipped fresh chives
¼ cup chopped fresh mint
2 tablespoons kimchee sauce (see note below)
¼ cup pomegranate molasses (or substitute balsamic vinegar)
½ cup virgin olive oil
Salt to taste
Tabasco sauce to taste

In a large pot, cover the beans with salted cold water. Bring to a simmer over medium heat and cook until tender, about 3 to 4 hours. Drain, then cool under running cold water. Refrigerate until cool.

In a large metal bowl, combine all the ingredients. Refrigerate until ready to serve or up to 3 days. (It tastes better after a minimum of 1 hour.)

VARIATIONS: This salsa is great if you substitute an equal amount of roasted tomatoes and 1 cucumber for the tomatillos and peppers. Fresh blanched corn will improve the flavor of the salsa or its variations.

COOKING NOTES: If you can't find kimchee, this makes an adequate substitute: In a small bowl, combine 1 tablespoon garlic powder, 1 teaspoon Ginger Puree (see page 66), 1 tablespoon Tabasco sauce, and ½ cup Hunt's chili sauce. Use sparingly. Keep refrigerated for up to 2 weeks.
∎ To roast tomatillos, remove the husks and place the tomatillos in an ovenproof skillet. Add enough olive oil just to coat them, then place in a preheated 400°F oven and cook until lightly browned, about 30 minutes. Allow to cool before dicing.

MAKES 2 CUPS ∎

Veal Chops with Tomatoes and Arugula

  1 cup Veal Stock (see page 64)
 ¼ cup balsamic vinegar
  4 large cloves garlic, roasted (see page 62) and minced
  2 cups trimmed and julienned arugula
 ½ cup julienned fresh basil
 ½ cup Tomato Concasse (see page 65)
    Salt to taste
    Freshly ground black pepper to taste
  2 tablespoons virgin olive oil (optional)
  4 veal chops, about 8 ounces each
  2 tablespoons grated Pecorino Romano cheese
  4 sprigs fresh basil for garnish

Preheat the grill or broiler.

In a small saucepan, bring the stock to a simmer over high heat. Cook until reduced to ¼ cup, about 5 minutes. Add the vinegar and cook until reduced enough to lightly coat the back of a spoon, about 3 minutes.

Add the garlic, arugula, basil, and Tomato Concasse to heat. Adjust the salt and pepper, then stir in the olive oil to enrich. Remove from the heat.

Place the chops on the grill and cook until well seared, about 5 minutes. Turn over and cook to the desired doneness, about 10 minutes for medium, depending on thickness.

Spoon the sauce onto warm serving plates, reserving ¼ cup for garnish. Position the chops over the sauce, then spoon the remaining sauce over them. Top with the cheese, garnish with a basil sprig, and serve.

VARIATION: You may also marinate the chops for up to 12 hours in a mixture of olive oil, chopped garlic to taste, ½ teaspoon salt, ½ teaspoon freshly ground black pepper, and basil stems before proceeding with the recipe.

COOKING NOTE: Remember, for thicker chops, high heat to sear, low heat to penetrate.

MAKES 4 SERVINGS ∎

Grilled Beef Tenderloin with Tomato and Anchovy Butter

This compound butter works on just about any meat, and is especially nice during the summer.

 ½ cup Beef or Veal Stock (see page 63 or 64), optional
 ½ cup balsamic vinegar
 ½ pound (2 sticks) unsalted butter, at room temperature
 ¼ cup minced roasted garlic (see page 62)
  2 tablespoons tomato paste
 ½ cup minced anchovy fillets (see note below) or to your taste
  1 teaspoon freshly ground black pepper
 ½ cup Tomato Concasse (see page 65)
 ½ cup chopped fresh basil
  4 tenderloin steaks, about 8 ounces each (see note below)
  2 tablespoons virgin olive oil or corn oil
  4 sprigs fresh basil for garnish

Preheat the grill or broiler.

In a medium-size saucepan, combine the stock and vinegar. Bring to simmer over medium heat, cooking until reduced enough to coat the back of a spoon, about 10 minutes. Remove from the heat and allow to cool.

With a mixer, whip the butter until light, then add the

garlic, tomato paste, anchovies, and black pepper. Stir in the reduced stock-vinegar. Fold in the tomatoes and chopped basil, then refrigerate until ready to use or up to 5 days. (The flavors will improve after 24 hours.)

Rub the surfaces of the steaks with the oil. Grill until well seared on the surface, about 5 minutes. Turn over and cook until you reach the desired doneness, about 5 minutes for medium-rare, depending on the thickness of the steaks.

Position the steaks on warm serving plates and spoon the tomato-anchovy butter on top, allowing it to melt over them. Garnish with the basil and serve.

COOKING NOTES: Choose tender anchovies rather than the firm, canned fishy ones from dusty shelves. They make a big difference.
■ Avoid very dark colored beef for the cow may have been excited prior to its termination. This raised activity depletes the muscles of their glycogen supply, resulting in less lactic acid, yielding gummy textured meat that spoils quickly.

MAKES 4 SERVINGS ■

Seasoned Steak

4 steaks or chops of your choice
Seasoning compounds (recipes follow)
2 tablespoons virgin olive oil (optional)

Preheat the grill or broiler as hot as possible.

Rub the surfaces of the steaks with the seasoning compound. Rub with olive oil first if you choose a dry compound. Grill until well seared on the surface, about 5 minutes. Turn over and lower the temperature on the broiler or raise the grate on the grill. Cook until you reach the desired level of doneness. How long this takes depends on the thickness and density of the meat. When done, remove to a platter and let rest 3 to 5 minutes before serving to allow the juices to settle. (Do not stack meats atop each other, as the juices will be forced out.) Serve and enjoy.

COOKING NOTES: The technique for great grilling is quite simple: high heat to sear, low heat to penetrate, thus cooking through. The high heat sears in the juices and flavors, the low heat cooks the meat without drying out the juices.
■ Thin cuts of meat require little penetration of heat to cook, so keep heat high throughout cooking. Thick cuts of meat require more penetrating heat to achieve temperatures of medium-rare or more without burning the outside of the meat.
■ Allow the meat to rest to keep the juices in before you cut the meat. If you remove the meat from the grill and cut immediately, all the juices will escape, leaving a dry piece of meat. Allow resting time proportional to the cooking time: little time for rare, additional time for medium temperatures, and more time for well done meats.

MAKES 4 SERVINGS ■

Steak Salt

¼ cup citrus salt (or substitute grated rind of 3 lemons—see note below)
1 tablespoon garlic salt
¼ cup kosher salt
3 tablespoons coarsely ground black pepper
3 tablespoons coarsely ground white pepper
1½ teaspoons ground cayenne pepper
1½ teaspoons ground cumin

In a small bowl, thoroughly combine all the ingredients. Store in a covered jar for up to 1 month. Use sparingly before searing meat for strongest flavor or after searing for softer flavor.

COOKING NOTE: Citrus salt or sour salt ($C_6H_8O_7$) is used primarily to add tartness to pickling compounds and soups or sauces. It is produced from the fermentation of crude sugars and lemon or pineapples and is then dehydrated to produce water-soluble crystals. It is available in specialty spice stores.

MAKES 1 CUP ■

In a small saucepan over medium heat, sauté the garlic, poblano pepper, and chili powder in the olive oil until the pepper is tender, about 5 minutes. Add the chipotle peppers. Remove from heat. Refrigerate until ready to use or up to 1 week.

COOKING NOTE: Chipotle peppers canned in adobo sauce are available at Mexican specialty stores.

MAKES 1 CUP ■

Garlic-Onion Rub

½ **cup minced garlic**
½ **cup minced onion**
2 **tablespoons virgin olive oil**
1 **tablespoon lemon pepper**
1 **tablespoon hot Hungarian paprika**

In a small saucepan over medium heat, sauté the garlic and onion in the olive oil until tender, about 5 minutes. Add the lemon pepper and paprika. Refrigerate until ready to use or up to 1 week.

MAKES 1 CUP ■

Rattleburgers

1½ **pounds beef chuck, trimmed and cubed**
½ **pound sirloin fat trimmings, cubed**
2 **large egg yolks**
¼ **cup Garlic-Onion Rub (see left)**
½ **teaspoon salt**
½ **teaspoon freshly ground black pepper**

Chill the meat and meat grinder in a freezer for 1 hour, then force the beef and fat through the large disc of the grinder into a large bowl. Mix in the eggs, then force the mixture through the medium disc of the meat grinder into another bowl. Fold in the Garlic-Onion Rub, salt, and pepper with your fingertips. Avoid mashing the meat. Form into four patties and refrigerate until ready to grill.

Preheat the grill or broiler as hot as possible.

Place the burgers on the grill and cook until well seared on the surface, about 4 minutes. Turn over and lower the temperature on the broiler or raise the grate on the grill. Cook until you reach the desired level of doneness, about 4 minutes for medium-rare for 8- to 10-ounce patties, depending on their thickness. When done, remove to a platter and allow to rest 3 minutes before serving to allow the juices to settle. (Do not stack them atop each other!) Serve on the bread of your choice and enjoy.

Snake Bite Compound

½ **cup minced garlic**
½ **cup roasted, peeled (see page 62), seeded, and diced poblano pepper**
1½ **teaspoons chili powder**
2 **tablespoons virgin olive oil**
2 **tablespoons minced chipotle peppers in adobo sauce or to taste (or substitute Tabasco sauce to taste—see note below)**

VARIATIONS: For a milder burger, omit the Garlic-Onion Rub. For a spicier burger, substitute an equal amount of Snake Bite Compound (page 144) for the rub.

COOKING NOTE: Do not prepare the patties too far ahead for the Garlic-Onion Rub can oxidize the meat, causing it to lose its bright red color, especially if you add a lot of it.

MAKES FOUR 8-OUNCE BURGERS ■

Spiced Baby Back Ribs

Though hot and spicy, this recipe does leave you able to talk after eating.

4 slabs baby back ribs, about 1¼ pounds each trimmed weight

BRAISING LIQUID

1 gallon Beef or Veal Stock (see page 63 or 64)—optional, see note below)
¾ cup red wine vinegar
½ cup achiote paste (see note below)
3 tablespoons ground cayenne pepper
1 cup mild Hungarian paprika
1½ cups ground cumin

3 tablespoons Tabasco sauce
4½ teaspoons garlic powder
1 tablespoon ground ginger
1 cup tomato paste
¼ cup honey
1 tablespoon salt

SPICED MIXTURE

¼ cup garlic salt
1 cup mild Hungarian paprika
¼ cup dry mustard
¼ cup red wine vinegar
½ cup Worcestershire sauce
½ cup beer
Barbecue Sauce (recipe follows)
Swami Sauce (recipe follows)

In a large pot, combine all the braising liquid ingredients. Bring to a simmer over medium heat. Add the ribs and simmer until tender, but *not* falling apart, about 1 hour and 45 minutes. Carefully transfer the ribs to a cookie sheet.

In a medium-size bowl, combine the spiced mixture ingredients to form a paste. (Add more beer if dry.) Rub the paste over all the surfaces of the ribs. (Reserve under refrigeration any extra rub for up to 2 weeks.) Wrap each slab of ribs in aluminum foil, dull-side out. Refrigerate until ready to cook. (Can be prepared 2 to 4 days ahead.)

Preheat oven to 400°F. Preheat grill.

Place the ribs, in the foil, on a cookie sheet. Position in the center of the oven and leave until hot, about 10 minutes. Remove the foil and place the ribs under the broiler or on the grill to char. Serve immediately with sauces. Add more cayenne pepper if you like it red hot!

COOKING NOTES: Achiote paste is a Central American condiment made from ground annatto seed (the achiote), garlic, vinegar, salt, and sometimes chiles. The flavor is similar to a rich, mild paprika. It is available in Mexican or Spanish markets. If you can't locate it, substitute 1 tablespoon mild paprika mixed with 1 tablespoon red bell pepper puree and 1 teaspoon red wine vinegar for 2 tablespoons of achiote. *Do not* substitute the annatto seed itself as it has a very strong flavor.

■ It is not necessary to use stock in this recipe. For the stock substitute water and a couple of bouillon cubes. After using the seasoned liquids, skim the fat and refrigerate for up to 1 week or freeze until you make the recipe again. To use the liquid again, add water to return to the original volume and adjust the seasonings with a *little* spice. The liquids may be used over and over as long as they are stored properly.

MAKES 4 SERVINGS ■

Barbecue Sauce

    1 cup Hunt's chili sauce
    1 cup ketchup
 1/4 cup A-1 sauce
    1 tablespoon tamarindo (or substitute grenadine)
    1 tablespoon garlic juice (derived from straining pureed garlic)
 1/4 cup finely grated fresh horseradish (see note below)
    3 tablespoons dry mustard
    2 tablespoons Tabasco sauce
    1 tablespoon molasses (see note below)
    1 tablespoon prepared hot salsa
    1 tablespoon red wine vinegar

Combine all the ingredients in a bowl. Whisk until smooth. Adjust the Tabasco to taste. Refrigerate until ready to use or up to 2 weeks.

COOKING NOTES: When grated, horseradish's flavor dissipates quickly into the air, so use immediately.
■ Select a light molasses from the first distillation. Unless you love harsh flavors, avoid blackstrap molasses, which is from the third and last distillation and thus contains the most impurities.

MAKES 3 CUPS ■

Swami Sauce

Serve hot or cold with fresh or fried vegetables, grilled meats, and fish. Everyone loves this sauce.

    2 tablespoons dry mustard
    1 tablespoon ground ginger
    1 tablespoon ground fennel seeds
    1 tablespoon minced garlic
 1/4 cup mayonnaise
    1 cup Hunt's chili sauce
    1 cup ketchup
 1/4 cup honey
    1 tablespoon Worcestershire sauce
 1/4 cup finely grated fresh horseradish (see note below)
    3 tablespoons extra-strong Dijon mustard (such as Pommery)
    2 tablespoons minced drained capers
    1 teaspoon Tabasco sauce

In medium-size bowl, combine the dry mustard, ginger, fennel, garlic, and mayonnaise until smooth. Mix in all the remaining ingredients. Adjust the pepper and Tabasco to taste. Refrigerate until ready to use or up to 2 weeks.

COOKING NOTE: When grated, horseradish's flavor quickly dissipates into the air, so use immediately.

MAKES 3 CUPS ■

Grilled Pork Chops and Corn Salsa

    4 pork loin chops, about 10 ounces each
    2 tablespoons virgin olive oil
1 1/2 cups Grilled Corn Salsa (recipe follows)
    4 sprigs fresh cilantro for garnish

Preheat the grill or broiler.

Rub the surfaces of the chops with the olive oil. Place on the grill and cook until well seared, about 5 minutes. Turn over and cook to the desired doneness, about 10 minutes for medium depending on thickness.

In a small skillet over medium heat, warm the salsa. Position the chops on warm serving plates, spoon the salsa over, then garnish with the cilantro and serve.

MAKES 4 SERVINGS ∎

Grilled Corn Salsa

Grilled corn develops a nutty flavor and the richness of the dried tomatoes and mushrooms makes this an unusual and special salsa. Try a mixture of white and yellow sweet corn, as well as some grilled and some just blanched.

3 ears sweet corn
½ cup virgin olive oil
¼ cup chopped oil-packed sundried tomatoes
1 clove garlic, minced
½ cup chopped wild mushrooms, sautéed over high heat until golden, about 5 minutes, and drained
2 tablespoons chopped fresh cilantro
2 tablespoons fresh lime juice
1 chipotle pepper in adobo sauce, finely chopped (or substitute Tabasco sauce to taste)
Salt to taste

Preheat the oven to 450°F. Preheat the grill.

Brush the corn with ¼ cup of the olive oil. Wrap in aluminum foil, dull-side out. Bake on the lower rack of the oven for 15 minutes, then unwrap and broil until evenly browned. (If you don't use a grill or broiler, brown the corn. In a large, heavy skillet, heat an additional ¼ cup of olive oil, then add the corn and cook until evenly browned, about 5 minutes.)

Cut the corn from the cob and in a large bowl, combine it with the remaining ingredients. Refrigerate until ready to serve or up to 3 days.

MAKES 2 CUPS ∎

Ann's Bread and Butter Pickles

These are crunchy and great!

1 gallon small pickling cucumbers, sliced
4 cups sliced red onions
6 medium-size green or red bell peppers, diced
½ cup salt
16 cups ice cubes
2 teaspoons salt
4 cups cider vinegar
3 cups sugar
1 tablespoon mustard seed, toasted (see page 61)
1 tablespoon celery seed, toasted
1 teaspoon ground turmeric

In a large bowl, combine the cucumbers, onions, peppers, and salt, and cover with ice. Allow flavors to develop for 3 hours at room temperature. Drain well.

In a large pot, combine the remaining ingredients and bring to a boil over high heat. Add the cucumber mixture and return to a boil. Let cool. Divide into sealing jars. Refrigerate until ready to serve or up to 1 month.

VARIATION: To create that extra "bite," add roasted and chopped jalapeño peppers after bringing the vinegar mixture to a boil the first time.

MAKES 4 QUARTS ■

Rattlesnake Coleslaw

1 **cup sugar**
2 **teaspoons salt**
1 **tablespoon ground caraway seed**
1 **tablespoon freshly ground black pepper**
1 **tablespoon ground celery seed**
1 **medium-size head green cabbage (or substitute red cabbage)**
1 **cup cider vinegar**
2 **cups red wine vinegar**
1 **cup virgin olive oil**

In a small bowl, combine the sugar, salt, caraway, pepper, and celery seed. Shred the cabbage about 1/16th inch thick. Spread a thin layer of it over a large colander. Sprinkle it with some of the spice mix. Repeat with layers of cabbage and spice mix until all the cabbage and spice is used. Allow to weep for 2 hours. Transfer to a large bowl and add the vinegars and olive oil. Mix well. Refrigerate overnight or up to 1 week. Mix again, then adjust the salt and pepper to your taste. Serve.

VARIATION: To create that extra "bite," add roasted and chopped jalapeño peppers with the olive oil. The following day add chopped fresh mint to balance the heat.

MAKES 2 QUARTS ■

Rainbow Flavor Chips

This recipe shows the wide range of root vegetables that can be made into chips. Wild roots such as burdock, boniato, and salsify can offer very interesting flavors. My personal favorite is the large purple taro root for its nutty taste.

1 **large beet, peeled**
1 **large taro root, peeled**
1 **large sweet potato (Orange Louisiana yam), peeled**
1 **large true yam, peeled**
1 **large russet potato, peeled**
1 **lotus root, peeled**
1 **celery root, peeled**
1 **large parsnip, peeled**
  Corn or virgin olive oil for frying
  Salt to taste
  Freshly ground black pepper to taste (optional)

Slice the vegetables to the thickness of potato chips. Rinse separately under cold running water to remove starch. Dry thoroughly on paper toweling.

Fill a large skillet with 3 inches of oil. Heat to 350°F. Add each vegetables separately, piece by piece, to prevent them from sticking to each other. Stir with a slotted metal spoon until golden and crisp, about 1 minute. Remove to paper toweling to drain. Repeat with remaining vegetables. Adjust salt and pepper. Combine the chips and serve.

Different oils will produce different flavors and saturated fat levels. The lower saturated fat oils are my preference: rapeseed (canola), safflower, sunflower, corn, and olive oil. For spicy chips, add dried hot peppers to the hot oil for 10 minutes. Remove the peppers, then add the vegetables and fry. You can also do the same with garlic and other intense dried spices, preferably seeds for easy removal from the oil.

MAKES 16 SERVINGS ■

Baby Potato Salad

1/2 **cup raspberry vinegar**
1/2 **cup coarse-grained prepared mustard**
3/4 **cup virgin olive oil**
     Salt to taste
     Freshly ground black pepper to taste
1 **bunch fresh parsley, chopped**
2 **pounds new potatoes, cut about 1 inch in diameter**

In a medium-size bowl, combine the vinegar, mustard, and olive oil, and season with salt and pepper. Add the parsley.

In a large pot of cold water, bring the potatoes to a boil over medium-high heat and cook until tender, about 15 minutes. Drain. Cut into halves or quarters. Pour the vinaigrette over them while still warm. Refrigerate overnight, then serve chilled.

COOKING NOTE: When boiling starchy vegetables, begin with cold water and bring up to boil. This way the vegetables heat up gradually, just like the water, which eliminates the development of a chalky exterior section.

MAKES 8 SERVINGS ■

Cucumber and Dill Salad

Great technique to get a crunchy salad.

2 **English cucumbers, peeled, cut in half lengthwise, seeded, and cut into 1/4-inch slices**
2 **tablespoons salt**
1/4 **cup champagne vinegar (or substitute cider vinegar)**
     Freshly ground white pepper to taste
1 **cup sour cream (or more if you like)**
1/2 **cup plain yogurt**
1/4 **cup chopped fresh dill**
2 **tablespoons chopped fresh mint**

In a colander, combine the cucumbers and salt. Place a bowl on top of the cucumbers and weight down. Allow to drain until the cucumbers are limp, about 1 hour. Rinse under cold running water, then submerge in ice water until recrisped, about 5 minutes. Drain well and pat dry with paper towels. Taste the cucumber to verify they are not salty; if they are, repeat the rinsing steps. Transfer to a medium-size bowl.

Add the vinegar, mixing well. Stir in the pepper, sour cream, and yogurt, then the dill and mint. Adjust the salt and pepper to taste. Refrigerate until ready to serve.

MAKES 4 SERVINGS ■

Chocolate Sorbet

7 ounces extra bittersweet chocolate (do not use baking chocolate)
2 tablespoons unsalted butter (optional—see note below)
2 cups brewed coffee, as strong as you like
1 cup sugar
1 ounce extra bittersweet chocolate, shaved (do not use baking chocolate)
2 ounces white chocolate, shaved

In the top of a double boiler over simmering water, melt the chocolate and butter together. Stir until smooth.

In a medium-size saucepan, combine the coffee and sugar over medium heat. Cook until the sugar is dissolved, then remove from the heat. Whisk the coffee mixture slowly into the melted chocolate, making sure the chocolate does not lump. Strain through a fine sieve.

Process in an ice-cream maker according to the manufacturer's instructions, until just about solid. Add the chocolate shavings, then freeze in a container until firm, at least overnight.

VARIATIONS: Substitute 1 cup maple sugar or syrup for the white sugar or different flavored coffees for lots of fun flavors.

COOKING NOTE: The butter simply enriches the sorbet.

MAKES 3 CUPS ■

Watermelon Sorbet

3 pounds watermelon, scooped and seeded
½ cup fresh lemon juice
1 cup sugar
½ cup chopped fresh mint

In a blender puree the watermelon and lemon juice until smooth. Transfer to a saucepan, add the sugar, and bring to a simmer over high heat. Remove after one short boil. Return to the blender, add the mint, and puree for exactly 10 seconds. Allow to steep until room temperature, about 10 minutes. Strain through a very fine sieve, then process the mixture in an ice-cream maker according to the manufacturer's instructions. Freeze until firm, at least overnight.

MAKES 1 QUART ■

Peach Sorbet

Try peach sorbet over shortbread with fresh peaches and Caramel Pecan Sauce (see page 193–94). Select very ripe fruit with great fragrance. White peaches make a killer sorbet.

1 cup sugar
½ cup water
¼ cup fresh lemon juice
1 pound peaches, pitted and peeled

In a small saucepan, combine the sugar with the water and lemon juice, and bring to a simmer over high heat. Remove from the heat.

In a blender, combine the fruit and sugar syrup and puree until smooth. Strain through a fine sieve. Process the fruit mixture in an ice-cream maker according to the manufacturer's instructions. Freeze until firm, at least overnight.

VARIATION: To make a raspberry sorbet follow the directions above, substituting raspberries for the peaches and reducing the water to ¼ cup. This is a great way to use bruised fruit, but avoid using moldy raspberries as the mold flavor will come through in the sorbet.

MAKES ½ QUART ■

Cassis Sorbet

Choose berries with the deepest color and fewest bruised fruits. Use a fork to pull the berries off the stems. Black currants are even better but are outlawed in most states because they carry a destructive tree disease.

> **1 pound red currants, stemmed**
> **1 cup sugar**
> **1 cup water**
> **¼ cup fresh lemon juice**

In a heavy saucepan, combine the currants, sugar, water, and lemon juice. Bring to a simmer over medium heat and cook until the fruit is soft, about 4 minutes.

Transfer to a blender and puree until smooth. Strain through a fine sieve, then process in an ice-cream maker according to the manufacturer's instructions. Freeze in a container until firm, at least overnight.

MAKES ½ QUART ■

Pear and Cinnamon Basil Sorbet

Cinnamon basil has a very pleasant flavor, more toward the spice cinnamon than the traditional sweet taste of basil. This recipe really works when simply framed by wonderful pears.

> **3 pounds pears (Comice or bartlett are best), peeled and cored**
> **½ cup fresh lemon juice**
> **1 cup sugar**
> **1 cup packed fresh cinnamon basil leaves**

In a blender, combine the pears and lemon juice, and puree until smooth. Transfer to a saucepan, add the sugar, and bring to a simmer over high heat. Remove from the heat after one short boil.

Return the puree to the blender, add the cinnamon basil, and puree for exactly 10 seconds. Allow to steep until room temperature, about 10 minutes. Strain through a very fine sieve, then process in an ice-cream maker according to the manufacturer's instructions. Freeze until firm, at least overnight.

VARIATIONS: Variations without the basil can be made with 4 cinnamon sticks, 1 crushed nutmeg, or ½ cup whole black peppercorns added to the pears after pureeing. Be sure to strain through a fine sieve after steeping.

MAKES 1 QUART ■

Red Zinger Sorbet

Great served with fresh strawberries.

> **9 cups water**
> **One 2-ounce box Red Zinger tea**
> **2¾ cups sugar**
> **½ cup fresh lemon juice**

In a large pot, bring the water to a boil. Remove from the heat and add the tea bags. Steep until the flavor is well developed, about 20 minutes, then add the sugar and lemon juice. Strain through a fine sieve.

Process in an ice-cream maker according to the manufacturer's instructions. Transfer to a freezer container and allow to harden overnight before serving.

MAKES 2½ QUARTS ■

Ginseng-Honey Sorbet

Great served with fresh or baked summer pears.

    8 cups water
One 2-ounce box ginseng tea
2½ cups sugar
    ½ cup honey
    ½ cup passion fruit juice or orange juice

In a large pot, bring the water to a boil. Remove from the heat and add the tea bags. Allow to steep until the flavor is well developed, about 20 minutes, then add the sugar, honey, and juice. Strain through a fine sieve.

Process in an ice-cream maker according to the manufacturer's instructions. Transfer to a freezer container and allow to harden overnight before serving.

MAKES 2½ QUARTS ■

Orange-Pekoe Sorbet

Great served with fresh peaches.

    8 cups water
One 2-ounce box orange pekoe tea
      Rind of 1 large orange, without the pith
    4 cups sugar
    1 quart orange juice

In a large pot, bring the water to a boil. Remove from the heat, then add the tea bags and orange rind. Steep until the flavors are well developed, about 20 minutes, then add the sugar and juice. Strain through a fine sieve.

Process in an ice-cream maker according to the manufacturer's instructions. Transfer to a freezer container and allow to harden overnight before serving.

MAKES 2½ QUARTS ■

Mint–Rose Hip Sorbet

Great served with a baked apple.

    8 cups water
    2 bunches fresh mint
    2 ounces dried rose hips (see note below)
    4 cups sugar
    ¼ cup fresh lemon juice

In a large pot, bring the water to a boil. Remove from the heat. Add the mint and rose hips. Steep until the flavors are well developed, about 20 minutes. Add the sugar and juice, then strain through a fine sieve.

Process in an ice-cream maker according to the manufacturer's instructions. Transfer to a freezer container and allow to harden overnight before serving.

COOKING NOTE: Rose hips are the rose plant's seed pods and an excellent source of vitamin C. They are available at specialty spice and tea shops or at health food stores.

MAKES 2½ QUARTS ■

Peach-Pecan Ice Cream

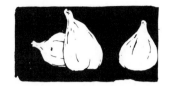

3 cups peeled, pitted, and chunked very ripe
   peaches
2 cups heavy cream, scalded
8 large egg yolks
1¼ cups sugar
   Pinch of salt
1 teaspoon vanilla extract
½ cup water
1 cup pecans, coarsely chopped

In a blender, combine the peaches and hot cream, and
puree until smooth.

In a medium-size saucepan, combine the egg yolks,
¾ cup of the sugar, the salt, and vanilla. Whisk in the
puree. Stir over medium-low heat until the custard thickens enough to coat the back of a spoon, about 10 minutes; *do not boil*. Remove from the heat and strain
through a fine sieve into a medium-size bowl. Cover and
refrigerate until well chilled.

Meanwhile, in a small saucepan, combine the remaining sugar and the water. Bring to a simmer over high heat,
cooking to the caramel stage, between 320° and 345°F on
a candy thermometer. Add the pecans, mixing well to
coat. Remove from the heat.

Process the custard in an ice-cream maker according
to the manufacturer's instructions until just thickened,
then add the sugar-coated pecans. Freeze in a covered
container overnight. If frozen solid, soften slightly before
serving.

VARIATION: Try using the sweet spiced pecans in the loin
of lamb recipe (see pages 184–85).

MAKES 1 QUART ■

Pistachio-Fig Ice Cream

Great served with fresh raspberries.

2½ cups half-and-half, scalded
2 cups pistachios, toasted (see page 60) and
   chopped
1 cup diced fresh figs
¼ cup vodka
14 large egg yolks
½ cup sugar
   Pinch of salt
1 teaspoon vanilla extract
2 cups heavy cream

In a blender, combine the hot half-and-half and 1 cup of
the pistachios, processing until minced. Cover and refrigerate overnight.

In a small saucepan, combine the figs and vodka.
Bring to a simmer over medium-low heat and cook gently
until the vodka is absorbed by the figs, about 5 minutes.
Refrigerate until cool.

In a medium-size saucepan, combine the egg yolks,
sugar, salt, and vanilla. Whisk in the half-and-half mixture. Stir over medium-low heat until the custard thickens
enough to coat the back of a spoon, about 10 minutes;
do not boil. Remove from the heat, then whisk in the
heavy cream. Strain into a medium-size bowl, cover, and
refrigerate until well chilled.

Process the custard in an ice-cream maker according
to the manufacturer's instructions, until just thickened.
Add the figs and remaining pistachios. Freeze in a covered container overnight. If frozen solid, soften slightly
before serving.

MAKES 1¼ QUARTS ■

Papaya Ice Cream

8 **large egg yolks**
1¼ **cups sugar**
 Pinch of salt
1 **teaspoon vanilla extract**
1 **cup half-and-half, scalded**
1 **cup heavy cream, scalded**
3 **large ripe papaya, peeled, seeded, and cut into pieces**
¼ **cup fresh lime juice**

In a medium-size saucepan, combine the yolks, sugar, salt, and vanilla. Whisk in the half-and-half and heavy cream. Stir over medium-low heat until the custard is thick enough to coat the back of a spoon, about 10 minutes; *do not boil*. Remove from the heat and combine in a blender with the papaya and lime juice. Puree until smooth, about 5 minutes. Strain through a fine sieve, then cover and refrigerate until well chilled.

Process the custard in an ice-cream maker according to the manufacturer's instructions, until thickened. Freeze in a covered container overnight. If frozen solid, soften slightly before serving.

VARIATION: *Papaya–Green Peppercorn Ice Cream:* For those strong of heart, combine 2 tablespoons drained water packed green peppercorns with the papaya in the blender, and then proceed with the recipe as outlined. It is a terrific combination. Use more peppercorns to make a hot summer day seem cool!

MAKES 1¾ QUARTS ∎

Spicy Beet Ice Cream

Absolutely, under penalty of death, do not tell your guests what they are eating until after they have taken a bite!

3 **large beets**
1 **cup orange juice**
12 **large egg yolks**
½ **cup sugar**
 Pinch of salt
1 **teaspoon vanilla extract**
2½ **cups half-and-half, scalded**
1 **cup heavy cream**
1 **teaspoon ground cinnamon**
¼ **teaspoon ground cayenne pepper**

Preheat the oven to 400°F.

Place the beets in a small baking pan, set in the lower third of the oven, and cook until a skewer inserted into the beets meets no resistance, about 1½ hours. Remove and allow to cool to room temperature. Peel the toughened outer skin off and cut into small pieces. In a food processor, combine the beets and orange juice, and puree until smooth, about 5 minutes. Strain through a fine sieve.

In a medium-size saucepan, combine the yolks, sugar, salt, and vanilla. Whisk in the half-and-half. Stir over medium-low heat until the custard thickens enough to coat the back of a spoon, about 10 minutes; *do not boil*. Remove from the heat. Add the heavy cream, beet puree, cinnamon, and cayenne. Cover and refrigerate until well chilled.

Process the custard in an ice-cream maker according to the manufacturer's instructions, until thickened. Freeze in a covered container overnight. If frozen solid, soften slightly before serving.

VARIATION: Make with blood-orange juice.

MAKES 1½ QUARTS ∎

Almond-Praline Ice Cream

8 **large egg yolks**
1 **cup sugar**
 Pinch of salt
1 **teaspoon vanilla extract**
2½ **cups half-and-half, scalded**
2 **cups heavy cream**
½ **cup water**
¾ **cup sliced almonds, toasted (see page 61)**

In a medium-size saucepan, combine the yolks, ½ cup of the sugar, the salt, and vanilla. Whisk in the half-and-half. Stir over medium-low heat until the custard thickens enough to coat the back of a spoon, about 10 minutes; *do not boil*. Remove from the heat and whisk in the heavy cream. Strain through a fine sieve into a medium-size bowl, cover, and refrigerate until well chilled.

Meanwhile, in a small saucepan, combine the remaining sugar and the water to dissolve. Bring to a simmer over medium-high heat, cooking to the caramel stage, 340°F on a candy thermometer. Add the almonds, stirring to coat, but cooking for only 1 minute. Remove from the heat, pouring directly onto a buttered cookie sheet to allow to cool.

Break into small pieces, transfer to a food processor, and pulse the processor on/off to achieve ½-inch chunks of praline. Freeze.

Process the custard in an ice-cream maker according to the manufacturer's instructions, until just thickened. Add the almond praline. Freeze in a covered container overnight. If frozen solid, soften slightly before serving.

MAKES 2 QUARTS ■

Hazelnut–Chocolate Chip Ice Cream

8 **large egg yolks**
¾ **cup sugar**
 Pinch of salt
1 **tablespoon vanilla extract**
2½ **cups half-and-half, scalded**
2 **cups heavy cream**
½ **cup hazelnuts, toasted (see page 60) and chopped**
½ **cup bittersweet chocolate chips**

In a medium-size saucepan, combine the yolks, sugar, salt, and vanilla. Whisk in the half-and-half. Stir over medium-low heat until the custard thickens enough to coat the back of a spoon, about 10 minutes; *do not boil*. Remove from the heat and whisk in the heavy cream. Strain through a fine sieve into a medium-size bowl, cover, and refrigerate until well chilled.

Process the custard in an ice-cream maker according to the manufacturer's instructions, until just thickened. Add the hazelnuts and chocolate chips. Freeze in a covered container overnight. If frozen solid, soften slightly before serving.

MAKES 1½ QUARTS ■

White Chocolate–Macadamia Ice Cream

Macadamias are originally from Australia. Now a major export from Hawaii, their flavor is terrific, especially with white chocolate.

8 **large egg yolks**
¾ **cup sugar**
Pinch of salt
1 **teaspoon vanilla extract**
2½ **cups half-and-half, scalded**
10 **ounces white chocolate, broken into ½-ounce pieces**
1 **cup heavy cream**
1 **cup macadamia nuts, toasted (see page 60) and chopped**

In a medium-size saucepan, combine the egg yolks, sugar, salt, and vanilla. Whisk in the half-and-half. Stir over medium-low heat until the custard thickens enough to coat the back of a spoon, about 10 minutes; *do not boil.* Remove from the heat. Whisk in the white chocolate just until melted, then add the heavy cream. Strain into a medium-size bowl, cover, and refrigerate until well chilled.

Process the custard in an ice-cream maker according to the manufacturer's instructions, until just thickened. Add the macadamia nuts. Freeze in a covered container overnight. If frozen solid, soften slightly before serving.

MAKES 1½ QUARTS ∎

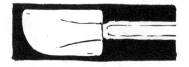

Dark Chocolate and Strawberry Ice Cream

Select the ripest and sweetest fruit for the best flavor with the chocolate. You can also try substituting raspberries for the strawberries.

8 **large egg yolks**
1 **cup sugar**
Pinch of salt
1 **teaspoon vanilla extract**
3½ **cups half-and-half, scalded**
12 **ounces extra bittersweet chocolate, coarsely chopped (do not use baking chocolate)**
½ **cup dark rum**
¼ **cup water**
1½ **cups quartered strawberries**

In a medium-size saucepan, combine the yolks, ¾ cup of the sugar, the salt, and vanilla. Whisk in the half-and-half. Stir over medium-low heat until the custard thickens enough to coat the back of a spoon, about 10 minutes; *do not boil.* Remove from the heat, and whisk in the chocolate just until melted. Strain through a fine sieve into a medium-size bowl. Add the rum, cover, and refrigerate until well chilled.

In a small saucepan, combine the remaining sugar and the water. Bring to a simmer over medium heat, then add the strawberries and cook until tender, about 3 minutes. Remove from the heat and cool.

Process the custard in an ice-cream maker according to the manufacturer's instructions, until just thickened, then add the strawberries. Freeze in a covered container overnight. If frozen solid, soften slightly before serving.

MAKES 1½ QUARTS ∎

Summer Berries with Shortcake

1 pint strawberries
1 pint raspberries
1 pint blueberries
1/2 cup crème de cassis
2 tablespoons cognac
    Sugar (optional)
4 Shortcakes (recipe follows)
1/2 cup heavy cream, whipped to firm peaks
4 sprigs fresh mint for garnish

In a medium-size bowl, combine the fruit, then add the cassis and cognac. Allow to mellow for a few minutes. Add sugar if necessary.

Split the shortcakes in half. Place the bottoms on the serving plates, spoon the berries over the shortcakes, divide the whipped cream over the berries, position the shortcake tops over the whipped cream, garnish with the mint, and serve.

MAKES 4 SERVINGS ■

Shortcake

A very light, easy shortcake that is extra flaky.

2 cups all-purpose flour
1/4 cup maple sugar (or substitute white granulated)

Pinch of salt
1 tablespoon baking powder
1/2 pound (2 sticks) unsalted butter
2 large egg yolks
1/4 cup orange juice

Preheat the oven to 400°F. Butter a cookie sheet.

In a medium-size bowl, sift together the flour, sugar, salt, and baking powder. Cut in the butter with a pastry cutter until the texture resembles small peas. Mix in the egg yolks and orange juice as necessary until the pastry sticks together. Flatten into a disc.

Dust the dough with flour or sugar and roll it out to a thickness of 1/2 inch. Transfer to the prepared cookie sheet and bake on the middle rack of oven until golden, about 15 minutes. Cut into 4 large pieces.

MAKES 4 LARGE SERVINGS ■

Phyllis's Famous Apple Pie

2 cups sifted all-purpose flour
3/4 cup vegetable shortening
1 teaspoon salt
8 to 10 tablespoons ice water
3 pounds tart Granny Smith apples, peeled, cored, and sliced
1 cup sugar (more if apples are too tart)
2 teaspoons ground cinnamon
4 tablespoons (1/2 stick) unsalted butter, cut into small pieces

Preheat the oven to 425°F.

In a medium-size bowl, cut the shortening into the flour and salt with a pastry cutter until the texture resembles small peas. Add the water tablespoon by tablespoon, working with your fingertips until the dough forms a ball. Scrape the edges and bottom of the bowl. Divide the dough in half and shape into discs.

Roll the first pastry disc out to 1/4-inch thick on a

floured counter. Place into a 9-inch pie tin, allowing the edges to fall over the sides of tin. Place half of the apples into the pie, then sprinkle with half of the sugar, cinnamon, and butter. Repeat with the remaining apples, sugar, cinnamon, and butter.

Roll out the second pastry disc to the same thickness. Fold in half. Cut on the folded edge three times. Cut three more times next to the first cuts to form vents. Place the pastry on top of the apples. Trim and finish the edges.

Place the pie on the lower rack of the oven for 15 minutes, then turn the temperature down to 375°F and bake for 30 minutes or until golden. Cool on a cake rack. Slice and serve.

MAKES ONE 9-INCH PIE ■

Chocolate Sauce

My preference is bittersweet chocolate, but try your own favorites and adjust the amount of sugar syrup accordingly.

3 ounces extra bittersweet chocolate (do not use baking chocolate)
1 ounce milk chocolate
4 tablespoons (1/2 stick) unsalted butter
1/2 cup sugar syrup (see note below)
1/4 cup condensed milk
Brewed coffee to thin, if necessary

In the top of a double boiler over simmering water, combine the chocolates and butter and melt. Remove from the heat, and add the sugar syrup and milk. Add coffee to thin, if necessary.

COOKING NOTE: To make sugar syrup, combine 1/2 cup sugar, 1/4 cup water, and 2 tablespoons fresh lemon juice in a small saucepan. Bring to a simmer over high heat, then remove from the stove. Can store in the refrigerator for up to one month. Makes 1/2 cup.

MAKES 1 CUP ■

Caramel Sauce

2 cups sugar
2 cups water
1/4 cup fresh lemon juice
2 cups heavy cream
1 cup condensed milk

In a heavy medium-size saucepan, combine the sugar, water, and lemon juice. Bring to a simmer over high heat, cooking to the caramel stage, 310° to 320°F on a candy thermometer. Remove from the heat. Carefully whisk in the cream; avoid boiling over. (Caution: This is very hot— do not touch or taste!) Return to a boil and cook until thickened enough to coat the back of a spoon, about 10 minutes. Remove from the heat and allow to cool and thicken. As the sauce thickens, thin with condensed milk to a sauce consistency. Serve warm.

Refrigerate till ready to use or up to 2 weeks.

MAKES 1 CUP ■

SUMMER MENUS

Grilled Squid and Vegetable Salad
Edna Valley Vin Gris

◆

Veal Chops with Tomatoes and Arugula
Rainbow Flavor Chips
Chalone Vineyard Pinot Noir

◆

White Chocolate–Macadamia Nut Ice Cream

Squash Blossoms with Pepper Tapenade
Joseph Phelps Vineyards Sauvignon Blanc

◆

Soft-Shell Crabs with Capers and Lemon
Shoestring Potatoes
Beringer Vineyard Private Reserve Chardonnay

◆

Summer Berries with Shortcake

Salmon Carpaccio
Sonoma-Cutrer Russian River Ranches
Chardonnay

◆

Lamb Loin Chops with Mint Pesto
Grilled Baby Squashes and Peppers
La Crema Pinot Noir

◆

Chocolate Sorbet

SUMMER BARBECUE

◆

HORS D'OEUVRES
Grilled Tomato, Caper, and Basil Pizza
Grilled Eggplant, Pepper, and Goat Cheese Pizza

THE BUFFET
Mussel, Scallop, and Corn Salsa Salad
Terrine of Corn, Squash, and Peppers with
Roasted and Sundried Tomato Salsa
Chilled Cucumber and Dill Soup
Willy's Salad

◆

Grilled Chicken with Misantle Butter
Spiced Baby Back Ribs
Lamb and Papaya Tortillas

◆

Rattlesnake Coleslaw
Ann's Bread and Butter Pickles
Baby Potato Salad

DESSERTS
Phyllis's Famous Apple Pie
Ice Creams to Mix and Match

◆

Assorted Beers
Blush Wines
Edna Valley Vin Gris
Mastroberardino Lacrimarosa

F A L L

Fall is the celebration of the harvest. The plants, trees, livestock, game, and poultry have matured through the summer season to produce their bounty for the coming year. The harvest emits an aura of completion, of the struggle of life won. Life's productivity is reflected in the sounds and smells of chilly days and nights. The fall flavors are richer from maturity. They tempt us to cook again within the kitchen, to warm the house and our souls with their fragrances. The glorious shellfish emerging after a summer of fattening are sublime as oysters on the half shell, grilled plump mussels, and Hot and Spicy Shrimp with Green Papaya. Salmon, fat from summer feedings, are perfect with the exotic flavors of prickly pears and with parsley sauce. The pumpkins, squashes, peppers, and roots offers their golden flavors in wonderful ravioli, rich bisques, and chowders to fortify us for the winter to come. Swordfish with Beaujolais Sauce heralds the arrival of the first of the year's wines, while the rest of the new wines are still happily bubbling through their fermentation to offer promise for many years to come.

Poultry is paired with the harvest of apples and cranberries for their fruity flavor and high acid values. Veal and beef explore the nuances of the pepper family with a glowing sunset of colors only fall can share. The subtle flavors of persimmon and the richness of dried cherries highlight the special quality of pork.

The desserts fall brings will warm us through the cooler nights. Fruits abound in Grilled Comice Pears, Pumpkin and Maple Sugar Crème Brûlée, and Apple Tart with Cassia-Vanilla Ice Cream. The return of chocolates in more intense proportion are very satisfying in The Brujo. The arrival of citrus is glorified in the Grapefruit and Pomegranate Tart.

Fall is very special to me, holding memories of foraging for black walnuts, butternuts, hickory nuts, and other annual treats. As a child, our family would collect the walnuts, lay them across the country road, and run over them with the car to remove the green exteriors, or drupes, before the trip home. The fall frost brought out the rifles for hunting special game for Thanksgiving and winter. The fall harvest was a time to rejoice for the gifts nature had so generously shared with us.

Grilled Mussels with Garlic and Tomatoes

The fall mussels, plump from the rich summer waters, are wonderful with grilled tomatoes, garlic, and parsley root butter.

48 mussels, scrubbed, debearded, and opened on
    half shell
    Rock salt
 2 cups Grilled Tomato Butter (recipe follows)
½ cup finely chopped almonds

Preheat the broiler.

Place the mussels on the half shell in a shallow oven-proof pan on a bed of rock salt to keep them upright. Spoon the butter over the mussels, and top with the ground almonds.

Place the mussels under a broiler and cook until golden, about 7 minutes. Without spilling the butter, carefully distribute the mussels on a serving platter and serve.

VARIATION: Try topping with different chopped nuts, such as hazelnuts or pistachios.

MAKES 4 SERVINGS ∎

Grilled Tomato Butter

 1 large, ripe tomato, cut in half widthwise and
    seeds squeezed out
 6 tablespoons virgin olive oil
 4 cloves garlic, roasted (see page 62) and
    minced
 1 tablespoon tomato paste
 2 tablespoons chopped fresh parsley

¼ cup diced blanched (see pages 57–59) parsley
    root (optional)
 2 tablespoons chopped fresh basil
    Salt to taste
    Freshly ground black pepper to taste
 2 tablespoons red wine vinegar
 4 tablespoons (1 stick) unsalted butter

Preheat the grill or the broiler.

Rub the tomato halves with 2 tablespoons of the olive oil. Place on the grill or under the broiler, skin-side toward the heat, and cook until well seared, about 10 minutes.

In a food processor, finely chop the tomatoes, garlic, tomato paste, parsley greens and root, and basil. Add salt and pepper. Mix in the vinegar, butter, and remaining olive oil. Refrigerate until ready to serve.

VARIATION: Substitute roasted peppers for the tomatoes in the butter or mix with sundried tomatoes.

MAKES 2 CUPS ∎

Seared Scallops with Marjoram

½ cup dry white wine, preferably chardonnay
 1 cup heavy cream
 1 large red bell pepper, roasted, peeled (see
    page 62), seeded, and diced
    Salt to taste
    Freshly ground white pepper to taste
 2 tablespoons corn oil
 1 pound large sea scallops, foot removed (see
    note below)
¼ cup chopped fresh marjoram or oregano

In a medium-size saucepan over medium-high heat, combine the wine and cream, and cook until thickened enough to coat the back of a spoon, about 10 minutes. Transfer the sauce to a blender, add half of the red pepper and puree until smooth. Return to the saucepan and the medium-high heat. Add salt, pepper, and the remaining pepper. Reduce the heat to low.

In a large skillet, heat the corn oil over high. Add the scallops and cook until opaque, about 2 minutes. Turn over and finish cooking until slightly firm, about 1 minute, depending on their size.

Spoon the sauce into the center of the serving plates and sprinkle the marjoram over it. Position the scallops in the center of the sauce and serve.

VARIATION: You can substitute bay scallops for the sea scallops but adjust the cooking time by half, depending on their size.

COOKING NOTES: The "foot" is the tough muscle on the side of the scallop.
- I prefer fresh marjoram in this recipe for its special rich flavor. Marjoram is milder than oregano and worth looking for. Fresh marjoram is very different in flavor than the dried, so use only the fresh for this recipe.

MAKES 4 SERVINGS ∎

Shrimp with White Beans and Thyme

The crunchy shrimp and silky beans are a terrific combination.

½ **cup dried white beans, soaked in water overnight and drained**
1 **medium-size onion**
1 **bunch fresh thyme, stems and leaves separated**
 Salt to taste
 Freshly ground black pepper to taste
2 **tablespoons virgin olive oil**
1 **pound large shrimp, peeled and deveined**
1 **clove garlic, minced**

1 **cup Tomato Concasse (see page 65)**
½ **cup dry white wine**
½ **cup Fish Stock (see page 65, or substitute clam juice)**
2 **tablespoons balsamic vinegar**
2 **tablespoons snipped fresh chives**

In a large pot, combine the white beans, onion, and thyme stems, the latter either wrapped in cheesecloth or tied together. Add cold water to cover and bring to a boil over medium-high heat. Add salt and pepper. Reduce the heat to low and simmer for 3½ to 4 hours, until the beans are tender. Remove the onion and thyme stems, and drain.

In a large heavy skillet over high heat, add the olive oil. Add the shrimp and cook until seared, about 2 minutes. Add the garlic, tomato, wine, and stock, and cook until the liquids are thickened enough to coat the back of a spoon, about 10 minutes. Add the beans and vinegar, adjust the salt and pepper, then add half of the chives and thyme leaves.

Divide the shrimp mixture onto warm serving plates. Sprinkle with the remaining chives and thyme, and serve.

COOKING NOTE: Cook the beans to a silky texture, still slightly firm but smooth when bitten into. The beans should be softer than the shrimp to accentuate their crunchy texture. Start cooking the beans in cold stock to develop the starches. Adding the beans to hot water or liquid makes them quite tough.

MAKES 4 SERVINGS ∎

Hot and Spicy Shrimp with Green Papaya

This riesling wine and vinegar reduction increases the acid levels of the sauce. This acid will enhance the heat from the peppers, making the dish seem hotter than it actually is and leaving less of an afterburn on the palate.

The green papaya provides a firm texture and light fruit flavor. The cucumber with the papaya offers a cool contrast to the heat of the peppers. This sauce works wonderfully with oysters, scallops, and mussels.

3 tablespoons chopped shallots
½ pound (2 sticks) unsalted butter, at room temperature
1 cup dry riesling wine
1 cup cider vinegar
1 bay leaf
½ bunch fresh parsley
¼ cup heavy cream
Salt to taste
Freshly ground black pepper to taste
1 cup peeled, seeded, and diced green papaya
1 cup peeled, seeded, and diced cucumber
1 cup all-purpose flour
½ cup crushed red pepper (hot!)
2 large eggs, lightly beaten
1 cup milk
1½ pounds large shrimp, peeled and deveined
½ cup virgin olive oil
2 tablespoons chopped fresh mint
2 tablespoons diced scallion greens

In a medium-size saucepan over medium-high heat, sauté the shallots in 2 tablespoons of the butter until tender, about 3 minutes. Add the wine, vinegar, bay leaf, and parsley, and simmer until the liquid is reduced to ½ cup, about 12 minutes. Strain through a fine sieve into another saucepan. Return the sauce to a boil, then whisk in the remaining butter and the cream. Cook until the sauce is reduced enough to coat the back of a spoon, about 3 minutes. Add salt and pepper to taste, then add the papaya and cucumber. Keep warm over very low heat while stirring occasionally to stabilize the sauce texture.

In a medium-size bowl, sift together the flour, red pepper, and ½ teaspoon salt.

In another medium-size bowl, combine the eggs and milk. Drench the shrimp in it, then shake off the excess and dredge in the seasoned flour. Coat evenly, then shake to remove excess flour.

In a medium-size skillet over high heat, heat the olive oil to 350°F. Add the shrimp and cook until golden, about 2 minutes. Turn over and finish, cooking about 2 minutes. Remove to paper toweling to drain. Keep warm in a low oven.

Spoon the sauce onto warm serving plates. Arrange the shrimp over the sauce, sprinkle with the mint and scallions, and serve.

MAKES 4 SERVINGS ∎

Seared Beef with Roast Peppers and Olives

A thin carpaccio-like rare beef salad with smoky flavors.

One 10-ounce tenderloin steak
½ cup hoisin sauce (see note below)
½ cup red wine vinegar
½ cup Dijon mustard
1 head red oakleaf lettuce, trimmed and pulled apart into leaves
1 red bell pepper, roasted, peeled (see page 62), seeded, and julienned
½ cup Mustard Vinaigrette (recipe follows)
24 niçoise olives, pitted
2 tablespoons snipped fresh chives
½ cup shaved Parmesan cheese
Toasted Croutons (see page 70)

Place the tenderloin in a dish. In a small bowl, combine the hoisin sauce, vinegar, and mustard, then pour it over the tenderloin. Marinate under refrigeration for at least 4 hours.

Preheat the grill or broiler.

Grill the tenderloin on all sides until well seared but rare, about 5 minutes. Remove from the heat.

Distribute the lettuce leaves onto serving plates. Slice the tenderloin very thin, then, between pieces of waxed or parchment paper, flatten with a meat bat or the side of a knife until paper thin. Lay the slices across the lettuce, then add the julienne of peppers. Drizzle with the vinaigrette and distribute the olives, chives, and Parmesan across the top. Serve with Toasted Croutons.

VARIATIONS: You can substitute any tender meat, such as lamb, in this recipe. It also works well with leftover cooked meat, preferably rare. If you like your meat more well done, cook according to your taste. You can also choose other marinades, even barbecue sauce.

COOKING NOTES: Avoid very dark colored beef for the cow may have been excited prior to termination. This raised activity depletes the muscles of their glycogen supply, resulting in less lactic acid, yielding gummy textured meat that spoils quickly.

▪ Hoisin sauce is available in Chinese markets.

MAKES 4 SERVINGS ▪

Mustard Vinaigrette

Serve this as a salad dressing or with smoked salmon and chilled crab or other shellfish.

¼ **cup red wine vinegar**
2 **cloves garlic, roasted (see page 62)**
¼ **teaspoon salt**
¼ **teaspoon freshly ground black pepper**

¾ **cup virgin olive oil**
2 **tablespoons coarse-grained prepared mustard**
2 **tablespoons chopped fresh parsley**

In a blender, combine the vinegar, garlic, salt, pepper, and olive oil, and puree until smooth. Strain through a sieve into a small bowl, then add the mustard and parsley. Refrigerate until serving or up to 2 weeks.

MAKES 1½ CUPS ▪

Crab and Avocado Fritters

Great for hearty cocktails. No need for sauce as the salsa is in the fritters.

2 **pounds crab meat, carefully picked over for shells**
1 **cup diced scallion greens**
1 **medium-size ripe avocado, peeled and cut into ¼-inch pieces**
2 **large eggs**
½ **cup prepared hot chili salsa**
Salt to taste
¼ **cup plain dry bread crumbs**
Corn oil for deep frying
All-purpose flour for dusting
Thinly slivered scallion greens for garnish (optional)

Line a baking sheet with parchment. Combine the crab, scallions, and avocado in a large bowl. In another bowl, combine the eggs, salsa, and salt. Add the egg mixture to the crab, then mix in the bread crumbs. Form the mixture into 1½-inch balls. Place on the baking sheet, cover with plastic, and refrigerate for 3 hours.

Fill a large skillet with corn oil to a depth of 3 inches. Heat to 350°F over medium-high heat. Preheat the oven to the lowest setting. Line another baking sheet with paper towels.

Dust the fritters with flour. Carefully add to the oil in batches (do not crowd) and cook until golden brown, turning on all sides, about 2 minutes. Drain on paper towels. Transfer to the prepared sheet and keep warm in the oven until all the fritters are cooked. Garnish with the scallion slivers. Serve immediately.

VARIATION: Use other moist, firm shellfish. Remember to partially cook shellfish if raw as the cooking time of the fritter is short and mostly for heating purposes only.

MAKES ABOUT 4 DOZEN ∎

Chilled Oysters on the Half Shell with Two Sauces

Fall is time for oysters bathed with two variations of traditional sauces.

> **Seaweed for the serving dishes**
> 24 **oysters, scrubbed and opened on half shell (see note below)**
> ½ **cup Rooster Sauce (recipe follows)**
> ½ **cup Green Peppercorn Mignonette sauce (see page 68)**

Place the seaweed on the serving dishes, then place the oysters on the seaweed to keep them level. Spoon the Rooster Sauce over half of the oysters. Stir the Mignonette Sauce and spoon over the remaining oysters. Serve. (Serve the sauces on the side, if you wish.)

COOKING NOTE: Avoid shucking the oysters more than 30 minutes prior to serving; otherwise, the adductor muscle will harden and detract from the overall silky oyster texture.

MAKES 4 SERVINGS ∎

Rooster Sauce

A roast pepper variation that shows the lengths I will go to avoid serving the notorious cocktail sauce.

> 2 **large red bell peppers, roasted, peeled (see page 62), seeded, and chopped**
> 1 **cup dry white wine**
> ½ **cup Hunt's chili sauce**
> 2 **tablespoons prepared white horseradish**
> 2 **tablespoons fresh lemon juice**
> ¼ **cup chopped fresh parsley**
> 1 **large yellow bell pepper, roasted, peeled, seeded, and finely diced**
> 1 **large poblano pepper, roasted, peeled, seeded, and finely diced**
> **Salt to taste**
> **Tabasco sauce to taste**

In a small saucepan, combine the red peppers and wine. Bring to a simmer over medium heat and cook until the peppers are tender and the wine reduced by half, about 15 minutes. Transfer to a food processor and puree until smooth. Strain through a medium sieve.

In a medium-size bowl, combine the pepper puree, chili sauce, horseradish, lemon juice, parsley, and diced peppers. Adjust the salt and Tabasco.

Refrigerate until ready to serve or up to 2 weeks.

MAKES 2 CUPS ∎

Green Peppercorn Mignonette Sauce

This green peppercorn recipe is a subtle variation of the classic mignonette sauce.

½ cup finely chopped shallots
½ cup green waterpacked peppercorns, drained and minced
½ cup cider vinegar
½ teaspoon salt
¾ cup virgin olive oil
¼ cup snipped fresh chives

Place the shallots in a lint-free towel, then rinse in the towel under cold running water, while squeezing their juices from them. Wring out the towel until the shallots are dry.

In a small bowl, combine the shallots, peppercorns, vinegar, and salt. Gradually whisk in the olive oil. Add the chives and adjust the salt.

Serve on shellfish or on the side. Stir well before serving.

COOKING NOTE: Rinsing the shallots under cold running water removes the strong flavor.

MAKES 2 CUPS ■

Smoked Chicken Blue Corn Chips

My favorite smoked chicken comes from Plath's Market in Rogers City, Michigan. It is unique for the chickens have been brined before smoking, creating a moist "ham-like" texture.

24 Blue Corn Tortilla Chips (see page 67)
½ cup Adobo Mayonnaise (recipe follows)
1 cup diced smoked chicken

½ cup roasted, peeled (see page 62), seeded, and diced red bell pepper
½ cup peeled and diced blanched (see pages 57–58) chayote
¼ cup chopped fresh cilantro

Preheat the oven to 400°F.

Place the chips on a cookie sheet and spread generously with the mayonnaise. Distribute the chicken, peppers, and chayote on top. Bake on the lower rack of the oven until hot, about 5 minutes. Sprinkle with the cilantro and serve.

VARIATION: This recipe adapts to any topping. Use the mayonnaise to adhere the toppings to the chips.

MAKES 2 DOZEN ■

Adobo Mayonnaise

The spunky chipotle peppers help keep the chill of fall away.

2 large egg yolks
2 tablespoons fresh lemon juice
1 tablespoon cracked or coarse-grained prepared mustard
1 tablespoon sherry wine vinegar
1 tablespoon achiote paste (see note below)
½ cup corn oil
½ cup virgin olive oil
2 tablespoons minced chipotle peppers in adobo sauce (see note below)
Salt to taste

With a mixer, combine the egg yolks, lemon juice, mustard, vinegar, and achiote paste. On high speed, slowly add the corn and olive oils, then the chipotle peppers. Adjust the salt. If necessary, thin with warm water.

COOKING NOTE: Achiote paste is a Central American condiment made from ground annatto seeds (the achiote), garlic, vinegar, salt, and sometimes chiles. The flavor is similar to rich mild paprika. It is available in Mexican or Spanish markets, as are chipotle peppers in adobo sauce. If you can't locate it, substitute 1 tablespoon mild paprika mixed with 1 tablespoon red bell pepper puree and 1 teaspoon red wine vinegar for 2 tablespoons achiote. *Do not* substitute the annatto seed itself as it has a very strong flavor.

MAKES 1 1/2 CUPS ■

Duck and Pheasant Ravioli

1/2 **pound boneless duck breast**
1/2 **pound boneless pheasant breast**
1/4 **pound (1 stick) unsalted butter**
1/4 **cup diced shallots**
1/2 **cup wild mushrooms, diced**
1/4 **cup snipped fresh chives**
  2 **tablespoons chopped fresh tarragon**
  2 **tablespoons chopped scallion greens**
  2 **tablespoons plain dry bread crumbs**
1/2 **teaspoon salt**
1/2 **teaspoon coarsely ground black pepper**
  3 **large egg yolks**
1/2 **pound pasta (flavor of your choice; see page 68)**
  2 **tablespoons heavy cream**
    Wild Mushroom Sauce (recipe follows)

Preheat the grill or broiler.

Place the duck and pheasant breasts skin-side toward the heat on the grill or under the broiler, cooking until well seared, about 5 minutes. Turn over and cook until rare to medium-rare, testing by making a small incision into the thickest part of the breast and looking for a pinkish color, about 4 minutes. Do not overcook for the breasts will continue to be cooked in the filling and serving steps. Remove to a plate and allow to cool to room temperature. Remove and discard the skin. Cut the breasts into 1/8-inch dice.

To make the filling, in a medium-size skillet, cook the butter over high heat until very brown, almost burnt and smoking. Add the shallots and mushrooms and cook for 30 seconds. Add the duck and pheasant and cook for 2 minutes. Transfer to a medium-size bowl. Mix in 2 tablespoons of the chives, the tarragon, scallions, bread crumbs, salt, and 1/4 teaspoon of the black pepper. Mix in 2 of the egg yolks. Set aside.

Using a pasta machine, roll out the pasta to make a very thin 2 1/2-inch by 24-inch sheet. Repeat the process to yield 4 sheets. Lay a pasta sheet flat on the table.

Place 1 tablespoon of filling mixture every 2 1/2 inches down the center of the sheet of pasta. In a small bowl, mix the remaining egg yolk with the heavy cream and brush the egg wash on the pasta around the filling. Cover with another sheet of pasta, pressing together to seal in the filling. With a crinkle ravioli cutter, cut the filled pasta into ravioli. Repeat with the other sheets of pasta. Refrigerate to firm for at least 1 hour.

Cook the ravioli in a large skillet in 3 inches of boiling salted water until al dente, about 4 minutes. With a slotted spoon, remove to paper towels to drain. Position the ravioli in the center of the warm serving plates, spoon the sauce around the ravioli, sprinkle with the remaining chives, and serve.

COOKING NOTE: Remember to keep the filling rare so that the meats are cooked when the pasta is tender. Also keep the filling well seasoned, for the boiling depletes much of the seasonings.

MAKES 4 SERVINGS ■

Wild Mushroom Sauce

Keep the sauce light in texture and strong in flavor.

½ **pound wild mushrooms, sliced**
2 **tablespoons unsalted butter**
½ **cup dry white wine**
1 **cup Poultry Stock (see page 63)**
1 **cup heavy cream**
  Salt to taste
  Freshly ground black pepper to taste

In a medium-size saucepan, sauté the mushrooms in the butter until tender. Add the wine and stock and bring to a boil over high heat. Reduce to ¼ cup, about 8 minutes. Add the cream and cook until reduced enough to coat the back of a spoon, about 6 minutes. Transfer to a blender and puree until smooth. Strain through a fine sieve into another saucepan. Adjust salt and pepper. Return to a simmer before serving.

MAKES 1 CUP ■

Pumpkin, Leek, and Mushroom Ravioli

2 **tablespoons unsalted butter**
¼ **cup diced leeks, white part only**
½ **cup wild mushrooms, diced**
1 **cup pumpkin puree (see note below)**
¼ **cup grated Parmesan cheese**
¼ **cup snipped fresh chives**
½ **teaspoon salt**
½ **teaspoon coarsely ground black pepper**
3 **large egg yolks**
½ **pound pasta (flavor of your choice; see page 68)**
2 **tablespoons heavy cream**
¾ **cup Rosemary Sauce (recipe follows)**
½ **cup shaved Parmesan cheese**

To make the filling, heat the butter in a medium-size skillet. Add the leeks and mushrooms and sauté until the juices have evaporated, about 5 minutes. Transfer to a medium-size bowl and mix in the pumpkin puree, grated cheese, chives, salt, pepper, and 2 of the egg yolks. Reserve.

Using a pasta machine, roll out the pasta to make a very thin 2½-inch by 24-inch sheet. Repeat the process to yield 4 sheets. Lay a pasta sheet flat on the table. Place 1 tablespoon of the filling mixture every 2½ inches down the center of the sheet of pasta. In a small bowl, mix the remaining egg yolk with the heavy cream and brush the egg wash on the pasta around the filling. Cover with another sheet of pasta, pressing together to seal in the filling. With a crinkle ravioli cutter, cut the filled pasta into ravioli. Repeat with the other sheets of pasta. Refrigerate to firm for at least 1 hour.

Cook the ravioli in a large skillet in 3 inches of boiling salted water until al dente, about 4 minutes. With a slotted spoon, remove to paper towels to drain. Position the ravioli in the center of 4 warm serving plates, spoon the sauce around the ravioli, top with the shaved Parmesan, and serve.

COOKING NOTES: My favorite eating pumpkins are the calabaza, a large, fine-grained, nonwatery variety native to the Americas, and the kabocha, a Japanese fiberless variety.
■ To make pumpkin puree, roast fresh pumpkin for about an hour. For additional flavor, grill it in large pieces. Then dice or puree as you choose. One pound of raw pumpkin yields about 1 cup puree.

MAKES 4 SERVINGS ■

Rosemary Sauce

1/2 **cup dry white wine**
1 **cup Vegetable Stock (see page 64)**
1 **cup heavy cream**
1 **bunch fresh rosemary**
  Salt to taste
  Freshly ground black pepper to taste

In a medium-size saucepan, combine the wine and stock and bring to a boil over high heat. Reduce to 1/4 cup, about 8 minutes. Add the cream and rosemary and cook until reduced enough to coat the back of a spoon, about 6 minutes. Strain through a fine sieve into another saucepan, adjust salt and pepper, and return to a simmer before serving.

MAKES 1 CUP ■

Pheasant and Wild Mushroom Pizza

This pizza is requested more than any other served at The Rattlesnake Club.

1 **ball Pizza Dough, rolled out (see page 123)**
2 **tablespoons Hoisin-Mustard Sauce (recipe follows)**
1/2 **cup diced cooked pheasant meat**
1/4 **cup grated smoked gouda cheese**
1/4 **cup grated mozzarella cheese**
1/4 **cup roasted, peeled (see page 62), seeded, and diced poblano peppers**
1/4 **cup sliced wild mushrooms, sautéed until tender over high heat and drained**
1 **tablespoon chopped fresh tarragon**
2 **tablespoons scallion greens, sliced on an angle**

Preheat the oven to 550°F, with a pizza stone in the lower third of oven. When the stone is hot, carefully pull it out of the oven.

Dust the bottom of the crust with cornmeal, then lay the crust onto the stone. Spread the hoisin sauce across the dough. Distribute the pheasant, then cover with the cheeses and sprinkle the diced pepper and mushrooms on top.

Place the stone back in the oven and bake 8 to 12 minutes, until the crust is golden. Remove from the oven, top with the tarragon and scallions, cut, and serve.

VARIATION: You can substitute duck or squab for the pheasant.

MAKES ONE 9-INCH PIZZA ■

Hoisin-Mustard Sauce

This works well with shrimp, tenderloins, and duck.

1/4 **cup Coleman's Dry English mustard**
1/4 **cup red wine vinegar**
1/4 **cup hoisin sauce (see note below)**

In a small bowl, whisk the mustard and vinegar together until smooth. Mix in the hoisin. Refrigerate until ready to use or up to 1 month.

COOKING NOTE: Hoisin sauce is available in Chinese markets.

MAKES 1/2 CUP ■

Shrimp and Pepper Pizza

1 **ball Pizza Dough, rolled out (see page 123)**
3 **tablespoons virgin olive oil**
1 **cup shelled and deveined cooked shrimp, cut in half lengthwise**
¼ **cup grated fontinella cheese**
¼ **cup grated mozzarella cheese**
¼ **cup roasted, peeled (see page 62), seeded, and large-diced red bell peppers**
¼ **cup thinly sliced and seeded jalapeño pepper (or to taste)**
2 **tablespoons chopped fresh cilantro**

Preheat the oven to 550°F with a pizza stone in the lower third of the oven. When the stone is hot, carefully pull it out of the oven. Dust the bottom of the crust with cornmeal, then lay it onto the stone.

Spread 2 tablespoons of the olive oil across the pizza. In a small bowl, combine the remaining olive oil and the shrimp. Distribute the shrimp across the pizza, cover with the cheeses, and distribute the peppers.

Place the stone back in the oven and bake 8 to 12 minutes, until the crust is golden. Remove from the oven, top with the cilantro, cut, and serve.

VARIATION: Also works well with cooked sea scallops, sliced ¼ inch thick.

MAKES ONE 9-INCH PIZZA ■

Hot and Sour Soup

This soup is Southwest in design. The flavors will warm you to your soul.

3 **cups Poultry Stock (see page 63)**
3 **cups Duck or Poultry Stock (see page 63)**
1¼ **teaspoons roasted, peeled (see page 62), seeded, and minced jalapeño peppers**
3 **tablespoons balsamic vinegar**
1 **tablespoon champagne vinegar**
½ **lime, juiced**
1 **teaspoon salt**
¼ **cup roasted, peeled, seeded, and diced poblano peppers**
¼ **cup roasted, peeled, seeded, and diced red bell peppers**
¼ **cup roasted, peeled, seeded, and diced yellow bell peppers**
½ **cup husked and diced tomatillos**
½ **cup diced rare duck breast (see note below)**
Twelve **½-inch-thick slices Red and Poblano Pepper Tamales (optional—see page 139)**
2 **tablespoons chopped fresh cilantro**

In a large saucepan, combine the poultry and duck stocks and bring to a short simmer. Remove from the heat. Strain the stocks through a coffee filter into another large saucepan. Bring to a gentle simmer over medium heat, then add the jalapeño, vinegars, and lime juice. Adjust the salt.

Add the peppers, tomatillos, and duck, and cook until tender, about 5 minutes. Add the tamales and cook until warm.

Ladle into warm serving bowls, sprinkle with the cilantro, and serve.

COOKING NOTE: Duck breast is best grilled or roasted. Be sure to remove the skin and all fat tissue before dicing.

MAKES 4 SERVINGS ■

Wild Mushroom Soup with Herbs

This soup is as woodsy as the great outdoors. Use those great wild mushrooms for this soup.

    3 tablespoons unsalted butter
    2 cups chopped shallots
    2 pounds chanterelles or other wild mushrooms,
       sliced
    4 cups Poultry Stock (see page 63)
  ¼ cup chopped fresh basil
    1 tablespoon chopped fresh tarragon
    1 tablespoon chopped fresh rosemary
    1 clove garlic, roasted (see page 62) and minced
    1 teaspoon grated lemon rind
    2 tablespoons grated aged Asiago cheese
    1 cup heavy cream
  ½ cup sour cream
       Salt to taste
       Freshly ground black pepper to taste
  ½ cup Amontillado or Fino sherry or to taste (see
       note below)

Melt the butter in a large saucepan over low heat. Add the shallots and sauté until they begin to soften, about 5 minutes. Add the mushrooms and sauté until they are browned and have released their juices, about 10 minutes. Add the stock and simmer until tender, about 1 hour.

Meanwhile, in a small bowl, combine the basil, tarragon, rosemary, garlic, lemon rind, and cheese. Mix until you form a paste. Refrigerate.

Puree the soup in a blender in batches. Strain through a coarse sieve into another saucepan. Whisk in the heavy cream and sour cream. Adjust the salt and pepper and stir in the sherry. Return to a simmer over high heat. Ladle the soup into warm bowls and garnish with the herb mixture. Serve.

COOKING NOTES: Browning the mushrooms concentrates and caramelizes the flavors, while the herb mix reinforces the woodsy flavor.

■ The Amontillado sherry is nutty and sweeter in flavor than the Fino, which is drier. Select according to your preference.

MAKES 8 SERVINGS ■

Pepper Bisque

The warm, rich peppers are highlighted in this simple but satisfying soup.

    2 tablespoons unsalted butter
    2 cups chopped shallots
    2 cups chopped onions
    8 large red bell peppers, seeded and chopped
       (see note below)
    4 cups Poultry Stock (see page 63)
    1 cup heavy cream
       Salt to taste
       Freshly ground white pepper to taste
  ½ cup snipped fresh chives
  ½ cup chopped fresh cilantro

Melt the butter in a large saucepan over low heat. Add the shallots, onions, and peppers, and sauté until the vegetables begin to soften, about 10 minutes. Add the stock and simmer until tender, about 1 hour.

Puree the soup in a blender in batches and strain through a fine sieve. Return to the saucepan. Whisk in the heavy cream, then adjust the salt and pepper. Return the sauce to a simmer over high heat. Ladle the soup into warm bowls and garnish with the chives and cilantro.

COOKING NOTES: Select the maturest, deepest red peppers possible. These will generate the best flavor. You can utilize all the pepper scraps from other preparations.
■ You can also thicken the soup with white or yellow cornmeal, like in the Corn Chowder recipe that follows, for a heartier variation.

MAKES 8 SERVINGS ■

Corn Chowder

This soup allows the true corn flavor to come through. It is simple and very fast to prepare.

- **3 tablespoons unsalted butter**
- **2 cups chopped onions**
- **4 cups Poultry Stock (see page 63)**
- **1 cup yellow cornmeal**
-    **Salt to taste**
-    **Freshly ground white pepper to taste**
- **¹/₂ cup fresh lemon juice**
- **4 cups sweet corn cut from the cob**
- **¹/₂ cup snipped fresh chives**

Melt the butter in a large saucepan over low heat. Add the onions and sauté until they begin to soften, about 10 minutes. Add the stock and simmer until tender, about ¹/₂ hour. Slowly whisk in the cornmeal and cook until thickened, about 5 minutes.

Puree the soup in the blender in batches and strain through a fine sieve. Return to the saucepan over medium-high heat, adjust the salt and pepper, then add the lemon juice and fresh corn and cook until the corn is tender, about 5 minutes. Ladle the soup into warm bowls and garnish with the chives.

VARIATIONS: To make special variations, use this soup as a base for any number of ingredients. Add a vegetable, such as 3 cups chopped pumpkin, or broccoli, or rapini, to the onions and stock and cook until tender. Add the cornmeal as necessary to thicken the soup. Puree if you choose and garnish with your imagination.

MAKES 8 SERVINGS ■

Radicchio, Mâche, and Dried Cherry Salad

A truly unusual winter salad with deep rich flavors.

- **¹/₄ cup red wine vinegar**
- **¹/₄ cup dried cherries (see note below)**
- **2 tablespoons finely diced shallots**
-    **Salt to taste**
- **¹/₂ cup virgin olive oil**
-    **Coarsely ground black pepper to taste**
- **1 head radicchio (see note below), trimmed**
- **4 bunches mâche, stemmed**
- **2 tablespoons snipped fresh chives, cut into 1-inch lengths**
- **¹/₂ cup crumbled Roquefort or blue cheese (optional)**

In a small saucepan, heat the vinegar, then add the cherries. Remove from the heat and allow to steep until softened, at least 2 hours. (Add a little water if the cherries are still firm.)

Place the vinegar, cherries, and shallots in a blender and puree until smooth. While the machine is running, add olive oil until thickened. Then add salt and pepper.

Carefully peel off the leaves from the head of radicchio. Select four of the best large leaves and place in the centers of the serving plates. Cut the remaining leaves into ¹/₄-inch chiffonade.

In a medium-size bowl, combine the chiffonaded radicchio and the mâche leaves. Add the dressing and toss. Arrange the tossed greens on the large radicchio leaves. Sprinkle with the chives and blue cheese and serve.

COOKING NOTES: Consider dried cherries as a spice rather than a fruit. When used sparingly, they season dishes very elegantly without being overly sweet or unbalanced. The dried fruit also has the characteristics of a good emulsifier, holding the oil in suspension in the dressing. You may need to thin the dressing with a little white wine if the dressing is too thick or begins to separate.
• Avoid soaking radicchio in water, as it will turn more bitter and lose flavor.

MAKES 4 SERVINGS ■

Escalope of Demi-Gravlax Salmon with Parsley Sauce

TO CURE THE FISH:

   8 large cloves garlic
1½ cups kosher salt
1½ cups packed dark brown sugar
1½ cups granulated white sugar
   ¼ cup hot Hungarian paprika
   1 complete fillet of salmon (1 side), about 2½ to 3 pounds

In a food processor, chop the garlic. Add the salt, both sugars, and paprika, and process until smooth. Distribute one quarter of the mix evenly across a cookie sheet.

Place the salmon fillet over the mix, skin-side down. Spoon the remainder of the mix over the flesh of the salmon, packing well. Refrigerate, covered, for 12 hours. After curing, scrape off all the curing mix. Cut the salmon on an angle about ¾ of an inch thick to form at least eight escalopes of approximately 3 ounces each. Reserve under refrigeration.

If you cure for 24 hours, the salmon will be ready to serve as gravlax without further preparation. You can serve it as prepared in the Salmon Carpaccio recipe on pages 115–16 or the Smoked Salmon with Radishes and Capers recipe on pages 230–31.

The cure can also be seasoned with fresh ginger, hot peppers, and other strong spices, such as cumin and coriander. Add these ingredients to the food processor with the garlic.

TO PREPARE THE DISH

½ cup Fish Stock (see page 65)
½ cup dry white wine
½ teaspoon hot Hungarian paprika
½ cup heavy cream
¼ pound spinach, throughly rinsed of grit and patted dry
3 bunches fresh parsley
Salt to taste
Freshly ground black pepper to taste

Preheat the grill or broiler.

In a large acid-resistant skillet, combine the stock and wine. Bring to a simmer over medium heat and cook until reduced to ¼ cup, about 5 minutes. Add the paprika and cream and cook until thickened enough to coat the back of a spoon, about 10 minutes. Add the spinach and parsley and cook until wilted. Transfer to a blender and puree until smooth. Strain through a fine sieve into another saucepan.

Return the sauce to a simmer and reduce until thickened enough to lightly coat the back of a spoon, about 3 minutes. Adjust the salt and pepper. Reduce the heat to low.

Place the salmon on the grill or under the broiler and cook until well seared, about 2 minutes for medium-rare. Turn over and cook to desired doneness, about 3 minutes for medium-rare; test by inserting a skewer to check firmness and warmth. Spoon the sauce across warm plates, position the salmon over it, and serve.

COOKING NOTE: Remember to trim the fatty darker flesh from the salmon as this carries the oily "fishy" flavor.

MAKES 4 SERVINGS ■

Salmon with Prickly Pear

This is a very interesting use of *ripe* prickly pears. Prickly pears are also know as cactus pears, Indian pears, and Barbary figs. They are very popular in the Mediterranean regions as well as Asia and other arid climates. Select supple ruby-red fruit with a smell similar to that of watermelon. They are also great for salsas and sorbets.

½ **cup Fish Stock (see page 65)**
½ **cup fresh lime juice**
 1 **clove garlic, roasted (see page 62) and minced**
 1 **tablespoon Ginger Puree (see page 66)**
 4 **prickly pears, peeled**
   Salt to taste
   Tabasco sauce to taste
 2 **tablespoons grated lime rind**
 2 **tablespoons virgin olive oil**
 8 **escalopes salmon, about 3 ounces each**
 2 **tablespoons snipped fresh chives**

Preheat the grill or broiler.

In a medium-size saucepan, combine the stock, lime juice, garlic, and ginger. Cook over high heat until reduced to ¼ cup, about 6 minutes. Transfer to a blender, add the prickly pears, and blend until pureed. Strain through a coarse sieve (to catch the seeds; avoid crushing them) into another saucepan. Reheat the sauce to a simmer and cook until thickened enough to coat the back of

a spoon, about 4 minutes. Adjust the salt and Tabasco. Add the lime rind and reduce the heat to low.

Rub the surfaces of the salmon with the olive oil. Place on the grill or under the broiler and allow to sear, about 3 minutes. Turn the escalopes over and cook until done, approximately 3 minutes, depending on thickness.

Spoon the sauce onto warm serving plates, sprinkle with the chives, then position the salmon over the sauce. Serve.

COOKING NOTE: Remember to trim the fatty darker flesh from the salmon as this carries the oily "fishy" flavor.

MAKES 4 SERVINGS ■

Grilled Tuna with Tamarillos

This is the start of the tamarillo season, with their bright, rich, citruslike flavor, and tuna are in season through late fall. The combination is wonderful.

½ **cup orange juice**
½ **cup dry white wine**
 1 **cup heavy cream**
   Salt to taste
   Freshly ground black pepper to taste
 2 **tamarillos, husked and diced**
¼ **cup snipped fresh chives**
 4 **tuna steaks, about 6 ounces each**
 2 **tablespoons virgin olive oil**
 4 **sprigs fresh chives for garnish**

Preheat the grill or broiler.

In a medium-size saucepan, combine the orange juice and wine. Bring to a simmer over high heat and cook until reduced to $1/4$ cup, about 3 minutes. Add the cream and cook until thickened enough to coat the back of a spoon, about 10 minutes. Remove from the heat and add salt and pepper. Return to the heat, add the tamarillos, and cook for 2 minutes. Add the snipped chives and reduce the heat to low.

Rub the surfaces of the tuna steaks with the olive oil. Place on the grill or under the broiler and allow to sear, about 3 minutes. Turn the tuna over and cook until done, approximately 3 minutes, depending on the thickness. Spoon the sauce onto warm serving plates, reserving $1/4$ cup for garnish. Place the tuna steaks over the sauce on each plate. Spoon the remaining sauce over the tuna, garnish with sprigs of chives, and serve.

COOKING NOTES: Cook tuna less than most fish for it becomes quite dry when fully cooked. Tuna lends itself to medium-rare doneness because of its fine texture.

■ Tamarillos develop their flavor with heat and acids. Their bright flavor and rich, meaty texture heightens that of the tuna.

MAKES 4 SERVINGS ■

Lake Trout with Shallots and Macadamias

This is a very rewarding sauce for use with any lean fleshed fish. The macadamia nuts offer a contrasting texture with a flavor complementary to the shallots.

- 1 **cup Fish Stock (see page 65)**
- 1 **cup dry white wine**
- 1 **cup heavy cream**
- 16 **medium-size shallots, roasted (see page 62)**

Salt to taste
Freshly ground white pepper to taste
- 2 **cups all-purpose flour**
- 2 **tablespoons paprika**
- 2 **large eggs, beaten**
- 1 **cup milk**
- 4 **lake trout fillets, about 7 ounces each, skinned and boned**
- $1/2$ **cup Clarified Butter (see page 70)**
- 2 **tablespoons chopped fresh parsley**
- $1/4$ **cup macadamia nuts, toasted (see page 60) and coarsely chopped**

In a medium-size saucepan, combine the stock and wine. Cook over high heat until reduced to $1/2$ cup, about 8 minutes. Add the cream and cook until thickened enough to coat the back of a spoon, about 10 minutes. Add the shallots, cooking until warmed through, about 2 minutes. Adjust the salt and pepper. Remove from the heat.

In a medium-size bowl, sift together the flour, paprika, 1 teaspoon salt, and $3/4$ teaspoon pepper.

In another medium-size bowl, combine the eggs and milk. Drench the fillets in the mixture, shake off any excess, then dredge in the seasoned flour. Coat evenly, then shake to remove any excess.

In a large skillet over high heat, warm the butter until just about smoking. Lay in the fillets one by one and cook until golden, about 3 minutes. Turn the fillets over and cook until done, about 3 minutes. Remove to a rack or paper toweling. Repeat with remaining fillets.

Return the sauce to a simmer, then spoon onto warm serving plates, reserving the shallots. Sprinkle with the parsley and macadamia nuts. Position the fillets on the sauce and spoon the shallots over them. Serve.

COOKING NOTE: Use this sauté technique for any lean fleshed fish. Sauté ingredients in clarified butter when they are to be served with a butter or cream sauce, and in olive oil when served with salsas and vinaigrettes, to keep the flavors of the cooking fats consistent with those of the sauce.

MAKES 4 SERVINGS ■

Swordfish with Beaujolais Sauce

The third Thursday of November at 12:01 A.M. is the release of the Nouveau Beaujolais throughout the world. Beaujolais is traditionally the first wine released of the current vintage year. It is bright, refreshing, and wonderful and is the first celebration of the harvest. The only Beaujolais released at this time are Beaujolais Nouveau and Beaujolais Villages Nouveau. The larger Grands Crus Beaujolais are released later. This dish matches the Beaujolais wine in flavor to celebrate its release. Cook with the Beaujolais Nouveau and drink the Beaujolais Villages.

1 **large leek, trimmed (reserve green trimmings for sauce)**
5 **tablespoons virgin olive oil**
1 **cup Fish Stock (see page 65)**
1 **cup Beaujolais Nouveau**
¼ **cup snipped fresh chives, cut 2 inches long, for garnish**
12 **tablespoons (1½ sticks) unsalted butter, at room temperature**
   Salt to taste
   Freshly ground white pepper to taste
2 **tablespoons snipped fresh chives**
4 **swordfish steaks, about 7 ounces each, trimmed of skin and fat (see note below)**

Preheat the grill or broiler.

Blanch the leek in boiling salted water until tender, about 8 minutes; test by inserting a skewer. Remove to paper toweling to drain. Dry well.

Rub the leek with 1 tablespoon of the olive oil, then place on the grill and cook until grill marks appear on the leek, about 3 minutes. Turn over and finish cooking, about 3 minutes. Remove from the heat and julienne cut.

In a medium-size saucepan, combine the stock, Beaujolais, and leek trimmings and cook over high heat until reduced to ½ cup, about 8 minutes. Strain through a fine sieve into another saucepan and return to a boil.

In a small pan over medium-high, heat 2 tablespoons

of the olive oil until hot. Add the long chive garnishes and cook until crisped, about 1 minute. Immediately pour through a strainer to collect the chives. Transfer to paper toweling to drain.

Whisk the butter into the Beaujolais reduction, one tablespoon at a time, and cook until thickened enough to coat the back of a spoon, about 4 minutes. Adjust the salt and pepper. Add the leek julienne and snipped chives. Reduce the heat to low.

Rub the surfaces of the swordfish with the remaining olive oil. Place on the grill or under the broiler and cook until seared, about 3 minutes. Turn over to finish, about 2 minutes, depending on the thickness of the swordfish. Position the swordfish on warm serving plates, spoon the sauce over it, garnish with the fried chives and leeks, and serve.

COOKING NOTE: Choose swordfish that has been cut into thick steaks so that during cooking more moisture is retained. If you prefer more well done fish, buy wider, thinner steaks that will cook through faster.

MAKES 4 SERVINGS ■

Shrimp Cakes with Two-Pepper Sauce

These shrimp cakes and peppers have the great flavors of the Southwest.

½ **pound sea scallops, foot removed (see note below)**
1 **large egg**
½ **pound (2 sticks) plus 1 tablespoon unsalted butter**
½ **teaspoon salt**
¼ **teaspoon freshly ground white pepper**
1 **tablespoon tomato paste**
4 **cloves garlic, roasted (see page 62) and minced**
1 **cup heavy cream**

½ pound shrimp, shelled, deveined, and cut into
    ½-inch pieces
¼ cup chopped fresh cilantro
    All-purpose flour for dusting
2 large green bell peppers, roasted,
    peeled (see page 62),
    seeded, and chopped
2 cups dry white wine
½ cup water
2 large red bell peppers, roasted, peeled,
    seeded, and chopped
4 sprigs fresh cilantro for garnish

In a food processor, puree the scallops. Add the egg and continue to puree until smooth. Refrigerate until ready to use.

With a mixer, cream together 1 stick of the butter with the salt and pepper. Gradually add the scallop puree, mixing until homogeneous. Add the tomato paste and 2 cloves of the garlic. With the mixer on slow speed, gradually add the cream until just incorporated. (Do not overwork the mousse or it will become grainy.) Fold in the shrimp and cilantro. Form into eight cakes and coat with flour. Place on a cookie sheet lined with parchment paper and refrigerate for at least 2 hours.

In a small saucepan, combine the green peppers, 1 garlic clove, 1 cup of the wine, and the water. Bring to a simmer over medium heat and cook until the peppers are tender, about 5 minutes. Transfer to a food processor and puree until smooth. Return to the saucepan. Repeat the exact procedure with the red bell peppers.

Bring each of the pepper sauces back to a simmer in separate saucepans over medium-high heat. Cook until thickened enough to coat the back of a spoon, about 5 minutes. Adjust the salt and pepper to taste. Reduce the heat to low.

In a heavy skillet, heat the remaining butter over medium-high. Add the shrimp cakes (flouring again if necessary) and cook until golden, about 3 minutes. Turn over, cover the skillet, and cook until done, about 5 minutes. Remove and drain on paper towels. Spoon the red pepper sauce onto half of the serving plate. Repeat with the green pepper sauce on the other half of the plate. Place the shrimp cakes in center, garnish with sprigs of cilantro, and serve.

VARIATION: For a spicy pepper sauce, substitute red and green poblano peppers for the mild bell varieties.

COOKING NOTES: The "foot" is the tough muscle on the side of the scallop.
■ Select the peppers by color, flavor, and heat. The roasting process will only condense and round out those flavors.

MAKES 4 SERVINGS ■

Empañadas of Shrimp

1½ cups orange juice
½ cup fresh lime juice
1 cup finely diced red onion
1 clove garlic, minced
½ pound shelled, deveined, and cooked shrimp
1 chili pepper, roasted, peeled
    (see page 62), seeded, and diced
½ cup diced scallion greens
    Salt to taste
8 Blue or Yellow Corn Tortillas,
    uncooked (see page 67)
    Corn oil for frying
1 cup Asian Pear Salsa (recipe follows)
4 sprigs fresh basil for garnish

In a medium-size saucepan, combine the orange and lime juices, onions, and garlic. Bring to a simmer over medium-high heat and cook until thickened enough to coat the back of a spoon, about 15 minutes.

In a medium-size bowl, combine the reduced juices, the shrimp, chili pepper, and scallions. (If the mixture is very wet, drain before continuing.) Add salt.

Lay the uncooked tortillas flat. Distribute the filling to the centers of each. Brush the edges of the tortilla with warm water. Fold the tortilla over the filling to form a half moon. Press the edges to seal. Refrigerate for at least 1 hour before cooking.

In a large, heavy skillet, heat 3 inches of corn oil over medium-high heat to 350°F.

Carefully slide the empañadas into the hot oil. Cook until evenly golden, about 2 minutes. Turn over and cook until done, about 2 minutes. Position two empañadas on each plate, spoon the salsa over them, garnish with the basil, and serve.

VARIATION: For a richer filling, add a soft cheese such as mozzarella or fontina.

COOKING NOTE: Remember to make a good seal at the empañada edges or it will come apart when fried. For the best results, press the tortillas thin so they are crisp when cooked. Cook the fillings until almost done, so that when the empeñadas are cooked the filling will be completely done *and* hot.

MAKES 4 SERVINGS ∎

Asian Pear Salsa

The Asian pear, or apple-pear, originates from China, and has the texture of an apple and mild flavor of a pear. There are more than thirty varieties of Asian pears under cultivation in the United States. My two favorites are the Nijisseiki, a large, smooth-skinned green-yellow variety, and the Kosui, a dull green-gold variety of medium size.

 2 **ripe Asian pears, diced**
 ½ **cup virgin olive oil**
 1 **teaspoon ground cumin**
 1 **large red bell pepper, roasted, peeled (see page 62), seeded, and diced**
 ¼ **cup fresh lime juice**
 ¼ **cup chopped lemon grass (or substitute chopped sorrel)**
    Salt to taste
    Freshly ground black pepper to taste

In a medium-size skillet, heat 2 tablespoons of the olive oil over high heat. Add the Asian pears and cook until browned on the edges, about 3 minutes. Sprinkle with the cumin and cook for 2 more minutes. Add the pepper and toss. Transfer to a bowl and allow to cool to room temperature.

Add the remaining olive oil, the lime juice, lemon grass, salt, and pepper. Refrigerate until ready to serve or up to 1 week.

COOKING NOTE: It is very important to cook the cumin to develop its flavor as well as eliminate the chalky texture from the raw ground seed. The same technique should be applied to most spices, especially curry powder.

MAKES 2 CUPS ∎

Slow Baked Lobster with Tomatoes

The moistest dry-heat lobster around. Lobsters molt or shed their shells in the spring. After molting, the shell is soft when squeezed and the meat stringy. For this reason, one must be very selective during the summer and early fall months, avoiding any late molters. Select hard-shelled lobsters by squeezing the shell; hard shells do not move when pressure is applied. The largest landings of lobsters take place in October.

 1 **large red bell pepper, roasted, peeled (see page 62), seeded, and diced**
 ¼ **cup minced oil-packed sundried tomatoes**
 ½ **cup dry white wine**
 ½ **cup cider vinegar (or substitute white wine vinegar)**
 12 **tablespoons (1½ sticks) unsalted butter**
 1 **large tomato, roasted (see page 163), seeded, and diced**
    Salt to taste

Freshly ground white pepper to taste
¼ cup plain dry bread crumbs
2 tablespoons chopped fresh basil
2 tablespoons snipped fresh chives
2 tablespoons chopped fresh parsley
Four 1¼- to 1½-pound hard-shelled lobsters,
halved lengthwise and cleaned
Sprigs fresh basil for garnish

Preheat the oven to 350°F.

In a small saucepan, combine the pepper, sundried tomatoes, wine, and vinegar over medium-high heat. Bring to a simmer and cook until the sauce is thickened enough to coat the back of a spoon, about 10 minutes. Whisk in 1 stick of the butter, tablespoon by tablespoon, cooking until thickened. Add the tomato and allow to heat through, about 2 minutes. Add salt and pepper. Remove from the heat.

Melt the remaining butter. Set aside.

In a small bowl, combine the bread crumbs, basil, chives, and parsley. Mix well.

Arrange the lobsters cut-side up on a baking pan. Dust with the bread crumb mixture. Spoon 1½ teaspoons of the melted butter over each lobster half. Place on the lower rack of the oven and cook until done, about 10 minutes. Transfer to warm serving plates. Return the sauce to a simmer, then spoon over the lobsters, garnish with sprigs of basil, and serve.

MAKES 4 SERVINGS ■

Duck Breasts with Figs

The ducks are a natural for the figs and pineau.

2 cups Poultry or Veal Stock (see page
63 or 64)
1 cup orange juice
½ cup fresh lemon juice

1 cup dry white wine
Salt to taste
Freshly ground black pepper
¼ cup Pineau des Charentes (see note below)
4 tablespoons (½ stick) unsalted butter
4 boneless duck breasts, about 10 ounces each
12 medium-size figs, almost quartered to form
stars
2 tablespoons pistachios, toasted (see page 60)
and chopped
2 tablespoons snipped fresh chives

Preheat the oven to 425°F.

In a medium-size saucepan over high heat, bring the stock, juices, and wine to a simmer. Cook until thickened enough to coat the back of a spoon, about 15 minutes. Adjust the salt and pepper, then add the pineau and reduce until thick enough to coat the back of a spoon, about 6 minutes. Whisk in the butter, tablespoon by tablespoon. Remove from the heat.

Place the duck breasts skin-side up on a broiler pan. Place on the lower rack of the oven and cook until medium-rare to medium, about 20 minutes. Remove from the oven and allow to rest for 3 minutes.

Return the sauce to a simmer and spoon the sauce onto warm serving plates. Arrange three figs per plate on the sauce. Remove the skin from the duck breast, then slice each breast on an angle into four or five pieces. Lay in a fan shape across the sauce and sprinkle with the pistachios and chives. Serve.

COOKING NOTE: Pineau des Charentes is an aperitif made from new wine whose fermentation has been stopped with cognac. Substitute with 2 tablespoons white wine and 2 tablespoons cognac.

MAKES 4 SERVINGS ■

Breast of Chicken with Apples and Mushrooms

The spinach and radicchio under the chicken offer a silky and slightly bitter contrast to the crunchy, sweet apples.

¼ **pound (1 stick) unsalted butter**
2 **Granny Smith apples, peeled, cored, and sliced**
1 **pound chanterelles or other wild mushrooms (or substitute white or brown mushrooms)**
4 **boneless chicken breasts, about 8 ounces each**
2 **cups Poultry or Veal Stock (see page 63 or 64)**
1 **cup apple cider**
2 **tablespoons Calvados or brandy**
  Salt to taste
  Freshly grated nutmeg to taste
  Freshly ground black pepper to taste
¼ **cup snipped fresh chives**
1 **pound baby spinach, stemmed**
1 **head radicchio, trimmed and julienned (see note below)**

In a medium-size skillet over high heat, cook 3 tablespoons of the butter until just about smoking. Add the apples and cook until browned on both sides, about 3 minutes. Add the mushrooms and sauté until browned, about 5 minutes.

In another medium-size skillet, heat 2 more tablespoons of the butter over medium-high heat. Add the chicken, skin-side down, and cook until well browned, about 3 minutes. Turn over and cook until the other side is browned, about 3 minutes. Add the stock, cider, and apple-mushroom mixture. Reduce the heat to low, cover, and let simmer for 10 minutes. Remove the lid and return to a boil, cooking until the liquids thicken enough to coat the back of a spoon, about 3 minutes. Add the Calvados and season with the salt, nutmeg, and a generous amount of black pepper. Remove from the heat and add the chives.

In a medium-size skillet, cook the spinach in the remaining butter over high heat until wilted, about 2 min-utes. Add the radicchio to warm. Season with salt, nutmeg, and pepper.

Position the spinach and radicchio in the center of warm serving plates. Spoon on the sauce, then place the chicken breasts on top. Spoon any remaining sauce over the chicken and serve.

VARIATIONS: You can substitute pheasant or veal chops teamed up with other fruits, such as pears, Asian pears, or even lemons. Adjust the herbs and spirits according to your personal taste preferences.

COOKING NOTES: Avoid soaking radicchio in water as it will turn more bitter and lose flavor.
■ This basic sautéing technique can be used on all poultry and smaller veal cuts. The cooking process allows the flavors to blend and create wonderful marriages. Remember to brown the poultry well to sear in the juices.

MAKES 4 SERVINGS ■

Chicken Empanadas

1 **small red onion, diced**
2 **tablespoons virgin olive oil**
1 **pound chicken, grilled and diced into ½-inch pieces**
½ **cup grated jarlsberg or smoked gouda cheese**
¼ **cup hot chunky prepared salsa**
  Salt to taste
  Freshly ground black pepper to taste
8 **Blue or Yellow Corn Tortillas, uncooked (see page 67)**

Corn oil for frying
¾ **cup Pumpkin–Blue Cheese Sauce (recipe follows)**
4 **sprigs fresh parsley for garnish**

In a medium-size skillet over medium-high heat, sauté the onion in the olive oil until tender. Drain. Transfer to a medium-size bowl and add the chicken, cheese, and salsa. Adjust the salt and pepper.

Lay the uncooked tortillas flat. Distribute the filling to the center of each. Brush the edges of the tortilla with warm water, then fold the tortilla over the filling to form a half moon. Press the edges to seal. Refrigerate for at least 1 hour before cooking.

In a large, heavy skillet, heat 3 inches of corn oil over medium-high heat to 350°F. Carefully slide the empañadas into the hot oil. Cook until golden, about 2 minutes, then turn over and cook until done, about 2 minutes.

Position two empañadas on each plate, spoon the sauce over, and garnish with the parsley.

COOKING NOTE: Remember to make a good seal at the empañada edges or it will come apart when fried.

MAKES 4 SERVINGS ∎

Pumpkin–Blue Cheese Sauce

Try it. You will be amazed how well it goes with the empañadas. It also goes great with smoked meats.

2 **large egg yolks**
1 **tablespoon Dijon mustard**
1 **tablespoon fresh lemon juice**
½ **cup corn oil**
  Salt to taste
  Freshly ground white pepper to taste
½ **cup pumpkin puree (see note on page 170)**
½ **cup crumbled blue cheese**

With a mixer, combine the egg yolks, mustard, and lemon juice. On high speed, gradually add the corn oil in a steady stream. Adjust the salt and pepper. Mix in the pumpkin puree and cheese. Refrigerate until ready to serve or up to 5 days.

MAKES 1½ CUPS ∎

Grilled Squab with Dried Cranberries

4 **squabs, boned except for drumsticks and wings (your butcher can do this)**
1 **teaspoon salt**
1 **teaspoon freshly ground black pepper**
½ **bunch fresh thyme, coarsely chopped**
2½ **cups virgin olive oil**
¼ **cup balsamic vinegar**
¼ **cup red wine vinegar**
¼ **pound dried cranberries (see note below)**
1 **head baby red oakleaf lettuce, trimmed**
1 **head mizuni (baby mustard greens), trimmed**
1 **head baby frisée lettuce, trimmed**
2 **tablespoons fresh tarragon leaves**
1 **large leek, trimmed and blanched (see page 62)**
4 **tablespoons (½ stick) unsalted butter**
1 **pound chanterelles and other wild mushrooms**

In a shallow pan or bowl, sprinkle the squabs with the salt and pepper. Add the thyme and 2 cups of the olive oil until evenly coated. Marinate under refrigeration for approximately 24 hours.

In a small saucepan, combine the vinegars. Bring to a short boil, then add the cranberries and remove from the heat. Allow to soften for at least 2 hours.

Preheat the grill or broiler.

Pour the cranberries and vinegars into a blender and puree until smooth. Add the remaining olive oil slowly with the blender running to emulsify the sauce. Add a little water as necessary to thin. Adjust the salt and pepper to taste. Reserve at room temperature.

Arrange the greens on serving plates. Sprinkle the tarragon across them.

Place the leek on the grill or under the broiler and cook until lightly browned. Remove and cut on the bias into bite-size pieces.

In a medium-size sauté pan, melt the butter until browned over high heat. Add the chanterelles and other mushrooms and sauté until well seared, about 5 minutes. Adjust the salt and pepper to taste. Distribute the mushrooms and the leek across the greens.

When the grill or broiler is very hot, place the squabs skin-side toward the heat and allow to sear but not burn. Cook the squabs until the skin is crisp and golden, about 5 minutes. Turn over and finish to your desired doneness, about 1 minute for medium-rare. Remove from the grill.

Spoon a little sauce over the greens, position the squab atop the greens and mushrooms, then spoon more sauce in a band across squab. Serve.

COOKING NOTES: The squab is an immature pigeon. The breast bone, an indication of age, is the most flexible when young, firming as the bird matures to a pigeon. The marinade is used here primarily to flavor the squab. The squabs do seem to tenderize while marinating but this tenderizing effect is actually the result of the aging process. The squabs may be marinated for up to 3 days. Grill the squab medium-rare to medium for the moistest textures; after that you will be cooking out the moisture, making the meat dry.

▪ If you can't locate dried cranberries, substitute an equal volume of Cranberry Puree as prepared on page 66. Because of their concentrated flavor, use dried cranberries as a spice rather than as fruit. The dried fruit also enhances the emulsification of the sauce, holding the oil in suspension.

MAKES 4 SERVINGS ▪

Loin of Lamb with Sweet Spiced Pecans

This recipe calls for an unusual slicing of the meat. This slice reveals different presentation opportunities worthy of the larger loin sizes. You can slice into medallions if you prefer.

½ cup pecan halves
1 teaspoon ground Szechuan pepper (or substitute ground coriander)
1 teaspoon ground cassia (see note below—or substitute ground cinnamon)
1 teaspoon freshly grated nutmeg
1 cup diced red onions
2 tablespoons virgin olive oil
½ cup balsamic vinegar
1 cup Lamb, Veal, or Poultry Stock (see page 63 or 64)
Salt to taste
Freshly ground black pepper to taste
1½ pounds loin of lamb, completely trimmed
1 papaya, peeled, quartered, seeded, then sliced into a fan
½ cup diced scallion greens

Place the pecans in a wire strainer. Rinse with cold water to moisten only. Spread the pecans across a cake rack or on parchment paper. In a small bowl, mix the spices together, then sprinkle across the pecans, turning them over and repeating until completely coated. Allow to dry at room temperature.

Preheat the oven to 400°F.

In a heavy nonstick skillet over medium-high heat, sauté the onions in 1 tablespoon of the olive oil until translucent, about 5 minutes. Add the balsamic vinegar and simmer until almost completely reduced, about 5 minutes. Puree in a food processor.

In a medium-size saucepan, bring the stock to a simmer over medium-high heat and cook until reduced by half, about 10 minutes. Add the onion puree and cook until thickened enough to coat the back of a spoon, about

5 minutes. Strain through a medium sieve into another saucepan and return the sauce to a simmer. Adjust the salt and pepper. Reduce the heat to low.

In a small, heavy ovenproof skillet, heat the remaining olive oil over high. Add the lamb and sear all the surfaces until browned, about 5 minutes. Place the skillet with the lamb in the lower third of the oven and cook until a meat thermometer inserted in the center registers 130°F (medium-rare), about 20 minutes, or until your desired temperature is reached. Remove the lamb from the skillet and allow to rest 3 minutes before carving.

Place the papaya fans in a pie tin and heat in the oven until warmed through, about 3 minutes.

Cut the loin in half. Carve each piece lengthwise into ¼-inch slices.

Position a papaya fan in the upper half of a warm plate. Spoon the sauce onto the lower half of the plate. Distribute the pecans across the sauce. Arrange the lamb slices across the sauce, top with the scallion greens, and serve.

COOKING NOTE: Cassia is the dried flower bud of the cassia tree, whose bark is sold commercially as cinnamon. Cassia buds have a pronounced flavor, much like that of "red hots" candy. Cassia can be bought in spice or specialty food stores.

MAKES 4 SERVINGS ■

Veal Scaloppine with Poblanos, Tomatillos, and Cilantro

> 1 cup Veal Stock (see page 64)
> ½ cup dry white wine
> 1 tablespoon achiote paste (see note below)
> 1 cup heavy cream
> 1 cup husked and diced tomatillos
> ½ cup roasted, peeled (see page 62), seeded, and diced poblano peppers
> ½ cup roasted, peeled, seeded, and diced red bell peppers
> Salt to taste
> Freshly ground black pepper to taste
> 2 tablespoons chopped fresh cilantro
> 1 cup all-purpose flour
> 1 tablespoon hot Hungarian paprika
> 2 tablespoons virgin olive oil
> 1½ pounds veal, thinly sliced and pounded for scaloppine (see note below)

In a small saucepan, combine the stock, wine, and achiote. Bring to a simmer over medium-high heat and cook until thickened enough to coat the back of a spoon, about 10 minutes. Strain through a sieve into another saucepan, pressing the achiote through.

Meanwhile, in another small saucepan, combine the cream and tomatillos. Bring to a simmer over medium heat and cook until reduced by half, about 10 minutes. Add to the reduced stock mixture and return to a simmer over medium heat. Add both peppers and cook until thickened enough to coat the back of a spoon, about 3 minutes. Adjust the salt and pepper. Reduce the heat to low and add the cilantro.

In a small bowl, sift together the flour and paprika.

Quickly dredge the veal in the seasoned flour and shake to remove excess. In a large skillet, heat the olive oil over high heat until just about smoking. Immediately place the veal in the hot oil and cook until well seared, about 1½ minutes. Turn the veal over to finish, about 30 seconds. Remove to paper toweling to drain. Season with salt and pepper.

Spoon half of the sauce onto warm serving plates. Position the veal slices over the sauce slightly overlapping each other. Spoon the remaining sauce over the veal. Garnish with a sprig of cilantro.

COOKING NOTES: Achiote paste is a Central American condiment made of ground annatto seed (the achiote), garlic, vinegar, salt, and sometimes chiles. The flavor is similar to rich, mild paprika. It can be found in Mexican and Spanish markets, but if you can't locate it, for 2 tablespoons achiote paste, substitute a mixture of 1 tablespoon mild Hungarian paprika, 1 tablespoon red bell pepper puree, 1 teaspoon minced garlic, and 1 teaspoon red wine vinegar. *Do not* substitute the annatto seed itself, as it has a very strong flavor.

■ Select the scaloppine from the top round of veal, which is from the leg. Slice as thin as possible. Using a meat bat, pound out the veal even thinner than the cut. I prefer a smooth meat bat over the pointed or textured one. The textured bat breaks the surface of the veal, releasing moisture and making the veal tender but dry. The real secret to great scaloppine is to cook it over very high heat for a very short period of time. The thin veal cooks almost instantly.

MAKES 4 SERVINGS ■

Grilled Beef Tenderloin with Roast Peppers and Olives

Great fall colors and grilled flavors.

1 cup Beef or Veal Stock (see page 63 or 64)
1 cup dry red wine
2 tablespoons minced roasted garlic
  (see page 62)
1 small zucchini, grilled (see page 62) and julienned
2 large red bell peppers, roasted, peeled (see page 62), seeded, and diced
  Salt to taste

Freshly ground black pepper to taste
2 tablespoons chopped fresh thyme
2 tablespoons chopped fresh parsley
4 tenderloin steaks, about 8 ounces each (see note below)
2 tablespoons virgin olive or corn oil
¼ cup pitted and finely chopped niçoise olives
4 sprigs fresh thyme for garnish

Preheat the grill or broiler.

In a large saucepan, combine the stock and wine. Bring to a simmer over medium heat and cook until reduced enough to coat the back of a spoon, about 10 minutes. Add the garlic, zucchini, and peppers. Adjust the salt and pepper, then add the thyme and parsley. Reduce the heat to low.

Rub the surfaces of the steaks with the oil. Grill or broil until well seared on the surface, about 5 minutes. Turn over and cook until you reach your desired temperature, about 7 minutes for medium-rare, depending on the thickness of the steaks.

Spoon the sauce onto warm serving plates and position the steaks in the center of it. Top each steak with 1 tablespoon of chopped olives. Garnish with a thyme sprig and serve.

COOKING NOTE: Avoid very dark colored beef for the cow may have been excited prior to termination. This raised activity depletes the muscles of their glycogen supply, resulting in less lactic acid, yielding gummy textured meat that spoils quickly.

MAKES 4 SERVINGS ■

Grilled Pork Chops and Dried Cherries

1 cup Veal Stock (see page 64)
1 cup balsamic vinegar
1 cup diced dried sour cherries (see note below)
½ cup pearl onions, roasted (see page 62)
4 tablespoons (½ stick) unsalted butter
  Salt to taste
  Freshly ground black pepper to taste
4 pork loin chops, about 10 ounces each, completely trimmed
2 tablespoons virgin olive oil
¼ cup packed fresh sage leaves, finely julienned
4 sprigs fresh sage or parsley for garnish

Preheat the grill or broiler.

In a large saucepan, combine the stock and vinegar. Bring to a simmer over medium heat and cook until reduced to 1 cup, about 6 minutes. Add the cherries and continue to simmer until thickened enough to coat the back of a spoon, about 4 minutes. Add the pearl onions, then whisk in the butter. Adjust the salt and pepper. Reduce the heat to low.

Rub the chops with the olive oil. Place them on the grill or under the broiler and cook until well seared, about 5 minutes. Turn over and cook to desired temperature or medium, about 10 minutes, depending upon the thickness of the chop.

Spoon the sauce onto warm serving plates, reserving ¼ cup. Sprinkle the sage across the sauce and position the chops on it. Spoon the remaining sauce over the chops, garnish with herb sprigs, and serve.

COOKING NOTE: The dried sour cherries are very rich in flavor. Select supple cherries, for the hard ones have been overdried. Balance any sweet fruit qualities with the acids of the vinegar to taste.

MAKES 4 SERVINGS ■

Tenderloin of Pork with Persimmons

1 cup Veal Stock (see page 64)
1 cup heavy cream
2 ripe persimmons, diced
  Salt to taste
  Freshly ground black pepper to taste
¼ cup Sercial Madeira or Marsala Solera (see note below)
2 tablespoons virgin olive oil
4 pork tenderloins, about 6 ounces each
¼ cup scallion greens, cut on an angle

Preheat oven to 400°F.

In a large saucepan, combine the stock and cream. Bring to a simmer over medium heat and cook until reduced to 1 cup, about 6 minutes. Add the persimmons and cook until thickened enough to coat the back of a spoon, about 4 minutes. Add salt and pepper. Transfer to a blender and puree until smooth. Strain through a fine sieve into another saucepan and return to a simmer over medium. Add the madeira, then reduce the heat to low.

In a medium-size ovenproof skillet, heat the oil. Add the tenderloins, and cook until browned on all sides over high heat, about 4 minutes. Transfer the skillet to the lower rack of the oven and cook until done, about 9 minutes for medium. Remove from the oven and allow to rest 2 minutes before slicing. Slice each tenderloin on an angle into five pieces. Lay the slices in a fan shape on warm serving plates and spoon the sauce over them. Sprinkle with the scallions and serve.

COOKING NOTE: Sercial Madeira is the driest of the madeiras while Marsala Solera is a bone-dry marsala. If you prefer a sweeter variety, please follow your own tastes.

MAKES 4 SERVINGS ■

Pumpkin Polenta

3 pounds pumpkin, cut into pieces
   and seeded
1 cup water
2½ cups milk
3 cups Poultry Stock (see page 63)
1 tablespoon salt
1 teaspoon freshly ground black
   pepper
1 teaspoon freshly grated nutmeg
3½ cups yellow cornmeal
¼ pound (1 stick) unsalted butter, plus
   more for sautéing

Preheat the oven to 400°F.

Place the pumpkin and water in a roasting pan on the lower rack of the oven. Bake until very well done and tender, about 1 hour; test by inserting a skewer to see if it meets with any resistance. Remove and allow to cool slightly. Scoop the meat of the pumpkin into a food processor, add ¼ cup of the milk, and puree until smooth. Reserve in a warm area.

In a large saucepan, combine the remaining milk, the stock, salt, pepper, and nutmeg. Bring to a simmer over medium-high heat, then gradually whisk in the cornmeal. Stir with a spatula or wooden spoon until the polenta is thick enough to allow the spoon to stand up in it, about 15 minutes. Add the pumpkin puree and butter. Adjust the salt and pepper.

Pour the polenta mixture into a parchment-lined 16- by 12- by 1-inch sheet pan. Smooth and level the surface, cover with plastic wrap, and refrigerate until firm, about 4 hours.

Remove the plastic wrap, and with a knife or cookie cutter, cut the polenta into desired shapes (triangles, rectangles, diamonds, moons, etc.). Invert the pan to unmold. Refrigerate until ready to cook, covering with plastic wrap if more than 1 hour.

In a nonstick skillet, heat butter (as much as is necessary to cover the bottom of the pan) over high heat. Carefully add the polenta and cook until seared, about 2

minutes. Turn over to lightly brown, about 2 minutes. Pat with paper towels, then serve immediately.

MAKES TWENTY-FOUR 2-INCH PIECES ∎

Anaheim Pepper Polenta

8 large ripe Anaheim chiles, roasted, peeled
   (see page 62), and seeded
2½ cups milk
3 cups Poultry Stock (see page 63)
1 tablespoon salt
1 teaspoon freshly ground black pepper
2 tablespoons hot Hungarian paprika
3½ cups yellow cornmeal
¼ pound (1 stick) unsalted butter, plus more for
   sautéing

Preheat the oven to 400°F.

In a food processor, puree the peppers with ¼ cup of the milk until smooth.

In a large saucepan, combine the remaining milk, the stock, salt, pepper, and paprika. Bring to a simmer over medium-high heat, then gradually whisk in the cornmeal. Stir with a spatula or wooden spoon until the polenta is thick enough to allow the spoon to stand up in it, about 15 minutes. Add the pepper puree and butter. Adjust the salt and pepper.

Pour the polenta mix into a parchment-lined 16- by 12- by 1-inch sheet pan. Smooth and level the surface, cover with plastic wrap, and refrigerate until firm, about 4 hours.

Remove the plastic wrap, and with a knife or cookie cutter, cut the polenta into desired shapes (triangles, rectangles, diamonds, moons, etc.). Invert the pan to unmold. Refrigerate until ready to cook, covering with plastic wrap if more than 1 hour.

In a nonstick skillet, heat butter (as much as is necessary to cover the bottom of the pan) over high heat.

Carefully add the polenta, and cook until seared, about 2 minutes. Turn over to lightly brown, about 2 minutes. Pat with paper towels, then serve immediately.

MAKES TWENTY-FOUR 2-INCH PIECES ■

Pepper Fritters

½ **cup half-and-half**
3 **large eggs, beaten**
1¼ **cups all-purpose flour**
½ **cup chopped scallion greens**
1 **cup roasted, peeled (see page 62),**
   seeded, and diced red bell peppers
   (or substitute pimientos)
½ **cup roasted, peeled, seeded, and diced**
   poblano peppers
1 **teaspoon salt**
¼ **teaspoon ground cayenne pepper**
1 **tablespoon hot Hungarian paprika**
   Corn oil for frying

In a medium-size bowl, combine the half-and-half and eggs, then mix in 1 cup of the flour. In a large bowl, combine the scallions and peppers. Sift the remaining flour, the salt, cayenne, and paprika over the vegetables and fold to coat. Mix in the half-and-half mixture.

Line baking sheet pans with parchment. Spoon the fritter batter into 2½-inch rounds on the parchment. (If the batter is too loose, adjust its texture with additional flour.) Freeze until firm, at least 4 hours.

Fill a large skillet with 2 inches of corn oil and heat to 350°F over high heat. Remove the fritters from the freezer, loosen from the parchment, and place directly into the oil. Cook until browned, about 2 minutes. Turn over to finish cooking, about 2 minutes. Remove to drain on paper toweling. Keep warm in a low oven until ready to serve.

MAKES EIGHTEEN 2½-INCH FRITTERS ■

Corn Fritters

4 **cups sweet corn, blanched**
   (see pages 57–58)
3 **tablespoons half-and-half**
2 **large eggs, beaten**
¾ **cup all-purpose flour**
½ **cup diced scallion greens**
½ **cup snipped fresh chives**
1 **teaspoon crushed red pepper**
1 **teaspoon salt**
   Corn oil for frying

In a food processor, puree 2 cups of the corn with the half-and-half until smooth. Strain through a medium sieve to remove the corn hulls. Blend in the eggs and ½ cup of the flour.

In a large bowl, combine the scallions, chives, red pepper, and remaining corn. Sift the remaining flour and salt over the vegetables and fold to coat. Mix in the batter.

Line baking sheet pans with parchment. Spoon the fritter batter into 2½-inch rounds on the parchment. (If the batter is too loose, adjust its texture with additional flour.) Freeze until firm, at least 4 hours.

Fill a large skillet with 2 inches of corn oil. Bring the oil to 350°F over high heat. Remove the fritters from the parchment and place directly into the oil, cooking until browned, about 2 minutes. Turn over to finish cooking, about 2 minutes. Remove to drain on paper towels. Keep warm in a low oven until ready to serve.

MAKES TWELVE 2½-INCH FRITTERS ■

Grapefruit and Pomegranate Tart

¾ cup white grapefruit juice
¾ cup pink grapefruit juice
½ cup fresh lime juice
1 cup sugar
¾ cup heavy cream
6 large eggs
3 large egg yolks
One 10-inch prebaked pastry crust (recipe follows)
1 pomegranate, juiced
Sprigs fresh mint for garnish

Preheat the oven to 375°F. To make the custard, combine the grapefruit juices, lime juice, sugar, and cream in a large bowl. Whip the eggs and two of the egg yolks together in another large bowl until foamy, then add to the juice mixture. Strain through a fine sieve.

Pour the custard into the prepared crust. Bake until almost set, about 20 minutes. Mix the pomegranate juice (about ¼ cup) and the remaining egg yolk together. Spoon across the top of the tart in a free-form pattern. Put back in the oven and bake until set, about 5 minutes. Let cool on a rack.

Garnish with the mint and serve.

COOKING NOTES: In this recipe, the acid of the grapefruit balances the sweetness of the custard.
▪ When juicing the pomegranate, you may find it easier if you roll the whole pomegranate on the counter top to crush the berries, then cut it open and collect the juice.

MAKES ONE 10-INCH TART ▪

Pastry Crust

2 cups all-purpose flour
6 tablespoons sugar
Pinch of salt
12 tablespoons (1½ sticks) unsalted butter, chilled
1 large egg, beaten

In a medium-size bowl, combine the flour, sugar, and salt. Cut in the butter until the mixture resembles fine meal. Add the egg and mix until just combined. Gather the dough into a ball, then flatten slightly. Wrap with plastic and refrigerate for at least 2 hours.

Roll out the pastry onto a lightly floured surface to a thickness of ⅛ inch. Fit into a 10-inch tart pan with removable sides. Trim the edges.

Preheat the oven to 375°F. Line the pastry crust with aluminum foil, shiny-side down. Fill with pie weights or dried beans. Bake until set, about 20 minutes. Remove the weights and foil and continue baking until crust is lightly browned, about 10 to 12 minutes.

MAKES ONE 10-INCH CRUST ▪

Apple-Calvados Bavarois

Almond oil for mold
5 cups unsweetened apple cider
2 sticks cinnamon
1 tablespoon unflavored gelatin
4 large egg yolks
¼ cup sugar
Pinch of salt

1 cup heavy cream
½ cup Calvados, plus a splash for the sauce
2 tablespoons unsalted butter
2 large greening apples, peeled, cored, and sliced
  Sprigs fresh mint for garnish

Wipe eight 6-ounce custard molds with the almond oil. Turn upside down on paper toweling until ready to fill.

In a large saucepan, combine the cider and cinnamon. Bring to a simmer over high heat and cook until reduced to 2½ cups, about 15 minutes. Strain through a fine sieve.

In a small bowl, combine 1 cup of the apple cider reduction and the gelatin. Heat in a water bath until the gelatin is dissolved.

In a medium-size saucepan, combine the egg yolks, half the sugar, the salt, and the remaining cider reduction. Warm over medium heat, stirring constantly, until thickened enough to coat the back of a spoon; *do not boil.* Remove from the heat, stir in the gelatin mixture, then strain through a fine sieve into a metal bowl.

In a large bowl, whip the cream until thickened but still fluid. Add the Calvados and whisk the mixture to a thickened consistency.

Fold the cream into the cider base. Place the bowl over an ice bath and stir constantly with a rubber spatula until heavily thickened, about 6 minutes. Immediately pour into the prepared molds. Refrigerate overnight.

To prepare the apples, heat the butter over high heat in a small skillet. Add the apples and cook until lightly browned on both sides. Add the remaining sugar and a splash of Calvados, and cook until the apples are coated with the sugar syrup.

To serve, unmold the bavarois onto serving plates and arrange the apple slices over it and on the plate. Garnish with the mint and serve.

MAKES 8 SERVINGS ■

Grilled Comice Pears with Persimmon White Chocolate Sauce

¾ cup persimmon puree (see note below)
½ cup honey
¾ cup fresh lemon juice
5 large egg yolks
1 cup half-and-half
5 ounces white chocolate, finely chopped
¼ cup heavy cream
4 large Comice pears, peeled, cored, and quartered (see note below)
¼ cup coarsely chopped unsalted pistachios
4 sprigs fresh mint for garnish

To make the sauce, combine the persimmon puree, honey, and ½ cup of the lemon juice in a medium-size saucepan. Bring to a simmer over medium heat and cook until the honey and persimmon are well blended, about 5 minutes. Remove from the heat and whisk in the egg yolks and half-and-half. Return to medium heat and stir until thick enough to coat the back of a spoon, about 6 minutes; *do not boil.* Remove from the heat, add the chocolate, and stir just until melted. Fold in the heavy cream, then refrigerate until chilled or up to 5 days.

Preheat the broiler.

Cut the pear quarters lengthwise into ¼-inch-thick slices, without cutting through the narrow ends. Brush them with the remaining lemon juice. Place on a baking sheet and broil until heated through, about 3 minutes.

To serve, spoon the sauce onto the serving plates. Fan two pear quarters across each plate, sprinkle with the pistachios, garnish with the mint, and serve.

COOKING NOTES: Pears brown when cut or peeled because of enzyme oxidation. Rubbing the exposed surfaces with lemon slows this process because the enzymes slow their activities under high-acid conditions. This is the case with most all fruits and vegetables that brown in this manner.

■ Frozen or fresh persimmon puree is available from specialty food stores. To make the puree yourself, remove the skin and pit from a very ripe persimmon. Combine in a food processor with 2 tablespoons fresh lemon juice per persimmon, pureeing until smooth. Strain through a coarse sieve. Cover with plastic and refrigerate until ready to use or up to 6 hours. Freeze to hold longer.

MAKES 8 SERVINGS ■

Dry Poached Pears with Cranberry Sauce

This recipe is great for capturing the ripe "just picked" flavors of fruits. Quince is a very special treat when prepared in this fashion.

 ¼ **cup sugar**
 1 **cup fresh cranberries**
 5 **large egg yolks**
 1¼ **cups half-and-half, scalded**
 1 **tablespoon vanilla extract**
 2 **tablespoons balsamic vinegar**
 One 3-**pound box kosher salt**
 4 **large Comice pears**
 ½ **cup pomegranate seeds**
 4 **sprigs fresh mint for garnish**

In a medium-size saucepan, combine the sugar and cranberries. Bring to a simmer over medium heat and cook until the cranberries are soft, about 30 minutes. Transfer to a blender and puree until smooth. Strain through a fine sieve into another saucepan.

Add the egg yolks, then whisk in the half-and-half and vanilla. Stir over medium heat until thick enough to coat the back of a spoon, about 6 minutes; *do not boil*. Re-

move from the heat, then stir in the vinegar. Refrigerate to cool.

Preheat oven to 425°F.

Select a medium-size ovenproof pot large enough to later accommodate all four pears. Fill the pot with all of the salt and place in the oven for 1 hour to thoroughly heat. Remove the pot from the oven. *Carefully* remove two thirds of the salt to another pan (remember, the salt is 425°F!!). Position the pears on the remaining salt so that they do not touch each other. Completely bury the pears with the salt you took out. Return the pot to the oven and cook until tender, about 15 minutes. Remove from the oven and carefully remove the salt from around one pear; test for tenderness by inserting a skewer. If ready, remove the salt from around the remaining pears and transfer them to a plate. Carefully brush any remaining salt from the pears. Allow to cool.

Spoon the sauce onto the serving plates. Position a pear in the center of the sauce. Garnish with the pomegranate seeds and mint, and serve.

VARIATIONS: You can also select a few cooked whole cranberries to use as a garnish in place of the pomegranate seeds.

You can use this dry poaching technique on a number of firmer fruits similar to the pear. The quince is perfect. Select quince that are unblemished. Allow to ripen at room temperature until the quince has a fragrant aroma and the texture is soft. Proceed with the recipe. *Glazed Dry Poached Pears:* Rub four dry poached pears with 2 tablespoons unsalted butter to lightly coat the skins. Then rub the skins with ½ cup dark brown sugar, allowing the sugar to stick to the butter. Using tongs, hold the pear over an open burner or under the broiler to heat the sugar and caramelize it onto the skin of the pear, about 2 minutes. Allow to cool, then serve with the cranberry sauce.

COOKING NOTE: Cooked in this manner, the pear is seared by the salt, causing the juices to be trapped within. The salt must be hot or the pear will be salty. For the same reason, do not allow the pear to cool in the salt. A properly cooked pear will have no taste of the salt.

MAKES 4 SERVINGS ■

Cranberry Sorbet

1 pound fresh cranberries
1 cup sugar
1 cup water
¼ cup fresh lemon juice
2 tablespoons Grand Marnier

In a large heavy saucepan, combine the cranberries, sugar, water, and lemon juice. Bring to a simmer over medium heat and cook until the fruit is soft, about 40 minutes.

Transfer to a blender and puree until smooth. Strain, then add the Grand Marnier. Process in an ice-cream maker according to the manufacturer's instructions. Transfer to a freezer container and allow to harden overnight before serving.

MAKES 2 CUPS ■

Pumpkin and Maple Sugar Crème Brûlée

2 cups heavy cream
½ cup half-and-half
10 large egg yolks
½ cup superfine sugar
1 tablespoon vanilla extract
1 cup pumpkin puree (see note on page 170)
¼ cup maple sugar

Preheat the oven to 300°F.

In a medium-size saucepan, combine the cream and half-and-half and scald over medium heat. Remove from the heat.

In a large bowl, combine the egg yolks, sugar, and vanilla, and beat rapidly with a wire whisk until light. Slowly add the hot cream and pumpkin puree while continuing to whisk until smooth. Strain through a fine sieve. Fill four custard dishes to ¼ inch below the top edge and place, in a water bath, into the lower third of the oven. Cook until lightly tanned on top and a skewer inserted in the center is hot to the touch, about 15 to 20 minutes. Remove to a cake rack and allow to cool. Cover with plastic wrap, then refrigerate for at least 8 hours before serving.

To serve, preheat the broiler. Evenly spread the maple sugar across the tops of the custards. Place the custards under the broiler and allow the tops to caramelize but not burn. Let cool for several minutes before serving.

MAKES FOUR 6-OUNCE SERVINGS ■

Pumpkin Ice Cream with Caramel Pecan Sauce

FOR THE ICE CREAM

15 large egg yolks
1 cup plus 2 tablespoons sugar
1 teaspoon vanilla extract
Pinch of salt
1 quart half-and-half, scalded
1 cup plus 2 tablespoons heavy cream, scalded
3½ cups pumpkin puree (see note on page 170)
½ cup pure maple syrup

FOR THE SAUCE

4 cups sugar
3 cups water
¼ cup fresh lemon juice
1 quart heavy cream
2 cups pecan halves

For the ice cream, combine the egg yolks, sugar, vanilla, and salt in a heavy medium-size saucepan. Whisk in the half-and-half and cream, then stir over medium-low heat until the custard thickens enough to coat the back of a spoon, about 10 minutes; *do not boil*. Remove from the heat and whisk in the pumpkin puree and syrup. Strain through a fine sieve into a large bowl, cover, and refrigerate until chilled.

Process the pumpkin mixture in an ice-cream maker according to the manufacturer's instructions, until firm. Freeze in a covered container at least 2 hours to harden.

For the sauce, cook the sugar, water, and lemon juice in a heavy medium-size saucepan over low heat, swirling the pan occasionally, until the sugar dissolves. Increase the heat to between 325° and 340°F and boil until the mixture is a rich caramel color, about 13 minutes. Remove from the heat and gradually whisk in the cream (the mixture initially will bubble up).

Return to medium-low heat and stir until the sauce thickens slightly, about 10 minutes. (The sauce can be prepared up to this step four days ahead of time and refrigerated. Rewarm it in the top of a double boiler over simmering water.) Mix in the pecan halves.

To serve, scoop the ice cream into bowls and top with the warm pecan sauce.

MAKES 8 SERVINGS ∎

Apple Tart with Cassia-Vanilla Ice Cream

This tart starts out upside down, then is turned over to right the apples on top of the puff pastry crust.

  2 **tablespoons unsalted butter**
1¼ **cups sugar**
  ¼ **cup fresh lemon juice**
  ½ **cup water**
  ½ **cup blanched, sliced almonds**
  8 **large greening apples, peeled, cored, and cut into ¼-inch slices**
  ½ **pound Puff Pastry (see page 69)**
     Cassia-Vanilla Ice Cream (recipe follows)
     Sprigs fresh mint for garnish

Preheat the oven to 400°F. Rub a 10-inch nonstick saucepan with the butter. Set aside.

In a medium-size saucepan, combine 1 cup of the sugar, the lemon juice, and water. Bring to a simmer over high heat and cook until light caramel in color, about 320°F on a candy thermometer. Add the almonds and stir to coat. Pour into the buttered saucepan.

Layer the apples over the almond-caramel sauce. Sprinkle each layer of apples with the sugar. Continue building layers of apples with the remaining sugar.

Roll out the pastry to ⅛ inch thick. Lay over the apples in the pan. Trim the pastry ½ inch from the edge of the pan. Bake on the lower rack of the oven until the pastry is golden, about 30 minutes. Remove from the oven and carefully invert onto a serving platter.

To serve, cut into slices, top with a scoop of ice cream, and garnish with the mint.

MAKES ONE 10-INCH TART ∎

Cassia-Vanilla Ice Cream

The vanilla-and-cassia combination ignites the apple tart flavors.

  ¼ **cup cassia buds (see note below)**
2½ **cups half-and-half, scalded**
  1 **cup sugar**
  8 **large egg yolks**
     Pinch of salt
  ¼ **cup vanilla extract**
  ½ **cup heavy cream**

Cook the cassia buds in a small, heavy skillet over medium-low heat until aromatic, stirring occasionally, about 4 minutes. Mix with the hot half-and-half and let cool completely.

Combine the sugar, eggs, and salt in a medium-size bowl. Stir in the half-and-half mixture, then pour into a saucepan. Stir over medium-low heat until the custard thickens enough to coat the back of a spoon, about 10 minutes; *do not boil.* Remove from the heat and whisk in the vanilla and heavy cream. Strain through a fine sieve. Cover and refrigerate until well chilled.

Transfer the custard to an ice-cream maker and process according to the manufacturer's instructions, until firm. Freeze in a covered container overnight to mellow the flavors. If frozen solid, soften slightly before serving.

COOKING NOTE: Cassia is the dried flower bud of the cassia tree, whose bark is sold commercially as cinnamon. Cassia buds have a pronounced flavor, much like that of "red hots" candy. Cassia is sold in spice and specialty food stores, in both the ground and dried whole bud forms.

MAKES 1 QUART ■

The Brujo with Dark and White Chocolates and Fire

Brujo is Spanish for sorcerer, the perfect word to convey the magical flavors of this dessert.

¼ cup sugar
6 large egg yolks
   Pinch of salt
1 teaspoon vanilla extract
1 cup half-and-half, scalded
7 ounces white chocolate, broken into
   ½-ounce bits
½ cup buttermilk
3 tablespoons tequila
½ cup unsweetened cocoa powder
1 tablespoon ground cayenne pepper
2 tablespoons mild paprika
1 batch Chocolate Tequila Ice Cream (recipe
   follows)
½ cup finely julienned, packed fresh mint for
   garnish

To make the sauce, combine the sugar, eggs, salt, and vanilla in a medium-size saucepan. Whisk in the half-and-half. Cook over medium-low heat, stirring continuously, until thickened enough to coat the back of a spoon, about 6 minutes; *do not boil.* Transfer to a bowl, add the chocolate, and stir to melt. Stir in the buttermilk and tequila, then strain through a fine sieve and chill.

In a small bowl, sift together the cocoa, cayenne, and paprika. Spoon the sauce onto the serving plates to cover the center. Scoop the ice cream into balls and roll in the cocoa mixture to just coat. Position the ice cream in the center of the sauce, sprinkle the mint over the sauce, and serve.

MAKES 6 TO 8 SERVINGS ■

Chocolate Tequila Ice Cream

12 large egg yolks
 5 tablespoons sugar
 1 teaspoon vanilla extract
   Pinch of salt
3½ cups half-and-half
 5 tablespoons honey
12 ounces extra bittersweet chocolate (do not
   use baking chocolate)
½ cup unsweetened cocoa powder, sifted
¼ cup tequila

Combine the egg yolks, sugar, vanilla, and salt in a heavy saucepan, then whisk in the half-and-half and honey. Stir over medium-low heat until the custard thickens enough to coat the back of a spoon, about 8 minutes; *do not boil.* Remove from the heat, add the chocolate, and stir until dissolved. Whisk in the cocoa and tequila, then strain through a fine sieve. Process the custard in an ice-cream maker according to the manufacturer's instructions, until firm. Freeze in a covered container until firm, at least 2 hours. If frozen solid, allow to soften slightly before serving.

MAKES 1½ QUARTS ■

FALL MENUS

Seared Scallops with Oregano
Château Woltner Chardonnay

◆

Swordfish with Beaujolais Sauce
Mixed Flavors of Polentas
Duboeuf Beaujolais Village Nouveau
Charles Shaw Gamay Beaujolais

◆

Apple Tart with Cassia-Vanilla Ice Cream

Seared Beef with Roast Peppers and Olives
Trimbach Pinot Gris

◆

Slow Baked Lobster with Tomatoes
Corn Fritters
Talbott Vineyard Chardonnay

◆

Pumpkin and Maple Sugar Crème Brûlée

Duck and Pheasant Ravioli
Far Niente Chardonnay

◆

Loin of Lamb with Sweet Spiced Pecans
Pumpkin Polenta
Knudsen Erath Pinot Noir

◆

Grapefruit and Pomegranate Tart

Grilled Mussels with Garlic and Tomatoes
William Hill Reserve Chardonnay

◆

Pepper Bisque

◆

Breast of Duck with Figs
Couscous with Wild Rice
Silver Oak Cabernet Sauvigon

◆

Dry Poached Pears with Cranberry Sauce

W I N T E R

Winter is the time for renewal. The earth lies asleep under a protective blanket of snow while preparing its seeds for their new life. The fall harvest has been plowed under to nourish the next generation. The winter winds bring rain or snow for the lakes, rivers, and streams.

Winter holds many longer maturing specialties and treasures that need time to develop. Patience in seeking them out yields wonders such as truffles, radicchio, endive, icicle pears, and exotic fruits.

Vibrant appetizers such as Crab Lumps with Cabbage and Chardonnay-Mustard Sauce, Poultry and Leek Terrine, and Onion and Lemon Vodka Tart offer new light twists on old traditions. Soups reign supreme with their full body and hearty flavors. In Spicy Black Bean or Navy Bean with radicchio, soups are elevated to new frontiers. Onions and squashes offer silky warmth and soul-satisfying depth.

Firm textured fish from the turbulent seas are paired with the bright essences of grapefruit, lime, and passion fruit. The intense, clean flavors of citrus bring their glow to the snowy season. This time of year is especially warm with the mature flavors of braised meats, reinforcing our spirits against the north winds. Veal Shanks with Fennel and

Radicchio, Deviled Lamb Shanks, and Beef Short Ribs with Celery Root will fend off winter's wildest storm. Roasts and other oven cooking fill the kitchen with warmth from the stove and scents for the spirit. These communal dishes are meant to be shared by family and friends.

The desserts of winter are full of flavor satisfaction. Pear Bread Pudding with Bourbon Sauce and Cherimoya and Banana Fritters are served warm. The exotic fruit treasures are grilled to bring forward their innermost flavors, then bathed in ginger and chocolate. To me winter has a sense of permanence. Winter regenerates my soul and spirit for the next year of growth.

Crab Lumps with Cabbage and Chardonnay-Mustard Sauce

The silky crab and crisp cabbage make a wonderful flavor contrast.

½ cup Fish Stock (see page 65)
1½ cups dry chardonnay
1 cup heavy cream
6 tablespoons (¾ stick) unsalted butter
4½ teaspoons coarse-grained prepared mustard
Salt to taste
Pinch of ground cayenne pepper
½ cup water
1 pound back fin crab lumps or crab meat, carefully picked over for shells
1 ripe avocado, peeled, quartered, and sliced into fan shapes
2 cups finely julienned red cabbage
Freshly ground white pepper to taste
2 tablespoons snipped fresh chives

In a heavy medium-size saucepan, combine the stock and 1 cup of the wine. Bring to a simmer over high heat and cook until reduced to ¼ cup, about 6 minutes. Add the cream and cook until thickened enough to coat the back of a spoon, about 10 minutes. Whisk in 2 tablespoons of the butter, then add the mustard, salt, and cayenne. Reduce the heat to low to keep warm.

In a medium-size steamer pan, combine the remaining wine and the water. Place the crab and avocado in the steamer tray, cover, bring to a simmer over medium heat, and cook until hot.

Meanwhile, in a medium-size skillet, heat the remaining butter over high heat. Add the cabbage and sauté until just limp, about 3 minutes. Add the salt and pepper. Remove to a strainer to drain.

Arrange the cabbage in a mound in the center of the serving plates. Position the avocado fans on the cabbage toward the edge of the plate. Place the crab atop the cabbage. Spoon the sauce over the crab and around the cabbage. Sprinkle with the chives and serve immediately.

VARIATION: For another combination, substitute shrimp and scallops for the crab.

COOKING NOTE: The moist heat method of steaming brings out the shellfish flavor and gently warms the avocado.

MAKES 4 SERVINGS ■

Crab, Chayote, and Papaya Salad

A great contrast of flavors and textures between the vegetables and crab.

2 large egg yolks
2 tablespoons fresh lemon juice
2 tablespoons extra-strong mustard (such as Pommery)
¾ cup corn oil
¼ cup passion fruit puree (see note below)
Salt to taste
Guinea pepper paste (see note below) or ground cayenne pepper to taste
1 pound crab meat, carefully picked over for shells
¾ cup peeled and julienned chayote, blanched (see pages 57–58, also see note below)
¾ cup roasted, peeled (see page 62), seeded, and julienned red bell pepper
¾ cup peeled, seeded, and diced papaya
12 small leaves red oakleaf lettuce
2 tablespoons chopped fresh cilantro

With a mixer on medium-high speed, combine the egg yolks, lemon juice, and mustard. Slowly add the oil in a steady stream until thickened, then add the passion fruit puree. Adjust the seasonings to just slightly hot. Reserve in the refrigerator.

In a medium-size bowl, combine the crab, chayote, pepper, and papaya. Arrange three leaves of the lettuce on each serving plate. Spoon the sauce across the plates, reserving ¼ cup for the garnish.

Mound the crab mixture in the center of each serving plate. Spoon 1 tablespoon sauce atop the crab. Sprinkle with the cilantro and serve.

COOKING NOTES: Frozen passion fruit puree is available in specialty food stores at a relatively modest price; fresh passion fruit yields only about 2 to 3 tablespoons of puree per average-size fruit and will result in greater expense.
■ Guinea pepper paste is available in Oriental markets. It is a condiment prepared from the berries of a tree related to cardamom. It's usually blended with hot peppers, vinegar, and sometimes garlic.
■ The chayote seed is edible and can be added to the salad or eaten by the chef. I prefer the latter technique for it tastes like a tender almond.

MAKES 4 SERVINGS ■

Add the shrimp and cook until opaque and firm, about 5 minutes. Season with salt and pepper. Remove to a strainer to drain. Cool the scallops and shrimp to room temperature in the refrigerator.

Transfer the scallops and shrimp to a bowl and combine with the pepper and mayonnaise. Adjust the salt and pepper. On serving plates, arrange the lettuce, then position the scallop and shrimp salad atop. Serve.

COOKING NOTES: The "foot" is a tough muscle on the side of the scallop.
■ When cooking the shellfish, keep it slightly undercooked, then remove from the heat. The stored heat energy will finish the cooking and will keep the textures silky. For best flavor and texture, bring shellfish to room temperature before mixing with mayonnaise. The shellfish can also be poached following the technique used for Chilled Poached Salmon Medallions on page 132.

MAKES 4 SERVINGS ■

Shrimp, Scallop, and Saffron Salad

    4 **tablespoons (½ stick) unsalted butter**
   ¾ **pound scallops, foot removed (see note below)**
       Salt to taste
       Freshly ground white pepper to taste
    1 **pound medium- to large-size shrimp, peeled and deveined**
    1 **large red bell pepper, roasted, peeled (see page 62), seeded, and cut into diamonds**
   ¾ **cup Orange-Saffron Mayonnaise (recipe follows)**
    2 **heads red oakleaf lettuce, trimmed**

In a large skillet, heat 2 tablespoons of the butter over medium heat. Add the scallops and cook until opaque and slightly firm, about 3 minutes. Season with salt and pepper. Remove to a strainer to drain. Add the remaining butter to the skillet and turn the heat up to medium-high.

Orange-Saffron Mayonnaise

Saffron is expensive but be generous in this sauce and you will taste the richness. This dressing is terrific on mild flavored, simply prepared shellfish.

    1 **cup orange juice**
  1½ **teaspoons saffron threads, finely chopped**
    2 **large egg yolks**
    1 **tablespoon fresh lemon juice**
   ¼ **teaspoon salt**
   ¼ **teaspoon freshly ground white pepper**
  1½ **teaspoons Dijon mustard**
   ¾ **cup corn oil**
   ¼ **cup virgin olive oil**
  4½ **teaspoons Grand Marnier**
    2 **tablespoons snipped fresh chives**

In a small saucepan over high heat, bring the orange juice to a boil. Cook until reduced to ¼ cup, about 5 minutes. Add the saffron and allow to steep for 5 minutes.

In a medium-size bowl, combine the egg yolks, lemon juice, salt, pepper, and mustard. Slowly add the oils in a steady stream while continuously whisking. As the sauce thickens, add the orange juice mixture and Grand Marnier. Add the salt and pepper, then add the chives. Refrigerate until ready to use, or up to 5 days.

MAKES 2 CUPS ■

Black Bean Ragout with Snails

- **1 cup dried black beans, soaked in water overnight and drained**
- **1 smoked ham hock**
- **4½ teaspoons Chinese fermented black beans (see note below)**
- **1 tablespoon unsalted butter**
- **¼ cup trimmed and finely julienned fennel bulb**
- **1 clove garlic, minced**
- **¼ cup prepared hot salsa**
- **4½ teaspoons red wine vinegar**
- **28 canned helix snails, drained**
- **¼ cup roasted, peeled (see page 62), seeded, and finely julienned red bell pepper**
- **Salt to taste**
- **1 tablespoon chopped fresh cilantro**
- **8 Bucheron Croutons (recipe follows)**

In a large pot, combine the black beans, ham hock, and fermented black beans. Add water to cover and bring to a boil over medium-high heat. Reduce the heat to low and simmer for 3½ to 4 hours, until the beans are tender. Remove the ham hock and discard.

In a large, heavy skillet, melt the butter over medium-high heat. Add the fennel and sauté until tender, about 4

minutes. Add the beans, garlic, salsa, and vinegar. Simmer over medium-heat for 20 minutes, then add the snails and cook until heated through, about 5 minutes. Add the peppers and allow to heat through, about 3 minutes. Then season with salt and remove from the heat.

Divide onto serving plates and sprinkle with the cilantro. Position two croutons on the plate. Serve.

COOKING NOTES: Chinese fermented black beans are rich in bean flavor and salt from the curing process. They should be used to enrich the bean flavor and as "salt" in a dish.

Select beans that are supple, not overdried. If the beans are accompanied by spices, such as ginger or citrus rind, remove and discard the spices for they are usually harder than the beans. If the beans are heavily salted, rinse them under cold running water. They are available in Oriental markets.
■ The flavors of the ragout mature when refrigerated overnight. To reheat, add a little stock or wine, return to a simmer, and cook until thickened enough to lightly coat the beans and snails.

MAKES 4 SERVINGS ■

Bucheron Croutons

- **¼ cup crumbled bucheron cheese**
- **8 thin slices French bread**

Spread the cheese on one side of the bread slices. Place on a cookie sheet and heat under a preheated broiler until golden, about 2 minutes.

Onion and Lemon Vodka Tart

A great appetizer with full flavor to chase away those winter chills.

One 11-inch Short Pastry Tart Shell (recipe follows)
- **4 tablespoons (½ stick) unsalted butter**
- **2 large onions, julienned**
- **½ cup citron vodka (or substitute regular vodka)**
- **4 large eggs**
- **½ teaspoon salt**
- **¼ teaspoon freshly ground black pepper**
- **1 tablespoon Ginger Puree (see page 66)**
- **2 tablespoons grated lemon rind**
- **2 cups half-and-half, scalded**
- **¼ cup snipped fresh chives**

Preheat the oven to 325°F.

Line the crust with aluminum foil, shiny-side down. Fill with pie weights or dried beans. Bake until set, about 30 minutes. Remove the weights and foil.

Meanwhile, in a large skillet over high heat, melt the butter. Add the onions and sauté until lightly browned, about 10 minutes. Add the vodka and cook until reduced enough to coat the onions, about 3 minutes. In a bowl, combine the eggs, salt, pepper, Ginger Puree, and lemon rind. Add the hot half-and-half, then stir in the onion mixture and chives.

Pour the onion mixture into the tart shell. Bake until the custard sets, about 40 minutes. Cool on a cake rack for 15 minutes. Cut into pie-shaped wedges and serve.

VARIATIONS: You can substitute other spirits for the vodka that have flavors that complement onions. One of my favorite variations is the Martini-Onion Tart created for one of our best customers, Mr. Minnowitz, which incorporates regular vodka with garnishes of anchovies and green olives. Have fun!

COOKING NOTES: The pastry weights or beans produce an even conduction of the heat so that the crust cooks evenly from the top as well as the bottom for the best texture, and the crust does not buckle.

■ To ensure a crisp crust, coordinate the custard preparation with the crust cooking time. The preparation should be done just as the crust finishes prebaking. Poured immediately over the crust, the hot custard and onions will cook in the shortest time, minimizing the crust's exposure to the liquid of the custard. The result will be a flaky, not soggy crust.

MAKES ONE 11-INCH TART ■

Short Pastry Tart Shell

- **1½ cups all-purpose flour**
- **¼ pound (1 stick) unsalted butter**
- **Pinch of salt**
- **1 large egg**
- **1 tablespoon grated lemon rind**
- **About ¼ cup ice water**

In a medium-size bowl, combine the flour, butter, and salt with your fingertips until the butter is broken into small pieces. Mix in the egg and lemon rind. Add as much of the water as is necessary until the pastry just sticks together. Flatten into a disc and refrigerate for at least 15 minutes. Dust the dough with flour, then roll out between sheets of parchment to a thickness of ¼ inch. Transfer to an 11-inch tart pan. Trim and finish the edges, then refrigerate at least 30 minutes before baking.

COOKING NOTE: The egg helps with the moisture resistant qualities of the crust. Delete the egg if you choose, replacing it with a little more water. The crust will be flakier if consumed immediately, but may become a little softer if the tart is held before for serving for more than 1 hour.

MAKES ONE 11-INCH TART SHELL ∎

Assorted Cheese Fritters

   3 **tablespoons unsalted butter**
  ½ **cup arborio rice**
1½ **cups hot Poultry Stock (see page 63)**
      Salt to taste
      Freshly ground white pepper to taste
  ¾ **cup grated fontinella cheese**
  ¼ **cup crumbled blue cheese**
  ¼ **cup crumbled bucheron cheese**
      Corn oil for frying
   1 **large egg**
  ½ **cup milk**
   1 **cup all-purpose flour**
1¼ **cups Spinach-Parsley Sauce (recipe follows)**
   4 **sprigs fresh mint for garnish**

In a heavy, medium-size saucepan over high heat, melt the butter. Add the rice, stirring continuously, and cook until hot, about 2 minutes. Add ½ cup of the stock and simmer until it is absorbed, about 5 minutes. Repeat the stock addition twice, cooking until the rice is creamy and all stock is used, about 10 minutes. Season with salt and pepper. Remove to a bowl and refrigerate until chilled.

Combine the cold rice and ½ cup of the fontinella. Divide the rice into twelve parts, flattening each into 3-inch circles on wax paper. Divide the remaining fontinella between the centers of four of the rice circles. Form the rice around the cheese into a ball. Repeat the

procedure with the blue and bucheron cheeses, keeping each flavor of cheese separate for later identification. Reserve in the refrigerator.

Fill a large, heavy skillet with 3 inches of corn oil and heat to 350°F over high heat.

In a small bowl, combine the egg and milk. Place the flour in another bowl.

Roll one flavor cheese fritters in the egg wash, then in the flour to coat. Slip them into the skillet and turn frequently until golden, about 5 minutes. Drain on paper towels. Keep warm in a low oven. Repeat with remaining flavors of cheese fritters.

To serve, spoon Spinach Parsley Sauce onto the serving plates and place one of each cheese flavor fritter atop the sauce. Garnish with the mint and serve.

VARIATIONS: You can substitute any cheese or spice in the rice and fillings with great success. Always a hit with cocktails.

COOKING NOTE: Cook the rice a little more rather than keeping too firm; it will allow you to form the balls more easily.

MAKES 4 SERVINGS ∎

Spinach-Parsley Sauce

   2 **large egg yolks**
   1 **tablespoon Dijon mustard**
   1 **tablespoon fresh lemon juice**
   1 **cup spinach, blanched for 1 minute in boiling water and drained**
   1 **cup fresh parsley, blanched for 1 minute in boiling water and drained**
  ½ **cup corn oil**
      Salt to taste
      Freshly ground white pepper to taste
      Freshly grated nutmeg to taste

In a food processor, combine the egg yolks, mustard, and lemon juice. Add the spinach and parsley and puree until smooth. Gradually add the corn oil in a steady stream. Adjust the salt, pepper, and nutmeg to taste. Refrigerate until ready to serve or up to 3 days.

MAKES 1 1/2 CUPS ∎

Poultry and Leek Terrine

2 **tablespoons virgin olive oil**
1 **cup morel mushroom pieces (or substitute dried rehydrated morels or wild mushrooms of your choice)**
14 **ounces trimmed leg of veal, cut into 1/2-inch cubes**
14 **ounces skinless chicken meat, cut into 1/2-inch cubes**
12 **ounces pork fatback, cut into 1/2-inch cubes**
1 **cup shallots, roasted (see page 62)**
1 **cup leeks, coarse leaves peeled, roasted, and cut into 1-inch pieces**
6 **large eggs, lightly beaten**
1/4 **cup waterpacked green peppercorns, drained and minced**
1/2 **cup Pineau des Charentes (see note below)**
1/2 **cup pistachios, toasted (see page 60)**
1/2 **cup snipped fresh chives**
1/2 **cup chopped fresh tarragon**
2 **teaspoons salt**
1 **teaspoon freshly ground white pepper**
1 **teaspoon Quatre Épices (see page 66)**
1/4 **cup plain dry bread crumbs**
Sprigs of fresh herbs
French bread toast
Lentil and Radish Salad (recipe follows)

In medium-size nonstick skillet, heat the olive oil over medium-high heat until just about smoking. Add the mushrooms and cook, while occasionally stirring, until browned, about 5 minutes. Remove to a plate and let cool to room temperature. In a large bowl, combine the veal, chicken, fatback, 1/2 cup of the shallots, and 1/2 cup of the leeks. Force the mixture through the large disc of a meat grinder. Mix in the eggs, then force again through the medium disc of the meat grinder. Fold in the remaining shallots and leeks, the peppercorns, Pineau des Charentes, mushrooms, pistachios, chives, tarragon, salt, pepper, Quatre Épices, and bread crumbs. Pinch off a small piece of the mixture and fry until cooked through. Taste, then season the mixture with salt and pepper as necessary.

Preheat the oven to 375°F. Spoon the mixture into an 11 by 3 1/2-inch terrine, smoothing the surface. Cover with aluminum foil, shiny-side down. Place the terrine in a large roasting pan and add hot water to the pan until it comes halfway up the sides of the terrine. Bake for 45 minutes.

Remove the foil and continue cooking until a skewer inserted in the center comes out hot, about 45 minutes. Place the terrine on a rack over a cookie sheet. Top with another pan filled with 2 pounds of weight (use food cans). Cool to room temperature, then remove the top pan. Cover the terrine with plastic wrap and refrigerate overnight. (Can be prepared 4 days ahead.)

To unmold, run a knife between the meat and pan. Invert onto a platter. Cut the terrine into 1/2-inch slices (an electric knife works best). Arrange the slices on a platter and garnish with herb sprigs.

Serve with toast and lentil salad.

COOKING NOTES: Pineau des Charentes is an aperitif made from new wine whose fermentation has been stopped with cognac. Substitute with a mixture made from 1/4 cup white wine and 1/4 cup cognac.

∎ For the best texture, keep the meats well chilled so that the fat stays combined. It will be the easiest to handle during this stage. When shaping the terrine, dip your hands in cold water; this will prevent it from sticking to your hands.

MAKES 8 TO 10 SERVINGS ∎

Lentil and Radish Salad

The earthy flavor of the lentils makes a great contrast to the crisp, spicy bite of the radish.

   1 **cup dried lentils, soaked in water overnight and drained (see note below)**
   1 **large onion, quartered**
 ¼ **cup red wine vinegar**
   1 **teaspoon salt**
 ½ **teaspoon freshly ground black pepper**
 ½ **cup virgin olive oil**
   2 **tablespoons snipped fresh chives**
 ½ **cup sliced red radishes (see note below)**

In a medium-size saucepan, combine the lentils and onion, then cover with salted water. Bring to a boil over medium-high heat, then reduce the heat to low and simmer until the lentils are tender, about 30 minutes. Remove the onion and discard. Drain and cool.

   In a medium-size bowl, combine the lentils, vinegar, salt, pepper, and olive oil. Add the chives and radishes. Adjust the salt and pepper to taste, and serve.

COOKING NOTES: Lentils have been cultivated since 7000 B.C. A number of colors and flavors are available so you can mix and match them for wild effects. Select colored lentils of about the same size so they cook in the same amount of time.

■ The smallest radishes have the most spice. The spicy flavor comes from the skin and the smallest radishes have proportionally more skin to meat. You can also slice off and use only the skins for more red color and spicy flavor. For the hottest radish flavor, try black radishes grated or diced into the salad. The black radish can be pungent like horseradish. Whatever the type, select firm radishes with deep color and unblemished skin. The more vinegar you add, the hotter the radish flavor will be. The vinegar heightens the heat on our palates for more heat and less burn.

MAKES 4 SERVINGS ■

Crispy Gratin of Sweet Potatoes and Artichokes

This crispy gratin with mousse of sweet potatoes is very untraditional but makes a wonderful appetizer or side dish. It is worth the time to make.

   1 **large sweet potato, Louisiana Orange yam variety if possible**
   2 **cloves garlic**
 ½ **cup balsamic vinegar**
   1 **teaspoon salt**
 ¼ **cup roasted, peeled (see page 62), seeded, and diced poblano peppers**
 ½ **cup roasted, peeled, seeded, and diced red bell peppers**
 ¼ **cup blanched (see pages 57–58), trimmed and diced artichokes**
   2 **tablespoons finely diced red onion**
   2 **tablespoons snipped fresh chives**
   2 **tablespoons chopped fresh parsley**
 ½ **cup virgin olive oil**
   2 **large potatoes, about 2 pounds, peeled**
   9 **tablespoons unsalted butter**
 ½ **cup water**
   1 **teaspoon achiote paste (see note below—or substitute paprika)**
      Salt and freshly ground black pepper to taste
 ¼ **cup finely grated Parmesan cheese**

Preheat the oven to 400°F.

   Place the sweet potato and garlic in an ovenproof pan and place in the lower third of the oven and cook for 1 hour. Remove to a warm area. Leave the oven on.

In a medium-size bowl, combine the vinegar and salt. Add the peppers, artichokes, onions, chives, parsley, and olive oil. Adjust the seasonings to taste. Set aside.

Slice the potatoes with a mandolin or slicer to the thickness of a potato chip. Rinse under cold water and pat dry with paper towels. Rub the inner surfaces of a 12-inch saucepan heavily with 3 tablespoons of the butter. Layer the potatoes, partially overlapping each other, to cover the bottom of the pan. Continue layering until all the potatoes are used.

Place the pan with the potatoes over high heat and cook until well browned, about 5 minutes. Turn the potatoes over or into a second pan to cook the top, first adding 3 more tablespoons of the butter to the pan. Cook until the other side is well browned, about 3 minutes. Remove from the heat, add the water, and place in the oven. Cook until the center of the potatoes is tender, as tested by inserting a skewer, and the outside is very crisp and golden, about 10 minutes. Remove from the oven and keep warm.

Scoop the flesh from the sweet potato into a food processor. Add the garlic, the remaining butter, and the achiote, and puree until smooth. Adjust the salt and pepper to taste.

Cut the potato pancake into eight pie-shaped pieces. Place the potato wedges on the serving plates and spread evenly with the puree. Top with another potato wedge and spread with the remainder of the puree. Spoon on the artichoke-pepper sauce. Garnish with a spoonful of cheese and serve.

COOKING NOTES: Achiote paste is a Central American condiment made with ground annatto seeds (the achiote), garlic, vinegar, salt, and sometimes chiles. It is found in Spanish and Mexican food stores. If you can't locate it, for 2 tablespoons of achiote paste, substitute 1 tablespoon mild Hungarian paprika, 1 tablespoon red bell pepper puree, 1 teaspoon minced garlic, and 1 teaspoon red wine vinegar. *Do not* substitute the annatto seed itself as the flavor is too strong.

▪ The potato pancakes are great served by themselves as a side dish without the puree.

MAKES 4 SERVINGS ▪

Endive, Spinach, and Orange Salad

A refreshing hearty winter salad.

¼ **cup red wine vinegar**
¾ **cup virgin olive oil**
¼ **cup snipped fresh chives**
  Salt to taste
  Coarsely ground fresh black pepper
½ **pound spinach, stemmed**
1 **small red onion, finely julienned**
3 **large blood oranges, separated into segments**
2 **large Belgian endives (see note below)**

In a small bowl, combine the vinegar, olive oil, and chives. Season with salt and pepper. In a medium-size bowl, combine the spinach, onion, and oranges. Add the dressing and toss.

Arrange the Belgian endive leaves with points outward on serving plates. Distribute the spinach mixture in the center of the endive. Serve.

VARIATIONS: You can substitute just about any type of orange but try mandarins or sevilles (bitter) for different taste sensations.

COOKING NOTE: Avoid soaking Belgian endive in water or exposing it to sunlight as both will result in bitterness.

MAKES 4 SERVINGS ▪

COOKING NOTES: Cook the beans just until tender, without losing their shape, so that when bitten into the bean is not starchy inside. Cook them in cold stock to develop the starches. Adding beans to hot stock makes them quite tough.

■ Add the radicchio and herbs at the last minute to preserve their bright colors and flavors. The taste will cook out and become dull if left in the hot soup for long. Avoid soaking radicchio in water as it will become more bitter and lose its flavor.

■ Do not add the cheese until you're ready to serve for it will become grainy if exposed to heat too long.

MAKES 16 SERVINGS ■

Navy Bean Soup

This navy bean soup is anything but plain and boring.

- **3 tablespoons unsalted butter or virgin olive oil**
- **2 cups diced shallots**
- **2 cups dried navy beans, soaked in water overnight and drained**
- **16 cups cold Poultry Stock (see page 63)**
- **1 smoked ham hock**
   Salt to taste
   Freshly ground black pepper to taste
- **½ cup balsamic vinegar**
- **4 cloves garlic, roasted (see page 62) and minced**
- **1 head radicchio, trimmed and finely julienned (see note below)**
- **½ cup snipped fresh chives**
- **½ cup chopped fresh basil**
- **½ cup grated Parmesan cheese**

In a large pot over high heat, melt the butter. Add the shallots and sauté until tender, about 3 minutes. Add the beans, stock, ham hock, salt, and pepper. Bring to a simmer, reduce the heat to medium, and cook until the beans are tender, about 3½ to 4 hours. Remove the ham hock and discard, then stir in the vinegar and garlic. Adjust the salt and pepper to taste. Remove from the heat and stir in the radicchio, chives, basil, and Parmesan. Ladle into warm bowls and serve immediately.

Spicy Black Bean Soup with Ribs and Ginger

- **3 tablespoons unsalted butter or virgin olive oil**
- **1 large red onion, diced**
- **4 cloves garlic, minced**
- **1 cup Chinese fermented black beans (see note below)**
- **16 cups cold Poultry Stock (see page 63)**
- **2 cups dried black turtle beans, soaked in water overnight and drained**
- **2 slabs baby back ribs**
   Salt to taste
   Tabasco sauce to taste
- **½ cup Ginger Puree (see page 66)**
- **1 cup Fino or other dry sherry**
- **2 cups chopped scallion greens**
- **½ cup packed fresh cilantro leaves for garnish**

In a large pot over high heat, melt the butter. Add the onions and garlic and sauté until tender, about 3 minutes. Add the Chinese black beans. Just cover with some stock, bring to a simmer over medium heat, and cook until the beans are tender, about 15 minutes. Transfer to a blender and puree in batches until smooth. Return to the pot.

Add the soaked black beans, ribs, the remaining stock, salt, and Tabasco. Return to a simmer over medium-high heat and cook until the ribs are tender, about 2 hours. Remove the ribs, pick the meat from them, dice, and set aside. Discard the bones.

Continue cooking the beans until tender, about 2 more hours. (Add water if necessary.) Add the Ginger Puree, sherry, scallions, and rib meat. Adjust the salt and pepper to taste. Garnish with the cilantro.

VARIATIONS: The ribs can also be spiced as on page 145 or with a blend of your own choosing before they are added to the soup. After they have been cooked, you can season the rib meat to complement the soup with hoisin or barbecue sauce.

COOKING NOTES: Chinese fermented black beans are rich in bean flavor and salt from the curing process. They should be used to enrich the bean flavor and as "salt" in a dish.

■ Cook the dried black beans to a silky texture, still slightly firm but silky when bitten into. Cook the beans in cold stock to develop the starches. Adding them to hot stock makes them quite tough.

MAKES 8 SERVINGS ■

Chayote and Butternut Squash Soup

This soup is great with all squashes, especially pumpkin. You can vary or eliminate the spices as you desire.

    2 chayotes, peeled
    1 large butternut squash, peeled, quartered, and
       seeded
    8 cups Poultry Stock (see page 63)
    4 tablespoons (½ stick) unsalted butter
   ¼ cup all-purpose flour
    1 cinnamon stick
   ½ teaspoon ground cardamom
    2 teaspoons ground allspice
    1 teaspoon ground coriander
   ½ teaspoon freshly grated nutmeg
   ½ cup balsamic or sherry wine vinegar
       Salt to taste
       Freshly ground black pepper to taste
    2 tablespoons chopped fresh cilantro

In a medium-size pot, combine the chayote and butternut squash with the stock. Bring to a simmer over medium heat and cook until tender, about 30 minutes. Remove the chayote and butternut and dice 2 cups of each for garnish and set aside.

In a large stock pot over low heat, heat the butter until the foam recedes. Whisk in the flour and cook for 5 minutes. Slowly add the stock while whisking to prevent lumps. Add the spices, the undiced chayote and butternut squash, and cook until thickened, at least 20 minutes. Add additional stock if the soup becomes too thick.

Transfer to a blender and puree in batches. Strain through a medium sieve, then add the vinegar. Add the salt and pepper. Add the squash and chayote garnishes and the cilantro. Serve.

COOKING NOTES: In variations using starchier vegetables, reduce or delete the flour to adjust the consistency.
■ The technique for making a common roux or flour bound soup/sauce is as follows. Heat butter until the foam recedes, whisk in flour, cooking for approximately 5 minutes for a light colored soup; add hot liquid off the heat. Return to a simmer and skim as necessary. Cook for 20 minutes, adding additional cold liquids as necessary to maintain the desired consistency. Strain.

MAKES 8 SERVINGS ■

Six-Onion Soup with Red Wine

The red wine adds depth and richness to this winter soup.

- **4 tablespoons (½ stick) unsalted butter**
- **2 large leeks, white part only, diced**
- **4 medium-size red onions, diced**
- **2 cups diced shallots**
- **¾ cup minced garlic**
- **½ cup red wine vinegar**
- **2 cups dry red wine**
- **8 cups Poultry or Vegetable Stock (see page 63 or 64)**
- **Salt to taste**
- **Freshly ground black pepper to taste**
- **1 bunch scallion greens, coarsely chopped**
- **1 cup snipped fresh chives**
- **1 cup chopped fresh parsley**

In a large pot over high heat, melt 3 tablespoons of the butter. Lightly sauté the leeks, onions, shallots, and garlic until browned, about 10 minutes. Add the vinegar and wine and cook until the liquids are reduced over the onions, about 8 minutes. Add the stock, salt, and pepper. Simmer over medium heat for 2 hours. Add the scallions, chives, and parsley, and serve.

MAKES 8 SERVINGS ■

Mako Shark with Lime and Carambola

- **1 cup fresh lime juice**
- **½ cup Fish Stock (see page 65)**
- **½ cup dry white wine**
- **2 tablespoons Ginger Puree (see page 66)**
- **1 cup heavy cream**
- **¼ cup grated lime rind**
- **2 tamarillos, husked and diced**
- **4 mako shark steaks, about 6 ounces each (or substitute blue shark)**
- **2 tablespoons virgin olive oil**
- **2 carambola, sliced into 12 pieces (see note below)**
- **¼ cup snipped fresh chives**
- **Salt to taste**
- **Freshly ground black pepper to taste**

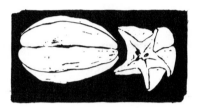

Preheat the broiler or grill.

In a medium-size saucepan, combine the lime juice, stock, and wine. Bring to a simmer over high heat and cook until reduced to ¼ cup, about 3 minutes. Add the ginger and cream and cook until thickened enough to coat the back of a spoon, about 10 minutes. Remove from the heat and strain through a fine sieve into another saucepan.

Rub the surfaces of the steaks with the olive oil. Place under the broiler or on a grill and allow to sear, about 3 minutes. Turn the shark over and cook until done, approximately 3 minutes for medium-rare to medium, depending on the thickness.

Lay the carambola slices on a pie tin. Place on the grill or under the broiler to warm, about 2 minutes.

Return the sauce to a simmer. Add the lime rind, tamarillos, chives, salt, and pepper.

Spoon the sauce onto warm serving plates, reserving ¼ cup for garnish. Place the steaks over the sauce and spoon the remaining sauce over them. Place the carambola atop the shark and serve.

COOKING NOTE: The carambola, or star fruit, is growing in popularity. There are two principal varieties in major production that find their way to your markets. The arkin is the sweetest, while the golden star has a tart flavor. There is a big difference between the flavors of the two species. I prefer the arkin for this recipe. If you select the golden star, reduce the lime juice by half to balance the tartness of the dish. Select firm supple fruit, without browned edges or points of the star, with a sweet fragrance.

MAKES 4 SERVINGS ■

Pompano with Passion–Green Peppercorn Sauce

¼ **cup dry white wine**
¼ **cup Fish Stock (see page 65)**
½ **cup heavy cream**
¼ **cup passion fruit juice**
1 **tablespoon waterpacked green peppercorns, drained**
1 **tablespoon snipped fresh chives**
  Salt to taste
2 **pompano steaks, about 6 to 8 ounces each, trimmed**
2 **tablespoons virgin olive oil**
2 **sprigs fresh chives for garnish**

Preheat the grill or broiler.

In a medium-size saucepan, combine the wine, stock, and cream over medium-high heat. Cook until reduced to ½ cup, about 5 minutes. Add the passion fruit juice and cook until thickened enough to coat the back of a spoon, about 5 minutes. Add the green peppercorns, chives, and salt. Remove to low heat.

Rub the pompano with the olive oil. Place on the grill or under the broiler and cook until seared, about 4 minutes. Turn over and cook to desired doneness, about 3 minutes for medium.

Spoon half of the sauce onto warm plates. Position

the pompano across the sauce and pour over the remaining sauce. Garnish with the chives and serve.

MAKES 2 SERVINGS ■

Swordfish with Champagne Grapes

The tiny champagne grapes are wonderful with the marc and swordfish. Champagne marc is a distillation from the leftover must and last pressing of the wine. This fruity alcohol works well with the vinegar in pickling the grapes. The grapes also make a great dessert topping when a little sugar is added while sautéing.

1 **cup Fish Stock (see page 65)**
1 **cup champagne or chardonnay**
1 **cup heavy cream**
¼ **cup Szechuan peppercorns**
  Salt to taste
  Freshly ground black pepper to taste
4 **swordfish steaks, about 7 ounces each, trimmed of skin and fat (see note below)**
2 **tablespoons virgin olive oil**
1 **tablespoon unsalted butter**
½ **cup champagne grapes**
2 **tablespoons Marc de Champagne (or substitute brandy or armagnac, if you wish)**
1 **tablespoon champagne vinegar (or substitute cider vinegar)**
½ **cup chopped fresh chervil or parsley**

Preheat the grill or broiler.

In a medium-size saucepan, combine the stock and champagne and cook over high heat until reduced to ½ cup, about 8 minutes. Add the cream and peppercorns and cook until thickened enough to coat the back of a spoon, about 6 minutes. Strain through a fine sieve into another saucepan and return to a boil over medium heat. Add the salt and pepper and reduce the heat to low.

Rub the surface of the swordfish with the olive oil. Place on the grill or under the broiler and cook until seared, about 3 minutes. Turn over to finish, about 2 minutes, depending on the thickness of the swordfish.

In a small pan, warm the butter over high heat, add the grapes, and cook until hot, about 1 minute. Add the marc and vinegar and cook until evaporated, about 1 minute. Add to the sauce. Spoon the sauce onto warm serving plates. Sprinkle with the chervil, then position the swordfish over the sauce and herbs, and serve.

COOKING NOTE: Choose swordfish that has been cut into thick steaks so that during cooking more moisture is retained. If you like more well done fish, buy wider, thinner steaks that will cook through faster.

MAKES 4 SERVINGS ■

Mahi Mahi with Grapefruit and Pine Nuts

    3 **tablespoons achiote paste (see note below)**
 ¼ **cup corn oil**
    8 **escalopes of mahi mahi, about 3 ounces each**
    2 **cups Fish Stock (see page 65)**
 ¾ **cup finely chopped scallion greens**
 ¾ **cup finely chopped fresh parsley**
    1 **tablespoon kimchee sauce (see note below)**
    1 **cup large fresh grapefruit segments with juice (see note below)**
       Salt to taste
 ½ **cup pine nuts, toasted (see page 60)**
    4 **sprigs fresh parsley for garnish**

Preheat the grill or the broiler.

In a small bowl, combine the achiote and corn oil to form a smooth paste. Rub over all the surfaces of the fish.

In a medium-size saucepan, bring the stock to a simmer over medium-high heat and cook until reduced to ¾ cup, about 8 minutes. Remove from the heat and stir in the scallions, parsley, kimchee sauce, and juice from the grapefruit. Adjust the salt.

Grill or broil the mahi mahi, searing it well, about 4 minutes. Turn over and continue cooking until done, about 4 minutes for medium-rare to medium, depending on the thickness of the fish.

Return the sauce to a boil over high heat. Add the grapefruit segments and cook until slightly thickened, about 2 minutes. Add the pine nuts.

Spoon the sauce onto warm serving plates. Position two escalopes, slightly overlapping, on the sauce, garnish with the parsley sprigs, and serve.

COOKING NOTES: Achiote paste is a Central American condiment made from ground annatto seed (the achiote), vinegar, garlic, salt, and sometimes chiles. The flavor is similar to rich, mild paprika. It is sold in Spanish and Mexican food stores. If you can't locate it, for 2 tablespoons achiote paste substitute 1 tablespoon mild Hungarian paprika, 1 tablespoon red bell pepper puree, 1 teaspoon minced garlic, and 1 teaspoon red wine vinegar. *Do not* substitute the annatto seed itself as the flavor is too strong.
■ Select Indian River grapefruit of any color for the best depth of flavor. Avoid sour grapefruits since they are cooked very little in the sauce.
■ This unusual sauce is thickened by the scallions and parsley. The kimchee sauce and pine nuts are for flavor.
■ If you can't find kimchee sauce, here's a substitute. Combine 1 tablespoon garlic powder, 1 teaspoon Ginger Puree (see page 62), 1 tablespoon Tabasco sauce, and ½ cup Hunt's chili sauce. Keep refrigerated.

MAKES 4 SERVINGS ■

Scallop and Oyster Stew

This silky stew is spiced with the riesling wine and tarragon. The shellfish is poached in the last minutes of cooking for terrific textures.

6 cups Fish Stock (see page 65)
4 tablespoon (½ stick) unsalted butter
½ cup all-purpose flour
2 cups dry riesling wine
1 cup heavy cream
2 tablespoons fresh lemon juice
1 cup shallots, roasted (see page 62)
¼ cup chopped fresh tarragon
  Salt to taste
  Freshly ground black pepper to taste
½ pound bay scallops, foot removed (see note below)
24 medium- to large-size oysters, shucked, oyster liquor strained through a fine tea strainer and reserved (see note below)

In a large saucepan, bring the stock to a boil over high heat.

In a large stock pot, over low heat, melt the butter. Whisk in the flour and cook for 5 minutes. Remove from the heat and slowly add the boiling stock while whisking to prevent lumps. Add 1¾ cups of the wine, return to a simmer over medium heat, and cook until thickened, at least 20 minutes. Skim the surface as necessary. Add additional stock if the soup becomes too thick.

Strain through a fine sieve into another pot. Return to a simmer over medium heat, add the cream, lemon juice, shallots, tarragon, and the remaining wine. Add the salt and pepper, then add the scallops, oysters, and oyster juices, and cook until the oyster edges begin to curl, about 2 minutes. Ladle into soup plates and serve immediately.

COOKING NOTES: The "foot" is the tough muscle on the side of the scallop. Sea scallops can be substituted but should be cut into ½-inch pieces so they cook in the same time period as the oysters.

■ If the oysters are shucked more than 30 minutes ahead of time, cut the tough adductor muscle. This muscle hardens after shucking and will detract from the overall smooth oyster texture.

MAKES 4 SERVINGS ■

Chicken and Cabbage with Juniper

Juniper is used in the making of gin and is a perfect seasoning for cabbage. The gin, the juniper, and the cabbage are a great combination.

¼ pound (1 stick) unsalted butter
1 small onion, julienned
1 small green cabbage, trimmed and julienned (use about 4 cups)
3 cups dry gewürztraminer wine (or substitute riesling)
1 cup Poultry Stock (see page 63)
1 roasting chicken, about 4 pounds
1 head baby bok choy, trimmed of coarse outer leaves and quartered on core
½ cup juniper berries, wrapped in cheesecloth
  Salt to taste
  Freshly ground black pepper to taste (be generous)
¼ cup English style dry gin
4 sprigs fresh parsley for garnish

Preheat the oven to 400°F.

In a large, deep, ovenproof skillet over high heat, melt half the butter. Add the onion and cabbage and sauté until softened, about 6 minutes. Add the wine and cook until reduced to 1 cup, about 10 minutes. Add the stock and bring to a boil. Add the chicken, bok choy, juniper, salt, and pepper. Cover the skillet and place on the lower rack of the oven. Cook until done, about 1 hour or until an instant meat thermometer inserted in the chicken's thigh reads 160°F and its juices run clear. Remove the skillet from the oven. Set the chicken and bok choy aside. Remove the juniper and discard. Bring the cooking liquids to a simmer over high heat and cook until thickened enough to coat the back of a spoon, about 8 minutes. Add the remaining butter, adjust the salt and pepper to taste, then stir in the gin. Remove from the heat.

Carve the chicken. Divide the cabbage and some of the sauce onto warm serving plates, place a piece of bok choy on each plate, then position the chicken over the cabbage. Spoon the remaining sauce over the chicken. Garnish with sprigs of parsley and serve.

COOKING NOTES: Gewürztraminer wine is produced in the United States, as well as Germany, France, and Northern Italy. Select a dry rather than sweet or residual sugar wine. Substitute riesling, although the gewürztraminer makes a big flavor difference.

■ The baby bok choy is perfect for providing different cabbage flavors and textures as well as creating a stunning presentation. It is found in Chinese markets.

■ The purpose of the gin in this recipe is to finish the sauce with the distilled juniper flavor.

MAKES 4 SERVINGS ■

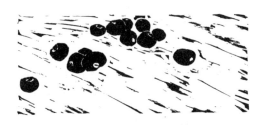

Deviled Lamb Shanks with Rosemary

 1 **cup plain dry bread crumbs**
¼ **cup dry mustard (Coleman's is my choice)**
 2 **tablespoons minced roasted (see page 62) garlic**
 1 **bunch fresh parsley, chopped**

¼ **cup grated Asiago cheese (or substitute Parmesan)**
    Tabasco sauce to taste
 4 **tablespoons (½ stick) unsalted butter**
 4 **lamb shanks, about 12 ounces each**
 2 **cups dry white wine**
 4 **cups Lamb or Veal Stock (see page 64)**
    Salt to taste
    Freshly ground black pepper to taste
½ **cup corn oil**
 4 **sprigs fresh rosemary for garnish**
 2 **cup shallots, roasted**
¼ **cup chopped fresh rosemary**

Preheat the oven to 375°F.

In a food processor, combine the bread crumbs, mustard, garlic, parsley, cheese, and Tabasco. Set aside.

In a large ovenproof skillet, melt the butter over high heat. Add the shanks and cook until browned on all sides, about 8 minutes. Add the wine and cook until reduced by half, about 5 minutes. Add the stock and bring to a boil. Add the salt and pepper. Float a sheet of aluminum foil, dull-side down, on the surface of the stock. Cover the skillet with a lid. Place on the lower rack of the oven and cook until the lamb is tender, about 1 hour and 45 minutes. The shanks are done when a skewer inserted into the thickest section of the meat can be removed without resistance.

In a small skillet over high heat, heat the corn oil to 350°F. Add the rosemary sprigs and cook until crisp, about 45 seconds. Remove with a slotted spoon or strain. Drain on paper toweling.

Remove 1½ cups of the stock and strain through a fine sieve into a small saucepan. Add the shallots. Bring to a simmer over high heat and cook until the sauce is thickened enough to coat the back of a spoon, about 6 minutes. Add salt and pepper. Add the chopped rosemary and simmer for about 6 minutes. Roll the shanks in the bread crumb mixture to coat. Place in a pie tin under a preheated broiler and cook until golden, about 3 minutes per side.

Spoon the sauce onto warm serving plates. Position the shanks over the sauce, garnish with a rosemary sprig, and serve.

COOKING NOTES: The spring lamb of last February and March is now a yearling mutton. Although most of the cuts have a stronger lamb flavor, the shanks are perfectly matured for braising. Covering the liquid with aluminum foil will prevent it from boiling and result in more tender meat. The braising technique of long, slow cooking will further tenderize the meat. The crisping of the shank with the deviled crumbs offers a contrast of textures.

▪ The fresh rosemary when fried briefly retains its green color without becoming tough. It is best to select the younger rosemary growths as they are the most tender.

MAKES 4 SERVINGS ▪

Lamb Chili with Papayas and Avocados

¼ **cup virgin olive or corn oil**
3 **pounds lamb shoulder, trimmed and tied into a roast**
2 **cups diced red onions**
2 **tablespoons minced garlic**
Rattlesnake Chili Powder to taste (see pages 66–67: 3 tablespoons = mild / 4 tablespoons = warm / 6 tablespoons = hot!)
Two **28-ounce cans Italian plum tomatoes, drained**
2 **tablespoons tomato paste**
2 **cups Lamb or Veal Stock (see page 64)**
Salt to taste
2 **papayas, peeled, seeded, and diced**
2 **ripe avocados, peeled, stoned, and diced**

¼ **cup crumbled goat cheese**
½ **cup sour cream**
½ **cup chopped fresh cilantro**

Preheat the oven to 375°F.

In a large ovenproof skillet or pot, over high heat, heat the oil until hot. Add the lamb and brown on all sides. Transfer to a warm dish and set aside. Add the onions and garlic to the oil and sauté until browned, about 4 minutes. Add the chili powder to your taste. Return the lamb to the skillet and add the tomatoes, tomato paste, and stock, and bring to a boil. Add the salt. Float a sheet of aluminum foil, dull-side down, on the surface of the stock and shoulder. Cover the skillet with a lid. Place on the lower rack of the oven and cook until tender, about 1 hour and 45 minutes. The lamb is done when a skewer inserted into the thickest section of the meat can be removed without resistance.

Remove the lamb to a cutting board and dice. Bring the braising liquids to a simmer over high heat and cook until thickened enough to coat the back of a spoon, about 10 minutes. Adjust the salt, then add the papaya, avocado, and diced meat.

In a small bowl, whisk the goat cheese and sour cream together until smooth.

Ladle the chili into bowls, spoon a dollop of the sour cream mixture onto it, top with the chopped cilantro, and serve.

COOKING NOTES: I prefer using the shoulder of lamb for stews and chilis, saving the legs for roasting. The cut is more economical as well as moister. Covering the liquid with aluminum foil prevents it from boiling and results in a more tender meat. Trim the shoulder well and braise it whole to capture the juices. Only after it cools slightly should you dice the meat for the chili, otherwise the juices will drain from the meat. I prefer the diced style chili because the meat plays a more important role.

▪ I finish the chili with ½ cup tequila when the chili is seasoned hot. The tequila rounds out the sharp hot flavors.

▪ You can use toasted papaya seeds atop the sour cream. Prepare them as shown in the Salmon Carpaccio recipe on pages 115–16.

MAKES 8 SERVINGS ▪

Veal Shank with Fennel and Radicchio

A terrific winter or summer recipe.

    4 tablespoons (½ stick) unsalted butter
    4 veal shanks, 12 to 14 ounces each, tied around
       the middle (see note below)
    3 cups dry red wine
    4 medium-size heads radicchio (see note below)
    2 large bulbs fennel, trimmed
    1 cup roasted (see page 62) shallots
    4 cups Veal Stock (see page 64), or to cover,
       depending on the size of the pot
       Salt to taste
       Freshly ground black pepper to taste
  ¼ cup chopped fresh parsley
  ¼ cup chopped fresh mint
    2 tablespoons minced garlic
    4 sprigs fresh parsley for garnish

Preheat the oven to 375°F.

In a large ovenproof skillet, melt the butter over high heat. Add the veal shanks and brown on all sides. Transfer the shanks to a warm dish and set aside. Add the wine and heads of radicchio to the skillet, still over high heat, and cook until the wine is reduced to ¾ cup, about 10 minutes. Arrange the shanks, fennel, and shallots in the skillet. Add the stock and bring to a boil. Add the salt and pepper. Float a sheet of aluminum foil, dull side down, on the surface of the stock. Cover the skillet with a lid, place on the lower rack of the oven, and cook until tender, about 1 hour and 45 minutes. The shanks are done when a skewer inserted into the thickest section of the meat can be removed without resistance.

Remove 1½ cups of the stock to a small saucepan. Bring to a simmer over high heat and cook until thickened to coat the back of a spoon, about 6 minutes. Adjust the salt and pepper.

In a small bowl, combine the parsley, mint, and garlic. Transfer the veal shanks to serving plates. Remove the string. Distribute the vegetables across the plates, spoon the reduced sauce over the shanks, and sprinkle with the herb mixture. Garnish with the parsley sprigs and serve.

COOKING NOTES: Veal shanks are a true luxury. Two servings are usually produced from each shank of the mature large veal. The shank is cut in half, yielding one smaller tall shank and one shorter wide shank. I prefer the shorter wide shank toward the knee of the veal. The veal shanks are tied around the middle of the meat to keep the meat attached to the bone during the handling.

■ Avoid soaking radicchio in water as it will become more bitter and lose its flavor.

■ Covering the liquid with aluminum foil prevents it from boiling and results in more tender meat.

MAKES 4 SERVINGS ■

Veal Chops with Vermouth and Romano

    4 tablespoons (½ stick) unsalted butter
    4 veal chops, about 10 ounces each
    2 cups shallots, roasted (see page 62)
    2 cups dry vermouth
    1 cup Veal Stock (see page 64)
       Salt to taste
       Freshly ground black pepper to taste (be
       generous)
  ½ cup chopped fresh basil
  ¼ cup snipped fresh chives
    1 cup shaved Pecorino Romano cheese
    4 sprigs fresh chives for garnish

Preheat the oven to 375°F.

In a large ovenproof skillet, melt the butter over high heat. Add the veal chops and brown on both sides, about 6 minutes. Set aside. Add the shallots and vermouth and cook until the vermouth is reduced to ½ cup, about 6 minutes. Add the stock and return to a boil.

Add the salt and pepper. Position the veal chops on the shallots. Place the skillet on the lower rack of the oven and cook until done, about 8 minutes for medium, depending on the thickness of the chop.

Remove the chops from the oven and set aside. Bring the cooking liquids to a simmer over high heat and cook until they are thickened enough to coat the back of a spoon, about 4 minutes. Stir in the basil and chives. Adjust the salt and pepper.

Transfer the veal chops to warm serving plates. Spoon the reduced sauce over. Top with the Romano cheese, garnish with the chives, and serve.

COOKING NOTES: The veal, through this method of pan roasting, will be very tender due to the old rule of high temperature to seal, low temperature to penetrate. You can apply this technique to lamb or veal chops without any other ingredients in the pan with superior results. It is a great alternative to broiling or grilling, although it does require a little more oil or butter to sear the meat in.
▪ The sharp Romano cheese is a great contrast to the sweet shallots. If you prefer, mix the Romano with milder Parmesan to your taste.

MAKES 4 SERVINGS ▪

Beef Short Ribs with Celery Root

4 tablespoons (½ stick) unsalted butter
4 beef short ribs, tied lengthwise, about 12 ounces each
1 medium-size onion, diced
1 cup malt vinegar (or substitute red wine vinegar)
2 medium-size celery roots, peeled
2 medium-size sweet potatoes, Louisiana Orange yams if possible, peeled

4 cups Beef or Veal Stock (see page 63 or 64)
   Salt to taste
   Freshly ground black pepper to taste
¼ cup prepared white horseradish
¼ cup chopped fresh parsley
4 sprigs fresh parsley for garnish

Preheat the oven to 375°F.

In a large ovenproof skillet, melt the butter over high heat. Add the short ribs and brown on all sides. Transfer to a warm plate and set aside. Add the onions and sauté until browned, about 5 minutes. Add the vinegar and cook until reduced over the onions, about 4 minutes. Return the short ribs to the skillet and add the vegetables and stock. Bring to a boil. Add the salt and pepper. Float a sheet of aluminum foil, dull-side down, on the surface of the stock. Cover the skillet with a lid, place on the lower rack of the oven, and cook until tender, about 1 hour and 45 minutes. The short ribs are done when a skewer inserted into the thickest section of the meat can be removed without resistance.

Remove 1½ cups of the stock to a small saucepan. Bring to a simmer over high heat and cook until it is thickened enough to coat the back of a spoon, about 6 minutes. Add the horseradish and parsley, then transfer to a blender. Puree until smooth, about 30 seconds. Adjust the salt and pepper.

Transfer the short ribs to serving plates. Remove the string. Cut the celery roots and yams into ¼-inch sticks and distribute around the ribs. Spoon the horseradish sauce over, garnish with parsley sprigs, and serve.

COOKING NOTES: Covering the liquid with aluminum foil prevents it from boiling and results in more tender meat.
▪ Once the horseradish has been added to the sauce, it should not be reheated extensively or the horseradish flavor will dissipate.
▪ For a fun presentation carve the celery root into shapes resembling the short-rib bones. Before serving, remove the short-rib bones and replace with the celery root "bones."

MAKES 4 SERVINGS ▪

Porterhouse with Guinness Compote

This sauce is also known as Forty Thieves Sauce.

- **2 tablespoons unsalted butter**
- **4 large onions, quartered and julienned**
- **One 10-ounce bottle Guinness stout**
- **½ cup Beef or Veal Stock (optional, see page 63 or 64)**
- **¼ cup coarse-grained prepared mustard**
- **¼ cup extra-strong Dijon mustard (such as Pommery)**
- **¼ cup snipped fresh chives**
- **Salt to taste**
- **Freshly ground black pepper to taste**
- **4 porterhouse steaks, about 24 ounces each (see note below)**
- **2 tablespoons virgin olive or corn oil**
- **4 sprigs fresh parsley for garnish**

Preheat the grill or broiler.

In a large saucepan, melt the butter over high heat. Add the onions and sauté until browned, about 8 minutes. Add the beer and stock and cook until thickened enough to coat the back of a spoon, about 12 minutes. Reduce to low heat. Stir in the mustards and chives, then add the salt and pepper.

Rub the surfaces of the steaks with the oil. Grill or broil until well seared on the surface, about 5 minutes (see note below). Turn over and cook until the meat reaches your desired temperature, about 7 minutes for medium-rare, depending on the thickness of the steaks. Season with salt and pepper.

Position the steaks on warm serving plates. Spoon the sauce over the steak or serve on the side. Garnish with the parsley and serve.

COOKING NOTES: Selection of a good porterhouse is very important. The sirloin should be twice the size of the tenderloin. The cut should be thick unless you prefer your meat well done. The marbling should be evenly dispersed throughout the sirloin if you like rich, fatty meat. Select a steak that does not have a large coarse fiber that runs through the center of the sirloin, commonly called the "spider." The spider is always tough.

■ The tenderloin cooks quicker than the sirloin. After a good sear, remove the porterhouse from the heat. Wrap the tenderloin with foil, shiny-side out, to protect the tenderloin while you continue cooking the sirloin. Shortly before reaching the desired temperature, remove the foil and finish cooking. Both pieces of meat on the porterhouse should be perfect.

MAKES 4 SERVINGS ■

Venison with Pomegranate and Tarragon

- **1 cup Veal Stock (see page 64)**
- **1 cup pomegranate juice**
- **1½ teaspoons juniper berries, crushed**
- **2 oranges, pulp only**
- **1 tablespoon black peppercorns**
- **4 venison steaks, tenderloin or sirloin, trimmed to 6 to 8 ounces each (see note below)**
- **2 tablespoons virgin olive oil**
- **4 tablespoons (½ stick) unsalted butter**
- **½ cup cleaned pomegranate seeds (see note below)**
- **2 tablespoons snipped fresh chives**
- **2 tablespoons fresh tarragon leaves**
- **2 tablespoons chopped toasted (see page 60) pistachios**
- **Sprigs of fresh tarragon for garnish**
- **4 small clusters pomegranate seeds**

Preheat the broiler or grill.

In a medium-size saucepan, combine the stock, pomegranate juice, juniper berries, orange pulp, and peppercorns. Bring to a simmer over medium-high heat and cook until reduced to ½ cup, about 15 minutes. Strain through a fine sieve.

Rub the surfaces of the steaks with the olive oil. Place on the broiler pan or grill and cook until well seared, about 5 minutes. Turn over and cook until desired doneness is reached. Check with an instant meat thermometer inserted into the center of the steak: 130°F for medium-rare. Allow to rest for 3 minutes before serving.

Return the sauce to a simmer over medium heat. Whisk in the butter 1 tablespoon at a time. Adjust the seasonings, then spoon the sauce into the center of warm serving plates. Sprinkle the pomegranate seeds, chives, tarragon, and pistachios over and around the sauce. Lay the steaks over the sauce, garnish with tarragon sprigs and pomegranate clusters, and serve.

COOKING NOTES: Avoid very dark venison for the animal may have been excited prior to its termination. This raised activity depletes the muscles of their glycogen supply, resulting in less lactic acid, yielding gummy textured meat that spoils quickly.

▪ Clean pomegranate seeds by removing all the white membrane from the red seeds. Clean seeds have a cleaner taste and better appearance.

MAKES 4 SERVINGS ▪

Pork Loin Roast with Fennel and Mâché

¾ **cup virgin olive oil**
One **3-pound pork loin, trimmed and tied for roasting**
2 **large bulbs fennel, trimmed and halved (reserve 1 cup fennel greens for garnish)**
¼ **cup fennel seeds**
1 **cup dry white wine**
2 **cups Veal Stock (see page 64)**
¼ **cup balsamic vinegar**
Salt to taste
Freshly ground black pepper to taste
4 **cups mâché, trimmed and torn apart (or substitute watercress)**
2 **tablespoons snipped fresh chives**

Preheat the oven to 375°F.

To a large ovenproof skillet over high heat, add ¼ cup of the olive oil. Add the pork and brown on all sides. Transfer the loin to a warm dish and set aside. Add the fennel, fennel seeds, and wine, and cook until the wine is reduced to ½ cup, about 4 minutes. Add the stock and return to a boil. Position the pork on the fennel and place the skillet on the lower rack of the oven and cook until done, about 1 hour or until an instant meat thermometer inserted into the thickest part of the meat reads 160°F. Add water as necessary to keep the fennel from burning on the bottom of the skillet.

Remove the pork from the oven. Set the pork and fennel aside. Bring the cooking liquids to a simmer over high heat and cook until they are thickened enough to coat the back of a spoon, about 4 minutes. Strain through a fine sieve. Whisk in the vinegar, the remaining olive oil, salt, and pepper.

Julienne the fennel. Transfer to a medium-size bowl and combine with the mâché and half of the sauce. Toss to coat and arrange on serving plates. Slice the pork and lay it over the greens. Spoon the remaining sauce on top, sprinkle with the chives, and serve.

COOKING NOTES: Pork being produced now has 50 percent less fat than it did twenty years ago. Selecting a lean cut such as the loin, trimming off the remaining fat, and roasting it produces a great meal with little of the greasiness people associate with pork.

When cooking today's leaner pork, be wary of long cooking times or else it will end up being overcooked and dry. Cook to your desired temperature, monitoring with a quick-response pocket thermometer, allowing for the stored heat energy that continues to cook the meat even after it is removed from the oven.

MAKES 4 SERVINGS ■

Preheat the oven to 350°F.

Place the sweet potatoes on the lower rack of the oven and cook until soft, about 1 to 1½ hours. Scoop the sweet potatoes out of their skins and mash into walnut-size pieces with a fork.

Combine the salt, pepper, cornstarch, baking powder, and flour. Stir in the egg yolks, eggs, and honey. Fold in the hazelnuts, sweet potatoes, and celery root.

Divide the mixture into 3-tablespoon portions and place on cookie sheets covered with wax paper. Flatten the pancakes with a fork to 2½ inches wide and ¼ inch thick. Freeze for at least 2 to 3 hours. (Can be frozen 3 days ahead.)

In a wide, deep skillet, heat 3 inches of corn oil over medium-high heat to 350°F. Fry the pancakes until golden brown, about 3 minutes. Remove to paper towels to drain. Keep warm in a low oven until ready to serve.

COOKING NOTE: Avoid the temptation to add more baking powder for lighter pancakes. The additional powder will cause more browning and an "off" chemical taste.

MAKES 36 PANCAKES ■

Celery Root and Sweet Potato Pancakes

2 large sweet potatoes (Louisiana Orange yam variety if possible)
1 teaspoon salt
½ teaspoon freshly ground white pepper
¼ cup cornstarch
1 tablespoon baking powder
¾ cup all-purpose flour
2 large egg yolks, beaten
1 large egg, beaten
1 tablespoon honey
½ cup blanched, toasted (see page 60), and chopped hazelnuts
1 medium-size celery root, peeled and grated
Corn oil for frying

Potato and Onion Pancakes

1 pound Idaho potatoes, peeled and shredded
¼ cup all-purpose flour
1 large egg, lightly beaten
¼ cup minced onions
½ teaspoon baking powder
½ teaspoon salt
¼ teaspoon freshly ground white pepper
Corn oil for frying

Rinse the potatoes under cold running water until the water is clear. Drain well. Dry with paper toweling, squeezing out the water.

In a medium-size bowl, combine the potatoes, flour,

egg, onion, baking powder, salt, and pepper.

Divide the mixture into 3-tablespoon portions and place on cookie sheets covered with wax paper. Flatten the pancakes with a fork to 2 1/2 inches wide and 1/4 inch thick and freeze for at least 2 to 3 hours. (Can be frozen 3 days ahead.)

In a wide, deep skillet, heat 3 inches of corn oil over medium-high heat to 350°F. Fry the pancakes until golden brown, about 3 minutes. Remove to paper towels to drain. Keep warm in a low oven until ready to serve.

MAKES 24 PANCAKES ■

Spinach Risotto

6 tablespoons (3/4 stick) unsalted butter
1/2 pound spinach, stemmed and finely chopped
3 cups hot Poultry Stock (see page 63)
1/2 teaspoon salt
1/4 teaspoon freshly ground white pepper
1 cup arborio rice

In a large saucepan over medium heat, melt 4 table-spoons of the butter. Add the spinach and sauté until tender. Set aside. Bring the stock to a simmer, then add the salt and pepper.

In another large saucepan, over high heat, melt the remaining 2 tablespoons of butter. Add the arborio rice and stir until coated and heated, about 3 minutes.

Reduce the heat to medium and add the hot stock, 1/2 cup at a time, to the rice, stirring until the stock is absorbed after each addition. Continue to add stock and stir until all of it is absorbed, approximately 25 minutes. Remove from the heat, stir in the spinach, and serve.

VARIATIONS: Variations of this simple risotto are endless. Choose complementary flavors in vegetables, fish, shell-fish, and meats.

MAKES 4 SERVINGS ■

Grilled Exotic Fruits

1 Asian pear, sliced
1 carambola, sliced
1 cherimoya, peeled, seeded, and cut into chunks
1 feijoa, peeled and quartered
1 guava, peeled, seeded, and diced
1 mango, peeled, seeded, and diced
1 pepino, peeled and sliced
1 cup Ginger White Chocolate Crème Anglaise (recipe follows)

Divide the fruit among four ovenproof soup plates. Heat under a preheated broiler until warm and a perfume de-velops. Serve with the sauce on top or on the side.

COOKING NOTE: Be selective in buying the exotic fruit, looking for ripe, supple fruit. Avoid bruised, soft, or shriv-eled fruit.

MAKES 4 SERVINGS ■

Ginger White Chocolate Crème Anglaise

Great over a fruit tart or any fruit, raw, grilled, or poached.

1/4 cup sugar
    Pinch of salt
2 tablespoons Ginger Puree (see page 66)
5 large egg yolks
2 tablespoons fresh lemon juice
2 tablespoons passion fruit or orange juice
1 cup half-and-half, scalded
1 tablespoon vanilla extract
5 ounces imported white chocolate

In a medium-size saucepan, combine the sugar, salt, ginger, egg yolks, and citrus juices. Whisk in the scalded half-and-half. Stir over medium heat until the sauce is thickened enough to coat the back of a spoon, about 5 minutes; *do not boil.* Remove from the heat. Add the vanilla and chocolate. Stir just until melted. Strain through a fine sieve into a metal container. Refrigerate until ready to serve or up to 1 week.

MAKES 1½ CUPS ∎

Baked Pears with Espresso-Chocolate Sauce

---

1 cup pure maple syrup (or to your taste)
5 large egg yolks
1 cup half-and-half, scalded
1 tablespoon vanilla extract
6 ounces extra bittersweet chocolate (do not use baking chocolate)
2 tablespoons instant espresso powder
½ cup pear liqueur or light rum
4 large Comice pears (see note below)
4 sprigs fresh mint for garnish

In a medium-size saucepan, combine ½ cup of the syrup and the egg yolks. Whisk in the scalded half-and-half and the vanilla. Stir over medium heat until the sauce is thickened enough to coat the back of a spoon, about 5 minutes; *do not boil.* Remove from the heat. Add the chocolate and stir just until melted. Add the espresso and whisk until dissolved. Adjust the sweetness to your taste with additional syrup. Strain through a fine sieve, then refrigerate to cool.

Preheat the oven to 375°F.

In a small bowl, combine the remaining syrup and the liqueur.

Place the four pears in a medium-size ovenproof pot large enough to accommodate them. Bake on the lower rack of the oven, basting frequently with the syrup and liqueur mixture. Cook until golden and tender, about 1 hour. Remove from the oven to a rack to cool.

Spoon the sauce onto a serving plate. Position a warm pear in the center of the sauce. Garnish with the mint and serve.

VARIATION: Make another favorite recipe for baked pears with a basting liquid of 1 cup honey and 1 cup rum. After baking and basting with this mixture, cool the pears. Combine the cooking liquids with 1 cup heavy cream and 1 cup dry white wine and simmer until the liquids are thickened enough to coat the back of a spoon. To serve, spoon the sauce over the pear and garnish with toasted poppy seeds.

COOKING NOTE: For the best results, select ripe pears for baking. If they are too firm, the flavors will not be developed. Use the firmer pears for the bread pudding recipe that follows.

MAKES 4 SERVINGS ∎

Pear Bread Pudding with Bourbon Sauce

---

3 Comice pears, peeled, cored, sliced ⅛ inch thick, and rubbed with lemon juice (see note below)
1 cup sugar
4½ teaspoons ground cinnamon
4½ teaspoons freshly grated ground nutmeg
1 cup dry red wine
2 cups milk
Pinch of salt
5 large eggs, beaten
1 teaspoon vanilla extract
½ cup dark rum
4 cups ½-inch wheat bread cubes, dried
1½ cups Bourbon Sauce (recipe follows)
6 sprigs fresh mint for garnish

Preheat the oven to 325°F.

In a medium-size saucepan, combine the pears, ½ cup of the sugar, 2¼ teaspoons each of the cinnamon and nutmeg, and the wine. Bring to a simmer over medium heat and cook until the liquid is reduced enough to coat the pears, about 45 minutes.

In another saucepan, scald the milk, then add the remaining sugar and the salt. Stir in the eggs, vanilla, rum, and remaining spices. Place the bread cubes in a 9- by 9- by 2-inch pan. Cover with the custard, pushing the cubes down to soak up the liquid. Bake in a water bath in the lower third of the oven until half set, about 20 minutes. Spoon the pears over the top. Continue baking until done, about 20 minutes. Cool on a cake rack.

Cut the warm pudding into six square pieces. Spoon the warm sauce around the pudding, garnish with mint, and serve.

VARIATIONS: Select different breads and seasonings, such as pumpkin with allspice. Each new bread and fruit will create another flavor combination.

COOKING NOTES: Select firm pears that are just beginning to turn or ripen. If the pears are sweet, reduce the sugar slightly to balance the sweetness of the compote.
■ To completely rehydrate the bread cubes, bake the custard immediately after mixing with the scalded milk.

MAKES 6 SERVINGS ■

Bourbon Sauce

Great over chocolate or apple pie.

  2 **cups sugar**
  2 **cups water**
 ¼ **cup fresh lemon juice**
  2 **cups heavy cream**
  1 **cup bourbon (my preference is Maker's Mark) or to your taste**

In a heavy medium-size saucepan, combine the sugar, water, and lemon juice. Bring to a simmer over high heat and cook to the caramel stage, 310° to 320°F on a candy thermometer. Remove from the heat. Carefully whisk in the cream; avoid boiling over. (Caution: This is very hot—do not touch or taste!) Return to a boil and cook until thickened enough to coat the back of a spoon, about 10 minutes. Remove from the heat. Allow to cool and thicken. As the sauce thickens, thin it with the bourbon, back to a sauce consistency. Serve warm. Refrigerate until ready to use or for up to 2 weeks.

COOKING NOTES: The technique above, of adding the bourbon as the sauce cools, does not evaporate the alcohol. You will consume the raw bourbon with alcohol so be aware of the normal effects and hazards of drinking alcohol.

If you prefer the taste of the bourbon without the bite, add all the bourbon as soon as the caramel is removed from the heat. The heat of the caramel will evaporate most of the alcohol. Adjust the sauce consistency with warm water or condensed milk as necessary.
■ You can reheat the sauce over boiling water in a double boiler or microwave just to warm.

MAKES 1 CUP ■

Cherimoya and Banana Fritters with Ginger Ice Cream

 ½ **cup pastry flour**
 ⅛ **teaspoon sugar**
 ⅛ **teaspoon salt**
  1 **large egg**
 ½ **cup dry white wine**
 ½ **teaspoon ground cassia (see note below, or substitute cinnamon)**
  1 **large egg white**
  1 **tablespoon sugar**

Pinch of cream of tartar
2 cherimoyas, peeled, seeded, and cut into chunks
4 bananas, cut in half lengthwise
Corn oil for frying
All-purpose flour for dusting
1 quart Ginger-Szechuan Ice Cream (recipe follows)
8 sprigs fresh mint for garnish

In a medium-size bowl, combine the flour, sugar, and salt. Mix in the egg, then the wine and cassia.

With a mixer, beat the egg white with the 1 tablespoon sugar and the cream of tartar. Fold into the batter.

Line a cookie sheet with parchment. Dip the cherimoya and bananas in the batter, coating thoroughly. Lay on the parchment and freeze until firm, at least 3 hours.

In a large skillet, heat 3 inches of oil over medium-high heat to 350°F. Working quickly, dust the frozen cherimoya and banana fritters with flour. Fry until golden brown, then turn over and fry until done, about 2 minutes each side. Drain on paper towels. Keep warm.

Scoop the ice cream into serving bowls or plates. Arrange the cherimoya and banana fritters around the ice cream. Garnish with the mint and serve.

VARIATIONS: The bananas can be substituted with plantains which have more depth of flavor. Most plantains must be quite ripe and dark in skin color before they develop their rich flavors. Do not refrigerate the plantains before they are ripe for they will not continue to ripen.

COOKING NOTES: Cassia is the dried flower bud of the cassia tree, whose bark is sold commercially as cinnamon. It has a pronounced flavor, much like that of ''red hots'' candy. You can buy it in spice or specialty food stores.

• The freezing step makes handling the fritter much less messy and also easier for party use. You can easily make the fritters fresh by adding ¼ cup more flour to the batter, which will make it slightly thicker.

MAKES 8 SERVINGS ■

Ginger-Szechuan Ice Cream

¼ cup Szechuan peppercorns (see note below)
2½ cups half-and-half, scalded
½ cup peeled and diced fresh ginger
¾ cup sugar
1 cup water
8 large egg yolks
1 teaspoon vanilla extract
Pinch of salt
½ cup heavy cream

Cook the peppercorns in a small heavy dry skillet over medium-low heat, stirring occasionally, until aromatic, about 4 minutes. Mix with the scalded half-and-half in a medium-size saucepan. Allow to cool completely.

Cook the ginger with the sugar and water in a heavy medium-size saucepan over low heat, swirling the pan occasionally, until the sugar dissolves. Bring to a simmer over medium heat and cook until the ginger is tender, about 15 minutes. Stir into the half-and-half mixture, then add the egg yolks, vanilla, and salt. Return to the saucepan. Stir over medium-low heat until the custard is thickened enough to coat the back of a spoon, about 10 minutes; *do not boil.* Remove from the heat and whisk in the heavy cream. Strain through a fine sieve. Cover and refrigerate until well chilled.

Transfer the custard to an ice-cream maker and process according to the manufacturer's instructions, until firm. Freeze in a covered container overnight to mellow the flavors. If frozen solid, soften slightly before serving.

VARIATION: The Szechuan pepper is spicy, not hot. If you prefer the heat, add crushed red peppers, by placing them in a strainer and dipping them into the cooked ice cream while it's still warm, until you have achieved your desired heat. The heat develops quickly, so be careful!

MAKES 1 QUART ■

WINTER MENUS

Crab, Chayote, and Papaya Salad
Barrow Green Chardonnay

◆

Pork Loin Roast with Fennel and Mâché
Potato and Onion Pancakes
Duckhorn Vineyards Merlot

◆

Pear Bread Pudding with Bourbon Sauce

Shrimp, Scallop, and Saffron Salad
Girard Winery Sauvignon Blanc

◆

Veal Chops with Vermouth and Romano
Spinach Risotto
Grgich Hills Cellar Chardonnay

◆

Grilled Exotic Fruits

Endive, Spinach, and Orange Salad
Preston Sauvignon Blanc

◆

Deviled Lamb Shanks with Rosemary
Celery Root and Sweet Potato Pancakes
Hacienda Cabernet Sauvignon

◆

Baked Pears with Espresso-Chocolate Sauce

Crab Lumps with Cabbage and
Chardonnay-Mustard Sauce
Fetzer Special Reserve Chardonnay

◆

Veal Shank with Fennel and Radicchio
Château Montelena Cabernet Sauvignon

◆

Cherimoya and Banana Fritters with Ginger Ice Cream

HOLIDAYS

H olidays'' is the season of the mind in celebration with nature. The most natural is
Thanksgiving, originating with the harvest. With the other holidays of Christmas,
Hanukkah, and New Year's it is a time to harvest our emotions, celebrating the
end of one year and the beginning of the next, with family, and friends. It is a time to share,
to give of oneself for others' nourishment, like nature's gifts to us. This is a time for fun
and celebration. Responsibilities should be pushed aside to enjoy the final completion of
another year and to welcome the future. Holidays shared with friends are the rewards of
a good life.

The foods of "holidays" reflect the best of the season. The techniques are more
complicated, requiring a little more time, but with fabulous results. This is food for the eye,
the mind, and the soul. The appetizers could be the entire meal with their rich and
completely satisfying flavors. It is hard to beat Buckwheat Blinis with Caviars, Oysters
Poached in Champagne, Smoked Salmon with Radishes and Capers, Lobster and Ginger
Bisque, and Scallop Chowder. The salads are masterpieces, such as Duck, Mâché, and
Radicchio or spinach and fried oysters.

The firm cold-water fish offer incredible textures for unique taste pairings. Salmon paired with sesame is stunning to the eye and crunchy on the palate. The swordfish seems to swim to meet coriander and pomegranate as a leaf or two of cilantro grace the surface. The Ragout of Lobster and Scallops with Couscous excites the palate with its spices and ingredients. Finally, endive and taro root masquerade as silky and crunchy noodles to complement the glory of sea scallops.

Poultry are plump from the long bountiful fall. They are blended with the best of late fall and early winter for special results. Glorious turkey glazed with maple and Calvados or spiced with pears and black pepper feeds large family gatherings. Stuffings are blended with wild mushrooms and pumpkin bread to redefine the traditional.

Meats also take the larger scale in their splendor as racks and prime cuts. This is the time of year to splurge on those tender cuts, served with robust sauces of Campari, red wine, and herbs, and seasonings of hazelnuts, chiles, and mustards.

With the desserts of the holidays, your guests will be stunned by the many forms chocolate can take, most spectacularly as ravioli and lasagne. Cake batters are sautéed as playful blini and served with the richest of chocolate ice creams. Fruits lead the crusade and raise hot soufflés beyond logic.

Holidays are food scents, tastes, and memories with the most important spices of all, laughter and friendship. When laughter and friendships are mixed with great food the experience will create memories for a lifetime!

Oysters Poached in Champagne

These are the silkiest oysters around.

- ¼ pound (1 stick) unsalted butter
- ½ cup sliced shallots
- ¾ cup brut champagne (see note below) or dry white wine
- ½ cup clam juice
- ¾ cup heavy cream
- 20 oysters, scrubbed and shucked (save lower half of shell)
  Seaweed to cover serving plates
  Salt to taste
  Freshly ground white pepper to taste
- ¼ cup snipped fresh chives

Preheat the oven to 300°F.

In a medium-size saucepan, melt 2 tablespoons of the butter over high heat. Add the shallots and sauté until tender, about 3 minutes. Add ½ cup of the champagne and the clam juice and cook until reduced by half, about 15 minutes. Add the cream and cook until thickened enough to coat the back of a spoon, about 10 minutes. Strain through a fine sieve into another saucepan.

Heat the shells on a cookie sheet in the oven, then place on seaweed-covered serving plates.

Return the sauce to a simmer. Add the oysters and cook until the edges just begin to curl. Remove the oysters to the shells. Whisk the remaining butter into the sauce. Add the remaining champagne and cook until thickened enough to coat the back of a spoon, about 3 minutes. Adjust the salt and pepper. Transfer to a metal bowl, add the chives, and spoon over the oysters. Serve immediately.

COOKING NOTES: If the oysters are shucked more than 30 minutes ahead of time, cut the tough adductor muscle from the oyster. This muscle hardens after shucking and will detract from the overall silky oyster texture.
- Brut champagne is one of the driest and will balance the sweetness of the shallots and cream.

MAKES 4 SERVINGS ∎

Buckwheat Blini with Caviar

- 1½ cups warm milk (at about 110°F)
- 1 package dry yeast
- 1 teaspoon sugar
- 1 cup all-purpose flour
- 1 cup buckwheat flour
- 3 large egg yolks
- ¼ pound (1 stick) unsalted butter, at room temperature
- ⅓ cup heavy cream
- ½ teaspoon salt
- ½ teaspoon freshly ground black pepper
- 2 large egg whites
- ¾ cup sour cream
- ½ cup pepper vodka
- ¼ cup finely diced red onion
- 2 tablespoons snipped fresh chives
- 4 ounces caviar of your choice (1 ounce of caviar per person is minimum, more is always great)

In a medium-size bowl, combine the milk, yeast, and sugar. Allow to develop until foamy, about 10 minutes. Whisk in the flours.

With a mixer on high speed, combine the egg yolks and 4 tablespoons of the butter. Whip until light and smooth, then add the flour mixture, whipping until fluid, about 10 minutes. Allow to rise, covered with a clean cloth, in a warm, draft-free spot, until double, about 1 hour.

In a separate bowl, whip the heavy cream on high speed until thickened but before peaks form. Fold into the batter, along with the salt and pepper.

In another bowl, whip the egg whites to soft peaks, then fold into the batter.

In a small bowl, combine the sour cream and vodka.

Melt 1 tablespoon of the butter in a 6-inch nonstick pan over medium-high heat. Add ¼ cup of the batter to form a 5-inch blini. Cook until golden, about 2 minutes. Turn over and cook until done, about 1 minute. Transfer to a plate, keeping separate and warm in a 150°F oven.

Repeat with the remainder of the butter and batter to form seven more blinis.

Position two blinis slightly overlapping in the center of each serving plate. Distribute the red onions and chives over them. Spoon the sour cream mixture into the center of the blinis, top with the caviar, and serve.

COOKING NOTE: Do not refrigerate blini batter for the yeast leavening will decrease, resulting in dense blinis.

MAKES 4 SERVINGS ■

Snails, Fennel, and Peppers

  3 **large red bell peppers**
  1 **large yellow bell pepper**
 ¼ **pound (1 stick) unsalted butter**
  4 **large cloves garlic, roasted (see page 62) and minced**
 ¼ **cup chopped roasted shallots**
 ½ **cup chopped fresh parsley**
 ¼ **cup chopped fennel greens**
  2 **tablespoons sherry wine vinegar**
    Salt to taste
    Freshly ground black pepper to taste
  2 **tablespoons virgin olive oil**
  1 **cup trimmed and julienned fennel bulb**
 28 **canned helix snails, drained**
  2 **tablespoons grated Parmesan cheese**
  4 **sprigs fresh parsley for garnish**

Preheat the grill or broiler.

Place the peppers on the grill or under the broiler and cook until the skin turns completely black, rotating to cook evenly on all sides. While still warm, peel the skin. Cut two of the red peppers in half, then remove the seeds and core. Reserve on an ovenproof plate for presentation.

Seed and clean the remaining red and yellow peppers, then cut into ¼-inch dice.

With a mixer, whip the butter until light. Add the garlic, shallots, parsley, fennel greens, and vinegar. Adjust the salt and pepper. Reserve.

Reheat the pepper halves in the oven or on the grill.

In a medium-size skillet, sauté the julienned fennel in the olive oil until tender, about 2 minutes. Add the snails and diced peppers and cook until hot, about 3 minutes. Remove from the heat and mix in the garlic butter just to melt. Adjust the salt and pepper.

Position the pepper halves in the center of the serving plates. Spoon the snail mixture into peppers, sprinkle with the Parmesan, garnish with the parsley, and serve.

MAKES 4 SERVINGS ■

Blue Corn Blini with Smoked Salmon

A modern Southwest approach to the classic Russian blini.

 ⅜ **cup warm milk (at about 110°F)**
  1 **package dry yeast**
  2 **teaspoons sugar**
 ¼ **cup all-purpose flour**
 ¼ **cup blue cornmeal**
  1 **large egg yolk**
  6 **tablespoons (¾ stick) unsalted butter, at room temperature**
 ¼ **cup heavy cream**
  2 **large egg whites**
 ¾ **cup sour cream**
 ¼ **cup crumbled bucheron cheese**
  1 **jalapeño pepper, roasted, peeled (see page 62), seeded, and diced**

¼ teaspoon freshly ground white pepper
 2 tablespoons fresh lime juice
¼ cup roasted, peeled, seeded, and finely diced
     red bell pepper
¼ cup roasted, peeled, seeded, and finely diced
     yellow bell pepper
¼ cup finely diced red onion
 2 tablespoons chopped fresh cilantro
 2 tablespoons snipped fresh chives
½ pound sliced smoked salmon (see note below)

In a medium-size bowl, combine the milk, yeast, and sugar. Allow to develop until foamy, about 10 minutes. Whisk in the flour and cornmeal.

With a mixer on high speed, combine the egg yolk and 2 tablespoons of the butter. Whip until light and smooth. Add the cornmeal mixture, whipping until fluid, about 10 minutes.

In a separate bowl, whip the heavy cream on high speed until thickened but before peaks form. Fold into the batter.

In a separate bowl, whip the egg whites on high speed to soft peaks, then fold into the batter.

In a small bowl, combine the sour cream and bucheron cheese, then add the jalapeño, white pepper, and lime juice.

Melt 1 tablespoon of the butter in a 6-inch nonstick pan over medium-high heat. Add ¼ cup of batter to form a 6-inch blini. Cook until golden, about 2 minutes. Turn over and cook until done, about 1 minute. Transfer to a plate, keeping separated and warm in a 150°F oven. Repeat with the remainder of the butter and batter to form three more blinis.

Position the blinis in the centers of the serving plates. Distribute the red and yellow peppers, onions, cilantro, and chives over them. Arrange the slices of salmon in a circle in the center of each blini. Spoon the sour cream garnish in the center and serve.

VARIATIONS: Try any smoked fish, avoiding those that are overcooked and dry looking. A good smoked fish should be tender and delicious. See Smoking Fish on pages 73–74.

You can also mix a number of light vegetables, such as blanched corn, diced pepper, chayote, and even

pumpkin, into the blini for garnish. Remember to blanch the vegetables for they will only be warmed in the blini, not cooked.

COOKING NOTES: Do not refrigerate blini batter for the yeast leavening will decrease, resulting in dense blinis.
■ Remember to trim the fatty darker flesh from the salmon as this carries the oily "fishy" flavor.

MAKES 4 SERVINGS ■

Foie de Canard with Ginger and Greens

Like caviar, foie is revered as a true luxury.

 2 heads red oakleaf lettuce, trimmed
 1 bunch mizuni (baby mustard greens),
     trimmed
1½ pounds fresh foie de canard, sliced ½ inch
     thick
     Kosher salt to taste
     Cracked black pepper to taste
½ cup cornmeal
 2 tablespoons virgin olive oil
¾ cup Ginger Vinaigrette (recipe follows)
 2 tablespoons peeled and julienned fresh
     ginger, blanched in boiling water until tender
¼ cup snipped fresh chives

Arrange the greens on serving plates. Set aside.

Season the foie with the salt and pepper, then dredge in the cornmeal. In a large nonstick skillet, heat the oil. Add the foie and cook until seared, about 1 minute. Turn over and cook until golden and tender, about 1 minute more.

Position the slices of foie atop the greens. Spoon the vinaigrette across them, then top with the ginger and chives and serve.

COOKING NOTES: Foie is fattened duck liver. Although foie also refers to fattened goose liver in France, it is seldom found in the United States. There are three grades of foie, "A," the largest and best; "B," smaller and a little leaner; and "C," which are the irregulars mostly used for making pâtés. I use both the "A" and "B" livers, although I get more large slices from "A" livers.

Soak whole livers in water to draw out any remaining blood, then dry and devein. Slice with a thin, sharp, warm knife. Keep the livers cool during handling. Since they are quite bland, be liberal with the salt and pepper.

MAKES 4 SERVINGS ■

Ginger Vinaigrette

The ginger and balsamic vinegar go great with the greens and foie. This is also terrific with smoked salmon, chilled lobster and shrimp, or simply as a spicy salad dressing.

- ¼ **cup balsamic vinegar**
- ¼ **cup peeled and thinly sliced fresh ginger**
- 1 **cup virgin olive oil**
- ¼ **teaspoon salt**
- ½ **teaspoon coarsely ground black pepper**

In a small saucepan, heat the vinegar to a boil. Add the ginger, then remove from the heat and allow to steep until cool. Strain into a small bowl.

Whisk in the olive oil, then add the salt and pepper. Refrigerate for up to 2 weeks.

MAKES 1¼ CUPS ■

Chanterelles with Blue Corn Tortilla Chips

Blue corn chips are great with holiday cocktails.

- ½ **cup sour cream**
- ¼ **cup crumbled bucheron cheese**
   Freshly ground black pepper to taste
- 4 **tablespoons (½ stick) unsalted butter**
- 2 **cups chanterelles, stemmed**
- 24 **Blue Corn Tortilla Chips (see page 67)**
- ¼ **cup chopped fresh mint**
- ¼ **cup snipped fresh chives**

Preheat the oven to 400°F.

In a small bowl, whisk together the sour cream and bucheron cheese until smooth. Season with black pepper.

In a medium-size skillet, heat the butter over high. Add the chanterelles and sauté until golden, about 3 minutes. Drain.

Place the chips on a cookie sheet. Spread generously with the sour cream mixture. Bake on the lower rack until hot, about 5 minutes. Sprinkle the chips with the mint and chives. Position the chanterelles on top and serve.

MAKES 2 DOZEN ■

Smoked Salmon with Radishes and Capers

- 3 **tablespoons raspberry or currant vinegar**
   Salt to taste
- ½ **cup virgin olive oil**
- 2 **tablespoons finely diced red onion**
- ¼ **cup nonpareil capers, drained**

¼ cup finely diced radishes (see note below)
Freshly ground black pepper to taste
1 pound thinly sliced smoked salmon (see note below)
¼ cup snipped fresh chives
2 tablespoons yellow or brown mustard seeds, toasted (see page 61)
16 Lemon Croutons (see page 70)

In a medium-size bowl, whisk together the vinegar and ¼ teaspoon salt. Whisk in the olive oil, then add the red onions, capers, and radishes. Adjust salt and pepper. Lay the smoked salmon slices across the serving plates and sprinkle with the chives and mustard seeds. Drizzle the radish vinaigrette over the salmon, garnish with the croutons, and serve.

COOKING NOTES: The smallest radishes have the most spice. The spicy flavor comes from the skin, so the smallest radishes have proportionally more skin to flesh. You can also just slice off the skins for more red color and spicy flavor. The radishes will lose their color if left in the vinaigrette for long. For the best color, add them just before serving the vinaigrette.
■ Remember to trim the fatty darker flesh from the salmon as this carries the oily ''fishy'' flavor.

MAKES 4 SERVINGS ■

Shellfish Wontons

Great little crisp packages perfect for holiday entertaining.

4 tablespoons (½ stick) unsalted butter
½ pound shrimp, peeled, deveined, and diced
½ pound scallops, foot removed (see note below) and diced
1 clove garlic, minced

1 medium-size red bell pepper, roasted, peeled (see page 62), seeded, and diced
½ cup chopped fresh parsley
Salt to taste
Tabasco or Pick-A-Pepper sauce to taste
24 rice wonton wrappers, square or round (see note below)
Corn oil for frying
1 cup Lava Sauce (recipe follows)
4 sprigs fresh parsley for garnish

In a medium-size skillet over high heat, melt the butter. Add the shrimp and scallops and cook until opaque and firm, about 2 minutes. Add the garlic and peppers and cook until hot, about 1 minute. Transfer to a bowl and add the parsley, then adjust the salt and Tabasco.

Lay the wontons out on a flat surface. Distribute the filling to the center of each. Brush the edges of the wontons with warm water, then fold over the filling to form half moons (if round wontons) or triangles (if square). Press the edges to seal. Refrigerate for at least 1 hour before cooking.

In a large, heavy skillet, heat 3 inches of corn oil over medium-high heat to 350°F. Carefully slide the wontons into the hot oil. Cook until golden, about 4 minutes. Remove to paper toweling to drain. Keep warm in a low oven.

To serve, place a small bowl of Lava Sauce in the center of the serving plates and arrange the wontons around it. Garnish with the parsley and serve.

VARIATIONS: Wontons can be filled with almost any mixture. Keep in mind that it will be heated, not extensively cooked, so avoid raw fillings. Wonton wrappers can also be fried plain without fillings, then used like a corn chip with your favorite toppings.

COOKING NOTES: The "foot" is a tough muscle on the side of the scallop.
■ Wonton wrappers are available at Oriental markets. They can be frozen until ready to use.

MAKES 4 SERVINGS ■

Lava Sauce

This makes you feel like you've got hot lava rolling over your tongue. Great with grilled and fried vegetables and grilled shellfish.

- 2 large egg yolks
- 4½ teaspoons Coleman's dry mustard
- 2 tablespoons extra-strong Dijon mustard (such as Pommery)
- 2 tablespoons fresh lemon juice
- 1 cup corn oil
- ½ teaspoon salt
- 2 tablespoons Tabasco or guinea pepper paste (see note below)
- 4½ teaspoons wasabi powder, prepared according to directions on the can (see note below)

With a mixer, combine the egg yolks, mustards, and lemon juice. On high speed, gradually add the corn oil in a steady stream. Season with the salt and Tabasco. Mix in the wasabi. Refrigerate until ready to serve or up to 5 days.

COOKING NOTES: Guinea pepper paste is a condiment prepared from the berries of a tree related to cardamon. It's usually blended with hot peppers, vinegar, and sometimes garlic, and can be found in Oriental or African markets.

- Wasabi powder is ground green Japanese horseradish. When mixed with water it develops hot spicy flavors. It is available in Oriental markets.

MAKES 1 CUP ∎

Lemon Pasta with Smoked Salmon and Caviar

This pasta is a great way to clean up the leftover smoked salmon and caviar from the holidays. The lemon sauce is so warm and bright it goes well with any smoked fish or just by itself.

- ½ cup finely diced shallots
- ½ cup dry white wine
- 1¼ cups heavy cream
- ¼ cup grated lemon rind
- 2 tablespoons fresh lemon juice
  Salt to taste
  Coarsely ground black pepper to taste
- 1 pound angel hair pasta (see page 68)
- 2 ounces smoked salmon, julienned (see note below)
- ¼ cup snipped fresh chives
- 2 ounces caviar of your choice

In a medium-size saucepan over high heat, combine the shallots and white wine and cook until reduced to ¼ cup, about 6 minutes. Add the heavy cream and lemon rind and cook until thickened enough to coat the back of a spoon, about 10 minutes. Add the lemon juice and season with salt and pepper to taste. Keep warm over low heat.

In a large amount of boiling water, cook the pasta until al dente. Transfer to a strainer, rinse with warm water, and drain well.

In a medium-size bowl, combine the pasta, lemon sauce, and smoked salmon. Arrange the pasta on warm serving plates. Sprinkle with the chives, top with the caviar, and serve.

COOKING NOTE: Remember to trim the fatty darker flesh from the salmon as this carries the oily "fishy" flavor.

MAKES 4 SERVINGS ∎

Lobster and Ginger Bisque

A great lobster bisque with full flavors and light textures.

2   **hard-shelled lobsters, 1½ pounds each (see note below)**
8   **cups Fish Stock (see page 65)**
½   **head garlic, roasted (see page 62) and mashed**
1   **cup coarsely chopped roasted shallots**
1   **tablespoon Ginger Puree (see page 66)**
2   **orange rinds, grated**
½   **teaspoon saffron threads, crushed**
1   **medium-size red bell pepper, roasted, peeled (see page 62), seeded, and cut into ¼-inch dice**
½   **cup trimmed and diced fennel bulb**
¼   **cup peeled and finely diced fresh ginger, blanched in boiling water until tender**
    Salt to taste
    Freshly ground black pepper to taste
1   **tablespoon chopped fresh cilantro**
1   **tablespoon snipped fresh chives**

Heat a large amount of salted water to a vigorous boil. Add the lobsters and return to a simmer. Cook for exactly 5 minutes. Remove the lobsters and immediately cool under cold running water for 3 minutes. Remove the meat from the tail, cutting into eight pieces per tail. Set aside. Remove the meat from the claws and forearms, maintaining the claws' shape. Set aside. Pull the outer head shell from the body and discard. Remove and discard the sand sac and chop the remaining bodies.

In a large acid-resistant pot, combine the lobster shells and fish stock. Bring to a simmer over medium heat and cook for 25 minutes. Strain out the shells.

In a blender, combine the stock, garlic, shallots, and Ginger Puree. Puree in batches until well mixed. Add the orange rind and allow to steep for 10 minutes. Strain through a very fine sieve into a saucepan.

Return to a simmer over medium heat, then add the saffron and allow to steep for 2 minutes. Add the lobster meat, red pepper, fennel, and ginger, allowing to heat through, about 3 minutes. Adjust the salt and pepper. Ladle the soup into warm bowls and sprinkle with the cilantro and chives. Serve.

COOKING NOTES: Select hard-shelled lobsters as the meat will be firm. Soft-shelled lobsters (those which have recently molted) have stringy meat. To determine a hard shell, squeeze the lobster; if the shell doesn't give, it's a good choice.

▪ The soup is slightly thickened with the shallots, garlic, and Ginger Puree. If you would like it thicker, add a little arrowroot dissolved in cold liquid to the simmering broth, allowing it to thicken to your desired consistency.

MAKES 4 SERVINGS ▪

Scallop Chowder

A great fall and winter soup that will become your new favorite.

4   **tablespoons (½ stick) unsalted butter**
¼   **pound slab bacon, diced**
1   **cup diced onions**
6   **cups clam juice**
¼   **cup chopped fresh thyme**
2   **cups half-and-half**
2   **cups tablewater crackers, ground**
1½ **pounds scallops, foot removed (see note below) and diced**
1   **cup diced potatoes, blanched (see pages 57–59) al dente**
    Salt to taste
    Freshly ground black pepper to taste
¼   **teaspoon ground mace (or substitute nutmeg)**
½   **cup chopped fresh parsley**

Melt the butter in a large soup pot over medium-high heat. Add the diced bacon and sauté until browned, about 10 minutes. Remove with a slotted spoon to a strainer to drain. Add the onions to the pot over high heat and sauté until tender, about 4 minutes. Drain the onions and cooking fats. Return the onions and bacon to the soup pot. Add the clam juice and thyme and cook over medium-high heat until reduced to 4 cups, about 10 minutes. Add the half-and-half and let simmer for 10 minutes. While stirring, slowly add the ground crackers until just slightly thickened. Add the scallops and potatoes. Cook until the scallops are opaque, about 3 minutes. Season with the salt, pepper, and mace. Stir in the parsley and serve.

VARIATIONS: Adapt this recipe to make clam chowder or oyster chowder. Allow for the cooking time differences of those shellfish. You can also use whole bay scallops to substitute for the diced sea scallops.

COOKING NOTES: The "foot" is the tough muscle on the side of the scallop.

▪ This soup is actually thickened by the tablewater crackers. Add them just until the soup is slightly thickened, as the crackers will continue to absorb juices and thicken it even more. You can also substitute oyster crackers for the tablewater crackers. Keep the soup underseasoned prior to adding the oyster crackers for they are salted.

▪ Mace is the aril, or covering, of the nutmeg. Its flavor is brighter than that of nutmeg and accentuates the sweet scallop flavor.

MAKES 8 SERVINGS ▪

Duck, Mâche, and Radicchio Salad

This salad is made terrific with the Eastern flavor of ginger. It is perfect with leftover Peking duck from your favorite Chinese restaurant.

1 **roasted duck (Chinese style recommended), approximately 2 cups cleaned meat**
1 **head radicchio (see note below)**
3 **bunches mâche, stemmed (see note below)**
½ **cup snow peas, cut on an angle, ½ inch thick**
½ **cup sliced mushrooms**
½ **cup rapini, blanched by sautéing in 2 tablespoons virgin olive oil over medium heat until wilted (see note below)**
¼ **cup finely julienned red onion**
1 **cup Ginger-Citrus Vinaigrette (recipe follows)**
¼ **cup scallion greens, cut on an angle, ¼ inch thick**

Remove all the meat and skin from the duck. Trim away all the fat. Crisp the skin in a preheated 400°F oven or under the broiler. Julienne the meat and skin.

Carefully peel off the leaves from the head of radicchio. Select four of the best large leaves and place in the center of the serving plates. Cut the remaining leaves into ¼-inch julienne strips.

In a medium-size bowl, combine the duck meat and skin, julienned radicchio, mâche, snow peas, mushrooms, rapini, and red onions. Toss with the vinaigrette. Distribute the salad to the serving plates, top with scallions, and serve.

COOKING NOTES: Avoid soaking radicchio in water as it will turn more bitter and lose its flavor.

▪ Mâche, or corn salad, is a tender, mild winter green that gives this salad a tender, light texture. The rapini, or broccoli rabe, is a smaller and more bitter relative of broccoli. It becomes even more bitter when blanched in water, and for that reason is sautéed in olive oil instead. Select firm dark green vegetables with little flowering.

MAKES 4 SERVINGS ▪

Ginger-Citrus Vinaigrette

Great with smoked and grilled fish and paillards of veal.

1/4 cup fresh lemon juice
1 tablespoon Ginger Puree (see page 66)
2 cloves garlic, roasted (see page 62) and minced
3/4 cup virgin olive oil
Salt to taste
Coarsely ground black pepper to taste

In a small bowl, whisk together the lemon juice, ginger, garlic, and olive oil. Adjust the salt and pepper. Refrigerate until ready to use or for up to 2 weeks.

MAKES 1 CUP ■

Fried Scallop and Spinach Salad

The infused oil technique for the dressing is quite unique.

1 cup corn oil
1 3/4 tablespoons hot Hungarian paprika
1/4 cup balsamic vinegar
1 tablespoon extra-strong Dijon mustard (such as Pommery)
Salt to taste
Freshly ground white pepper to taste
1/4 cup finely diced shallots, rinsed under cold water and pressed dry (see note below)
2 cups all-purpose flour
1 1/2 teaspoons freshly ground white pepper
1 large egg, lightly beaten
3/4 cup milk
Corn oil for frying
1/2 pound scallops, foot removed (see note below)
2 tablespoons unsalted butter
3/4 cup julienned red onion
3/4 cup roasted, peeled (see page 62), seeded, and julienned red bell pepper
3/4 cup roasted, peeled, seeded, and julienned yellow bell pepper
4 cups spinach, stemmed and torn into bite-size pieces
2 tablespoons snipped fresh chives

In a small, heavy saucepan, heat the corn oil to 325°F. Remove from the heat, add 3/4 tablespoon of the paprika, and allow to cool to room temperature. Strain through a paper coffee filter to remove the paprika sediment.

In a small bowl, combine the vinegar and mustard. Slowly whisk in the paprika oil. Adjust the salt and pepper. Add the shallots and set aside at room temperature.

Sift together the flour, the remaining paprika, 1 tablespoon salt, and 1 1/2 teaspoons white pepper into a shallow cake pan. Set aside.

In a small bowl, combine the egg and milk, whisking until combined. In a large, heavy skillet, heat 2 inches of corn oil over medium-high heat to 350°F.

Dip the scallops in the egg mixture, then dredge in the seasoned flour to coat evenly. Carefully drop the scallops, one at a time, into the hot oil. Fry until brown, about 3 minutes. Remove to paper toweling to drain.

In a medium-size skillet, heat the butter over high heat. Add the onion and sauté until translucent, about 3 minutes. Add the peppers and cook until hot but still crisp, about 2 minutes. Add the paprika dressing and allow to just warm.

In a metal bowl, toss the spinach with the warm dressing. Distribute the wilted spinach salad between the serving plates. Apportion the scallops and spoon across the salads, sprinkle with the chives, and serve.

VARIATION: Substitute oysters for the scallops. To cook the oysters, dredge them in the flour without the egg wash since they are already quite moist. Then fry for 45 to 60 seconds until they begin to hiss. Serve immediately.

COOKING NOTES: Rinsing the shallots removes their strong flavor.
■ The "foot" is a tough muscle on the side of the scallop.

- You can infuse a number of spices such as Szechuan peppercorns, coriander, and cumin successfully into oil for dressings, using this method. Be careful not to overheat the oil for the spice flavor may become bitter. The spices should then be strained out so that the flavor, not the sediment, remains.
- Cook the scallops briefly so they are silkier than the spinach. The scallops will then accentuate the spinach texture.

MAKES 4 SERVINGS ■

Swordfish with Coriander

The nutty flavor of coriander is perfect with swordfish.

  1 cup Fish Stock (see page 65)
½ cup dry white wine
¼ cup shallots, roasted (see page 62)
  1 cup heavy cream
¼ cup coriander seed, toasted (see note below and page 61)
    Salt to taste
    Freshly ground white pepper to taste
  4 swordfish steaks, about 7 ounces each, trimmed of skin and fat (see note below)
  2 tablespoons virgin olive oil
¼ cup packed fresh cilantro leaves
¼ cup pomegranate seeds

Preheat the grill or broiler.

In a medium-size saucepan over high heat, combine the stock, wine, and shallots and cook until the liquid is reduced to ½ cup, about 10 minutes. Add the cream and reduce until thickened enough to coat the back of a spoon, about 8 minutes. Remove from the heat and transfer to a blender. Add the coriander and process just enough to chop the seeds. Allow to steep for 5 minutes. Strain through a fine sieve into another saucepan and return to a simmer. Adjust the salt and pepper, then reduce the heat to low to keep warm.

Rub the surfaces of the swordfish with the olive oil. Place on the grill or under the broiler and cook until seared, about 3 minutes. Turn over to finish, about 3 minutes for medium rare, depending on the thickness of the swordfish.

Spoon the sauce onto warm serving plates and sprinkle with the cilantro and pomegranate seeds. Position the swordfish in the center of the sauce and serve.

VARIATION: Substitute equal quantities of chopped hazelnuts and fresh chives for the coriander and cilantro. Then add poached oysters tossed in the chives as a garnish to finish the dish.

COOKING NOTES: Choose swordfish that has been cut into thick steaks so that during cooking more moisture is retained. If you prefer more well done fish, select wider, thinner steaks that will cook faster.
- To develop the nutty flavor of the coriander, toast the seeds under a broiler, removing every 15 seconds to shake the pan to rotate the seeds. Carefully heat them in this way until they are a deep tan color and a strong fragrance is achieved. The combination of the coriander and cilantro is a perfect match.

MAKES 4 SERVINGS ■

Escalope of Salmon with Black and White Sesame

The sesames create a wonderful crunchy surface on the salmon.

 1 medium-size leek, white part and
 2 inches of green, diced
 ½ cup finely diced shallots
 4 tablespoons (½ stick) unsalted butter
 1 cup Fish Stock (see page 65)
 1 cup dry white wine, preferably
 chardonnay
 Salt to taste
 Freshly ground black pepper to taste
 ¼ cup heavy cream
 ½ cup white sesame seeds, lightly toasted
 without coloring (see page 61)
 ½ cup black sesame seeds, lightly toasted
 8 escalopes salmon, about 3 ounces each
 Corn oil for cookie sheet
 ½ cup snipped fresh chives, cut 2
 inches long

Preheat the broiler.

In a large skillet, sauté the leeks and shallots in the butter over medium heat until tender, about 8 minutes. Add the stock and wine and bring to a simmer over high heat. Cook until thickened enough to coat the back of a spoon lightly, about 8 minutes. Adjust the salt and pepper. Remove from the heat and transfer to a food processor. Puree until smooth, adding heavy cream as necessary. Strain through a coarse sieve into a saucepan. Keep warm.

Spread the sesame seeds over two separate flat dishes. Press half of the top surface of each salmon escalope into one color of sesame and repeat with the opposite side in the other sesame seed. Lay the escalopes, seed-side up, on an oiled sheet pan.

Place the salmon on the middle rack of the oven and cook until medium-rare, about 6 minutes, or until desired doneness is reached. Do not brown the sesame seeds.

Spoon the sauce across warm plates, then position two escalopes on each plate, slightly overlapping. Sprinkle with the chives and serve.

MAKES 4 SERVINGS ▪

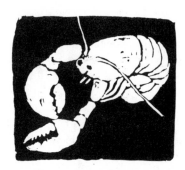

Ragout of Lobster and Scallops with Couscous

 2 hard-shelled lobsters, 1½ to 2 pounds each
 (see note below)
 1 tablespoon achiote paste (see note below)
 1 tablespoon corn oil
 ½ pound sea scallops, foot removed (see note
 below)
 1 cup Fish Stock (see page 65)
 1 cup dry white wine
1½ cups heavy cream
 1 dried pasilla pepper, seeded (or substitute
 dried anchos chile)
 Salt to taste
 Freshly ground white pepper to taste
 2 tablespoons unsalted butter
 2 large Asian pears, sliced ¼ inch thick with
 skin on
 1 recipe Spiced Couscous (see page 134)
 ¼ cup packed fresh tarragon leaves
 ¼ cup snipped fresh chives

Preheat the broiler to 475°F.

Heat a large amount of salted water to a vigorous boil. Add the lobsters and return to a simmer. Cook exactly 5 minutes. Remove the lobsters and immediately cool under cold running water for 3 minutes.

Cut the lobster in half lengthwise. Remove the tail meat and the meat from the claws and forearms, preserving the claws' shape. Pull the outer head shell from the body and rinse under water. Remove and discard the sand sac. Chop the body.

In a small bowl, combine the achiote and corn oil. Spread the mixture over the surfaces of the lobster meat and scallops, then set aside.

In a large saucepan, combine the lobster bodies, stock, and wine, and bring to a simmer over medium heat. Cook until reduced to 1/4 cup, about 10 minutes. Add the cream and cook until thickened enough to coat the back of a spoon, about 12 minutes. Remove and discard the lobster bodies. Transfer the mixture to a blender. Add the pasilla pepper and allow to steep for 15 minutes. Puree until smooth, then strain through a fine sieve into another saucepan. Return to a simmer. Adjust salt and pepper and reduce the heat to low.

In a medium-size skillet, heat the butter over high heat. Add the Asian pear slices and cook until golden, about 2 minutes. Turn over and cook the other side until golden. Remove to paper toweling to drain. Keep warm in a low oven.

Broil the lobster meat and scallops for about 3 minutes, then turn over and broil until tender, about 2 minutes.

Position the couscous on warm serving plates. Arrange three slices of the Asian pear on each plate, then spoon the sauce onto the plate around the couscous. Position the lobster and scallops over the sauce and couscous, then sprinkle with the tarragon and chives and serve.

COOKING NOTES: Select hard-shelled lobsters as the meat will be firm. Soft-shelled lobsters (those which have recently molted) have stringy meat. The shell of a hard-shelled lobster will not give when squeezed.

▪ Achiote paste is a Central American condiment made from ground annatto seed (the achiote), garlic, vinegar, salt, and sometimes chiles. The flavor is similar to a rich, mild paprika. It is available in Spanish and Mexican food stores. If you can't locate it, for 2 tablespoons achiote, substitute 1 tablespoon mild Hungarian paprika, 1 table-spoon red bell pepper puree, 1 teaspoon minced garlic, and 1 teaspoon red wine vinegar. *Do not* substitute the annatto seed itself, as its flavor is very strong.

▪ The "foot" is a tough muscle on the side of the scallop. You can substitute bay scallops for the sea scallops; just cut the cooking time in half or less, depending on their size.

MAKES 4 SERVINGS ▪

Scallops with Endive and Lemon

1 1/4 **cups corn oil**
  1 **small taro root, peeled and finely julienned**
  1/2 **cup snipped fresh chives, cut into 2-inch lengths**
  1/2 **cup dry white wine (see note below)**
  1/2 **cup fresh lemon juice**
  1 **tablespoon Ginger Puree (see page 66)**
  1 **cup heavy cream**
  1/4 **cup mixed grated rind of oranges and lemons**
    Salt to taste
    Freshly ground white pepper to taste
  2 **Belgian endives, cut 1/4 inch thick lengthwise**
1 1/2 **pounds large sea scallops, foot removed (see note below)**

In a medium-size skillet over medium-high heat, heat 1 cup of the corn oil. Rinse the taro under cold running water until the water is clear. Drain well, then dry with paper toweling. Add the taro to the oil and fry until golden, about 2 minutes. Remove with a slotted spoon to paper towels to drain. Keep warm in a low oven. Fry the chives in the same manner. Mix with the taro.

In a medium-size saucepan, combine the wine, lemon juice, and Ginger Puree. Bring to a simmer over high heat, then cook until reduced to 1/2 cup, about 6 minutes. Add the cream and grated rind and cook until thickened enough to coat the back of a spoon, about 6 minutes. Add salt and pepper. Add the endive and let wilt. Remove immediately from the heat.

In a large skillet, heat the remaining corn oil over high heat. Add the scallops and cook until browned and well seared, about 2 minutes. Turn over and finish cooking until slightly firm, about 1 minute, depending on the size. Season with salt and pepper. Spoon the sauce into the center of warm plates. Position the scallops in the center of the sauce, top with the taro and chives, and serve.

COOKING NOTES: Taro root is a high-starch root vegetable that fries up very crisp. Select the larger taro, preferably the Chinese variety with purple veining, that are firm with no mold. Be sure to rinse well under cold running water to remove the large amounts of starch it contains before cooking. The taro serves as a crispy pasta in this dish.

▪ The Belgian endive has a light, crisp, delicate flavor. Avoid soaking it in water or exposing it to sunlight as both will result in bitterness. In this preparation it serves as a silky pasta, contrasting with the crunchy taro.

▪ The Lacrimarosa wine by Mastroberardino in Italy is perfect for this dish, with its soft, dry, rosé characteristics. A good Vin Gris from Edna Valley Winery works well too. Serve the same wine with this dish.

▪ The "foot" is a tough muscle on the side of the scallop.

MAKES 4 SERVINGS ▪

Duck Breast with Pears and Pine Nuts

2 cups Poultry or Veal Stock (see page 63 or 64)
1 cup dry red wine, preferably pinot noir
½ cup honey
¼ cup balsamic vinegar
1 teaspoon Quatre Épices (see page 66)

Salt to taste
Freshly ground black pepper to taste
2 tablespoons unsalted butter
4 boneless duck breasts, about 10 ounces each
2 pears (see note below)
½ cup fresh lemon juice
2 tablespoons pine nuts
2 tablespoons snipped fresh chives

Preheat the oven to 425°F.

In a medium-size saucepan, bring the stock and wine to a simmer over high heat. Cook until thickened enough to coat the back of a spoon, about 15 minutes. Add the honey, vinegar, and Quatre Épices, then adjust the salt and pepper. Whisk in the butter, then reduce the heat to low.

Place the duck breasts skin-side up on a broiler pan. Place on the lower rack of the oven and cook until medium-rare to medium, about 20 minutes. Remove from the oven and allow to rest for 3 minutes.

Peel and quarter the pears, then remove the core. Slice the pear quarters almost completely through lengthwise to form a fan. Rub with the lemon juice, then dust with ground black pepper, if desired. Place on a sheet pan and broil to heat, about 2 minutes.

Spoon the sauce onto warm serving plates. Arrange two pear fans per plate on the sauce. Remove the skin from the duck breasts. Slice each breast on an angle into four or five pieces, then lay in a fan across the sauce. Sprinkle with the pine nuts and chives and serve.

COOKING NOTE: My choice for pears here would be the Comice or the Royal Riviera. Both have terrific flavor and texture for serving in this simple preparation. The icicle pear, which is late maturing, is also one of my favorites but is more difficult to find.

MAKES 4 SERVINGS ▪

Pheasant with Leeks and Vanilla

Domesticated pheasants, with their delicate flavor and tender flesh, are much milder than the wild variety and are gaining popularity. They can be cooked in a fraction of the standard time and the meat remains very moist.

2 medium-size leeks, trimmed
2 tablespoons corn oil
2 tablespoons unsalted butter
1 medium-size Asian pear, julienned
2 cups Poultry or Veal Stock (see page 63 or 64)
1 cup dry white wine
3/4 cup heavy cream
 Salt to taste
 Freshly ground black pepper to taste
4 boneless pheasant breasts, about 8 ounces each
2 tablespoons cognac or brandy
1 tablespoon vanilla extract
2 tablespoons snipped fresh chives

Preheat the grill and the oven to 425°F.

Blanch the leeks in boiling salted water until tender, about 7 minutes. Remove to paper toweling to drain. Dry well. Rub the leeks with 1 tablespoon of the oil, place on the grill, and cook until grill marks appear. Turn over and finish cooking, about 3 minutes. Remove from the heat and cut into 1-inch diamonds.

In a medium-size skillet, heat the butter over high heat. Add the Asian pear and sauté until slightly browned and tender, about 3 minutes. Drain on paper toweling.

In a medium-size saucepan over high heat, bring the stock and wine to a simmer. Cook until reduced to 1/2 cup, about 10 minutes. Add the cream and cook until thickened enough to coat the back of a spoon, about 6 minutes. Adjust the salt and pepper, then remove from the heat.

Place the pheasant breasts skin-side up on a broiler pan. Place on the lower rack of the oven and cook until medium-rare to medium, about 15 minutes. Remove from the oven and allow to rest for 3 minutes. Return the sauce to a simmer over medium heat. Add the leeks, pears, and cognac and reduce until thickened enough to coat the back of a spoon, about 2 minutes. Remove from the heat and stir in the vanilla.

Spoon the sauce onto warm serving plates. Remove the skin from the pheasant breasts, then slice each on an angle into four or five pieces. Lay the breast in a fan shape across the sauce, sprinkle with the chives, and serve.

COOKING NOTE: In this dish, the heady aroma of vanilla, added at the end to prevent being cooked off, is a perfect balance to the leeks and cognac.

MAKES 4 SERVINGS ■

Roast Chicken with Walnuts and Parsley

2 cups Poultry or Veal Stock (see page 63 or 64)
1 cup dry white wine
1 roasting chicken, about 3 to 3 1/2 pounds
 Salt to taste
 Freshly ground black pepper to taste
4 tablespoons (1/2 stick) unsalted butter
1/2 cup black walnuts, toasted (see page 60) and chopped
1/2 cup chopped fresh parsley
1 clove garlic, roasted (see page 62) and minced
2 tablespoons balsamic vinegar
1 recipe Celery Root and Fennel Puree (recipe follows)
4 sprigs fresh parsley for garnish

Preheat the oven to 400°F.

In a medium-size saucepan, combine the stock and wine and bring to a simmer over high heat. Cook until thickened enough to coat the back of a spoon, about 10 minutes. Remove from the heat.

Rinse the chicken and dry with paper towels. Season the chicken cavity with the salt, pepper, and fennel tops reserved from the puree. Place in a roasting pan in the lower rack of the oven. Cook until golden, about 1 to 1¼ hours. Larger chickens may take up to 15 minutes longer. Cook until an instant thermometer inserted into the thick section of the thigh registers 160°F. Remove from the oven and allow to rest 3 minutes before carving as you wish.

Return the sauce to a simmer over medium heat, then whisk in the butter. Adjust the salt and pepper, then add the walnuts, parsley, garlic, and vinegar, and cook for 2 minutes.

Position the chicken on warm serving plates. Divide the Celery Root and Fennel Puree on the plates. Spoon the sauce over the chicken, garnish with the parsley sprigs, and serve.

MAKES 4 SERVINGS ■

Celery Root and Fennel Puree

1 **large celery root**
1 **large fennel bulb, trimmed (reserve trimmed greens for chicken cavity)**
1 **medium-size boiling potato, scrubbed**
½ **cup shallots, roasted (see page 62) and chopped**
½ **cup half-and-half**
½ **cup walnut oil (or substitute a mild virgin olive oil)**
Salt to taste
Freshly ground white pepper to taste

In a large pot, combine the celery root, fennel, and potato, and cover with salted water. Bring to a boil and cook until the fennel is tender, about 45 minutes. Remove the fennel and let drain. Continue cooking until the celery root and potato are tender, about 15 minutes. Drain. Peel the celery root and potato, then cut all the vegetables into 1-inch cubes.

Combine the diced vegetables in a food processor with the shallots. Puree until smooth, adding the half-and-half and walnut oil as necessary to maintain the thick puree consistency. Season with salt and pepper. Strain, if lumpy, through a coarse sieve into a metal pan or bowl and cover. Keep warm in a 200°F oven until ready to serve.

MAKES 4 SERVINGS ■

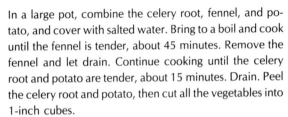

Roast Turkey with Maple Glaze, Apples, and Ginger Butter

My Thanksgiving favorite.

One **16-pound turkey (see note below)**
1 **tablespoon salt**
1 **tablespoon freshly ground black pepper**
1 **tablespoon chopped fresh rosemary**
4 **tablespoons (½ stick) unsalted butter**

FOR THE GLAZE

1 **cup pure maple syrup**
¼ **cup applejack or Calvados**

FOR THE SAUCE

2 **tablespoons unsalted butter**
3 **medium-size Granny Smith apples, peeled, cored, and sliced into wedges**
2 **cup Poultry Stock (see page 63)**
½ **cup applejack or Calvados**
1 **cup Ginger Butter (recipe follows)**

in the moisture while the low heat penetrates to cook the bird.

■ Avoid stuffing birds over 18 pounds because the stuffing never gets hot enough to kill the bacteria. The juices from the turkey do enter the stuffing, so contamination can easily occur.

MAKES 8 SERVINGS ■

Preheat the oven to 475°F with the rack in the lower third of the oven. Rinse the turkey and dry with paper towels. Sprinkle the cavity with the salt, pepper, and rosemary. Truss it, then rub the entire skin with the butter.

Place the turkey in a roasting pan and roast for 45 minutes breast-side up. Reduce the temperature to 375°F. Combine the syrup and applejack and frequently baste the turkey with it. Cook until an instant meat thermometer inserted into the thickest part of the thigh reads 160°F, about 1½ to 2 hours later. (Start your stuffing about ½ hour before the turkey is finished.) Transfer the turkey to a heated serving platter.

In a large skillet over high heat, melt the butter for the sauce, add the apples, and sauté for 3 minutes. Add the stock and reduce by three-fourths, about 10 minutes. Add the applejack and cook until the sauce is thickened enough to coat the back of a spoon, about 3 minutes. Whisk in the Ginger Butter. Remove to a metal bowl and continue whisking for 1 minute to stabilize before serving. Transfer to a sauceboat and immediately serve the sauce and turkey.

COOKING NOTES: Select your turkey by size and age. The older they get, the firmer fleshed they become. A fryer or roaster turkey is under 16 weeks old, a young hen or tom turkey is between 5 and 7 months of age (which is my preference), and a yearling turkey is 15 months old. I also select my bird on the basis of its diet, as what it has been fed will flavor the bird. Fresh turkeys are much moister than the frozen varieties. They must be stored very cold and for just a few days. The high initial heat helps to seal

Ginger Butter

This is also great with veal scaloppine or chops.

½ **cup peeled and diced fresh ginger**
½ **cup sugar**
¾ **cup water**
12 **tablespoons (1½ sticks) unsalted butter**

In a small saucepan, combine the ginger, sugar, and water. Bring to a simmer over medium heat and cook until tender, about 30 minutes. Transfer to a blender and puree until smooth. Strain through a medium sieve.

With a mixer, in a small bowl, beat the butter until light. Add the ginger puree and combine well. This can be made 3 days in advance and stored, covered, in the refrigerator.

MAKES 1 CUP ■

Roast Turkey with Pears and Black Pepper

One **16-pound turkey (see note below)**
1 **tablespoon salt**
1 **tablespoon freshly ground black pepper**
4 **tablespoons (½ stick) unsalted butter**

¼ **cup Poire William or vodka**
2 **tablespoons cracked black pepper**
½ **cup honey**

FOR THE SAUCE

4 **Comice pears**
2 **cup Poultry Stock (see page 63)**
2 **cups pear cider (or substitute apple-pear cider)**
2 **tablespoons unsalted butter**
½ **cup Poire William or other pear brandy**

Preheat the oven to 475°F with the rack in the lower third of the oven. Rinse the turkey and dry it with paper towels. Sprinkle the cavity with the salt and pepper. Truss it, then rub the entire skin with the butter.

Place the turkey in a roasting pan and roast for 45 minutes breast-side up. Reduce the temperature to 375°F. Combine the Poire William, cracked pepper, and honey, and frequently baste the turkey with it. Cook until an instant meat thermometer inserted into the thickest part of the thigh reads 160°F, about 1½ to 2 hours later. (Start your stuffing about ½ hour before the turkey is finished.) Transfer the turkey to a heated serving platter.

Meanwhile, place the whole pears in a baking dish on a rack in the oven. Baste frequently with the turkey glaze and bake until golden and tender, about 45 minutes. Remove to a rack to cool. When cool, cut in half, remove the core, and dice.

In a medium-size saucepan, combine the stock and cider. Bring to a boil over high heat and cook until thickened enough to coat the back of a spoon, about 10 minutes. Whisk in the butter. Adjust the salt and pepper, then add the Poire William and diced pears. Transfer to a sauceboat and immediately serve with the turkey.

COOKING NOTES: Select your turkey by size and age. The older they get, the firmer fleshed they become. A fryer or roaster turkey is under 16 weeks old, a young hen or tom turkey is between 5 and 7 months of age (which is my preference), and a yearling turkey is 15 months old. I also select my bird on the basis of diet, as what it has been fed will flavor the bird. Fresh turkeys are much moister than the frozen varieties and must be stored very cold and for just a few days. The high initial heat helps to seal in the moisture while the low heat penetrates to cook the bird.

▪ Avoid stuffing birds over 18 pounds because the stuffing never gets hot enough to kill the bacteria. The juices from the turkey do enter the stuffing, so contamination can easily occur.

MAKES 8 SERVINGS ▪

Rack of Lamb with Pomegranate and Herbs

1 **rack of lamb for four (16 ribs), trimmed and prepared for roasting**
2 **cups Lamb or Veal Stock (see page 64)**
3 **cups pomegranate juice (or substitute unsweetened cranberry juice)**
1 **tablespoon juniper berries**
1 **orange, pulp only**
2 **lemons, pulp only**
1 **tablespoon black peppercorns**
 Salt to taste
 Freshly ground black pepper to taste
2 **tablespoons unsalted butter**
½ **cup cleaned pomegranate seeds (see note below)**
2 **tablespoons snipped fresh chives**
2 **tablespoons chopped fresh tarragon**
2 **tablespoons chopped pistachios**
4 **sprigs fresh tarragon**
4 **small clusters pomegranate seeds**

Preheat the oven to 400°F.

Place the prepared rack of lamb in a roasting pan in the lower third of the oven. Cook until an instant meat thermometer inserted in the eye of the rack reads 130°F, for medium-rare, about 30 minutes. Allow to rest 5 minutes before carving.

Cut the racks in half and slice the meat between the bones to yield sixteen chops.

Meanwhile, in a medium-size saucepan, combine the stock, pomegranate juice, juniper, orange, lemons, and peppercorns. Bring to a boil over high heat, then cook until thickened enough to coat the back of a spoon, about 15 minutes. Adjust the salt and pepper. Strain through a sieve into another saucepan and return to a simmer. Whisk in the butter, then reduce the heat to low. Spoon the sauce into the center of warm plates and sprinkle the pomegranate seeds, chives, tarragon, and pistachios over the sauce. Lay four lamb chops over the sauce, garnish with the tarragon sprigs and pomegranate clusters, and serve.

COOKING NOTES: In December, the spring lamb is nearing 10 months old and full maturity. The racks will be filled out for the holiday season, with more pronounced flavor, perfect for pairing with full-bodied sauces and wines.
▪ Clean pomegranate seeds by removing all the white membrane from the red seeds. Clean seeds have a cleaner taste and better appearance.

MAKES 4 SERVINGS ▪

Veal Liver with Raspberry Vinegar

½ **cup Veal Stock (see page 64)**
½ **cup raspberry vinegar**
4 **tablespoons (½ stick) unsalted butter**
  Salt to taste
  Freshly ground black pepper to taste
¼ **cup corn oil**
2 **cups all-purpose flour**
8 **thin slices veal liver, about 3 ounces each (see note below)**
1 **pint raspberries**
2 **tablespoons snipped fresh chives**

In a small saucepan, combine the stock and vinegar. Bring to a boil over high heat and cook until thickened enough to coat the back of a spoon, about 5 minutes.

Whisk in the butter, then adjust the salt and pepper. Remove from the heat.

In a large skillet, heat the corn oil over high heat. Dredge the liver in the flour, shaking off the excess, then cook in the oil until seared and golden, about 2 minutes. Turn over and cook to desired doneness, about 2 minutes for medium-rare. Remove to paper toweling to drain. Season with salt and pepper.

Lay the liver slices on warm serving plates. Return the sauce to a simmer, add the raspberries and chives to the sauce, then spoon the sauce over the liver and serve.

COOKING NOTES: Veal liver is under 3 months of age. After this time it becomes calf liver. I prefer veal liver for sautéing and calf liver for broiling. The higher moisture content of the veal liver needs the hot oil to sear the juices in, while the structure of the calf liver firms up nicely under a very hot broiler. The veal liver has a milder, sweet flavor that is accentuated in this case by the fruit vinegar.
▪ Select the freshest liver possible. The texture should be firm, not mushy, with little or no blood. A number of years ago when fresh "just killed" liver was available in Detroit, we offered only the liver from the kill of the morning for lunch and the last kill of the day for dinner. Liver was less expensive at that time and the slaughterhouses were more active. That was fresh liver!

MAKES 4 SERVINGS ▪

Rack of Veal with Campari

1½ **cups Veal Stock (see page 64)**
½ **cup fresh lemon juice**
1 **cup blood orange juice (or substitute regular orange juice)**
2 **medium-size artichoke hearts, blanched (see pages 57–58), trimmed, and cut into ½-inch wedges**
1 **large yellow bell pepper, roasted, peeled (see page 62), seeded, and julienned**

Salt to taste

Freshly ground black pepper to taste

1 **rack of veal for four (4 ribs), about 3 pounds, trimmed and tied (see note below)**

¼ **pound (½ stick) unsalted butter, at room temperature**

½ **cup Campari**

½ **cup trimmed and julienned radicchio (see note below)**

2 **tablespoons chopped fresh basil**

4 **sprigs fresh basil for garnish**

Preheat the oven to 450°F.

In a medium-size nonaluminum saucepan, combine the stock and juices. Bring to a simmer over medium-high heat and cook until the sauce is thickened enough to coat the back of a spoon, about 10 minutes. Add the artichokes and peppers and cook until hot, about 2 minutes. Adjust the salt and pepper.

Place the veal in a roasting pan with a rack. Position in the lower third of the oven and cook for 15 minutes. Lower the oven temperature to 350°F and continue to cook for another 30 minutes or until an instant meat thermometer inserted into the eye of the rack registers 120°F. Remove from the oven and allow to rest for about 5 minutes. Trim the veal of fat and bones, then cut into eight slices.

Return the sauce to a simmer. Whisk in the butter and Campari. Remove from the heat and add the radicchio and chopped basil.

Spoon the sauce onto warm serving plates. Lay the veal slices over the sauce, garnish with the basil sprigs, and veal bone if you choose, and serve.

COOKING NOTES: Select a rack of veal for good pink/blush color and one that has not been raised in confinement. If you can locate true milk fed veal from Jamie Nichols of Summerfield Farm in Virginia, it is well worth it.

▪ Campari is an aperitif from Italy used in the famous cocktail Negroni. Made from distilled spirits and herbs, it has the flavor of bitters. The sweet blood orange juice and basil balance the more bitter Campari and radicchio, making for a full-flavored and rich combination. Remember to add the basil and radicchio after the sauce has

been removed from the heat to retain their fresh flavors. Avoid soaking radicchio in water as it will turn bitter and lose its flavor.

▪ Avoid using aluminum pots with artichokes as you will end up with aluminum-flavored artichokes.

MAKES 4 SERVINGS ▪

Venison with Mustards and Chiles

A spicy, unusual preparation for mustard and chile lovers.

2 **cups Veal Stock (see page 64)**

2 **cups dry red wine**

1½ **cups chopped shallots**

1 **tablespoon black peppercorns**

2 **tablespoons unsalted butter**

2 **tablespoons coarse-grained prepared mustard**

   Salt to taste

   Freshly ground black pepper to taste

4 **venison tenderloin steaks (or substitute venison sirloin or beef), trimmed to 6 to 8 ounces each (see note below)**

2 **tablespoons corn oil**

2 **tablespoons thinly sliced and seeded mild red chiles, blanched in boiling water for 1 minute (see note below)**

2 **tablespoons water**

2 **tablespoons peeled and julienned fresh ginger, blanched in boiling water until tender**

¼ **cup yellow mustard seeds, toasted (see page 61)**

¼ **cup Chinese brown mustard seeds, toasted**

Preheat the broiler or grill to the highest temperature.

In a medium-size saucepan, bring the stock to a simmer over medium-high heat. Cook until reduced to 1 cup, about 10 minutes. Add the wine, shallots, and peppercorns, and bring back to a simmer. Cook until thickened enough to coat the back of a spoon, about 10 minutes. Strain through a fine sieve into another saucepan set over medium-high heat. Whisk in the butter and mustard. Adjust the salt and pepper and reduce the heat to low. Rub the surfaces of the steaks with the oil. Place on the broiler pan or grill and cook until well seared, about 5 minutes. Turn over and cook until desired degree of doneness is reached. For medium-rare a small meat thermometer inserted into the center of the steak will read 130°F, about 4 minutes. Allow to rest for 3 minutes before serving.

Place the chiles in a small pan with 1 tablespoon of the water and quickly warm over high heat until hot. Remove from the heat. Repeat with the ginger in another pan.

Spoon the sauce in the center of warm plates, reserving 1 tablespoon for the top of each of the steaks. Sprinkle the chiles and ginger over the sauce. Position the gratin on the plates.

Position the steak in the center of the sauce. Working very quickly, spoon the remainder of the sauce lightly across the tops of the steaks. Sprinkle both mustard seeds over the top of the steak, allowing them to stick to the sauce. Serve.

COOKING NOTES: Avoid very dark venison for the animal may have been excited prior to its termination. This raised activity depletes the muscles of their glycogen supply, resulting in less lactic acid, yielding gummy textured meat that spoils quickly.

▪ Select serrano chiles for great flavor and good heat. They range from medium hot to very hot. They can be mature and green in color or ripened to the red stage which is milder. The blanching takes away some of the raw heat.

MAKES 4 SERVINGS ▪

Grilled Sirloin with Hazelnuts

Mixed with the peppercorns and fennel seed, hazelnuts offer a great flavor for any red meat. The crunchy contrast accents the texture of the sirloin steak.

½ **cup chopped toasted (see page 60) hazelnuts**
1 **teaspoon cracked black pepper**
1 **teaspoon cracked white pepper**
2 **teaspoons fennel seeds, coarsely chopped**
1 **cup Beef or Veal Stock (see page 63 or 64)**
1 **cup pomegranate juice (or substitute unsweetened cranberry juice)**
½ **cup red wine vinegar**
2 **tablespoons unsalted butter**
 Salt to taste
 Freshly ground black pepper to taste
4 **sirloin steaks, New York cut, about 12 ounces each (see note below)**
2 **tablespoons virgin olive or corn oil**
¼ **cup snipped fresh chives**
½ **cup cleaned pomegranate seeds (see note below)**

Preheat the grill or broiler.

In a small bowl, combine the hazelnuts, peppers, and fennel seed. Reserve at room temperature.

In a large saucepan, combine the stock, juice, and vinegar. Bring to a simmer over medium heat and cook until reduced enough to coat the back of a spoon, about 10 minutes. Whisk in the butter, then adjust the salt and pepper. Remove from the heat.

Rub the surfaces of the steaks with the oil. Grill or broil until well seared, about 5 minutes. Turn over and cook until they reach your desired temperature, about 7 minutes for medium-rare, depending on the thickness of the steaks.

Return the sauce to a simmer over medium heat. Spoon the sauce onto warm serving plates and sprinkle with the chives and pomegranate seeds. Center the steaks on the sauce and top with the hazelnut mix. Serve.

COOKING NOTES: Avoid very dark colored beef, for the cow may have been excited before its termination. This raised activity depletes the muscles of their glycogen supply, resulting in less lactic acid, resulting in gummy textured meat that spoils quickly.

- Clean pomegranate seeds by removing all the white membrane from the red seeds. Clean seeds have a cleaner taste and better appearance.

MAKES 4 SERVINGS ■

Gratin of Root Vegetables

- **1 pound baking potatoes, peeled**
- **1 pound sweet potatoes, peeled**
- **¾ cup heavy cream**
- **1 teaspoon salt**
- **¾ teaspoon freshly ground white pepper**
- **¼ teaspoon freshly grated nutmeg**
- **2 tablespoons unsalted butter**
- **½ cup snipped fresh chives**
- **½ cup grated Parmesan cheese**

Preheat the oven to 350°F.

Slice all the potatoes to the thickness of potato chips. Combine the cream, salt, pepper, and nutmeg in a small bowl. Rub an 8- by 8- by 2-inch baking dish with the butter. Cover the bottom of the baking dish with a single layer of the baking potatoes, allowing them to slightly overlap. Pour some of the cream mixture over the potatoes. Repeat with the sweet potatoes. Sprinkle with a layer of chives and Parmesan. Repeat this procedure until all ingredients are used.

Cover the pan with aluminum foil, dull-side out, and bake on the lower rack of the oven for 25 minutes. Remove the foil and continue baking until brown, about 15 to 20 minutes. Remove to a cake rack to cool slightly. With a sharp knife, cut into portions and serve.

MAKES 8 SERVINGS ■

Cranberry Compote

- **2 pounds fresh cranberries**
- **4 cups sugar**
- **¼ cup marsala (see note below)**
- **2 tablespoons Angostura bitters**
- **¼ cup Grand Marnier**

Combine the cranberries and sugar in a medium-size saucepan. Cook over medium heat until the cranberries are very soft and coated with the sugar syrup, about 30 minutes. Puree in a blender and strain through a medium sieve into a bowl. Whisk in the marsala, bitters, and Grand Marnier. Pour into a serving dish and refrigerate overnight before serving.

COOKING NOTE: Select a dry marsala to balance the sugar used in cooking the cranberries.

MAKES 8 TO 12 SERVINGS ■

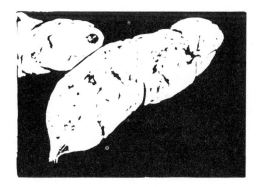

Pumpkin, Mushroom, and Parsley Stuffing

½ pound (2 sticks) unsalted butter
2 cups diced red onions
2 cups wild mushroom pieces (chanterelles, hedgehogs, or cepes)
1 cup diced parsley root, blanched (see pages 57–59)
2 teaspoon salt
1 teaspoon freshly ground black pepper
2 tablespoons chopped fresh rosemary
2 tablespoons chopped fresh tarragon
2 tablespoons snipped fresh chives
2 tablespoons chopped fresh parsley
1 loaf Pumpkin Wheat bread, diced and allowed to dry overnight (see page 249)
   Poultry Stock to moisten (see page 63)

In a large heavy skillet, melt the butter over medium-high heat. Add the onions and sauté until soft, about 5 minutes. Add the mushrooms and sauté until golden, about 6 minutes. Add the parsley root, seasonings, and herbs, and allow to heat through, about 1 minute. Remove to a large bowl. Mix in the bread and enough stock to moisten it. Transfer to a buttered 12- by 8- by 2-inch baking dish and cover with aluminum foil, shiny-side down. Refrigerate until ready to bake.

Bake in a preheated 375°F oven until hot, about 30 to 45 minutes.

VARIATIONS: Substitute different flavors of bread along with the herbs of your choice.

MAKES ABOUT 10 CUPS ■

Wild Mushroom, Leek, and Pepper Stuffing

½ pound (2 sticks) unsalted butter
2 cups diced red onions
2 cups wild mushroom pieces (chanterelles, hedgehogs, or cepes)
2 cups trimmed and ¼-inch sliced leeks
2 cups roasted, peeled (see page 62), seeded, and julienned red bell peppers
2 teaspoons salt
1 teaspoon freshly ground black pepper
2 tablespoons chopped fresh basil
2 tablespoons chopped fresh tarragon
2 tablespoons snipped fresh chives
2 tablespoons chopped fresh parsley
1 loaf wheat bread, diced and allowed to dry overnight
   Poultry Stock (see page 63) to moisten

In a large heavy skillet, melt the butter over medium-high heat. Add the onions and sauté until soft, about 5 minutes. Add the mushrooms, leeks, and peppers, and sauté another 6 minutes. Add the seasonings and herbs, then remove to a large bowl. Mix in the bread and enough stock to moisten it. Transfer to a buttered 12- by 8- by 2-inch baking dish and cover with aluminum foil, shiny-side down. Refrigerate until ready to bake.

Bake in a preheated 375°F oven until hot, about 30 to 45 minutes.

MAKES ABOUT 10 CUPS ■

Pumpkin Wheat Bread

Great for French toast.

2½ cups all-purpose flour
2 cups whole wheat flour
2 cups sugar
1 tablespoon baking powder
2 teaspoons baking soda
4 large eggs, at room temperature
2 cups canned solid-pack pumpkin
2 teaspoons salt
½ pound (2 sticks) unsalted butter, at room temperature
1 large egg yolk, beaten with ¼ cup heavy cream for glaze

Position the rack in the lower third of the oven and pre-heat to 350°F. Butter two 9- by 5-inch loaf pans.

Sift the flours, sugar, baking powder, and baking soda together into a large bowl. Combine the eggs, pumpkin, and salt in another bowl. Add to the dry ingredients and mix until smooth. With a mixer, blend in the butter, 1 tablespoon at a time.

Divide the batter between the pans. Brush the loaves with the egg glaze, then bake until golden brown, about 45 minutes. Invert onto racks and cool before using. (Can be prepared 2 days ahead. Wrap tightly.)

MAKES 2 LOAVES ■

Pear and Black Walnut Soufflé

Black walnuts are related to the hickory tree family and are highly regarded in the Midwest for their deep rich flavor.

Unsalted butter for soufflé dish
Granulated sugar for soufflé dish
Two 28-ounce cans bartlett pear halves, drained
¼ cup maple sugar (or substitute granulated white sugar)
¼ cup water
2 tablespoons grated lemon rind
2 teaspoon arrowroot (or substitute cornstarch)
2 tablespoons fresh lemon juice
¼ cup Poire William or other pear brandy
8 large egg whites
Pinch of salt
½ cup black walnut pieces, toasted (see page 60)
Confectioners' sugar to dust

Preheat the oven to 400°F. Butter and sugar an 8-cup soufflé dish.

Dice three pear halves. In a small saucepan, combine the pear dice, maple sugar, and water. Bring to a simmer over high heat and cook for 5 minutes. Remove the pear dice with a slotted spoon and reserve, along with the syrup.

In a food processor, combine the remaining pear halves and the lemon rind. Puree until smooth, then transfer to a large saucepan. Add the maple sugar syrup, bring to a simmer over medium heat, and cook until reduced to 2 cups, about 30 minutes.

Dissolve the arrowroot in the lemon juice. Add to the pear puree and cook until thickened, about 4 minutes. Stir in the pear brandy, then remove from the heat.

With a mixer, whip the egg whites with the salt to soft peaks. Gently stir a quarter of the whites into the warm pear puree, then fold in the remaining whites. Spoon half of the mixture into the prepared soufflé dish. Place the pear dice and walnuts in the center. Spoon the remaining mixture over them. Smooth the top with a spatula.

Place on the lower rack of the oven and cook until the soufflé has risen and is light brown, about 30 minutes. Dust with confectioners' sugar and serve immediately.

MAKES 8 SERVINGS ∎

Peach and Cranberry Soufflé

A great way to use leftover cranberry compote.

    Unsalted butter for soufflé dish
    Granulated sugar for soufflé dish
    Two 28-ounce cans peach halves, drained
  2 **tablespoons grated orange rind**
¼ **cup sugar**
  2 **teaspoon arrowroot (or substitute cornstarch)**
  2 **tablespoons orange juice**
  1 **tablespoon fresh lemon juice**
¼ **cup Southern Comfort**
  8 **large egg whites**
    Pinch of salt
½ **cup Cranberry Puree or Cranberry Compote (see page 66 or 247)**
    Confectioners' sugar to dust

Preheat the oven to 400°F. Butter and sugar an 8-cup soufflé dish.

In a food processor, combine the peaches and orange rind and puree until smooth. Transfer to a large saucepan and add the sugar. Bring to a simmer over medium heat and cook until reduced to 2 cups, about 30 minutes.

Dissolve the arrowroot in the orange and lemon juices. Add to the peach puree and cook until thickened, about 4 minutes. Add the Southern Comfort, then remove from the heat.

With a mixer, whip the egg whites with the salt to soft peaks. Gently stir a quarter of the whites into the warm peach puree, then fold in the remaining whites. Spoon half of the mixture into the prepared soufflé dish. Spoon the Cranberry Puree into the center. Spoon the remaining soufflé mixture on top. Smooth the top with a spatula.

Place on the lower rack of the oven and cook until the soufflé has risen and is light brown, about 30 minutes. Dust with confectioners' sugar and serve immediately.

MAKES 8 SERVINGS ∎

White Chocolate Ravioli

FOR THE CHOCOLATE MOUSSE FILLING

  8 **ounces imported extra bittersweet or semisweet chocolate, coarsely chopped (do not use baking chocolate)**
  4 **tablespoons (½ stick) unsalted butter**
  2 **large eggs, separated, at room temperature**
    Pinch of salt
    Pinch of cream of tartar
¼ **cup sugar**
¾ **cup heavy cream, well chilled**
  1 **teaspoon vanilla extract**

FOR THE RAVIOLI

Seven 3-ounce bars imported white chocolate (preferably Lindt), halved crosswise
  2 **cups Hazelnut Sauce (recipe follows)**
½ **cup chopped toasted (see page 60) hazelnuts**
  8 **sprigs fresh mint for garnish**

To make the chocolate mousse filling, melt the dark chocolate and butter in the top of a double boiler over barely simmering water. Stir until smooth. Transfer to a medium-size metal bowl and whisk in the egg yolks. Beat the whites, salt, and cream of tartar in another bowl until soft peaks form. Add 2 tablespoons of the sugar and beat until stiff but not dry. Fold into the chocolate. Beat the cream with the remaining sugar and the vanilla in another bowl until slightly thickened. Fold into the chocolate. Cover and chill overnight. (This can be made up to 3 days ahead.)

To make the ravioli, chill ravioli mold in the freezer. Preheat the oven at the lowest setting for 5 minutes, then turn it off. Place the white chocolate on a baking sheet, set in the turned-off oven, and let stand until soft enough to yield when pressed with a finger, about 5 minutes. Roll out one piece of the chocolate on a sheet of parchment paper to flatten slightly. Lift the chocolate off the paper, using a thin knife if necessary. Turn the pasta machine to its widest setting and run the chocolate through (or see note below). Adjust the pasta machine to the next narrower setting and run the chocolate through again. Repeat, narrowing the rollers after each run until the chocolate is $1/16$ inch thick. Quickly press the chocolate into the chilled ravioli mold. Fill each ravioli with 1 to $1\frac{1}{2}$ tablespoons of the mousse filling. Repeat rolling with a second piece of chocolate, resoftening in the oven as necessary. Place atop the ravioli. Seal with a rolling pin. Invert the mold, pressing to gently release the ravioli. Cut into separate pieces with a ravioli cutter or knife if necessary. Place on a chilled baking sheet and refrigerate. Repeat with the remaining white chocolate and filling, chilling the ravioli mold between batches. (This can be prepared up to 3 days ahead. Cover the white chocolate ravioli tightly.)

To serve, let the chocolate ravioli stand at room temperature for 30 minutes. Spoon $1/4$ cup of the Hazelnut Sauce onto each plate and arrange four ravioli over it. Sprinkle the nuts over the sauce and garnish with the mint.

COOKING NOTE: A blend of cocoa butter, milk solids, and sugars, white chocolate contains no cocoa solids. It is less stable and harder to melt, but is easy to mold. The

optimum temperature to soften it is 72°F. To melt easily for other preparations, melt in the top of a double boiler with a little half-and-half. White chocolate can be rolled by hand between two sheets of parchment or wax paper. Place the piece of chocolate in the center of the sheets and roll on a flat, hard surface until evenly thin and slightly larger than the ravioli mold you are using. Remove the top sheet of paper. Cool slightly to firm the chocolate, then remove from the paper and form into the ravioli mold. Do not chill the chocolate until hardened as it will become very brittle.

MAKES 8 SERVINGS ∎

Hazelnut Sauce

$1\frac{3}{4}$	**cups half-and-half, scalded**
$3/4$	**cup toasted blanched (see page 60) hazelnuts**
5	**large egg yolks, at room temperature**
$1/4$	**cup sugar**
$1/4$	**teaspoon vanilla extract**
	Pinch of salt
2	**tablespoons Frangelico or other hazelnut liqueur**

Process the hot half-and-half and hazelnuts in a blender until the nuts are coarsely chopped. Cool completely.

In a medium-size saucepan, combine the egg yolks, sugar, vanilla, and salt. Bring the nut mixture to a simmer in a heavy medium-size saucepan, then strain, pressing to extract as much liquid as possible, into a small bowl.

Whisk the nut cream into the yolk mixture and cook over medium heat until the custard is thickened enough to coat the back of a spoon, about 5 minutes; *do not boil.* Remove from the heat and whisk until cool. Strain the sauce through a fine sieve into a bowl and stir in the Frangelico. Refrigerate, tightly covered, until ready to serve, or for up to 3 days.

VARIATION: For Pistachio Sauce follow the above directions, substituting pistachios for the hazelnuts and pistachio liqueur or rum for the Frangelico.

MAKES ABOUT 2 CUPS ∎

Chocolate Pâté

15 **ounces extra bittersweet chocolate (do not use baking chocolate)**
1 **cup heavy cream**
4 **tablespoons (½ stick) unsalted butter**
4 **large egg yolks**
1 **cup confectioners' sugar, sifted**
½ **cup dark rum**
2 **cups Pistachio Sauce (see variation of previous recipe)**
½ **cup chopped pistachios**
  Sprigs fresh mint for garnish

Combine the chocolate, cream, and butter in the top half of a double boiler over simmering water, cooking until the chocolate is melted and warm, about 10 minutes. Transfer to a large warm bowl. Add the egg yolks, whisking until well blended. Add the sugar gradually while whisking until the chocolate is very shiny. Whisk in rum.

Completely line a small 3-cup terrine mold with parchment. Pour the chocolate mixture into the mold and refrigerate overnight. Invert the terrine and pull on the edges of the parchment to unmold. If the terrine sticks to the mold, loosen it by dipping the terrine in hot water for a few seconds, then inverting again. Refrigerate until ready to serve.

Cut the chocolate into "pâté" slices with a wire cheese cutter. Position the slices in the center of the serving plates and spoon the sauce around it. Garnish with the nuts and mint. Serve.

MAKES 8 SERVINGS ∎

Blini with Chocolate Velvet Ice Cream

For those who can't wait for the cake to bake—sauté it!

2 **large eggs**
¼ **cup sugar**
  Pinch of salt
¼ **teaspoon vanilla extract**
⅓ **cup all-purpose flour, sifted**
2 **tablespoons Clarified Butter (see page 70), melted**
3 **cups Chocolate Velvet Ice Cream (recipe follows)**
¾ **cup Chocolate Sauce (see page 158)**
6 **sprigs fresh mint for garnish**

In a medium-size bowl, whip the eggs on high speed until foaming. While continuously whipping, slowly add the sugar until the batter forms ribbons. Transfer to a wide bowl and add the vanilla. Fold in the sifted flour in three additions. Fold in the butter in two additions. Heat a 7-inch nonstick pan over medium heat and brush with unsalted butter. Add enough batter to cover the bottom of the pan. Cook until tan, about 1 minute. Carefully turn over. Cook until done, about 1 minute more. Transfer to a serving plate. Repeat with the remainder of the batter.

Scoop the ice cream into a ball and position in the center of each blini. Cover with chocolate sauce, garnish with the mint, and serve.

VARIATION: For a two-color variation, divide the batter in half after the ribboning step. In one bowl proceed with the instructions using only 3 tablespoons flour and 1 tablespoon butter. In another bowl proceed with 3 tablespoons unsweetened cocoa powder and 1 tablespoon butter. Spoon half of each color into the sauté pan for a great flavor and visual combination.

COOKING NOTE: Air is the most important ingredient of this genoise style cake. It is very important to trap air by ribboning the batter and to not deflate it by carefully folding in the flour and butter. Your effort will be rewarded by a very light textured and large volumed blini.

MAKES 6 SERVINGS ■

Chocolate Velvet Ice Cream

12 **large egg yolks**
 5 **tablespoons sugar**
 1 **teaspoon vanilla extract**
   Pinch of salt
3½ **cups half-and-half, scalded**
 5 **tablespoons honey**
12 **ounces extra bittersweet chocolate, broken into ½-ounce pieces (do not use baking chocolate)**
 ½ **cup unsweetened cocoa powder, sifted**
 ¼ **cup dark rum**

Combine the egg yolks, sugar, vanilla, and salt in a heavy medium-size saucepan. Whisk in the half-and-half and honey. Stir over medium-low heat until the custard thickens enough to coat the back of a spoon, about 5 minutes; *do not boil.* Remove from the heat, add the chocolate, and stir until dissolved. Whisk in the cocoa and rum. Strain through a fine sieve. Process the mixture in an ice-cream maker according to the manufacturer's instructions, until firm. Freeze in a covered container until firm, at least 2 hours. If frozen solid, soften slightly before serving.

MAKES 1½ QUARTS ■

Quadruple Chocolate Suicide

The deepest chocolate mousse and ice cream combination going. Four times the daily recommended dose of chocolate.

FOR THE BITTERSWEET CHOCOLATE ICE CREAM

1¾ **cups half-and-half**
 2 **tablespoons honey**
 6 **large egg yolks**
 2 **tablespoons sugar**
 1 **teaspoon vanilla extract**
   Pinch of salt
 6 **ounces extra bittersweet chocolate, broken into ½-ounce pieces (do not use baking chocolate)**
 3 **tablespoons unsweetened cocoa powder**
 2 **tablespoons dark rum**

FOR THE RICH CHOCOLATE MOUSSE

 2 **cups heavy cream**
 ¼ **cup honey**
12 **large egg yolks**
 ¼ **cup sugar**
 1 **teaspoon vanilla extract**
   Pinch of salt
12 **ounces extra bittersweet chocolate, broken into ½-ounce pieces (do not use baking chocolate)**

To make the ice cream, in a medium-size saucepan, scald the half-and-half, then add the honey. In a medium-size bowl, combine the egg yolks, sugar, vanilla, and salt. Slowly whisk in the half-and-half mixture, then return to the saucepan. Stir constantly over medium heat until the custard thickens enough to coat the back of a spoon, about 5 minutes; *do not boil.* Remove from the heat, add the chocolate, and stir until melted. Sift in the cocoa and whisk to blend. Stir in the rum.

Strain through a fine sieve into a container and refrigerate to cool. Cover and freeze until firm, at least 8 hours.

To make the mousse; in a medium-size saucepan, scald the cream, then add the honey. In a medium-size bowl, combine the egg yolks, sugar, vanilla, and salt. Slowly whisk in the cream mixture. Return to the saucepan. Constantly stir over medium heat until the custard thickens enough to coat the back of a spoon, about 5 minutes; *do not boil.* Remove from the heat and add the chocolate, stirring until melted. Strain into a bowl. Cool, then refrigerate until firm, at least 3 hours.

To assemble the Suicide, place four scoops of the ice cream in a bowl, allowing to soften if frozen solid. Add four scoops of mousse. Cut the ice cream and mousse together with a serving spoon until chunks of each are intermixed. Scoop the mixture into balls and place on serving dishes. Repeat with the remainder of the ice cream and mousse to serve your guests.

MAKES 8 TO 10 SERVINGS ∎

White Chocolate Lasagne

This dessert bends the imagination but it's good!

Three 3-ounce bars imported white chocolate, broken into halves
3 cups Peanut Ice Cream, cut into eight 5- by 3-inch rectangles (recipe follows)
¾ cup Rattlesnake Hot Fudge Sauce (see page 107)
4 sprigs fresh mint for garnish

Preheat the oven on the lowest setting for 5 minutes, then turn it off. Place the white chocolate on a baking sheet, set in the turned-off oven, and let stand until soft enough to yield when pressed with a finger, about 5 minutes. Roll out the chocolate, one piece at a time, on a sheet of parchment paper to flatten slightly. Lift the chocolate off the paper, using a thin knife if necessary. Adjust the pasta machine to its widest setting. Working with one piece of chocolate at a time, run the chocolate through (or see note below). Adjust the pasta machine to the next narrower setting and run the chocolate through again. Re-

peat, narrowing the rollers after each run through, until the chocolate is 1/16 inch thick. Lay the chocolate on a flat surface and cut into twelve 5- by 3-inch rectangles. Transfer to a parchment-lined sheet pan and keep cool until ready to use.

To assemble, lay four pieces of the chocolate on a parchment-lined sheet pan for the base. Place a Peanut Ice Cream rectangle atop each one. Follow with a second layer of chocolate, then another ice cream rectangle. Top with a piece of chocolate and return to the freezer until ready to serve.

To serve, position the chocolate lasagna on serving plates. Spoon the hot fudge sauce over, garnish with mint sprigs, and serve immediately.

COOKING NOTES: A blend of cocoa butter, milk solids, and sugars, white chocolate contains no cocoa solids. It is less stable and harder to melt, but is easy to mold. The optimum temperature to soften it is 72°F. White chocolate can be rolled by hand between two sheets of parchment or wax paper. Place the piece of chocolate in the center of the sheets and roll out on a flat hard surface until evenly thin and slightly larger than a 3- by 10-inch rectangle. Remove the top sheet of paper and trim to 3 inches by 10 inches. Cut the rectangle in half to form two 3- by 5-inch rectangles. Repeat the process to form ten more rectangles. Keep cool until assembly. If the chocolate sticks to the paper, cool slightly to firm but do not chill until hardened as it will become very brittle.

MAKES 4 SERVINGS ∎

Peanut Ice Cream

8 large egg yolks
¾ cup sugar
   Pinch of salt
1 teaspoon vanilla extract
3½ cups half-and-half, scalded
½ cup heavy cream
½ cup smooth peanut butter
1 cup unsalted dry roasted peanuts, very
   coarsely chopped (see note below)

In a medium-size saucepan, combine the egg yolks, sugar, salt, and vanilla. Whisk in the scalded half-and-half. Stir over medium-low heat until the custard thickens enough to coat the back of a spoon, about 6 minutes; *do not boil.* Remove from the heat and whisk in the cream and peanut butter. Strain through a fine sieve into a medium-size bowl. Stir the custard over an ice bath until cool. Cover and refrigerate until well chilled.

Process the custard in an ice-cream maker according to the manufacturer's instructions, until just thickened. Add the peanuts. Freeze until firm or, if making for White Chocolate Lasagne, pour into a parchment-lined ½-inch-deep sheet pan. Cover with parchment and freeze overnight.

With a pizza cutter or thin knife, cut the ice cream into eight 3- by 5-inch rectangles. Keep frozen until ready to use. Lift the rectangles out with a spatula when ready to assemble the lasagne.

COOKING NOTE: The peanut is actually not a nut but the seed of a small bush. It has only been a food crop since the 1940s. Dry roasting develops the flavor and texture. Select shelled, skinned, and dry-roasted peanuts for the easiest preparation and fullest flavor.

MAKES 1¼ QUARTS ∎

Chocolate Romance

Great love is many things, which is what this dessert was designed to reflect.

Four 3-ounce bars imported white chocolate,
      broken into halves
  ¼ recipe Dark Chocolate Mousse (recipe
      follows)
  ¼ recipe Grand Marnier Sabayon (see page
      257)
   2 pints raspberries
      Sugar to taste
   4 sprigs fresh mint to garnish

Preheat the oven on the lowest setting for 5 minutes, then turn it off. Place the white chocolate on a baking sheet set in the turned-off oven, and let stand until soft enough to yield when pressed with a finger, about 5 minutes. Roll out the chocolate, one piece at a time, on a sheet of parchment paper to flatten slightly. Lift the chocolate off the paper, using a thin knife if necessary. Adjust the pasta machine to its widest setting. Working with one piece of chocolate at a time, run the chocolate through (or see note below). Adjust the pasta machine to the next narrower setting and run the chocolate through. Repeat, narrowing the rollers after each run, until the chocolate is ¹⁄₁₆ inch thick by approximately 4½ inches wide. Immediately wrap the chocolate around molding tubes approximately 4 inches high and 2 inches wide, allowing the chocolate to overlap ¼ inch. Trim the excess away. Press gently on the seams to secure. Trim the tops and bottoms evenly to a length of 4 inches, so that the chocolate cylinders can stand on their own. Refrigerate for 5 minutes to firm the chocolate. Carefully remove the chocolate from the molds and place upright on a parchment-covered sheet pan. Refrigerate until ready to fill.

To assemble, fill the cylinders with the chocolate mousse to a height of 3 inches. Refrigerate for at least 1 hour.

Fill the remainder of the cylinder with the sabayon. Refrigerate until firm, about 2 hours.

Press 1 pint of the raspberries through a strainer to

puree and remove the seeds. Add sugar as necessary to sweeten.

Place the filled cylinders on serving plates and spoon the puree around the base. Top the cylinders with the remaining raspberries, garnish with sprigs of mint, and serve.

COOKING NOTES: A blend of cocoa butter, milk solids, and sugars, white chocolate contains no cocoa solids. It is less stable and harder to melt than chocolate, but is easy to mold. The optimum temperature to soften it is 72°F. White chocolate can be rolled by hand between two sheets of parchment or wax paper. Place the piece of chocolate in the center of the sheet and roll out on a flat hard surface until evenly thin and slightly larger than a 3- by 10-inch rectangle. Remove the top sheet of paper and trim to 3 inches by 10 inches. Proceed with the technique to wrap the chocolate around a molding tube.

If the chocolate sticks to the paper, cool slightly to firm and pull the paper off. Do not chill until hardened as it will become very brittle. Warm the chocolate with your hands to soften for the molding.

MAKES 4 SERVINGS ■

Dark Chocolate Mousse

16 **ounces extra bittersweet or semisweet chocolate, broken into pieces (do not use baking chocolate)**
¼ **pound (1 stick) unsalted butter**
 4 **large eggs, separated, at room temperature**
    Pinch of salt
    Pinch of cream of tartar
½ **cup sugar**
1½ **cups heavy cream, well chilled**
 2 **teaspoons vanilla extract**
 4 **sprigs fresh mint for garnish**

Melt the chocolate and butter in the top of a double boiler over barely simmering water. Stir until smooth, then transfer to a medium-size bowl. Whisk in the egg yolks. In another bowl, beat the egg whites with the salt and cream of tartar until soft peaks form. Add two tablespoons of the sugar and beat until stiff but not dry. Fold the egg whites into the chocolate mixture. In another bowl, beat the cream with the remaining sugar and the vanilla until slightly thickened. Fold into the chocolate mixture. Refrigerate overnight if it will be served alone. Can be made 3 days ahead. Spoon into chilled dishes, garnish with sprigs of mint, and serve.

VARIATIONS: Serve the mousse with fresh fruit, such as berries or white peaches. Top with the White Chocolate Crème Anglaise on page 257 for something special.

COOKING NOTE: After folding the chocolate into the mousse, use immediately in the preceding Chocolate Romance recipe.

MAKES 4 SERVINGS ■

Grand Marnier Sabayon

This gelatin-stabilized sabayon makes a firm chilled sauce great for dessert construction. To serve traditionally, omit the gelatin and pour the warm sabayon over chocolate or fresh fruit.

1/2 **cup Grand Marnier**
1 **tablespoon unflavored gelatin**
2 **large egg yolks**
1/4 **cup sugar**
 Pinch of salt
1 **teaspoon vanilla extract**

In a small custard cup, combine 1/4 cup of the Grand Marnier with the gelatin. Melt in a water bath over low heat.

In a medium-size saucepan, combine the egg yolks, sugar, salt, and vanilla. Whisk until light in color and thick in texture. Cook over medium heat while continuously whisking until thickened, about 3 minutes. Add the remaining Grand Marnier and cook until thick and silky, about 5 minutes. Remove from the heat and whisk in the melted gelatin. Allow to rest for 2 to 3 minutes.

COOKING NOTES: After adding the gelatin, do not continue to whisk. Use only a spoon from this point on for a cool whisk will collect the gelatin strands as they begin to firm.
■ If using for the Chocolate Romance recipe on pages 255–56, check the temperature of the sabayon before spooning it into the cylinders. If the sabayon is quite warm, the chocolate may melt. The 2- to 3-minute rest is to allow some cooldown of the sabayon without the gelatin firming.

MAKES 1 CUP ■

White Chocolate Crème Anglaise

1/4 **cup sugar**
 Pinch of salt
5 **large egg yolks**
2 **tablespoons fresh lemon juice**
1 **cup half-and-half, scalded**
1 **tablespoon vanilla extract**
5 **ounces imported white chocolate, broken into pieces**

In a medium-size saucepan, combine the sugar, salt, yolks, and lemon juice. Whisk in the scalded half-and-half. Stir over medium heat until the custard thickens enough to coat the back of a spoon, about 8 minutes; *do not boil*. Remove from the heat and add the vanilla and chocolate. Stir just until melted. Strain through a fine sieve into a metal container and refrigerate until ready to serve.

COOKING NOTE: The chocolate will melt in the hot sauce base.

MAKES 1 1/2 CUPS ■

Almond-Pistachio Tuiles

Unsalted butter for parchment
1½ **cups all-purpose flour**
¾ **cup sugar**
¾ **cup sliced almonds, toasted (see page 60)**
½ **cup pistachios, blanched, roasted, and coarsely chopped**
4 **large egg whites**

Preheat the oven to 300°F. Line a sheet pan with buttered parchment.

In a large bowl, combine the flour, sugar, nuts, and egg whites. Fold together until well blended. Spread the batter on the prepared sheet pan in 4-inch triangles. Place the sheet pan in the upper third of the oven and bake until the edges begin to brown, about 20 minutes.

Remove from the oven. While still hot, trim the edges of the tuiles with a sharp knife to form different sizes of triangles. Remove to a cake rack to cool. Repeat with the remainder of the batter. Reserve at room temperature.

MAKES 32 TUILES ■

Chocolate Truffles

7½ **ounces bittersweet chocolate, broken into pieces**
½ **cup heavy cream**
2 **tablespoons unsalted butter**
2 **large egg yolks**
¾ **cup confectioners' sugar**
¼ **cup liqueur of your choice**
½ **cup Dutch process unsweetened cocoa powder**

In a double boiler, over medium heat, combine the chocolate, cream, and butter. Stir occasionally until melted. Heat the chocolate to 100°F on a candy thermometer. Transfer the mixture to a large bowl. Whisk in the egg yolks, then sift in the sugar, ¼ cup at a time, while whisking. Add the liqueur and whisk until smooth and shiny. Pour the chocolate into a 1-inch deep cookie pan. Cover and refrigerate overnight.

Shape the truffles using a small scoop. Quickly roll into a ball with your hands and place in the cocoa. Roll to cover. Refrigerate until ready to serve. Serve chilled.

MAKES ABOUT 16 TRUFFLES ■

Grilled Grapefruit with Maple Sugar

Select large, heavy grapefruits, preferably the Indian River orchids.

¼ **cup maple sugar**
½ **teaspoon freshly grated nutmeg**
½ **teaspoon ground cassia (see note below)**
4 **grapefruit, cut in half and segments cut away from membrane**

Preheat the broiler.

In a small bowl, mix together the sugar and spices. Sprinkle on the grapefruit, then place the grapefruit on a broiler pan cut-side up toward the heat source. Heat under the broiler until the sugar is carmelized, about 5 minutes. Serve.

COOKING NOTE: Cassia is the dried flower bud of the cassia tree, whose bark is sold commercially as cinnamon. It has a very pronounced flavor, much like that of ''red hots'' candy. You can buy it in spice and specialty food stores.

MAKES 4 SERVINGS ■

Blueberry Bourbon Pancakes

FOR THE RASPBERRY-BOURBON BUTTER

⅛ **cup raspberries**
1 **tablespoon sugar**
6 **tablespoons (¾ stick) unsalted butter**
6 **tablespoons bourbon (my choice would be Maker's Mark)**

FOR THE PANCAKE BATTER

¾ **cup pastry flour**
2 **teaspoons salt**
2 **tablespoons sugar**
¾ **teaspoon baking soda**
2 **teaspoons baking powder**
2 **tablespoons unsalted butter**
¾ **cup milk**
6 **tablespoons bourbon**
1 **large egg, lightly beaten**
1½ **cups blueberries**

Corn oil for pan
Maple syrup for garnish
4 **sprigs fresh mint for garnish**

To make the raspberry-bourbon butter, puree the raspberries and strain. Combine the puree with the sugar. With a mixer, whip the butter until light. Add the raspberry puree and the bourbon. Refrigerate until ready to serve.

To make the batter, sift the flour, salt, sugar, baking soda, and baking powder together in a large bowl. Melt the butter and combine with the milk, bourbon, and egg. Slowly add the milk mixture to the flour mixture in a steady stream until a batter consistency is reached; do not overmix. Fold in the blueberries.

In a large nonstick skillet over medium-high heat, add as much corn oil as is necessary to lightly glaze the bottom of the pan. Spoon 3/4 cup of the batter into the skillet. Cook until the center of the pancake bubbles and the bottom is browned, about 2 minutes. Turn over and cook until evenly browned, about 1 minute. Reserve pancakes in oven on warm. Repeat three more times with the remaining batter.

Slip the pancakes onto warm serving plates. Serve with the raspberry-bourbon butter and warmed maple syrup. Garnish with sprigs of mint.

VARIATIONS: You can substitute preserves or dried fruit for the raspberries in the compound butter. Preserves can be added right out of the jar, but some dried fruits will need to be softened by soaking in a little fruit juice, then pureed or diced. To make strawberry Southern Comfort pancakes, substitute 1/4 cup strawberry preserves for the raspberries, Southern Comfort for the bourbon, and sliced strawberries for the blueberries.

MAKES 4 SERVINGS ■

Crab and Avocado Hash

FOR THE HASH

- **2 pounds crab meat, carefully picked over for shells**
- **1 large yellow bell pepper, roasted, peeled (see page 62), seeded, and diced**
- **1 large red bell pepper, roasted, peeled, seeded, and diced**
- **6 tablespoons prepared jalapeño salsa (hot!)**
- **3 large eggs**
- **3 large egg yolks**
- **1/2 cup plain dry bread crumbs, plus a little extra for dusting**
- **2 ripe avocados, peeled and diced**

FOR THE SAUCE

- **6 large egg yolks**
- **1/4 cup fresh lime juice**
- **1 1/2 cups Clarified Butter (see page 70)**
- **2 teaspoons salt**
  Tabasco sauce to taste
- **1 tablespoon grated lime rind**
- **2 tablespoons snipped fresh chives**
- **2 tablespoons chopped fresh cilantro**
- **4 tablespoons (1/2 stick) unsalted butter**
- **8 sprigs fresh cilantro for garnish**

In a large bowl, combine the crab meat, peppers, salsa, eggs, and yolks for the hash. Add the bread crumbs and mix well. Fold in the avocado. Mold into eight cakes, about 1 inch thick, on a parchment-covered sheet pan. Refrigerate to firm or up to 24 hours.

In a metal bowl or on top of a double boiler over simmering water, combine the egg yolks and lime juice for the sauce. Heat gently over a low flame while constantly whisking. Cook until slightly thickened. Remove from the heat. While whisking slowly, begin adding the clarified butter in a slow, steady stream. If the sauce becomes too thick, thin with a little warm water or lime juice. Season with salt and Tabasco. Garnish with the lime rind, chives, and chopped cilantro. Keep warm over tepid water.

In a large heavy skillet, heat the butter over medium-high heat. Dust the crab cakes with bread crumbs. Place in the skillet and cook until golden, about 3 minutes. Turn over, reduce the heat to low, and finish cooking, about 3 minutes more. Remove to paper towels to drain.

Position the crab on warm serving plates, spooning the sauce over. Garnish with a cilantro sprig and serve.

MAKES 8 SERVINGS ■

Curried Lamb Sausage with Compote and Pecan Pancakes

1½ cups orange juice
1½ cups passion fruit juice
 1 tablespoon sugar
 1 large papaya, peeled, seeded, and sliced ¼ inch thick
 2 large pears, peeled, cored, sliced ¼ inch thick, and rubbed with lemon juice to prevent discoloring
1½ teaspoons finely grated orange rind
 2 cups coarsely grated russet potatoes (or substitute baking potatoes)
 2 cups broken pecans
 1 cup diced red onion
 4 large eggs, beaten
 1 tablespoon baking powder
 1 tablespoon cornstarch
½ cup all-purpose flour, sifted
 1 teaspoon salt
½ teaspoon freshly ground white pepper
 4 tablespoons (½ stick) unsalted butter
 1 recipe Curried Lamb Sausage (recipe follows)
 4 sprigs fresh parsley for garnish

In a medium-size acid-resistant saucepan, combine the juices, sugar, papaya, and pears. Bring to a simmer over medium-high heat and cook until the fruit is tender, about 10 minutes. Remove the fruit and continue simmering the juices until they are thickened enough to coat the back of a spoon, about 10 minutes. Return the fruit to the juices, add the orange rind, and reduce the heat to low.

In a large strainer, wash the grated potatoes three times under cold running water. Drain well by squeezing the water from the potatoes. Dry in paper towels. Transfer to a medium-size bowl and add the pecans, onions, and eggs. Mix in the baking powder, cornstarch, flour, salt, and pepper.

In a large skillet over medium-high heat, melt the butter. Spoon the potato batter into four large pancakes and cook until golden, about 3 minutes. Turn over and cook 1 minute more.

Position the pancakes in the center of the serving plates. Spoon the compote over it, arrange two sausages atop each pancake, garnish with the parsley, and serve.

MAKES 4 SERVINGS ∎

Curried Lamb Sausage

¾ pound lamb leg meat, trimmed of fat and cut into 1-inch pieces
¼ pound veal or beef fat
 1 small red onion, cut into 1-inch pieces
1¼ teaspoons salt
¾ teaspoon freshly ground black pepper
 1 tablespoon Rattlesnake Curry Powder (see page 67)
 2 large egg yolks

In a medium-size bowl, combine the lamb, fat, and onion. Grind through the medium disc on a meat grinder. Add the salt, pepper, curry, and egg yolks. Grind again. Form into eight patties. Refrigerate until set, about 2 hours.

In a large heavy skillet over medium-high heat, cook the sausage until browned, about 5 minutes. Turn over and cook until done, about 5 minutes more. Drain on paper towels and serve.

MAKES 4 SERVINGS ∎

Smoked Salmon and Watercress Omelet

¼ pound (1 stick) unsalted butter
1 cup sliced shallots
½ cup dry white wine
1¼ cups heavy cream
   Salt to taste
   Freshly ground black pepper to taste
1 pound smoked salmon, julienned (see note below)
3 bunches watercress, stemmed
12 large eggs, lightly beaten

In a medium-size saucepan, combine 2 tablespoons of the butter and the shallots over medium-high heat and sauté until tender, about 8 minutes. Add the wine and cream and cook until thickened enough to coat the back of a spoon, about 10 minutes. Add salt and pepper. Add the smoked salmon and watercress, reserving 4 sprigs for garnish. Immediately remove from the heat.

In an omelet pan, heat 1½ tablespoons of the butter over a medium fire. Add a quarter of the eggs and cook until set, about 3 minutes. Spoon a quarter of the salmon filling onto the eggs and fold out of the pan onto a plate to form an omelet. Garnish with a sprig of watercress. Repeat with the remaining eggs and filling. Serve.

COOKING NOTE: Remember to trim the fatty darker flesh from the salmon as it carries the oily "fishy" flavor.

MAKES 4 SERVINGS ■

Poached Eggs with Corn Bread and Salsa Hollandaise

½ cup cider vinegar
   Salt to taste
   Freshly ground black pepper to taste
8 large eggs
4 Blue Corn and Pepper Muffins, halved (recipe follows)
1¼ cups Salsa Hollandaise (recipe follows)

In a medium-size saucepan, combine the cider with water to a level of 3 inches deep. Bring to a simmer over medium-high heat. Crack the eggs into a bowl. Add one at a time to the poaching liquid and adjust the heat to a very slow simmer. Cook until the white firms but the yolk is still soft, or to your taste. Remove with a slotted spoon. Pat dry with paper toweling.

Position the bottoms of the muffins on serving plates. Top each with 2 poached eggs. Spoon the hollandaise over the eggs and top with the other muffin halves. Serve.

MAKES 4 SERVINGS ■

Blue Corn and Pepper Muffins

1/2 **pound plus 6 tablespoons (2 3/4 sticks) unsalted butter**
1 **small zucchini, diced**
1 **small yellow squash, diced**
1 **large red bell pepper, roasted, peeled (see page 62), seeded, and diced**
1 **bunch scallion greens, diced**
  Tabasco sauce to taste
  Salt to taste
1/2 **cup milk**
1 **large egg**
1/2 **cup all-purpose flour**
3/4 **cup blue cornmeal (or substitute yellow cornmeal)**
1 **tablespoon light brown sugar**
1/2 **teaspoon salt**
2 **teaspoons baking powder**

Preheat the oven to 350°F. Grease a 2 1/2-inch muffin pan with 2 tablespoons of the butter.

In a medium-size skillet over high heat, melt 2 tablespoons of the butter. Add the zucchini and yellow squash and sauté until tender, about 4 minutes. Add the bell pepper and scallions and cook until tender, about 3 minutes. Season with the Tabasco and salt. Remove from the heat and drain.

In a small pan, melt the remaining butter. Combine with the milk and egg. Combine the flour, cornmeal, sugar, salt, and baking powder in a large bowl. Add the milk mixture until just combined. Add the vegetables until mixed. Do not overwork.

Pour the batter into the muffin pan. Bake until golden, about 30 minutes, testing for doneness by inserting a skewer to check for warmth and clean removal. Cool on a cake rack.

MAKES 8 MUFFINS ■

Salsa Hollandaise

3 **large egg yolks**
1/4 **cup fresh lime juice**
1 **cup Clarified Butter (see page 70)**
1/2 **cup prepared hot salsa or to your taste**
  Salt to taste

In a metal bowl or in the top of a double boiler over simmering water, combine the egg yolks and lime juice. Heat gently over a low flame while constantly whisking. Cook until slightly thickened, about 6 minutes; *do not boil*. Remove from the heat. While whisking, slowly begin adding the clarified butter in a slow, steady stream. If it becomes too thick, thin with a little warm water or lime juice. Add the salsa. Adjust the salt. Keep warm over tepid water.

MAKES 1 1/4 CUPS ■

Bran Muffins

4 tablespoons (½ stick) unsalted butter, plus extra for the pan
1½ cups whole wheat flour
2 cups bran flakes of your choice
2 tablespoons light brown sugar
⅛ teaspoon salt
1¼ teaspoons baking soda
1½ teaspoons ground cinnamon
1½ teaspoons freshly grated nutmeg
1 large egg
1½ cups buttermilk
¾ cup unsulfured molasses
¼ cup grated coconut
½ cup grated carrots
½ cup diced pineapple
¼ cup golden or regular raisins, soaked in orange juice, covered, for 1 hour to soften, and drained

Preheat the oven to 350°F. Grease a 2½-inch muffin pan with butter.

Combine the flour, bran, brown sugar, salt, baking soda, cinnamon, and nutmeg in a large bowl. With a mixer on medium speed, cream in the butter. Add the egg and buttermilk and combine. Add the molasses just to combine; do not overwork. Fold in the coconut, carrots, pineapple, and raisins.

Divide the batter into the muffin pan. Bake until golden, about 30 minutes, testing for doneness by inserting a skewer to check for warmth and clean removal. Cool on a cake rack.

MAKES 8 MUFFINS ■

Carrot Muffins

10 tablespoons (1¼ stick) unsalted butter, at room temperature
⅜ cup sugar
¼ cup packed light brown sugar
2 large eggs
1 cup all-purpose flour
1 teaspoon baking powder
⅛ teaspoon salt
1 teaspoon ground cinnamon
1½ cups grated carrots
½ cup roughly chopped walnuts

Preheat the oven to 350°F. Grease a 2½-inch muffin tin with 2 tablespoons of the butter. With a mixer, cream the butter, sugars, and eggs together. Add the dry ingredients, mixing until smooth. Fold in the carrots and walnuts.

Divide the batter into the prepared pan. Bake until golden, about 30 minutes, testing for doneness by inserting a skewer to check for warmth and clean removal. Cool on a cake rack.

MAKES 8 MUFFINS ■

HOLIDAY MENUS

Lemon Pasta with Smoked Salmon and Caviar
Iron Horse Blanc de Noirs

◆

Duck, Mâché, and Radicchio Salad
Beringer Chardonnay

◆

Pheasant with Leeks and Vanilla
Mixed Flavors of Polentas
Edna Valley Pinot Noir

◆

Chocolate Pâté

Oysters Poached in Champagne
Schramsberg Vineyards Blanc de Blancs

◆

Escalope of Salmon with Black and White Sesame
Schramsberg Vineyards Blanc de Noir

◆

Grilled Sirloin with Hazelnuts
Gratin of Root Vegetables
Joseph Phelps Vineyards Insignia

◆

Blini with Chocolate Velvet Ice Cream
Vichon Botrytis Semillon

Buckwheat Blini with Caviars
Krug Grande Cuvée Champagne

◆

Swordfish with Coriander
Krug Rosé Champagne

◆

Rack of Veal with Campari
Celery Root and Fennel Puree
Beringer Chabot Vineyard Cabernet Sauvignon

◆

Pear and Black Walnut Soufflé
Joseph Phelps Vineyards
Special Select Late Harvest Johannisberg Riesling

HOLIDAY MENUS

Hors d'Oeuvres
Chanterelles with Blue Corn Chips
Shellfish Wontons
Scharffenberger Blanc de Blancs

◆

Smoked Salmon with Radishes and Capers
Mayacamas Sauvignon Blanc

◆

Scallop Chowder

◆

Roast Turkey with Maple Glaze, Apples, and Ginger Butter
Pumpkin, Mushroom, and Parsley Stuffing
Cranberry Compote
Gratin of Root Vegetables
Fisher Coach Insignia Chardonnay

◆

White Chocolate Ravioli
Chocolate Truffles
Almond-Pistachio Tuiles
Bonny Doon Semillon Vin de Glacière

Sources

American Spoon Foods
411 East Lake Street
Petoskey, MI 49770
616-347-9030

■ *Dried cherries, cranberries,
nuts, maple sugar, mushrooms*

Blue Corn Connection
3825 Academy Parkway South NE
Albuquerque, NM 87109
505-344-9768

■ *Blue corn meal*

Gourmet Mushrooms
P.O. Box 391
SE Bastopol, CA 95472
707-823-1743

■ *Mushrooms*

Howard Duchacek
Maple Works
RFD 1 Box 502
Waterville, VT 05492
802-644-5838

■ *Maple syrup, maple sugar*

California Sunshine
144 King Street
San Francisco, CA 94107
415-543-3007

■ *Specialty foods*

Fox Hill Farms
444 West Michigan Avenue Box 9
Parma, MI 49269-0009
517-531-3179

■ *Fresh herbs and plants*

Marcel Akselrod Co.
530 West 25th Street
New York, NY 10001
212-675-7777

■ *Passion puree, fruit purees*

Ducktrap River Fish Farm, Inc.
RFD 2, Box 378
Lincolnville, ME 04849-9989
1-800-828-3825

■ *Naturally smoked seafood*

Giffords
Gifts of Fine Foods
60 Franklin Street
Boston, MA 02110
1-800-225-5800 ext. 77

■ *Specialty foods*

Paradise Farms
P.O. Box 436
Summerland, CA 93067
805-684-9468

■ *Specialty lettuces,. fresh herbs,
edible flowers*

Plath's Market
116 S. 3rd, P.O. Box 7
Rogers City, MI 49779
517-734-2232

■ *Smoked chicken, hams, bacons*

Summerfield Farm
HCR 4, Box 195 A
Brightwood, VA 22715
703-948-3100

■ *Summerfield veal*

Van Rex Gourmet Foods
120 Imlay Street
Brooklyn, NY 11231
718-858-8887

■ *Fruit purees, including passion and white peach*

VIV Food Products
2141 South Troop
Chicago, IL 60608
312-421-1020

■ *Mexican foods, dried chiles*

Wild Game, Inc.
1941 West Division
Chicago, IL 60622
312-278-1661

■ *Game*

Williams-Sonoma
P.O. Box 7456
San Francisco, CA 94120
415-421-4242

■ *Specialty foods, equipment*

Bibliography

Andrews, Jean. *Peppers: The Domesticated Capsicums.* Austin: University of Texas Press, 1984.

Clarke, Charlotte Bringle. *Edible and Useful Plants of California.* Berkeley: University of California Press, 1977.

Eekhof-Stork, Nancy. *The World Atlas of Cheese.* Paddington Press, 1975.

Fielder, Mildred. *Wild Fruits: An Illustrated Field Guide & Cookbook.* Chicago: Contemporary Books, 1983.

Kamman, Madeleine. *The Making of a Cook.* New York: Atheneum, 1971.

Larousse Gastronomique. New York: Crown Publishers, 1989.

Larousse Gastronomique. Paris: Librairie Larousse, 1938.

Lichine, Alexis. *Encyclopedia of Wines & Spirits.* New York: Alfred A. Knopf, 1951.

———. *Guide to the Wines and Vineyards of France.* New York: Alfred A. Knopf, 1979.

McClane, A. J. *The Encyclopedia of Fish Cookery.* New York: Holt, Rinehart and Winston, 1977.

———. *Field Guide to Freshwater Fishes of North America.* New York: Holt, Rinehart and Winston, 1965.

———. *Field Guide to Saltwater Fishes of North America.* New York: Holt, Rinehart and Winston, 1965.

McGee, Harold. *On Food and Cooking, The Science and Lore of the Kitchen.* New York: Charles Scribner's Sons, 1984.

McNulty, Henry. *Drinking in Vogue.* New York: The Vendome Press, 1972

Miller, Carey D., Katherine Bazore, and Mary Bartow. *Fruits of Hawaii.* Honolulu: The University Press of Hawaii, 1945.

Nagy, Steven, and Phillip E. Shaw. *Topical and Subtropical Fruits.* Westport, Connecticut: AVI Publishing, 1980.

Pacioni, Giovanni. *Simon & Schuster's Guide to Mushrooms.* New York: Simon & Schuster, 1981.

Popenoe, Wilson. *Manual of Tropical and Subtropical Fruits.* New York: Hafner Press, 1948.

Rinaldi, Augusto, and Vassili Tyndalo. *The Complete Book of Mushrooms.* New York: Crown Publishers, 1974.

Schneider, Elizabeth. *Uncommon Fruits & Vegetables, A Commonsense Guide.* New York: Harper & Row, 1986.

Thompson, Bob. *The Pocket Encyclopedia of California Wines.* New York: Simon & Schuster, 1985.

Smith, Alexander H., and Nancy Smith Weber. *The Mushroom Hunter's Field Guide.* Ann Arbor: The University of Michigan Press, 1958.

Weatherbee, Ellen Elliott, and James Garnett Bruce. *Edible Wild Plants, A Guide to Collecting and Cooking.* Ann Arbor, Michigan, 1982.

Winkler, A. J., James A. Cook, W. M. Kliewer, and Lloyd A. Lider. *General Viticulture.* Berkeley: University of California Press, 1962.

Index